AN ANTHOLOGY OF
Russian Folktales

AN ANTHOLOGY OF
Russian Folktales

Translated and edited by **Jack V. Haney**

M.E.Sharpe
Armonk, New York
London, England

Library of Congress Cataloging-in-Publication Data

An anthology of Russian folktales / translated and edited by Jack V. Haney.
   p. cm.
 Includes bibliographical references and index.
 ISBN-978-0-7656-2305-8 (cloth : alk. paper)
 1. Tales—Russia (Federation) I. Haney, Jack V., 1940–
 GR203.17.A58 2008
 398.20947—dc22   2008007916

Printed in the United States of America

BM (c)   10   9   8   7   6   5   4   3   2   1

For Barbara

The Provinces of European Russia in 1900

Cartography by Bill Nelson

Source: Reprinted from *Liberal Reform in an Illiberal Regime: The Creation of Private Property in Russia, 1906–1915,* by Stephen F. Williams, with the permission of the publisher, Hoover Institution Press. Copyright 2006 by the Board of Trustees of the Leland Stanford Junior University.

Contents

Map	vi
Preface	xi
Introduction: The Folktale	xiii
Glossary	xxxv

I. Animal Tales — 3

1. Sister Fox and the Wolf	3
2. The Peasant, the Bear, and the Fox	6
3. The Pig Set Off For the Games	8
4. The Fox as Keener	10
5. The Fox as Confessor	11
6. A Wolf—Gray and Daring	13
7. The Fox and the Jug	14
8. The Bear and the Beam	14
9. The Peasant, the Bear, the Fox, and the Gadfly	15
10. The Case of the Beekeeper and the Bear	17
11. The Bear	19
12. The Mushrooms	20
13. The Sun, the Wind, and the Moon	20

II. Tales of Heroes and Villains — 24

14. Nikita the Tanner	24
15. Ivan the Mare's Son	27
16. Maria Morevna	30
17. The Witch and the Sun's Sister	37
18. The Milk of Wild Beasts	39
19. Baba Yaga and the Nimble Youth	42

20. Ivan Tsarevich and the Gray Wolf — 44
21. The Maiden Tsar — 56
22. Elena the Wise — 59
23. The Frog Tsarevna — 64
24. The Petrified Tsarevna — 67
25. Fenist the Bright Falcon Feather — 70
26. How the Tsar's Daughter Came to Know Need — 74
27. Go Where You Know Not Where, Bring Back You Know Not What — 76
28. The Mare's Head — 81
29. Baba Yaga — 83
30. The Swan-Geese — 85
31. Vasilisa the Beautiful — 87

III. Tales of Magic — 89

32. A Prince and His "Uncle" — 89
33. The Golden Slipper — 94
34. Burenushka the Little Red Cow — 95
35. Sivko-Burko — 98
36. The Pig with the Golden Bristles — 101
37. Dirty Face — 107
38. Ivan Tsarevich, the Gray Wolf, and Elena the Most Beautiful — 110
39. The Rejuvenating Apples — 115
40. The Three Sons-in-Law — 119
41. The Everlasting Piece — 126
42. Little Boy Green — 127
43. The Fiddler in Hell — 129
44. The Snow Maiden — 131
45. The Armless Maiden — 135

IV. Legends — 139

46. The Poor Widow — 139
47. The Serpent — 141
48. The Hermit and the Devil — 142
49. The Proud Rich Man — 143
50. The Bigamist — 146
51. The Old Woman in Church — 147
52. The Golden Saucer and the Silver Apple — 147
53. Kas'ian and Nikolai — 149
54. Why Women Lost Their Rights — 150
55. A Tale of a Drunkard — 151

56. Who Brought Vodka to Rus 152
57. The Forest Spirit 153
58. The Skomorokh Vavilo 155

V. Tales of Love and Life **159**

59. The Self-Playing *Gusli* 159
60. About Ivan the Fool 161
61. The Philosopher and the Cripple 162
62. The Soldier Erema the Crafty 165
63. The Peasant and the Devil 171
64. The White-Bearded Old Man 176
65. The Tsar and the Two Craftsmen 180
66. The Wise Seven-Year-Old Girl 185
67. Tsar Peter and the Clever Woman 187
68. The Clever Daughter (or the Dispute over a Colt) 190
69. How I Became Head of the Division 191
70. The Merchant's Daughter 193
71. A Hunter Rescues a Maiden 197
72. The Woman from the Grave 200
73. About Savvushka 200
74. The Son-in-Law Teaches His Wife and Mother-in-Law 205
75. How Peter and a Hunter Went Hunting 208
76. Peter the Great Ate the *Murzovka* 210
77. The Carefree Monastery 210
78. Why There Is Treason in Rus 213
79. Eaten by a Wolf 216
80. How a Lad Bought Wisdom 216
81. Why They Stopped Banishing Old Men 221
82. How the Bear Killed the Robbers 223
83. The Soldier and Death 224
84. The Golden Pitcher 227
85. Peter the Great and the Three Soldiers 228
86. The Monk and the Abbess 230

VI. Tales of Clever Fools **231**

87. Balda the Laborer 231
88. The Laborer and the Priest 237
89. Horns 240
90. How Klimka Stole the Landlord's Wife 242
91. Shabarsha the Laborer 244

92. About a Sly Peasant and a Priest   246
93. About Egibikha (Baba Yaga)   247
94. A Lad Who Watched *Rusalki*   249
95. The Tsar and the Peasant   252
96. The Peasant and the Devil   253
97. The Devil Takes the Soldier's Watch   254
98. Whence Came Baba Yaga   256
99. The Wizard   257

VII. Anecdotes   **259**

100. The Dog Tsuvarnachka   259
101. Those Folk from Pskov   260
102. A Tailor or a Crayfish   260
103. The Mare's Egg   262
104. Kostia   262
105. The Lord of the Manor   264
106. How the Soldier Stole the Speck   267
107. Unsalted Custard   267
108. If You Don't Like It, Don't Listen!   268
109. The Turnip   270
110. Roundsides   271
111. The Sad Story of a Raven   273

VIII. Serial Tales from the Far North   **274**

112. Fear-Bogatyr   274
113. Ondrei the Shooter   285
114. Ivan Medvedevich the Bear's Son   302

Story Credits   322
Sources Cited in Russian   326
Selected Bibliography of Works in English   329
Index of Tale Types and Motifs   331
About the Editor   340

Preface

This anthology is intended for anyone who likes reading folktales. It includes ninety-nine tales selected from the seven volumes of *The Complete Russian Folktale* (CRF), which in turn were drawn from more than fifty sources including newspapers, journals, and books. The selection encompasses tales from North and South Russia, the Caucasus, Western and Eastern Siberia, Lithuania, the Urals, and the central regions of Russia. Rounding out the volume are twelve anecdotes as well as three "serial tales" collected from the remote Russian North. These three have never been translated before and are virtually unknown even to Russians. The North Russian tales are distinguished by their length, apparently a result of the special circumstances in which they were told. They are discussed fully in the Introduction.

The anthology includes examples of each of the major classificatory groups of tales: animal tales, wondertales (both heroic and magical), legends, tales of everyday life, sometimes called household tales or novellas, tales of the clever fool, and anecdotes or numbskull stories. The three North Russian tales mentioned above fall into the category of wondertales.

Several principles guided me in the selection. The originals must all have been told and recorded in Russian and each must be a well-told tale that will amuse or perhaps even instruct the reader; and in addition I attempt to show the breadth of the Russian folktale, both geographically and temporally. It is likely that not all of these tales will amuse all readers but most readers will discover, as the old saw has it, that "The right laughter is medicine to weary bones." I trust that most readers will manage at least a droll smile if not a belly laugh!

The translations do not pretend to replicate the language of the originals, but it is hoped that something of the flavor comes across. The oral nature of the tales means that, if they were accurately recorded in the first place, there will be all sorts of inconsistencies: repetitions, lacunae, ungrammatical utterances, and dialect vocabulary are some of the more common ones. In many cases the original editors "cleaned up the diction" of the tales with the result that some of them are recorded in more or less literary Russian. Although that is unfortunate for the scholar, it is less a hindrance to enjoying them in English, where the language is unavoidably smoothed out in many places. All the translations are my own, including those from the Afanas'ev collection.

The Introduction is relatively brief. The interested reader is encouraged to consult CRF, volume 1, *An Introduction to the Russian Folktale,* for a more complete treatment of the Russian folktale. Each of the subsequent volumes in that series contains a substantial introduction to each category of tales with the exception of the anecdotes and serial tales, which are discussed in the Introduction to the present volume.

My thanks are due to many friends and readers who encouraged me to compile this selection of Russian folktales. For technical assistance in preparing the typescript I am indebted to my son, Andrew, and to Farah and Vinit Sethi. My appreciation goes to Ana Erlic and Makiko Parsons for their roles in the editorial and production process of the book. The editor, Patricia Kolb, deserves especial thanks for the role she played in bringing this volume to its successful conclusion. I also owe a special debt of gratitude to I.P. Foote, of The Queen's College, Oxford University, who first introduced me to the Russian folktale.

Introduction:
The Folktale

> "In the evening I listen to folktales and thus compensate for the shortcomings in my cursed upbringing. How charming these tales are! Each one is a poem."
> —*A.S. Pushkin*

In the poet Alexander Pushkin's time (1799–1837), relatively few Russian folktales had been written down. Today thousands more are available to the reader. In this volume, I have gathered together some of the best examples of the various kinds of Russian folktale.

Probably more folktales have been recorded from among the Russian people than from any others. The likely reason for this is that until well into the twentieth century Russia remained an illiterate and basically peasant country where folk traditions were strong and carefully maintained.[1] The folktale was and is an integral part of this folk tradition. The rites, rituals, customs and beliefs, songs, music, and dances of the Russian people are all reflected to some degree in the tale.

Not only does Russia have vast numbers of recorded folktales, it also has the second largest number of tale types according to the international classificatory system. This can be attributed to a number of factors, notably the enormous territory settled by the Russians, the isolation of traditional Russian communities, and the diligence of Russian ethnographers and folklorists in recording the tales.

Today, however, the era of folktale telling and the recording of new tales have almost come to an end. Only in a few remote places such as the Far North of European Russia and the Lake Baikal region are tales still being recorded. The twentieth century was devastating for the Russian peasantry. Revolutions, civil war, collectivization and its associated policies, Stalin's purges, and World War II all took their toll. Millions were killed, exiled, and driven or forcibly removed to industrial centers. At the same time, illiteracy was drastically reduced. The result was that the ancient way of life in the countryside was transformed and the tradition of storytelling disrupted.

What Is a Folktale?

There are many kinds of oral narrative but four may easily be distinguished: myths, memorates, fabulates, and folktales proper. Our concern here is not with myths, which I define as oral narratives that the society as a whole believes to be true at a point in time. Some of these are obviously Christian, while others may be pre-Christian or even coexistent with Russian Orthodoxy. In the twenty-first century it would be difficult to point to any myths that would find anything like universal belief among the Russian rural population. That was probably not the case a century ago.

Memorates are narratives in which the narrator asks his audience to believe that the tale he is about to relate is true because he was a witness to the events described. At one step farther removed, the fabulate may be defined as a tale in which the narrator reports that his narrative is true because he has heard it from others whom he regards as trustworthy. By and large these kinds of oral narrative are not the subject of this anthology.[2]

The folktale is an oral narrative of no fixed length but shorter rather than longer, distinguished by its traditional nature, indeterminate authorship, and worldwide distribution. It may or may not be believed by the person who tells it or by the audience for whom it is intended. The folktale has no known author and thus it is a component of the oral tradition of the group that relates it.

With but very few exceptions no one knows who first told a particular folktale. We can be quite sure that the tale known as "Jack and the Beanstalk" was told long before it was recorded for posterity, and we can be quite sure that many versions of that favorite tale existed in English and in other languages as well. Some Russian tales may have become part of the Russian tradition as a result of their migrating orally from another culture, while others owe their presence to texts brought from Byzantium or the South Slavs, which then made their way into that oral tradition. A very few have been proved to have their roots in the Russian literary sources.[3]

No doubt, many have very ancient origins in the myths and rites of the pre-Christian East Slavs. That is especially true of the animal tales and wondertales. This ancient tradition is also the point of origin for many other genres of folklore: the folk dance and song, proverbs, spells and incantations, and obviously the famous folk epic, the *bylina*. Just how old any particular tale is cannot reasonably be determined because before the eighteenth century the folktales as such were rarely recorded in writing. There are minor exceptions. *The Primary Chronicle*, dating from the twelfth century, contains many narratives that might well be classified as folk legends, that is, they are about real people and sometimes about real events in general, but the factual contents of the legends cannot be established with any certainty. Thus, it is reasonably certain that there was a Prince Oleg ruling in Kiev in the early tenth century and no doubt he died there, but whether he died after being bitten by a serpent hiding in his favorite horse's skull, as a sorcerer had predicted, seems somewhat unlikely! There are many such quasi-historical accounts in the written record of the ancient Kievan Rus state and their ties to an oral tradition can scarcely be doubted.

The medieval Muscovite state produced a different type of tale showing the interaction of the oral tale with the literary. Beginning in the fifteenth century there appeared a considerable number of tales (*povesti*) that seem to have been derived from local legends. While they purport to be factual, and some are even found in the lives of saints, the majority of them contain the most wondrous episodes that can only reflect an oral tradition and the passing of the oral tale into the literary one. Again, many of the persons who figure in the tales are known from written sources to have existed but the rather fantastic accounts of their activities are unquestionably fictitious. The entire story of Peter and Fevroniia of Murom, for instance, consists of one folkloric theme followed by another.[4] A whole collection of tales known in the Sanskrit tradition as the *Panchatantra* made its way to Muscovy as the *Stefanit i Ikhnilat,* where it served as a source for moralistic episodes involving animals posing as the ruled and rulers of imaginary kingdoms, and at least some of these written tales found their way into the oral tradition.

Folktales are told throughout the world, by all peoples and, apparently, at all times in their cultural development.[5] But some folktales are unique to one particular people or group of people: there are many Russian tales not known among other peoples, even among other Slavic nations. One such tale is "Nikita the Tanner," found only among the Russians and included in this collection (no. 14).

Stories written in the style of the folktale are not true folktales. The tales of Hans Christian Andersen, Alexander Pushkin, and many others fall into this category of literary tales. They may indeed have oral analogues, not necessarily within the national tradition, but they are literary, written creations of their authors. Pushkin, for instance, not only wrote tales stylized in the manner of the folktale, for example, "The Tale of Tsar Saltan, of his Son the Glorious and Mighty Warrior Prince Guidon Saltanovich and of the Beautiful Tsarevna Lebed." He was also fond of using family legends and quasi-historical sources in his prose works.

By and large it is pointless to search for the origins of a particular folktale. The tale is linked inextricably to other kinds of oral narrative that served as an adhesive in preliterate societies. It is even suggested that some kinds of tale are derived from ritual dancing. Some scholars have argued that they are derived from myths, those narratives that expressed the group's religious beliefs.[6] There is no question that many of these narratives were regarded as indisputably true and even sanctioned by the god or gods. Such would include the Greek myths, those of the Judeo-Christian tradition, and many others. To the extent that these are regarded as sacred truths they are not folktales, but what is one to do with the apocryphal stories that "look" like folktales (legends) yet are rejected by the religious authorities of the society? Apparently all the world's great religions sanction "miracles," indeed may be founded on them. At the same time, they pick and choose which miracles they accept as plausible, even true, while rejecting others as implausible, even heretical. But then must the folktale be thought to be false? Some scholars have argued that this is a distinctive feature: that it is not regarded as true. Yet in Russia, in the twentieth century at least, it was quite possible to meet narrators who insisted that their tales were literally true. My favorite such evidence is the statement of a woman brought up in the years of Soviet communism who insisted that her tales were true because she had heard them from her grandfather, and "Would the old folks lie?" Yet it is quite clear that most narrators and their audiences did not regard the tales as true, while at the same time the lesson of the tales was upheld—one may say universally. The virtues bravery and honesty, loyalty and perseverance, nimbleness of foot and mind—all these were regarded as true and worthy of emulation. (Here an exception must be made for the memorate and fabulate, in which the narrator specifically states that he has personal knowledge of what he is about to narrate, thus asking the audience to believe that it is true.)

Classification of Tales

Needless to say, no one knows how many times a given tale has been told and retold. That is the nature of the tale. Collectors of tales eventually decided a system of classification was needed and folklorists have by and large agreed on one that is used throughout the world. This system is known as the A–T index after the two scholars who first devised it, Antti Aarne and Stith Thompson. It has recently been revised and expanded by Hans-Jörg Uther.[7] This ATU system assigns a number to each type (plot) of folktale recorded throughout the world, so that all Hansel and Gretel type tales are classified as ATU 327, and all Cinderella-like tales are classified 510A. The version covering the three East Slavic traditions (Belarusian, Russian, Ukrainian) is the *Comparative Index of Types. The East Slavic Folktale,* known by its Russian initials: SUS.

These indexes are far from perfect, as many commentators have pointed out. Many tales could reasonably be assigned to more than one type, while many contain multiple story lines or plots, and thus need to be classified under several numbers. For instance, "Sister Fox and the Wolf" (no. 1 in this collection) consists of no fewer than eight different tale types strung together one after another. While I know of no Russian folktale that is more complex than this one, most do in fact consist of more than one type. In this anthology I give the SUS number, which is the same as the A–T or ATU number for most of the tales. The ATU index should be used to find analogues to the Russian SUS numbers. In cases of tales published subsequent to the SUS index I use an SUS number supplied by the editors of the newer collections, when available.

Collections

Interest in collecting folktales does not appear in Russia until the eighteenth century although some Russian folktales appeared in foreign sources as early as the sixteenth. The earliest of the domestic versions seem to have been legends about tsars Ivan the Terrible and Peter the Great, both popular topics right into the twentieth century. In 1769, however, N. Kurganov published a small booklet, the *Pismovnik,* containing 321 folktales and anecdotes. It was extremely popular in its day and went through five editions in the eighteenth century alone. The quality of the tales is not especially noteworthy:

> Two men—a Russian and a Pole—were sitting in a tavern and they asked for some supper. The hostess told them that all she had left was a small piece of boiled mutton and one roast partridge. They both wanted to eat the game and for a long time they quarreled before they finally decided to eat just the boiled mutton and the one who had the best dream would eat the partridge the next day. They went to bed. The Russian, noting where the bird had been put, got up in the night and took it. The Pole decided to tell of an amazing dream in the morning:
>   "Brother, I was taken by angels to heaven to eternal bliss, and you could never dream such a fine dream!"
>   "But I saw that you had flown off to heaven," answered the Russian, "so then I ate the partridge, thinking that you would never come back from there."

This rather silly tale can actually be classified according to the SUS system as 2100, that is, an anecdote about two foreigners. Others in the collection appear to have been borrowed and Russified from various West European sources, including Italian and German.

S.V. Drukovtsov published a collection of thirty-one tales in 1778, titled "Grandmother's Tales," but these are not all folktales. The most interesting thing about this booklet is the title: it suggests that women were telling folktales, for which there had been no direct evidence before this time.

Drukovtsov published a second collection of "folktales" in 1779. In this volume were twenty-five anecdotes and tales, in general of mediocre quality. Nothing is known of the sources for Drukovtsov's selection, although some of the tales in the collection are known to have circulated at the court of Catherine II.

During the last years of the eighteenth century the number of collections of folktales and narratives purporting to be "of the folk" increased rapidly. Those by V. Levshin, P. Timofeev, and others with titles such as *A Treatment for Ennui, The Wanderings of a Certain Russian,* and so on, are notable for the inclusion of some tales that remained favorites throughout the nineteenth and twentieth centuries. Here we meet for the first time tales about Ivan the Fool in some of his various guises, animal tales, and wondertales, including those about Fenist the Bright

Falcon Feather and Ivan with Bear's Ears. Some of them went through several editions right into the middle of the nineteenth century.

The growing literacy and literary sophistication of the Russian public is evident in the publications of folktales in the later eighteenth and the first half of the nineteenth century. These were of two general kinds. The more sophisticated was a collection of tales on paper of generally poor quality. These "gray" booklets contained no illustrations. On the decidedly unsophisticated side were the *lubok* tales, engravings often printed on bast.[8] These tales reflect the reading tastes of the Russian peasantry and with their colorful illustrations were extremely popular.

In 1847 and 1849, Ivan Vanenko published two small volumes of folktales for schoolchildren. In an introductory note he stated that his aim was to provide accessible versions of tales Russians have always heard from their "nannies and grannies." Some of the actors in Vanenko's tales are indeed similar to the familiar characters known from the more extensive collections that were to appear in the second half of the nineteenth century.

The latter half of the nineteenth century and the first two decades of the twentieth saw the publication of the great collections of Russian folktales. First and foremost of these was that of Aleksandr N. Afanas'ev, which in its breadth takes first place among European collections of folktales.[9] It was first published in eight fascicles over the years 1855–63 and subsequently in three volumes, the last edition appearing in 1984. Unlike subsequent collections of Russian tales, Afanas'ev's represented tales from throughout the Russian empire and in languages that were then regarded as mere dialects of standard Russian, especially Ukrainian and Belarusian. These latter two languages together with Russian comprise the East Slavic branch of the Slavic languages.

Born in 1826, Afanas'ev spent his youth in the south of Russia in the Voronezh guberniia or province, where he completed his schooling in 1844. In that year he was admitted to Moscow State University to study law. He finished his studies in 1848, but while he was there, he was much involved in the social and political discussions of the time between the Slavophiles on the one hand and the Westernizers on the other. Afanas'ev apparently desired to remain at the University as a lecturer but was not offered a post, whereupon he took up a position in the archives of the Ministry of Foreign Affairs, where he remained until 1862. He used his time well at the ministry, writing for journals of all sorts on a vast array of topics, mostly having to do with Russian history and satire.

It was in the early 1850s that Afanas'ev began writing about Slavic mythology. These studies prompted the appearance of the famed *Narodnye russkie skazki* (Popular Russian Tales) and *Narodnye russkie legendy* (Popular Russian Legends), all within the first decade after his completion of the university. He was also actively collecting texts of folk songs and proverbs; indeed he collected any folkloric texts that came his way.

Not all of Afanas'ev's texts were printed in Russia initially. The legends were printed in London before being printed in Moscow, where they immediately ran afoul of the censorship. And the censors banned a considerable number of the so-called obscene folktales, although they were unable to stop their subsequent publication in Geneva. These tales were deemed pornographic and anticlerical, and it is worth noting that they were not published in Russia until after the fall of the Soviet Union. Their publication in the original Russian and in various European languages in the intervening century does not seem to have had a deleterious effect on their readers, and they were indeed well known in Russia despite the censors.

Afanas'ev was certainly not the only collector of Russian folktales active at this time. A student, I.A. Khudiakov, published a fine collection of tales in 1850, most from the central Moscow region, and he was only one of many. The list would include A.A. Erlenvein, a teacher who encouraged schoolteachers to collect tales that he would subsequently publish in a collection of forty-one tales in 1863, and E.A. Chudinskii whose little volume of fifty-four tales came out the following year.

By the late nineteenth century and in the prerevolutionary years, the pace of folktale collecting had increased but the collectors were no longer amateurs: they were highly trained ethnographers, philologists, and trained folklorists. D.K. Zelenin collected the tales of the Urals and Viatka regions, N.E. Onchukov and A.A. Shakhmatov worked in the Far North of European Russia, D.I. Sadovnikov compiled an outstanding book of tales from the Samara region of the south, and the list goes on and on, perhaps culminating in the two-volume collection of tales of the White Lake by the brothers B.M. and Iu.M. Sokolov.

After the revolutions of 1917 a great number of collections appeared from all over the new Soviet Union. M.K. Azadovskii was one of several collectors who, following D.K. Zelenin and D.I. Sadovnikov, showed an interest in collecting and publishing tales by narrator rather than by the geographic region where they had been told. Rather than the tales collected by such and such a folklorist, they were designated as the tales of Gospodarev, Korol'kova, or Vinogradova. The number of collections of all types increased rapidly until Stalin's liquidation and dispersal of the peasantry broke the folkloric tradition once and for all time. In the past half-century, tales have been collected primarily in only two areas: the remote European North and Eastern Siberia.[10]

Narrators

The narrators of the folktales recorded in the twentieth century were not all illiterate peasants, and both their speech and the contents of the tales often show traces of literacy. Often they introduce contemporary phenomena into traditional tales: a hero may rescue the princess in the tower by flying to her in an airplane! The collective farm is also a common locus for the tale. Other tales contain obvious anachronisms. Twentieth-century narrators felt perfectly at home telling tales set in Soviet Russia but featuring the tsars and grasping landlords of prerevolutionary times. On the whole, however, the Russian tales remain even today highly traditional.

Scholars have advanced various theories in trying to sort out an explanation for the manner in which folktales were passed on from generation to generation and retold. There is general agreement that each telling of a tale constitutes an artistic performance, although not all such repetitions are of equal quality. But there are certain criteria that seem to have been present when the Russian narrators told their tales in a natural setting. The setting itself was important. They preferred an isolated place, after dark, during certain times of the year, and with a carefully restricted audience. Tales were not told during the lengthy and frequent Orthodox fasts, and the absence or presence of women and children was certainly a factor in the decision of some male narrators to tell tales. Among the fishermen of the remote Russian North, the White Sea area, some narrators were employed to tell tales until all a ship's crew had fallen asleep. M.M. Korguev's tales reflect this practice.

Tales were also told at celebratory occasions such as weddings and baptisms, or at saint's day celebrations or country fairs, and the common ending of many tales indicates that the narrator expected to be rewarded for his efforts: "I was there; I drank wine and beer. It ran down over my moustache, but none got into my mouth." Women are known to have used this same formula to encourage donations!

When the general peasantry was still largely illiterate, the tales were handed down entirely by word of mouth. Usually boys learned from their fathers, uncles, or grandfathers, or from the semiprofessional storytellers operating on their ships or in their hunting groups, although some seem to have attached themselves to storytellers and walked with them from village to village, making their living, as it were, from telling tales. We also know that traveling tradesmen told tales as they moved from village to village, and that they expected to be rewarded for telling the tales. Before the eighteenth century, traveling minstrels, known as *skomorokhi*, may also have been purveyors of folk tales (no. 58).

The future teller of tales learned his story from the master in much the same way we learn a story today—by hearing it over and over. Of course, the tale was never memorized, but the plot remained recognizably the same. The simplest of the tales consist of but one such plot, known by folklorists as a "type." Many animal tales consist of just one type, and most anecdotes do as well. Something sets the characters in motion, there is an encounter or episode, and there is a conclusion. A more elaborate version of the same single tale type would have the central episode repeated or varied in repetition either to ornament the tale or merely to lengthen it. The type may thus be repeated (as in no. 114) or combined with other types. When even the language of a tale consisting of repeated episodes is the same, and it is usually rhythmic, the tale is called a cumulative tale. Such tales as "Chicken Little" or "The Gingerbread Man" in the English-language tradition are cumulative and each has its counterpart in Russian.

The more restricted lives of women suggest that the girls and women learned tales primarily from the older women of the village, although in time they came to hear tales from the older men of the village as well. They would also have heard tales at the public events mentioned above. All in all, storytelling was a very traditional activity.

Genres

This anthology contains examples of a number of genres of the folktale. These include the animal tales; the wondertales, both those of heroes and their adversaries and the tales of magic; legends; tales of everyday life, sometimes called novellas; and anecdotes. All in all, according to SUS, there are nearly 1,250 tale types in the Russian tradition, a number exceeded only in Ukrainian.

Most scholars will agree that among the various genres of tale the animal tales are most closely related to ancient belief and myth. Indeed, in some societies they are more or less identical. They are also the tales most widely distributed throughout the world.

The Russian animal tales can easily be subdivided into groups where the protagonists are solely wild animals, where wild and domestic animals interact, or where humans participate. There are also many tales involving birds, fish, the sun and the moon, and even mushrooms.[11]

The Russian index lists 119 animal-tale types. While this may seem a large number compared with West European repertoires, the Ukrainian tradition knows more than 336 types. How is one to explain this apparent anomaly? As a people, the Russians have for centuries been more numerous than the Ukrainians, and also more isolated, factors that ought to have produced more tale types. It has been suggested that the Ukrainians have borrowed more tales from their Central European neighbors or that traders and travelers passing through that other enormous land have shared their folktale heritage with the local raconteurs. The only plausible answer is that all these factors have come into play from time to time.

Among the wild animals in the Russian tales one most frequently encounters the fox, the wolf, and the bear. The fox has a well-earned reputation for slyness and guile. She (the gender follows that of the word for fox in Russian—*lisa*) is happiest when tricking the hapless wolf out of his dinner, or luring him into a trap from which there is rarely any escape. The fox can easily outwit the bear as well, and in many instances humans too.

If the fox can be admired for her slyness, and there is something lovable about the oaf that is the bear, the wolf seems to be without redeeming features. He is rapacious but stupid, brutal, and feared by all except the fox and bear. Even men fear him, and apparently not only in the folktales.

The bear was regarded as a symbol of Russia as early as Shakespeare's time, and he is the subject of the earliest recorded Russian folktale, one related in the sixteenth century in the Vatican, of all places. Generally known in folktales as Mikhail Potapovich, Old Pigeon-toes, or simply Misha, he is awkward and relies on his huge size rather than his brain to make his way through life. One oddity connected with the bear is that he often is depicted either as the parent of a human child or as the mate of a human. This is likely an echo of the ancient cult of the bear, widely documented throughout time and throughout Russia.

There is nothing particularly kind and gentle about the tales involving animals or animals and humans. Trickery and knavery are the least of the actions they perform. The animal tales are the most gruesome of the Russian folktales, featuring disemboweling, eating alive, bashing out a victim's brains, kidnappings, and the usual acts of promiscuity. For reasons best known to psychologists, children seem to love these animal tales and overlook the sadistic and murderous elements in them.

Not all so-called animal tales involve cruelty, however. Some of them are humorous or involve humorous situations. This is particularly true of tales in which the three wild beasts (the fox, the wolf, the bear) do not participate or in which they participate only marginally. Tales about talking birds, mushrooms going to war, or the sun, moon, and stars are generally lighter in tone. And it is only just punishment, one feels, when the rascally fox gets her head caught in a jug and drowns or when the bear is so stupid that he cannot figure out why a swinging beam continues knocking him in the head until it is too late.

Domestic animals tend to be victims, just as they are in real life. Pigs are meant to be eaten and they will be. So will the hen, the goose, the hare, and the goat unless they manage to escape in the nick of time.

Whether the animals in the animal tales depict real animal behavior in any significant way has been debated. Or does the animal behavior in the tales really reflect humans' often inhuman treatment of animals and of each other?

The first animal tale in this anthology also may be regarded as a classic example of the genre. As its SUS (ATU) numbers indicate, it is made up of no fewer than eight types woven together: 1 + 2 + 3 + 4 + 43 + 30 + 170 + 61A. In the first episode the vixen pretends to be lying dead by the side of the road. The peasant, riding home with a cartload of fish, thinks that the fox's coat will make a fine shawl for his wife and tosses the fox onto his cart. The fox proceeds to divest the peasant of his fish and then hops off the cart.

Soon the wolf comes along (ATU 2 usually features a bear outside of Russia) and begs the fox to share the booty. The fox suggests that the wolf can easily catch as many fish as he likes and she shows him how to dip his tail in an ice hole. The wolf's tail freezes solidly in the ice and his howling alerts the peasant women from a nearby village who come and beat the hapless wolf nearly to death.

Meanwhile, episode SUS 3 has the fox in the village where either purposely or accidentally she covers her head with dough or batter. This leads her in the next episode (SUS 4) to plead with the wolf to carry her away as she has had her brains beaten out.

There follows in some versions of this tale the curious story of how the fox builds an ice hut for herself. When it melts, she contrives to move into a bast hut and oust its rightful occupant or occupants (SUS 43). This may be followed by SUS 30, featuring a race between the fox and the wolf in which the wolf falls into a pit. There then follows a tale of the fox and her rolling pin, which she successfully exchanges for bigger and better objects (SUS 170). The tale concludes with the fox enticing a cock to come down out of a tree so that the fox–confessor may hear the confession of the cock, who has too many wives (SUS 61A). Other genres of folktale may combine tale types in exactly the same way, although I am not aware of any that are as elaborate as this one.

"Sister Fox and the Wolf" takes up about two pages in the original Russian, each episode being told in little more than a sentence or two. Indeed, there is no reason why the tale could not have been continued. Most of the individual tale types could easily have been elaborated.

The motifs one meets in the Russian animal tales suggest that they were part of a body of narrative extant before the coming of Christianity to the East Slavs in the tenth century. Those involving the bear and the horse (the latter especially in the wondertale) are particularly noteworthy. Though the bear is portrayed as clumsy and not overly bright in many tales, in others (no. 82) he is seen as a protector of humans and their property. In many, many tales, including some in this volume, the bear kidnaps a peasant woman and they have a child who goes on to become a mighty warrior or bogatyr. Note that horses and bulls can also fill this role with similar results. One of the best of the serial tales (no. 114), told by the renowned *skazochnik* or narrator M.M. Korguev, is about such a peculiar hero's animal parentage. Korguev tells another tale, "Ivan Sosnovich," in which the hero is made from a pine tree.

For many people it is the fairy tale that comes to mind when the topic of folktale is raised.[12] But here, and increasingly in the world of folktale scholarship, the term fairy tale is not used. I will refer to them as wondertales. Wondertales in the Russian tradition have no fairies at all, and magic plays a role in only some of them.

The Russian folktale knows more than 225 types of wondertale and there are literally thousands of recorded, different renditions of these. The number of such retellings continues to grow, albeit very slowly, but few new types have been uncovered in recent years.

The actors in the wondertale are limited in number and they have limited roles to play.[13] There is always a hero, always a villain. There may be a donor and/or a helper. The hero may well have rivals—sometimes his brothers, sometimes the villain. There has to be some impulse for the hero to set about performing his heroic deeds, and the object causes this. The object may be a princess or something valued, such as a treasure. Note that a villain can actually play a number of roles: villain, donor, helper, or rival. The hero, on the other hand, is limited to being the hero. In nearly all Russian wondertales this hero will be a young male. He is not perfect, at least not at the beginning of the tale. He may be lazy, illiterate, and wearing tattered clothes. He may even have some moral blemish—he is not above telling little white lies. But as a result of his struggle with the villainy that constitutes the core of the tale, the hero overcomes his imperfections; and as a result, at the end of the tale his physical and moral blemishes have disappeared as he is readied for marriage and rule over the tsardom.

The wondertale begins in a state of equilibrium, but it is a state of equilibrium that is doomed to be broken: "There lived and dwelt a tsar and his tsarevna with their only daughter." "There lived and dwelt a poor peasant woman and her only son." Inevitably, either of these situations just described will force the appearance of a potential hero who is equally inevitably an unpromising youth: he may be a stepson or an orphan; he may be destitute; he is always forced by circumstances beyond his control to do something, to act. He departs from home and in tales of magic he departs never to return to that initial situation and goes into another world, where he is to encounter the most bizarre beasts imaginable. He has no talents, no special knowledge, nothing that will promise him success in what he is about to endure. He must seek assistance and advice before he can succeed in his task and accomplish his goal. In no. 114 he learns to read and write, but he never makes use of these modern inventions. He is utterly dependent on chance encounters, often with otherworldly beings. Along the way he must learn and therefore we find our hero prone to transgressing boundaries, breaking interdictions. Oddly enough, failure to do so means failure to succeed. The hero is an actor, a doer, not a lad who asks "Why." But succeed he will and he will emerge unscathed at the end of the tale, often enough as the heir to the throne and the groom for that lonesome daughter of the tsar.

The villain may be the serpent, Baba Yaga the witch, a nasty dwarf, or a shape-shifting magician. Baba Yaga can also function as donor or helper, but obviously neither a rival nor the object of the hero's ultimate quest. In other words, the cast of characters is small, the roles they play are limited, and without exception they all exist only to further the hero's tasks.

The structure of the wondertale is also limited. More than half a century ago V.Ia. Propp proved that the syntax of the wondertale could theoretically contain no more than thirty-one units, or functions as he called them.[14] We can understand these as predicates in that they refer to the actions that may take place in a wondertale. As Propp showed, these can only occur in a specific order within a type and thus it may be said that there is but one overall structure to the wondertale. Furthermore, from the static beginning to the conclusion these functions tend to occur in pairs (negative/positive) with the climax occurring in the middle of the tale. The enormous number of combinations of the functions within the limited number of (ATU/SUS) tale types, which may be "chained" together by the skillful tale teller, makes possible the great variety of wondertales within a given tradition.

The great attraction of the wondertale in Russian has not, however, been its structure, but rather its ornamentation. The old stories were told with a richness of vocabulary, including various kinds of fixed epithets, and the common situations that allowed the storyteller to depict the location of the action in just a few sentences and leave much to the imagination of the audience. Nowadays the tales are nearly always presented to children in books, often lavishly illustrated, and the role of narrator is filled by the reader. The illustrator plays an important role in determining the way the characters and their various escapades are imagined by the young listeners. Such characters as Baba Yaga and her hut, the Firebird, Koshchei the Deathless, Prince Ivan, Princess Elena, the tsar, and all the rest have become part of the wondertale tradition in the art of Ivan Bilibin and other illustrators. Nor is there now any great distinction drawn between the true wondertales and those penned by Russian writers, whether Pushkin or Tolstoy or lesser lights.

The Russian tradition knows two kinds of wondertale: those about heroes and villains, and those in which the focus is on magic. There is never more than one hero, although he may have rivals such as his two older brothers. The hero in the Russian tradition is most frequently named Ivan Tsarevich, although in the wondertale as a whole the hero often enters the tale simply as Ivan and only becomes a tsarevich or heir to the tsar at the end of the tale. At the beginning of the tale the would-be hero is a marked youth: he is either disadvantaged or overly advantaged. If the former, he may be an orphan or the youngest brother, or have some undesirable physical characteristic. The overly advantaged youth is more often than not the tsar's son and yet he lacks something for his maturation. That may be proving himself in a struggle with a wicked adversary or even overcoming a reluctant bride. It is not difficult to see why so many readers have identified the wondertale as reflective of rites of initiation. Certainly, the struggles of the potential hero are indicative of a youth's struggles to become a man, albeit in a highly exaggerated form.

Tales in which the hero accomplishes his tasks by means of magic and the supernatural often feature animals, including those whom the hero has rescued at some point in his wanderings through the woods. But they also include tales told of superhuman heroes such as those met in the Russian folk epic, the *bylina*. In these tales, secret languages, disguises, magic rings and stones or hats and slippers may all play a role. Eating the hero's apples may make the tsarevna (tsar's daughter) grow horns, which will only fall off when she agrees to marry him and eats another of his apples. Magic carpets, purses that can never be emptied of their contents, tablecloths that magically provide the hero with all the food and drink he can possibly want, horses that leap rivers of fire—all of these are commonplace in tales of this kind. But any of these elements can and will appear in tales of heroes and villains as well: the line between these two divisions of the wondertale is anything but clear.

Whether anybody but children believes the wondertales are true is a matter of some dispute. The saying "Skazka—skladka, pesnia—byl'" (The tale is a fabrication, but the song is real) suggests that adults are not prone to believe them, but on the other hand, "Would the old folks lie?"

The legend is another matter. Usually based either on a historical event or a person known to have existed, the legend may sometimes be quite close to truth, while at other times completely unbelievable.[15] There are many legends about figures in the Orthodox Church that church officials might well regard as blasphemous and certainly as utterly fictitious. The Russians are fond of legends that portray days past when Christ or His disciples walked about Holy Mother Russia, enabling the poor and oppressed to eke out their meager existence, and there are a number that portray saints in various lights. Especially popular are those featuring Nikolai the Wonderworker and George, who does not always slay dragons.

Some historical figures are also popular, including tsars Ivan IV (the Terrible) and Peter the Great, although the episodes connected with these and well-known military leaders such as Ermak or Suvorov are far from any documented truth. A very few legends are connected to figures from premodern Russian culture. Such would include those about the *skomorokhi*, widely thought to have been associated with Russian paganism. Others reflect the deeds and misdeeds of contemporary Russian peasants, especially drunkenness. Many legends reflect a wistful desire for a better life, often enough depicted in the narrator's imaginary heaven, or his equally real imaginary hell where bigamists, fornicators, and again especially drunkards are known to dwell. There is much humor in the legends, but much gloom and despair as well.

What Russians call "tales of everyday life" or perhaps "household tales" or novellas (*bytovye skazki*) reflect social conditions of the late eighteenth and especially the nineteenth centuries.[16] For the most part, gone are the tsars and tsareviches, the fantastic settings, characters, and magic of the wondertale, and in their place one finds unscrupulous merchants, swaggering officers, soldiers returning from their twenty-five years in service (no exaggeration, this!), maidens whose virtue cannot always be guaranteed before their marriage, and priests whose morality is a shock to everyone.

Many of the tales in this general category resemble short stories, only they were told orally of course, and with all the inconsistencies, lapses, and repetitions that such narratives feature. One aspect of these tales that is totally absent from wondertales is social conflict between classes. When the tsar announces a competition for the hand of his daughter, the lower-class hero always triumphs over the ham-fisted efforts of rich landlords, nobles, or generals, using not only his wits but also his superior strength to determine the outcome.

Sometimes the novellas, as they may be called, are simply dirty stories. These could not be published by the guardians of public purity in tsarist Russia and the Soviet Union, but the "secret tales" were known abroad, one such collection appearing in Geneva, of all places, in 1872.[17] Since the fall of the Soviet Union, a number of such collections have appeared in Russian, but the newer ones await their translation into English.

Having stated earlier that these tales were devoid of the fantastic, I should exclude a special category—tales in which the devil or the devil's offspring appear.[18] These are almost always tales that feature a priest and the devil's adversary, Ivan the Fool. Now Ivan was no fool and he immediately takes advantage of the witless priest and the equally witless devil. These tales tend to be told in combinations of types: the priest encounters or hires Ivan; they make a bargain that the priest assumes Ivan will not be able to keep and thus the priest will not have to pay him; the time agreed by the priest and Ivan draws to a close and the priest fears he will have to pay up, so he sends Ivan on an impossible mission to collect the rents from the devil, who may inhabit a mill or dwell at the bottom of a lake. Ivan forces the devil to accede to his demands and returns to the priest with the rents and more. The priest and his wife decide to flee from Ivan rather than pay him. He hides from them and they cart him off in their baggage. In the end, he often does away with the hapless priest and occasionally marries the widow.

All these stories have well-thought-out plots and tended to be among the most frequently told of the Russian folk narratives, judging by the number of extant versions. In this they differ from the so-called anecdotes, which are farcical and often enough pointless.[19] In the opinion of many, these jokes are not really folktales at all. On the other hand, some of them are extremely similar to tales that are universally classified as folktales.

Their basic theme is stupidity, usually human stupidity, and if the outlandish means the narrator employs to prove the point are at all a guide, he succeeds remarkably well. They have always been popular among the Russians, just as their analogues have remained popular in the West. The problem with anecdotes is that in many cases they are extremely similar to the tales of everyday life, especially those involving the fool. Some Russian scholars have argued that the bulk of the tales classified as anecdotes are really traditional folktales. Conversely, some tales classified as folktales are really anecdotes (see SUS 664 and variants, for example). There are differences, however. The anecdote almost always consists of a single episode and is always humorous, even absurd. There is no disputing the fact that the anecdote is derived from the tales of everyday life, at least in the majority of instances.

More may be said about the serial tales told by Korguev, the Dmitrievs, and Kabrenov in the twentieth century.[20] Other than the actual texts of the tales themselves the best information we have about the circumstances surrounding the telling of this variety of tale comes from the Russian naturalist writer Mikhail Prishvin, who came across Osip Dmitriev in the Pudozh area of Karelia before the revolution. Dmitriev emphasized the physical setting: nighttime at certain times of the year (and never during the lengthy fasts of the Orthodox Church), a secluded place, the absence of women and small children—all to heighten the sense of the mystery surrounding the tales. As Russian scholars have pointed out, these features suggest ritual.

Dmitriev and his son Mikhail Osipovich were not associated with fishing, but they apparently were involved in hunting, the second activity that required long absences from home in the company of a group of men. These hunting associations or artels spent much of the winter and early spring months in communal activity that featured much traditional lore recorded since the early nineteenth century.

Apparently, those narrators who were hired on to accompany a fishing vessel for weeks at a time would begin a story late in the evening when the crew was preparing to go to sleep. After a period of time the narrator, Korguev in this case, would ask "Are you asleep?" If someone answered, he would continue the tale until a point when no one responded to his question. He would then continue the tale the following night. Thus, the tales are rather like chapters in a book or television serials.

Korguev, Kabrenov, and the Dmitrievs told only wondertales in this fashion, and primarily among these, tales of the epic struggles of heroes and their adversaries. The reader will readily recognize the familiar episodes from tales presented earlier in this book; they are not new, it is just that there are many more of them and the ornamentation is much more substantial. Though not all his tales are "serial" tales, Korguev related more than 120 tales between 1936 and 1938, while Kabrenov narrated more than 50. Limitations of space have determined that only three of these serial tales can be included in this collection (nos. 112, 113, 114). That these narrators were active until just before World War II is testimony to the isolated regions where they lived on the Kola Peninsula or in Karelia.

To this point the discussion has involved tale types and representative examples of them, which is how they are presented in this anthology. But any reader of folktales, especially one who reads tales from more than a single tradition, is well aware of the fact that within a type there may be wide variation. These variants reflect the individual narrator's art, perhaps his interest in the tale he is telling. In the first tale of this anthology not all eight tale types were equally well elaborated. Some indeed were represented only by a sentence or two, while others properly read like little chapters of a larger work. If one takes a look at the variants of a tale type, one will be struck by the uniformity exhibited by many of the variants as opposed to some others. The ways in which these variants are handled has a direct bearing on the interpretation of the tales, for the material of the variant is closely controlled by the narrator working within the given tradition. The fact is, as E.V. Pomerantseva has pointed out, narrators felt quite within their rights to alter not so much the structure of the tale, its type as it were, as the flesh they hung on that skeleton.[21] More often than not, they did this to suit their audience. Tales told to children differed from those told to young men or adults. One excellent example of this notion of variants is ATU/SUS 61A, found in two tales of this collection (nos. 1 and 5) but existing in more than fifteen other printed versions in the Russian tradition alone. The editors of ATU give this synopsis of the tale type:

Fox persuades cock to come down from a tree and confess sins to him. When cock comes down, fox seizes him. Cock begs to be released and tempts fox by saying that he will lead him to a feast of a rich bishop. Fox believes it, and the cock flies away and mocks him.

Excluding a *lubok* version of the late eighteenth century the oldest treatment is Afanas'ev 16, included in this volume (no. 5). This version reads like a parody of the gospel texts from Matthew and Luke, and the language is a parody of the Russian Church Slavonic, which was quite far removed from peasant speech. Other than our knowing that the tale was written down from an aged peasant working in a Perm factory in 1846, we know nothing further about the tale. The point here is that from the beginning the tale was regarded as anticlerical and it ran afoul of the censors.

Another Afanas'ev version (15), has only one reference to the church and that a most insignificant one. In fact, it could be regarded as the "standard" version of the tale with the sly, honey-tongued vixen and the flattering cock each attempting to outwit the other.

His third version is preceded by the tale of the wolf meeting up with a sow and devouring her piglets, which is only tangentially connected to type 61A, "The Fox as Confessor." This tale, recorded in Tula province, is rhymed, has the fox promising that "I will raise your soul to heaven" and the silly cock willy-nilly descending onto the ground. As the fox shakes the life out of the cock, the latter utters a prayer to as many "saints" as he finds time for. The effect is humorous, hardly anticlerical.

Yet another version was included in Afanas'ev's collection as the concluding episode to tale no. 1. In this tale, which Afanas'ev himself collected, we encounter nothing more than the barest outlines of the type: the fox encounters the cock, accuses him of sinning by having seventy wives, entices him to come down to the ground so that his confession might be heard, grabs him, and gobbles him up.

Kupriianikha, a twentieth-century narrator, has the fox wringing the cock's neck and then devouring him, but then a wolf happens along and devours the fox. The entire tale follows the usual pattern up to the final unexpected episode with the wolf (Kupriianikha, no. 33).

A version recorded by N.E. Onchukov from an extremely talented raconteur, G.I. Chuprov, who lived on the Pechora River in the north, tells of the fox, the cock, and the crane. As the fox is preparing to raid a nobleman's yard, the cock is alerted and awakens the household, which comes to the aid of the livestock. The fox and cock meet again in the woods where the cock has wandered to have a look around. The fox entices the "thieving cock" to descend from his perch in the tree "to confess as the last time is near." The cock is caught and castigated for having prevented the fox's getting a good meal at the boyar's expense and the cock responds with flattery, which is often the fox's downfall. The fox allows the cock to escape and then there follows an episode where the crane attempts to teach the fox to fly, which ends in the death of the fox. Meanwhile, the hens long for a cock and are not laying well. At the last moment one shows up and harmony is restored. Except for the unfortunate episode with the fox, who learns too late that he cannot learn to fly, the tale generally follows the expected pattern.

In 1859 a version was recorded (later published in Smirnov, no. 295) in a mixture of Church Slavonic and Russian. Here the fox invites the cock to join her and go into the service of the archimandrite, or head of a large Orthodox monastery. The cock is caught but again flattery wins out and once again from the treetop the cock mocks the hapless fox. End of tale.

A.I. Nikiforov published the tale in his collection from the Mezen in northern Russia in which the fox once more attempts to raid the henhouse but is thwarted by "thieving Petusha." The vixen barely escapes and lies three days beneath a willow. She meets with the cock and there ensues a lengthy conversation in which the fox attempts to convince the cock that it was not she who attempted the theft of the hens but another vixen. The vixen explains the cock's dilemma: "The peasant has but one wife and each year goes to confession, while you have seven wives and don't go to confession even once a year."

In Nikiforov's version the cock goes on to promise the fox a soft life in the communion bread bakery and as one expects, the fox releases her grip on the cock, who flies away and from a safe perch mocks the vixen. There then follows the episode with the crane trying to teach the fox to fly. This is one of the outstanding versions of the traditional tale, but one cannot find any appreciable variations from the standard.

D.M. Balashov collected the tale in the White Sea coast village of Strelna from one Fedora Stepanovna Nizovtseva, who was sixty-two years old. After the usual attempts on the part of the vixen to steal from a peasant, she meets the cock in the wood, where he has flown in "fine weather." The conversation concerns the cock's sinful past and his twenty, even thirty wives. Soon the cock is once more in the fox's clutches. The cock promises the fox soft loaves and sweet ales in the metropolitan's household. Back in the tree the cock says, "Congratulations, dear mother fox, on your new position! Eat white snow as if it were ham."

Two versions of SUS 61A have been recorded in Siberia, one in the Tomsk district and one in Chita. Only the former has been published, in 1993 by Matveeva and Leonova. It follows the ATU/SUS synopsis almost exactly and seems to have been intended for an audience of children. The language replicates that of children's tales right to the very end when the narrator states, "Then the fox went off to the woods and carried off the whole tale with her."

From these several variants we can draw some obvious conclusions: that the overall structure of the tale in all of them closely follows the expected; that only rarely does the cock fall victim to the fox in the end, and in those instances the fox may pay dearly for her trickery; that in the instance of obvious anticlerical tendency in the tale (Afanas'ev 16) someone for some reason was very concerned to deviate from the usual manner of telling the tale in choice of language and details from everyday life in a way not encountered even in tales told in the Soviet period. Afanas'ev 16 (no. 5 in this collection) is a tale splendidly told, but it is not entirely typical of its type. It does show how this narrator was clearly able to take a well-known tale type and elaborate on it, using a special language (the ecclesiastical) and parodying texts well known to his presumed audience (of which we have no direct knowledge). That Afanas'ev chose to include it in a collection of tales for children says more about his political and social views than it does about the narrator himself, and the same can be said about the ecclesiastical censors who found the tale objectionable precisely because the narrator had chosen to step outside the bounds of the given scheme.

But such is the art of the folktale. Kazakov, the narrator of our tale no. 5, is hardly an exception in altering the substance of a tale while sticking rather closely to its overall structure. Some of the well-known narrators of more recent times have even boasted about their ability, if such it is, to tell a tale to suit an audience. This is especially true of tales told in the Soviet period where tellers of tales freely substituted one social class for another or one national group for a more favored one. But the stability of the tales remains a striking phenomenon as the comparative and historical study of tale types shows. While the morphology of the tale remains constant, to use V.Ia. Propp's term, the narrator can and does alter the characters, their language, and their social background to suit himself and please his audience.

Art of the Tale

The repertoire of the narrator may vary greatly from just a single tale or just a handful of tales to well over a hundred. The most common ways in which the experienced and talented storyteller demonstrates his art are elaboration and ornamentation. By elaboration we mean the weaving into a single narrative of two or more tale types. As tales such as "Sister Fox and the Wolf" show, there is no particular limit on the number of tale types that the skilled narrator may include in a single tale. Here is the artistry the audience has been expecting, for although the theft of the fish from the hapless peasant sets the audience on the right track to guess the outcome of that particular episode, it has no way of knowing whether there will be subsequent tale types added to it. Nor can it predict the order that the additions might take: there is no fixed order. In fact, even the denouement is uncertain: is the wolf to die or the fox to be punished, or will the bear perhaps enter the scene and become the victim?

Simply stringing together tale types does not make an artful folktale, however, and the audience likely will become restless if that is all the narrator's art appears to be. The true folk artist knows the value of ornamentation and knows how to employ a variety of kinds. There are, for instance, fixed epithets. Here combinations of words used throughout the entire oral tradition help the audience identify characters and situations. Thus, Ivan in the wondertale may be Ivan the Tsar's Son, or Ivan the Handsome or Brave or Mighty Warrior, or even Ivan the Bear's Son, whereas in tales about the clever fool he is never any of these but invariably Ivan or Ivan the Peasant or

Laborer. The princess is always beautiful with beautiful hair or eyes, pathetically weak and incapable, and just waiting to be rescued by Ivan the Brave—but not in tales of the clever-fool type, where no such princesses are to be found. If her appearance goes beyond the barest outline, the maiden is always dressed in a red *sarafan*, while the handsome hero will be in a blue tunic. Falcons are bright-eyed, Baba Yaga is always described in the same horrific way, aged parents are either the tsar and tsarina or poor and unable to support their hapless son, who must therefore set off on an adventure to right the situation. Rivers tend to be swift, the sea is blue, all tsars reward the hero with the daughter and/or half the tsardom, and so on, and so forth.

The animals have their own particular names just as humans do. These may often describe their behavior or their appearance. Lisa Patrikeevna is the sly fox, the wolf is mangy and greedy, old Mikhail Potapovich the Pigeon-toed is the clumsy and rather stupid bear, and some animals end up being helpers to the human figure while others play roles that are the opposite. In wondertales the horse is the agent ensuring the hero's escape from the witch and his successful arrival in the Otherworld where he will encounter the death-dealing serpents. Sometimes the horse turns out to be his true guardian, as it were, stumbling to warn the hero of incipient danger. On the other hand, the horse in tales of the clever fool is often a castoff nag. All genres of the Russian oral tradition feature these fixed epithets and depictions, although the folktale employs somewhat fewer than do others, especially the *bylina* and the historical song.

Another form of ornamentation is the fixed situation or locus. The peasant hut (*izba*) is dominated by the enormous stove that serves not only its culinary purpose but also as a place for sleeping, hiding, or storytelling. The hut is also a place connected with myriad superstitions, many of which are still widely practiced among Russians today. So, too, is the bathhouse, inhabited by a special malevolent spirit, the *bannik*.

When the would-be hero departs his hut or the tsar's palace, he usually proceeds into a deep wood and there he stumbles upon a peculiarly Russian phenomenon, the little hut of the Russian witch Baba Yaga. Capable of revolving, it stands on cock's legs and apparently has no windows. The hero, instinctively as it were, knows the formula needed to gain entrance to the interior of this structure, which with its inhabitant resembles nothing so much as a tomb. Often depicted as having a palisade of skulls, Baba Yaga's *izbushka* is known to the audience as the locus of the testing of the wondertale hero.

Whether fleeing or flying, the hero must next cross over the well-known barrier between the world of Baba Yaga and the thrice-nine kingdom inhabited by the true villain of the tale, a multiple-headed serpent or some ogre. The cataclysmic struggle takes place either on or near the bridge, or in some place that remains featureless.

The hero is victorious—always. He returns to the real world and his reward, usually to the tsar's palace, which is just a place name. It, too, is featureless.

Most legends know real cities and real characters. Christ and his apostles walk about the vastness of Mother Russia, real tsars are met in Moscow or St. Petersburg or out on real campaigns, and real generals win important victories. However, other legends merely reflect the religious atmosphere or superstitions connected with religious beliefs.

In other kinds of tales, traders set up their tables in Red Square or on some village square and carry out their inevitable tricks and knavery. The village smithy, the bathhouse, and the mill with their sinister associations of devilry provide locations for superhuman feats and quite fantastic deeds that are completely familiar to the audience. These common locations of actions and associations on the one hand are a kind of shorthand the narrator uses to avoid describing the well known again and again, and at the same time they provide him with the opportunity for substantial ornamentation. The narrator does not have to tell his audience that the smithy has sinister associations: that is given. He can thus describe the outlandish size of the smith's anvil and hammer, or the wonder-working icons on the wall, or the incredible age of the smith's father, and so on.

A feature known as triplification is also commonly met in the Russian folktale. Here, a portion or even an entire episode may be repeated three times with slight variation. The purpose of this tripling is not always clear. It may merely be to lengthen a tale the narrator feels is too short, or perhaps it is a feature of ornamentation, or perhaps the narrator feels his audience needs to be reminded of the idea embedded in the part of the tale being repeated. Or all of the above!

The question of the meaning of the folktale is a perilous one. Many a scholar-editor has sought to impose his or her interpretation on the tales, often in accordance with a prevailing ideology. I would prefer to leave such questions for the reader to decide. In this anthology there are ample illustrations of tales open to many interpretations, but the reader is encouraged always to keep in mind that folktales were originally told by the elders both to instruct the young and to entertain the community or family in days when there were no books, no radio, and certainly no television.

Organization of the Anthology

As outlined in the table of contents, the tales are organized by genre, and each such grouping begins with a brief introduction. A headnote preceding each tale briefly describes what is known about its provenance—place and time, narrator and collector—and explains any unfamiliar features or terms. (Readers may also consult the Glossary in the front of the book.) At the end of each headnote we provide the appropriate SUS number (or numbers) from the comparative index of East Slavic tale types. The SUS number is based on the Aarne-Thompson (A–T) index of tale types, later expanded as the Aarne-Thompson-Uther (ATU) international index of tale types. Interested readers may consult these indexes to find analogues of the Russian tales. Story credits at the back of the book identify the source of each text with a short citation corresponding to a listing in the Sources Cited in Russian.

Notes

1. As late as the 1897 census, 87 percent of the Russian population were classified as peasants.

2. For discussion and examples see Linda J. Ivanits, *Russian Folk Belief* (Armonk, NY, 1989), especially Part 2.

3. Jack V. Haney, *An Introduction to the Russian Folktale.* Vol. 1 of *The Complete Russian Folktale.* (*CRF*).

4. Jack V. Haney, "On the 'Tale of Peter and Fevroniia, Wonderworkers of Murom,'" *Canadian-American Slavic Studies*, vol. 13, nos. 1–2 (1979): 139–62.

5. Stith Thompson, *The Folktale* (Berkeley, CA, 1977), p. 3.

6. See Jack Zipes, *Fairy Tale as Myth. Myth as Fairy Tale* (Lexington, KY, 1994), for an interesting approach to this question.

7. Hans-Jörg Uther, *The Types of International Folktales* (Helsinki, 2004).

8. An excellent English work on the *lubok* is Alla Sytova, *The Lubok. Russian Folk Pictures 17th to 19th Century* (Leningrad, 1984).

9. A representative selection of Afanas′ev's tales is to be found in *Russian Fairy Tales,* trans. by Norbert Guterman with commentary by Roman Jakobson (New York, 1973).

10. Full bibliographic information for these and other Russian collections through 1979 may be found in SUS.

11. On the animal tales see Thompson, *The Folktale*, 217–29, and Haney, *CRF*, vol. 2.

12. On the wondertales see Haney, *CRF*, vols. 3 and 4; Lüthi's several volumes; Thompson, *The Folktale,* pp. 21–188; and Zipes, *Fairy Tale as Myth.*

13. E.S. Novik, "Sistema personazhei russkoi volshebnoi skazki," in *Tipologicheskie issledovaniia po fol′kloru* (Moscow, 1975), pp. 214–46.

14. V.Ia. Propp, *Morfologiia skazki* (Moscow, 1969). The two English translations are faulty in places and should be used with considerable caution.

15. On the legends see Haney, *CRF*, vol. 5.

16. Haney, *CRF*, vols. 6, 7.

17. Aleksandr N. Afanasiev, *Russian Secret Tales. Bawdy Folktales of Old Russia* (Baltimore, 1998).

18. Haney, *CRF,* vol. 7.

19. Thompson, *The Folktale*, p. 188 ff., refers to the anecdotes as jests, anecdotes, and numbskull stories. There is no collection of translations of these simple narratives from the Russian. They are found labeled SUS 1200 and above. The anecdotes were very popular in Western Europe in medieval times, but in Russia we have scant evidence of them before the seventeenth century.

20. Little has been written on these serial tales, although T.I. Sen′kina, *Russkaia skazka Karelii* (Petrozavodsk, 1988), has some scattered comments.

21. E.V. Pomerantseva, *Russkaia narodnaia skazka* (Moscow, 1963), p. 17 ff.

Glossary

altyn	three kopecks
arshin	twenty-eight inches
ataman	headman, leader, especially in Southwest Russia and Ukraine
A–T	Aarne-Thompson tale-type index
ATU	Aarne-Thompson-Uther international tale-type index
Baba Yaga	Russian witch
bast	inner layer of bark, usually of birch, lime or linden, used to weave *lapti* (boots or shoes)
bathhouse	center of much ritual activity in old Russia
batiushka	Father, used of tsar and priest
bliny	thin pancakes
bogatyr	warrior, especially in the epics (*byliny*)
boyars	landed nobles of old Russia
bylina	heroic epic
Circassian	Cherkass, people of the Caucasus
CRF	*The Complete Russian Folktale* (Haney)
dead and living waters	the former ends "chaos" and brings form, while the latter provides the life force
grivennik, grivna	ten-kopeck coin
gubernia	province
gusli	traditional musical instrument resembling a small harp
hegumen	head of an Orthodox monastery
hegumeness	head of an Orthodox nunnery
Idolishche	giant, villain, hostile warrior, pagan warrior; a monster
izba, izbushka	peasant hut
kaftan	long robe worn by men, especially by merchants
kasha	porridge often made of buckwheat; staple of peasant life
koldun	sorcerer
kvass	slightly alcoholic brew made from stale rye bread

lapti	bast boots or shoes
leshii	forest spirit
lubok/lubki	booklet made of bast, woodcuts on bast often telling animal and other folktales
matushka	priest's wife
mizinets	little finger or toe; amputated in ancient times in initiatory rites
pan	gentleman, sir (Polish, west Russian)
pood	weight equivalent to thirty-three pounds
sarafan	pinafore dress of peasant women
sazhen	length equivalent to 2.3 yards
skazki	folktales
skazochnik	teller of folktales
skomorokh	minstrel, purveyor of pre-Christian lore, entertainer in Muscovite Russia
sleigh	means of conveyance of the bride in the peasant wedding or of a corpse
station	postal station where horses were changed, meals served, and beds provided
stove	heart of the peasant hut; the oven was at the bottom and this then heated several layers up to the rafters. The family slept on the top layers.
SUS	East Slavic tale-type index
tarantas	light carriage pulled by three horses
tsar, tsarina (tsaritsa), tsarevna, tsarevich	Russian royal family equivalent to king, queen, princess, prince
verst	length equivalent to 3,500 feet
vodianoi	undersea or underwater spirit or deity
voevoda	military commander or governor
wine/vodka	used interchangeably in the tales for vodka
wreathing	Christian wedding rite conducted by priest (also crowning)

AN ANTHOLOGY OF

Russian Folktales

Animal Tales

The East Slavic (Belarusian, Russian, and Ukrainian) animal tales comprise nearly 550 types according to the SUS, the index to the East Slavic folktale. Of these some 125 are recorded in Russian and some of them are unique to that tradition. Printed versions of the most popular tales exist from the late eighteenth century and the tales continue to find an audience even today. The most popular actors in the tales are the wily fox, the gluttonous wolf, and the affable if somewhat stupid and clumsy bear. The listener/reader also will encounter pigs, chickens, cows, horses, birds, and of course people. Even mushrooms and the sun, wind, and moon may make appearances. The roots of the animal tales are very ancient indeed, stretching back to the pre-Christian era and surviving in local customs and taboos even today. This selection of fourteen tales represents merely some of the more popular tales from this vast tradition. For more on the Russian animal tales see Haney, *CRF*, vol. 2.

1. Sister Fox and the Wolf

Recorded in 1848 by Afanas'ev in Voronezh province. The first two types are frequently combined in many folktale traditions, the first four frequently in East Slavic, but only in this single tale do we meet eight types combined into one tale. Not all of the episodes are fully represented. The tale was frequently reworked by nineteenth-century Russian writers and published in collections for children. SUS 1 + 2 + 3 + 4 + 43 + 30 + 170 + 61A.

There lived an old man and an old woman. The old man said to the old woman, "You, old woman, bake some pies, and I'll go catch some fish."

The old man caught the fish and was bringing home a whole cart full. On the way, he saw a fox curled up like a biscuit lying in the road. The old man got down from his cart and went up to the fox, but she didn't move; she just lay there as if dead. "Well, that'll be a present for the wife," said the old man, and he took the fox and put her in the cart. Then he rode on. Now the fox waited for just the right time and then began ever so gently to toss all the fish one after another from the cart. And when she had thrown them all off, she herself departed.

"Well, old woman," said the old man, "look what a collar I've brought you for your fur coat!"

"Where?"

"There, the fish and the collar are both in the cart."

The old woman went up to the cart: no collar, no fish, so she began to curse the old man. "You old horseradish, you so-and-so. Who did you think you could fool?" Just then the old man figured it out: the fox hadn't been dead. He grieved and was bitter, but there was nothing to be done.

Now the fox collected into a pile all the fish she had thrown off along the way, and then she sat down and began to eat. A wolf came up to her.

"Hello, dearie!"

"Hello, my dear!"

"Give me a bit of fishy!"

"Catch it yourself, then you'll eat."

"I don't know how."

"Oh, I've already caught my lot. You, dear, go out on the river and let your tail down into the ice hole. A fish will hook onto your tail by itself. Then you sit a bit longer, or you won't catch your lot."

The wolf went out onto the river and lowered his tail into the ice hole. It was winter, you see. And he sat and he sat, he sat a whole night through, and his tail was frozen solid. He tried to get up, but there was no way he could. There was just nothing to be done. "Oh, so many fish have clamped on, I can't even pull them out."

He looked up. Some women who were coming for water had caught sight of him and were shouting: "Wolf, wolf! Kill him!" They came and began to thrash the wolf, some with yokes, some with buckets or whatever was at hand. The wolf tried and tried to jump up; then he tore off his tail and ran away with nary a glance back.

"Very well then," he thought. "I'll pay you back, my dearie."

But sister fox, having eaten up the fish, decided to try getting something else. She climbed into a hut where the women were making pancakes and fell head first into a barrel of batter, got it smeared all over her, and fled. The wolf happened along and met her. "So this is what you taught me! I've just been thoroughly thrashed!"

"But my dear," said sister fox, "you've just lost a little blood, while I've had it far worse than you. My brains have been beaten out. I'm just staggering along."

"That is true," said the wolf. "Wherever you need to go, I'll carry you."

So the fox got on his back, and the wolf set off carrying her. So sister fox sat quietly and sang quietly, "The beaten one carries the unbeaten one, the beaten one carries the unbeaten one."

"What are you saying, dearie?"

"I'm saying, 'the beaten one carries the beaten one.'"

"Well, that's it, dearie, that's it."

"Say, let's build huts for ourselves, my dear."

"Let's, dearie."

"I'll build a bast house, and you build one of ice."

They set to work and built the huts: for the fox a bast one, and for the wolf one of ice. And they lived in them. Spring came, and the wolf's hut melted. "Oh, dearie," said the wolf, "you've deceived me once again, and now I'll just have to eat you for this."

"Let's go, friend, let's have another try to see who can find something to eat."

So sister fox led him into the forest to a deep pit and said, "Jump! If you jump across the pit, then you eat me, but if you don't jump across, then I'll eat you!"

The wolf jumped and fell into the pit. "Well," said the fox, "just sit there." And she went away.

She walked along, carrying her rolling pin in her paws, and invited herself into a peasant's hut. "Let sister fox spend the night."

"It's already crowded without you."

"I won't crowd you, I'll lie on the bench, my tail beneath the bench, the rolling pin next to the stove." They let her in. She lay down on the bench, her tail beneath the bench, her rolling pin next to the stove. Early the next morning the fox got up, burned up her rolling pin, and then asked, "Where's my rolling pin? I'll take nothing less than a goose for it!" There was nothing else the peasant could do, so he gave her a goose for the rolling pin. The fox took the goose and walked along singing:

> Sister fox went walking along the road.
> She was carrying a rolling pin
> And for that rolling pin got a goose!
> Knock, knock, knock!

She knocked at the door of another peasant's hut.

"Who's there?"

"It is I, sister fox, let me in to spend the night."

"It's already crowded without you."

"I won't crowd you. I'll lie on the bench, my tail beneath the bench, my goose next to the stove." They let her in. She lay herself down on the bench, her tail beneath the bench, and the goose next to the stove. The next morning she jumped up early, grabbed the goose, plucked her, ate her up, and said, "Where's my goose? I'll take nothing less than a turkey hen for her!" The peasant—there was nothing else he could do—gave her his turkey hen for the goose. The fox took the turkey hen and walked along singing:

> Sister fox went walking along the road.
> She was carrying a rolling pin
> And for that rolling pin got a goose!
> And for that goose she got a turkey hen!

Knock, knock, knock! She knocked at the door of a third peasant's hut. "Who's there?"

"I am, sister fox. Let me in to spend the night."

"It's already crowded without you."

"I won't crowd you. I'll lie on the bench, my tail beneath the bench, my turkey hen next to the stove." They let her in. She lay down on the bench, her tail beneath the bench, the turkey hen next to the stove. Early in the morning the fox jumped up, grabbed the turkey hen, plucked it and ate it up, and said, "Where's my turkey hen? For her I won't take less than your bride!" For the peasant there was nothing to do except give up his bride for the turkey hen. The fox put her in a bag and walked along singing:

> Sister fox went walking along the road.
> She was carrying a rolling pin
> And for that rolling pin got a goose!
> And for that goose she got a turkey hen!
> And for that turkey hen she got a bride!

Knock, knock, knock! She knocked at the hut of a fourth peasant. "Who's there?"

"It is I, sister fox. Let me in to spend the night."

"It's already crowded without you."

"I won't crowd you. I myself shall lie on the bench, my tail beneath the bench, my bag next to the stove." They let her in. She lay down on the bench, her tail beneath the bench, the bag next to the stove. The peasant stealthily let the bride out of the bag and kicked a dog into it. Well, next morning sister fox prepared for the road, took her bag, walked along, and said, "Oh bride, sing some songs!" And that dog started yelping! The fox was so frightened that she flung away the bag with the dog and ran.

So the fox was running and saw that on the gate there sat a cock. She went up to him and said, "Cock, oh cock! Come down here, and I'll hear your confession: you have seventy wives and are always sinning!" The cock came down, and she grabbed him and ate him up.

2. The Peasant, the Bear, and the Fox

Recorded in Lipetsk district of Tambov province. This popular tale often features the devil rather than the bear and is then classified SUS 1030 + 154. Afanas'ev edited this tale, judging from his notebooks. SUS 9 + 154.

A peasant and a bear were great friends. Once they took it into their heads to sow turnips. They sowed them, and then they began to discuss who should take what.

The peasant said, "I'll take the roots, and you, Misha, take the tops." So the turnips grew, and the peasant took the roots and Misha the tops.

Misha saw that he had made a mistake, and he said to the peasant, "You have tricked me, brother! When we sow something else, you won't fool me so easily."

A year passed. The peasant said to the bear: "Well, Misha, let's sow some wheat."

"Let's," said Misha.

So they sowed the wheat. And the wheat ripened, and the peasant said, "Now which will you take, Misha? The roots or the tops?"

"No, brother, you won't fool me now! Give me the roots, and you take the tops."

So they gathered in the wheat and divided it. The peasant ground some wheat and baked himself some fine wheat rolls. He went to Misha and said, "Well, Misha, and this is what the tops give."

"Well, peasant," said the bear, "now I am angry with you, and I'm going to eat you!"

The peasant went off and started crying.

Then a fox came along and said to the peasant, "Why are you crying?"

"Why should I not cry, why should I not be sad? The bear wants to eat me."

"Don't be afraid, uncle, he won't eat you." And the fox went off into the bushes, but she ordered the peasant to stay in the same spot. Then she came out and asked, "Peasant, aren't there any lobo wolves or bears around here?"

And so the bear came up to the peasant and said, "Well, peasant, don't say anything, I won't eat you."

The peasant said to the fox, "Nope."

The fox started laughing and said, "What's that lying in the cart there?"

The bear quietly said to the peasant, "It's a chopping block."

"If it were a chopping block," said the fox, "it would be tied to the cart." And she ran off into the bushes.

The bear said to the peasant, "Tie me up and put me in the cart." The peasant did just that.

So the fox came back again and asked the peasant, "Peasant, aren't there any lobo wolves or bears around?"

"Nope," said the peasant.

"Well, what's that lying in the cart?"

"It's a chopping block."

"If it were a chopping block, it would have an axe stuck in it."

So the bear quietly said to the peasant, "Well now, peasant, stick an axe in me." The peasant stuck an axe in his back, and the bear died.

Then the fox said to the peasant, "Well, now, peasant, what will you give me for my labors?"

"I'll give you a pair of white hens, and you carry them off, don't peek."

So she took the bag from the peasant and set off. She carried and carried it along and then thought, "Let me have a peek!" She looked in and there were two white dogs! The dogs jumped out of the bag after her. The fox ran and ran, then popped under a stump into her burrow, and she got away, and she sat there talking to herself, "What did you do, little ears?"

"We listened."

"And what did you do, little legs?"

"We just kept on running."

"And what did you do, little eyes?"

"We just kept on looking."

"And tail, what about you?"

"I kept you from running faster."

"So you bothered me, just you wait, I'll give you one." And she stuck her tail out at the dogs. The dogs grabbed hold of it, pulled out the fox, and tore her to bits.

3. The Pig Set Off for the Games

E.V. Pomerantseva recorded this tale in Bashkiriia in 1948 from U.I. Peskova. This is a popular tale in each of the East Slavic traditions. SUS 20A + 21 + 154.

An old man lived with an old woman. The old woman said, "Let's butcher the pig. Brother-in-law is coming, and there'll be nowhere to get any pork."

The pig heard and decided to run away. She was walking along when she met a dog. "Where are you off to, pig?"

"To the games."

"Take me along."

"Let's go, the more the merrier." They continued on. They met a hare. "Where are you going, pig?"

"To the games."

"Take me."

"Let's go! The more the merrier."

So the pig, the dog, and the hare set off again. They met a fox. "Where are you going?" asked the fox.

"To the games."

"Take me."

"Let's go. We'll go together. The more the merrier." So the pig, the hare, the dog, and the fox set off. They met a wolf. "Where, oh pig, are you going?"

"To the games."

"Take me with you."

"Let's go. The more the merrier."

So the pig, the dog, the hare, the fox, and the wolf set off again. They met a bear. "Where are you going, pig?"

"To the games."

"Take me with you."

"And why not? Let's go. The more the merrier."

The pig, wolf, bear, fox, hare, and dog set off again. They walked and walked. They came to a pit. How could they cross it? They laid down a thin pole. The pig set out first, behind the rest came the bear. When they came to the middle, the pole broke and they all fell in. They sat and sat. They wanted to eat. The fox said, "Let's all see who can drone a note the longest." They all stretched out their voices, but the hare didn't stretch his in the slightest, so they tore him up.

The fox put the guts under herself. But the bear didn't stretch his voice out either: he was master of them all. They sat there one day, a second day they sat. And again they started to drone out a note. The pig didn't quite stretch the note far enough, so they ate her, and then the dog and wolf were torn to bits. Each time the fox put the intestines under herself.

Finally the fox was left sitting with the bear. They sat and sat. The fox put her paw beneath her and sat there, eating the intestines. The bear asked her, "What are you eating, foxy?"

"I'm pulling out my intestines and eating them." The bear stuck his paw into himself, took out all the innards, and died. The fox ate him.

The fox sat in the pit, but she did not know how to get out. She looked and saw a woodpecker flying over the pit. "Woodpecker, dear little father! Let me out!"

"And how am I to let you out?"

"Peck out some steps for me!" So he pecked out the steps and out she crawled.

"Woodpecker, little father, bring me some beer."

"And how shall I?"

"Over there a peasant is carting some beer. Sit first on the horse, then on the barrel, then the horse, then the barrel."

The woodpecker flew off. The peasant began to use his whip chasing the bird, and he whipped the barrel apart, and the beer spilled out, and the fox drank it up.

Then the fox asked, "Woodpecker, dear little father! Feed me with pancakes."

"And how shall I feed you?"

"When the old woman has mixed the batter, drag away the pancakes." He fed her.

Again the fox asked, "Woodpecker, dear little father? Make me laugh!"

"And how shall I make you laugh?"

"Over there four peasants are threshing grain. Fly over there, alight on them, first one, then another, and they will whip each other with their flails."

The woodpecker flew off. Then the peasants did whip each other, crosswise. And the fox giggled behind the threshing floor. They heard it, and the dogs leapt after the fox. The fox ran and ran, got herself into a hollow tree, and asked, "Eyes, little eyes, what have you been doing?"

"We saw everything and helped you run, fox!"

"Feet, little feet, what have you been doing?"

"We kept on running, fox, and saved you from the dogs."

"And you, tail, what did you do?"

"I just twitched between your legs."

"So you twitched, intending to hand me over to the dogs to perish." She stuck her tail out of the hollow tree. The dogs tore off the tail. And so the fox started running about without a tail. The other foxes laughed, but she said, "You just tear yours off, and you'll find out how easy it is to run!" And that's all.

4. The Fox as Keener

The origins of this particular version of a very popular East Slavic animal tale are obscure. Extremely common throughout Europe, but known all over the world. Professional keeners were a common element in the Russian rural funeral service until quite recently. SUS 218B* + 1889K + 37 + 154.

There lived an old man with an old woman, and they had a daughter. Once she was eating beans and dropped one onto the ground. The bean grew and grew and grew right up to heaven. The old man climbed up to heaven. He climbed up and walked and walked about, admiring everything, and he said to himself, "Let me bring the old woman here; she would be overjoyed!" So he climbed down to the ground, placed the old woman in a sack, held the sack with his teeth, and climbed up again. He climbed and climbed, grew tired, and dropped the sack. He descended most quickly, opened the sack, and saw the old woman lying there, gnashing her teeth. Her eyes had popped out. And he said, "What are you laughing at, old woman? Why are you baring your teeth?" Then he noted that she was dead, and so he burst into tears.

They had lived alone, quite alone in the middle of a wilderness. There was no one to mourn the old woman. So the old man took a sack with three pairs of white hens and set out to look for a keener. And he saw a bear coming. So he said to the bear, "Weep, o bear, for my old woman! I'll give you two white hens!"

The bear roared out, "O you, my own grandmother! How I pity you!"

"No," said the old man, "you don't know how to keen." And he continued on. He walked and walked and met a wolf. He got him to keen, but the wolf didn't know how either.

So he continued on and met a fox, and he got her to keen for a pair of white hens. And she sang out, "Tra la, Grannie, tra la, your old man has killed you."

The peasant liked the song, and he got the fox to sing it a second, third, and fourth time, but then he was short a fourth pair of white hens. The old man said, "Fox, fox, I forgot the fourth pair at home. Come to my place." So the fox followed on his trail.

And they came home. The old man took the sack, put a pair of dogs in it, and on top put the fox's six hens and handed it over to her. The fox took it and ran. A little later she stopped beside a stump and said, "I'll sit on this little stump, and eat a white hen." She ate it and ran on. Then she again sat on a stump and ate another hen. Then a third, a fourth, a fifth, and a sixth. And then she opened the sack for the seventh time, and the dogs leaped out at her.

That fox did run! She ran and ran and hid beneath a log, she hid and asked, "Ears, ears, what did you do?"

"We listened and listened so that the dogs didn't eat the fox."

"Eyes, little eyes, what did you do?"

"We watched and watched so that the dogs wouldn't eat the fox."

"Legs, little legs, what did you do?"

"We ran and ran so that the dogs wouldn't catch the fox."

"And you, tail, what have you done?"

"Through stumps and bushes, through the logs, I got hung up so that the dogs would catch the fox and rip her apart!"

"So that's what you are! Well, take this, dogs! Eat my tail!" And she stuck out her tail, and the dogs grabbed her by the tail, dragged out the fox herself, and tore her apart.

5. The Fox as Confessor

A ninety-year-old factory worker, P.S. Kazakov, told this tale to L. Piterskii in 1846 and Afanas'ev published it in a collection of tales for children. Ecclesiastical censors in the 1870s found the tale objectionable for its parody of the Sermon on the Mount in the Gospel of St. Matthew and the parable of the rich man in that of St. Luke. The name Trunchinsk is likely derived from a verb meaning "to make fun of." SUS 61A.

It was most extraordinary: a fox was coming from a far-off wilderness. And having caught sight of a cock in a high tree, she spoke sweet words to him: "Oh, my dear child, oh, fine cock! You are sitting there in that tall tree, and you are thinking dirty thoughts, accursed thoughts. You cocks keep too many wives. Some keep ten, others twenty, still others even thirty, and from time to time the number goes up to forty! And whenever you get together, you quarrel over your wives as if they were concubines. Come down onto the earth, my dear child, and confess! I am coming from a far-off wilderness, I haven't drunk anything or eaten, and I have endured many hardships, and all because I wanted to hear your confession, my dear child."

"Oh, mother of mine and fox! I have not fasted nor have I prayed; come at some other time."

"Oh, my dear child, oh, fine cock! You have not fasted and you have not prayed, so come down onto the earth and confess so that you do not die in your sins."

"Oh, mother of mine and fox, honeyed are your lips and sweet your words, but

11

deceitful is your tongue. Judge not one another, and you will not be judged; whoever sows something will also reap. You wish to bring me to confession by force, not to save me but to devour my body."

"Oh, my dear child, oh fine cock! Why do you say such things? Would I do that to you? Have you not considered the parable about the publican and the Pharisee, where the publican was saved but the Pharisee perished on account of his pride? Now you, my dear child, will perish on that high tree without confession. Come down lower, onto the ground, and you will be closer to confession: forgiven and absolved and allowed into the heavenly kingdom."

The cock recognized the heavy sin on his soul, and he was deeply moved and weeping, and he began to descend from branch to branch, from bough to bough, from stump to stump, and the cock descended onto the ground and perched in front of the fox. The fox leaped up, like a sly bird, and grabbed the cock in her sharp claws; she looked at him with her fierce eyes and ground her sharp teeth; she intended to devour him alive, just like some renegade.

And the cock said to the fox, "Oh, mother of mine, fox, honeyed are your lips and sweet your words, but deceitful is your tongue! Are you going to spare me, or will you devour my body?"

"Neither your body nor your bright clothing is dear to me; what's dear is to repay you some friendship. Or don't you remember? I was going to visit a peasant; I just wanted to eat a little hen, and you, fool, idler, were sitting up on a high perch, and you started shouting and wailing with your loud mouth, you stamped your feet, you flapped your wings, and then all the hens started chattering, and then the geese started honking, and the dogs started barking, and the stallions started neighing, and the cows started mooing. And all the peasants and their wives heard it. The women came with brooms and the men with axes, and they wanted to cause my death on account of that hen; yet that owl lives from generation to generation there, always eating chicken! But you, fool, idler, shall live no longer!"

Then did the cock speak to the fox: "Oh, mother of mine, fox, honeyed are your lips and sweet your words, but deceitful is your tongue! You see, just yesterday I was called upon by the metropolitan of Trunchinsk to serve as a deacon; I was singled out of the choir for special praise, and the congregation said, 'He's a handsome lad, well-clad, reads a great many books, and has a fine voice.' Now could I not, oh, mother of mine and fox, use my influence to get you into the group of ladies who bake the communion loaves? There would be great profit for us in that. They would be giving us sweet buns, fine white loaves, and a bit of butter and eggs and cheese!"

The fox recognized the cock's plan and held the cock a little less firmly with her claws. The cock tore away and flew into a tall tree and started shouting and wailing with his loud mouth, "Dear madam bread baker, greetings! Is your profit large? Are your buns sweet? Have you worn away your hump carrying all the baked goods? Or wouldn't you like some nuts, you villain? But maybe you don't have any teeth?"

So the fox went off into the forest with a long face and began weeping bitterly: "As long as I have lived on this earth, I have never in my life seen such a disgrace. Since when do cocks become deacons or foxes bakers!" Glory to him and power, now and forever, and that's an end to the tale.

6. A Wolf—Gray and Daring

This tale is notable for its preamble. Briansk is a very rural province, located southwest of Moscow. SUS 61A.

In a certain tsardom in a certain country, in the one in which we are living, beneath the number seven where we are sitting, snow burned, and they put it out with straw; many people were destroyed, as a result of which nothing was decided.

Twelve wolves ran, and old men with pikes ran after the twelve wolves. One wolf—gray and daring—said, "Old men, turn back, take pity, my father ate a hundred of your sheep, but I will never touch your flock!" So they turned back, took pity, and went off home.

Then came that wolf—gray and daring. And a pig with her piglets went strolling by. So he took the pig. "Let me go, wolf—so gray and daring—and take my bob-tailed, chicken-assed piglet!"

So he took the bob-tailed, chicken-assed piglet by the back, stripped the skin off it, and sat down to eat. Up popped a fox out of nowhere: "Good health to you, cousin, dearest friend! I came to visit you to swallow up the piggy's bones."

"What kind of creature are you, to tell me such rubbish? In Riga I learned to read the Lenten books. What happened to the bob-tailed, chicken-assed piglet will happen to you, creature!"

That fox stretched out her legs running along the road. That fox set off for the Briansk woods, and in the Briansk woods a cock sat in an oak. "Good health, little cock, dearest friend! I have been in the city of Jerusalem, where they praised you: you see, they say, the cock has a silken beard, speckled wings, and bright red boots. I am your mother confessor and go around to all chicken coops to hear the confession of you cocks. You are a sinner; you are a lawbreaker; you have seventy-seven wives. Climb down here to me, confess to me. In the otherworld there is spring wheat and winter wheat, and I'll let you go there; I'll regale you with fine food."

That cock was seduced by the fox's patter, from branch to branch he descended, said farewell to the tree, and sat down on the fox's head. The fox took the rooster into her lips, carried him into some thick bushes, and proceeded to wring the cock's neck. She ate up the cock, just the guts were hanging out, and she went to the river to slake her thirst.

Up popped that wolf—gray and daring—grabbed the fox by the back, stripped the skin off her, ate her all up, and sweet it seemed to the wolf! And with that this fable is at an end.

7. The Fox and the Jug

This tale is often found in conjunction with other tales about the sly fox. Kretov's tale comes from the South Russian Voronezh area and was collected just before World War II. SUS 68B.

A certain peasant went into the field to work and took with him a clay jug. And in this jug there was some sour cream. A fox saw the peasant, and, the conniving good-for-nothing, she began thinking about how to get away with that sour cream.

She waited a while until the peasant turned his back, then zap! and she had the sour cream. The good-for-nothing ran away to a quiet spot, desirous of investigating that sour cream! So, you see, she stuck her head into the jug and lapped up some sour cream, and then she thought of pulling her head out of that jug. She wanted to pull her head out, she wanted to, but she couldn't. The head wouldn't budge; the jug's throat was narrow. She bashed her head against a stump, but the jug wouldn't break. And oh! how her head did hurt! The fox ran to the river. "I'll sink this wretched jug in the river." She sank her head in the water and started sinking together with the jug. And she drowned. And that's how an end came to that conniving fox.

8. The Bear and the Beam

No Russian version is recorded in SUS. Recorded in the Siberian district of Chita in the late 1980s. The informant was F.A. Balagurov. SUS 88*, according to Matveeva.

A bear wanted to satisfy his craving for honey. So off he went and hung around an apiary, but he was afraid. The owner took note of this, and hung a beam over the hive because the bear had already tricked him more than once on his hunts for honey.

And so it was that one fine day the bear got up the courage to satisfy his craving and went after the honey. And there's that beam hanging there. The bear took it in his paws and gave it an almighty shove away from him. The beam swung back and flew right at the bear and knocked him down. He got up and pushed it off again. And so it went on, time after time. The beam would swing away and then come flying back, and time after time it knocked the bear down. He got angry and gave it an even greater push, and he pushed it so hard that the beam came and hit him and knocked him off his feet. His legs could hardly carry him away. He lost all desire to go after honey and so never ventured there again.

9. The Peasant, the Bear, the Fox, and the Gadfly

This tale ran into problems with the imperial censors, who found it coarse. Its distribution is limited to Balto-Slavic and German traditions. SUS 152.

There lived and dwelt this peasant, and he had this dappled horse. The peasant harnessed it to a cart and set off into the forest for some wood. He had just come into the woods when a large bear came straight toward him. He exchanged greetings with the peasant and asked him, "Tell me, little peasant, who dappled your horse? She's such a dazzling and splendid one."

"Oh, brother Mishka!" said the peasant. "I dappled her myself."

"So you know how to dapple?"

"Who? Me? I'm the past master! If you like, I could probably make you more colorful than my horse."

The bear was overjoyed: "Be so kind, please! For your labor I'll drag over a whole hive for you."

"Well, why not! Fine. Only I'll have to bind you, you old devil, with some ropes; otherwise you won't lie still when I start dappling."

The bear agreed. "Wait," thought the peasant, "I'll swaddle him." He took the reins and ropes and wound them round; he bound the bear so that he began bellowing at the top of his lungs, and the peasant said to him, "Stop, brother Mishka! Don't move; it's time to do the dappling."

"Untie me, peasant!" the bear begged. "I don't want to be dappled anymore; please, release me."

"No, you old devil! You asked for it yourself, and that's how it's going to be." The peasant chopped some wood, laid a big fire, and got a hot, hot fire going; then he took his axe and placed it straight into the fire.

When the axe was red-hot, the peasant dragged it out and started dappling that bear. How it sizzled! The bear started roaring with all his might; he strained and broke all the ropes and reins and headed off running through the woods without a glance backward—and how that forest shook! The bear tore through the forest until his strength gave out. He wanted to lie down, but he couldn't: his belly and sides were scorched, so he bellowed and bellowed. "Oh, let me get my paws on that peasant; I'll give him something to remember me by!"

The next day the peasant's wife went into the fields to cut some rye, and she took a crust of bread and a jug of milk with her. She came to her strip of land and put the jug of milk to one side and began cutting. And the peasant thought, "I'll call in on the wife!" He harnessed his horse and was riding up to their strip when he caught sight of a fox strolling about in the rye. The good-for-nothing crept up to the jug of milk and somehow stuck her head in it, but no way could she pull it out again, so she was wandering about the stubble, shaking her head and saying, "Alright, jug, I was joking, that's enough! That's enough of this playing around. Let me go! Little jug! Little dove! That's enough fooling around, you've had your play and that's enough!" And she just kept on shaking her head.

So while the fox was trying to persuade the jug, the peasant got a chunk of wood, went up to her, and clobbered her legs. The fox rushed off to one side and banged her head against a stone, breaking the jug into tiny pieces. She saw the peasant chasing after her with the chunk of wood, so the fox increased her pace—never mind that she was on three legs, you couldn't have caught her with hounds—and she disappeared into the woods.

The peasant went back and started loading the sheaves onto the cart. Out of nowhere a gadfly appeared, landed on his neck, and bit him fiercely. The peasant grabbed at his neck and caught the gadfly. "Hey," he said, "what shall we do with you? Right! Just you wait, and I'll give you something to remember me by." The peasant took a straw and stuck it up the gadfly's ass. "Fly away now, wherever you know best!"

The poor gadfly flew off, dragging the straw behind it. "Well," it thought to itself, "I fell into his hands! Since the day I was born I've never had such a burden to carry around as I have now!"

On and on it flew, and it flew into the forest until it was quite out of breath. It wanted to land on a tree to rest, and it wanted to fly a little higher, but the straw dragged it down. It struggled and struggled and with great effort managed to sit down, panting, and it started breathing so heavily that the tree shook.

Beneath that very tree the bear was lying down, the very one the peasant had dappled. The bear took fright: What was making that tree shake so? He looked up and saw the gadfly sitting in the tree. So he shouted to it, "Hey, brother! Cousin! Come on down, please, or else you're going to topple this tree."

The gadfly obeyed and flew down. The bear looked at it and asked, "Who pounded that straw into your ass?"

And the gadfly looked at the bear and asked, "And you, brother, who's mutilated you? Look, in some places you've got some fur and in others you can see the bones!"

"Well, brother gadfly, it was that peasant who worked me over."

"Well, brother bear, my straw came from the same peasant."

They looked and saw a fox hopping by on three legs. "Who broke your leg?" asked the bear.

"Oh, cousin! I couldn't see very well myself. It looked like some peasant or other; he was chasing after me with a chunk of wood."

"Brothers, let's all three go after that peasant!" So the three of them got ready and set off for the field where the peasant was gathering in the sheaves. They started creeping up on him; the peasant caught sight of them, took fright, and didn't know what to do.

And so this peasant didn't know what to do. And then he thought of grabbing his wife in an embrace, and he knocked her down onto the ground. She shouted, and the peasant said, "Quiet!" and that was that. He pulled off her pinafore and shirt and raised her legs up as high as possible. The bear saw that the man was hurting some woman, and he said, "No, fox, you and gadfly do as you please, but no way am I going up to that peasant!"

"Why?"

"Because, just look, see how he's treating that person!"

The fox looked and looked: "You're absolutely right. In fact he is breaking someone's leg."

And the gadfly stared and stared and said, "That's not right; he's shoving a straw up somebody's ass."

Everyone, you see, understands his own misfortune his own way. But the gadfly figured it out best of all. The bear and the fox headed for the woods, and the peasant stayed on, in one piece and unharmed.

10. The Case of the Beekeeper and the Bear

This tale retains many of the ancient notions concerning the relationship between men and bears. SUS 154**.

There was once this case in Smolensk District of a grandfather beekeeper and a bear. This bear had the habit of going to the beekeeper's apiary and smashing up the beehives. The grandfather pondered what to do with this heathen. Every night the bear would break up one or two hives. The old man took it into his head to get the bear to drink himself to death on wine. So the grandfather took a quarter of a barrel of wine and dragged that wine into his apiary. He poured the wine into a trough and sweetened it with so much honey that the bear would drink the wine with gusto. And then the old man went home, as if to say, "Just let that bear come; he'll get drunk on the wine, and then, when he's dead to the world, I'll get him." That's what grandpa reckoned!

But the bear had another way of reckoning. He went to the apiary, scented that the old man had been there not long before, whistled through his nostrils, smacked his lips, and then set out to drink up the wine. The bear drank his fill of the wine and started considering things to himself: "Oh, what an old man! He's even started treating me to a little wine." But the bear wasn't content to leave things as they were, he wasn't. He took two casks from the apiary, dragged them out and broke them up, and then went away to his bear's lair.

The next morning the old man came after the fact, as it were. He had thought that the bear would be dead drunk. The old man looked in the trough—there was no wine and no bear, and two casks of honey were smashed to boot. So then the old man said that he was "a heathen, and he doesn't drink the way we do; he drank it all, but it didn't finish him off." The old man pondered to himself, "Well now, this next night I'll supply you with half a barrel. You're lying if you say you'll drink that down!" And that's how he reasoned to himself. So then the old grandpa got everything ready for the next night, just as he had the first time, only he added the extra quarter of a barrel of wine. And again the old man left the apiary and went home.

Well, that bear just had to come once more to grandpa's apiary. The bear looked again in the trough—there was more wine supplied than before and sweetened just as much with the honey. The bear thought to himself, "Oh, what a virtuous old man is my grandpa. Today he's given me even more wine."

So the bear drank up every bit of that wine. But that about finished him off. He had just left the apiary when he crashed to the ground with his paws sticking straight up. In the morning the old man came to have a look: the bear was lying there with his paws straight up. "Aha," the old man said with great joy. "You've given in, you heathen. Your paws are already swollen, so you've died." Then the old man ran off home happily to announce to his sons, "Well, my sons, hitch up the horse, fast, the bear has gotten drunk on the wine; he's lying there with swollen paws." The sons hitched the horse to a cart, and they set off to load up the bear. They loaded him onto the cart and tied him down in three places with a rope and carted him home. They put the cart next to the threshing floor gates and discussed among themselves what they should do with him: "There's no time to skin him now; we'll skin him toward evening. Now we've got to go cut the buckwheat." (It was, you know, already the month of September there.)

The old man went with the women to shock the buckwheat. But the bear hadn't really pegged out; he was just in a deep sleep from the booze, and he woke up. He looked here and there to see where he was and saw that he had been brought to the house and tied down. Whatever he did, struggling on the cart, he was tied securely and tightly. Somehow he got his front paws free (he was face down in the cart), and he moved the cart away from its front wheels so that they remained in place, and with the back wheels he set off through the hemp beds in the general direction of the forest! Then that bear went off with the cart and with the back wheels, laying down a road through the hemp with the cart, and that bear disappeared with the cart near the forest.

The old man came back with the women from the field and saw that there was no bear anywhere and no cart anywhere, just the front wheels remained. So the old man figured that somebody had unhitched the front wheels and taken the bear and the cart off somewhere. But then he got to reckoning: Why would they leave the front wheels? "Perhaps I'd better have a good look, see how the track lies." The old man looked. A road led through his hemp; the hemp was torn up. The old man walked along the track until he had passed through all the hemp. But there was no bear, no bear at all. So the old man began mumbling something to himself. "Oh, the very devil! I didn't kill him with drink; I just put him to sleep. He was probably just putting it on so that I wouldn't notice the heathen's breathing! Well, I'll carry on and follow the track."

So grandpa followed the track right up to the forest, and he went through a bit of the forest and then suddenly saw the bear, tangled up in the trees with the cart. The old man started shouting and howling at the bear. And people came running from all around, and from the steppe, and from their various jobs, all in response to his shouting. And they reported it to the old man's sons. The sons came running, and the whole bunch of them killed that bear. Then the old man said, "I thank you for killing this heathen of mine. He has recently drunk three-quarters of a barrel of wine and smashed nine hives of bees, but it's all right now because we've killed him." And then they all said to the old man, "If that bear drank up three-quarters of a barrel, then you can put out a barrel for us; we left our jobs and came running."

"Well, I won't argue with you; I'll put out a barrel for you, too. Here, help me load him up and cart him home, and then we'll have a memorial service for him." So the old man arranged it all, and they brought him home, and he put out the barrel, and the peasants drank it up, and for a whole month they talked about the story of what happened to the old man and the bear. And that's an end to this little tale.

11. The Bear

From Perm in the Ural Mountains. Most of the recordings among the East Slavs have come from Russia, where it was popular through the mid-twentieth century. It is also known as the "Bear on the Lime Leg" and appears in verse form in collections for children. SUS 161A*.

There lived and dwelt an old man and an old woman, and they had no children. The old woman said to the old man, "Old man, go get some firewood." So the old man set off after the firewood, and on the way he chanced upon a bear, and the bear said to him, "Old man, let's wrestle!" So the old man went and cut off the bear's paw with his axe, and then he went home with the paw and gave it to the old woman: "Here, old woman, cook this bear paw." So the old woman set about it and tore off the hide, and as she sat on it she began to pluck the fur, and she put the paw on the stove to cook. The bear roared and roared, then fell to thinking and made himself a limewood paw, and then he went to the old man in the village and sang:

> Squeak, paw
> Squeak, limewood!
> And the water sleeps,
> And the land it sleeps
> And they sleep throughout the hamlets,
> And throughout the villages they sleep.
> Only the woman doesn't sleep.
> She sits on my skin,
> She's spinning my fur,
> She's cooking my flesh,
> She's drying my hide.

At that the old man and old woman took fright. The old man hid in the loft beneath a trough and the old woman on the stove beneath some black clothes. The bear came into the hut. The old man wheezed beneath the trough in fear, and the old woman coughed. The bear found them and caught them and then ate them.

12. The Mushrooms

This tale, popular among children, is almost exclusively a Russian tale, recorded primarily in north and north central areas. SUS 297B.

A mushroom thought it up; the pine mushroom, sitting beneath a little oak tree, gazing at all the other mushrooms, resolved it. He began to give orders: "Come here, you boletes, come and fight me!"

But the boletes refused: "We are noble lady mushrooms; we will not go to war!"

"Come here, you saffron mushrooms, come and fight me!"

But the mushrooms refused. "We are rich men, ill-equipped to go to war."

"Come here, you coral mushrooms, come and fight me!"

But these coral mushrooms also refused: "We are gentlemen's chefs; we do not go to war."

"Come here, you honey mushrooms, come and fight me!"

But the honey mushrooms refused: "Our legs are too thin; we cannot go to war."

"Come here, you milky caps, come and fight me!"

"We milky caps are a friendly lot; we'll go to war!"

And so that's how King Pea fought with the mushrooms.

13. The Sun, the Wind, and the Moon

Related to 552B, the "Three Sons-in-Law" (or the "Three Brothers-in-Law"). Told by Irina Pavlovna Perkhina, born in 1926. The tale bears traces of literary influence and Perkhina was apparently literate in 1976 when the tale was recorded. SUS *299.

There lived and dwelt this old man and his old woman. Now once the old man went to the barn for some grain, and he didn't see that there was a hole in the bag. The old man carried the bag home, but all the grain trickled out along the way. The old man thought, "If only the moon looked out now, I could gather up all the grain." And the old man promised to give him his oldest daughter in marriage if he did it.

The moon looked out, and the old man gathered all the grain back up in the bag, carted it home, and the next morning handed over his eldest daughter.

A week, perhaps it was two, passed by, and the old man went to cut grass. He cut and he cut, and then there was such a downpour! And the old man said, "Oh, of only the sun would look out now, I would give my middle daughter in marriage to the sun!" He had just thought this when the sun looked out, bright and hot, and dried up all the old man's grass.

Well, maybe another week passed, but maybe it was two, and then the old man went to the field for the hay. He came and raked all the hay, and then he thought, "If only the wind were to blow, all my hay would fly home by itself!" He had barely thought this when a whirlwind came up! The old man's hay was lifted up and carried off home. And so the old man gave his youngest daughter in marriage to the wind.

He and the old woman were left alone, just the two of them. They lived, and life went on, but it was boring in the house, no one laughed, no one played. The old man said to the old woman, "Well, old woman, I'll visit my oldest son-in-law, the moon and our eldest daughter."

So he went there, and the daughter asked him, "Well, father, perhaps you'd like to steam in the bath?"

"What do you mean, bath? It's night outside. Better give me a place to lie down and sleep."

"No, father, let's go to the bathhouse; you'll steam a bit after the journey."

So they went. The old man set off for the bathhouse and said, "Give me a light, daughter; otherwise it's too dark to wash in there."

But the daughter said, "Don't worry about it, father, just go into the bathhouse."

The old man came into the bathhouse, and the moon's son stuck a finger in a crack, and it became as light as day in the bathhouse. The old man had a good wash and steam and then went home the next day. He came and demanded of his old woman, "Woman, heat up the bath."

"What do you mean, old one? It's already evening. How can we go to the bathhouse if it's so dark?"

"Heat it up," he said, "and don't chatter!"

So the woman heated up the bath, and she clambered in. She started to light a splinter, but the old man shouted, "Don't touch that splinter, don't waste it; just go into the bathhouse, take your birch branch, and climb up on the ledge."

So the woman climbed up onto the ledge, and the old man stuck his finger in the crack, but it was dark in the bathhouse! No matter how the old man tried—this finger, that, he tried all his fingers—it remained dark in the bathhouse. The old woman started down off the ledge, but she fell and bruised herself. Well, there was enough cursing for a second day for the old man! Poor old man!

Well then, a week passed, and maybe it was two, but then the old man got ready to go to his middle daughter. And the old woman said, "Go, go on, old man, go!"

She packed up a satchel of bread for him, and the old man set off. He was behind the sun for a whole day. Toward evening, just as the sun was about to hide behind a hill, the old man finally caught up to him. The sun said, "Why have you come, old man?"

And the old man said, "It was boring in our house, so I've come to visit you."

And then his middle daughter ran out and greeted her father and said, "Well now, father, what would you like to eat? Perhaps you'd eat some hot pancakes?"

But the old man said, "What do you mean 'hot pancakes' if it's already evening outside?"

"Why not, father, we can make hot pancakes at any time."

The sun sat down on the floor, the daughter mixed up the pancake batter and poured it onto his head, and the pancakes just flew off the sun—they flew off so soft, red, and buttery! The old man ate his fill. He slept the night or maybe he spent a week, and then he went home. He came home in the evening and demanded some pancakes of his old wife, but the old woman said to him, "What do you mean, old man, where can I get hot pancakes, if I only heat the stove in the morning?"

"Never mind," he said. "You mix up the pancakes."

The old woman mixed up the pancakes in a mixing bowl. The old man sat down on the floor and said to the old woman, "Pour the batter onto my bald spot!"

The old woman said, "Have you gone mad, old man, or what?"

"Pour it," he said.

The old woman began pouring the pancake batter onto the old man, and she covered the old man all over, but not a single pancake did she cook. The next day she forced the old man into the river to bathe.

Well, another week went by there, and then the old man went off to visit his third daughter. He came to the wind. He visited and visited, but they didn't show him anything amazing at all, and so he started to get ready to go home. And then his daughter said, "Why should you walk, father? My husband will take you; you'll be home ever so quickly."

"And how will he take me?"

"Let's go."

The daughter came and told her husband that the old man was ready to go home. They went out onto the shores of a vast lake, and she threw a kerchief onto the water and said, "Get in, father."

The old man got in, and the wind blew so that in an instant the old man turned up home. He came home and said to his wife, "Woman, let's go fishing."

"Where do you think you're going, old man, it's night!"

"Come on, listen to me."

So they went. The old woman started putting out the boat, she brought the oars up, and then the old man said, "Don't you dare touch anything. Let all that stay here. Just take that kerchief from your head and throw it onto the water."

The old woman said, "Have you gone completely crazy, old man?"

"Throw it down, I'm telling you."

The old woman threw her kerchief onto the water and the old man said, "Climb onto the kerchief!"

The old woman said, "No, I won't; you try to get in first."

So the old man jumped and went right into the water up to his head. The old woman was forced to pull him out, and did she shake him up! Since then the old man hasn't gone visiting his sons-in-law, and he hasn't been performing any miracles at home either. And that's the whole tale. There are no more lies!

Tales of Heroes and Villains

There are more than 225 types of Russian wondertales. Of these, somewhat fewer than half are tales of heroes and their opponents, while the remainder are tales in which magic is a major element. The opponents vary: serpents whose role is to devour maidens or children, or commit some other social crime; evil dwarves who live underground and who kidnap tsarevnas; giants who seek to possess treasure or kidnap the tsar's only daughter; the witch Baba Yaga; or even a bear who captures a peasant's wife and fathers a son who will become the cause of the bear's death. The villain may even be the tsar himself, seeking to possess the peasant lad's beautiful wife. The heroes are most frequently a poor peasant lad, the tsar's young son who seeks a bride; a strongman, a soldier, or a merchant. Occasionally, one will encounter Christ or a hermit as the hero. Heroes always begin the tale in need: of a bride, of some object, of a steed, for example. They often are associated with some peculiar feature at birth. They may have an animal parent, be crippled, or lack something necessary for their adult lives. The supernatural does not play an important role in most tales of this type. For more on the Russian wondertales see Haney, *CRF,* vol. 3.

14. Nikita the Tanner

This very popular tale is based on a legend contained in the twelfth-century *Primary Chronicle.* It is possible, however, that the chronicle legend and the folktale may both be derived from some earlier mythic and oral narrative. Prince Vladimir in the tale is probably a reference to the first Christian prince of the Rus', who ruled from ca. 980 until 1015. SUS 300_2.

In the times of the prince, of Bright-Sun Vladimir, there appeared near Kiev a terrible serpent and he took from the people a considerable tribute: from each household a beautiful maiden, from each chimney a berry, and when he had taken the maiden from the particular household, he would devour her, and memory of her would go cold. In such a pitiable time, sadness made all equal: be he householder or shooter, or trader or boyar, or mayor or even the tsar and grand prince himself—all were equal, none could avoid this fate, which was to be subject to the cannibal serpent, to humble oneself with a beautiful daughter, and on whomever the lot fell, that was the tribute.

And so the turn came for the tsar's daughter herself to go to that pagan serpent to be devoured—and she set off. The serpent grabbed the tsarevna and dragged her off to his lair. The people cried out in one voice. Each had wept for his own, now they groaned as one for the princess. All of them thought: the daughter of our Bright-Sun has perished, she is no longer on this earth, the serpent has devoured her. But the serpent had not started eating her, she was such a beauty that there was none other like her on earth, so he preserved her and took her as his wife, and so she lived.

When he would fly off, this pagan serpent, on his man-eating hunts, he would barricade the tsarevna up in his lair with logs so that she couldn't go anywhere without him. Now that tsarevna had a little dog, attached to her since her days in the royal household, and it lived with her in the lair. And whenever the tsarevna wrote a letter to her kind father and mother, she would tie it to the dog's neck and wave it off, in tears, and it would run straight off for the tsar's chambers and it would scratch at the gate and start barking and the guards would immediately open the gates, let the little dog in, and lead it into the bright royal and princely presence. The tsar and tsaritsa would read it and thank God that their daughter was still alive and then they would cry for a little while that she had been destroyed by the monster, the cannibal serpent, then they would hang a letter in answer on the little dog's neck and it would run straight back to the serpent's lair and secretly and silently go to the tsarevna and in a flash crawl up to her and she would unfasten the letter and look over the news and unburden her heart and soul.

Then once the tsar and tsaritsa wrote this to the tsarevna: "Find out who is stronger than the serpent." The tsarevna guessed what this was all about and she became even more pleasant to her fierce enemy, and she began, in women's fashion, to question him about what he was afraid of and not afraid of and who was stronger than he. Even though she fawned on him, for a long time he would say nothing. But it is most difficult to withstand a woman's wiles and once he let slip that "there is only one person on earth of whom I am afraid, but he doesn't even know his own strength himself, so he is not really terrifying to me as long as he doesn't know about it. You see, he lives in the capital city of Kiev, he's a peasant tanner and he's so strong and so fierce that tangling with him is something I'm not up to. If he had a daughter and her turn came to be given up to me, then probably this tanner wouldn't hand her over and that would be most unfortunate for me and I really wouldn't know what to do."

So when the tsarevna found out, her heart began to race. She waited until the serpent had flown away on his man-eating hunts, then she quickly called her trusty little dog and wrote a note: "Father, seek out a peasant tanner in the capital city of

Kiev and send him to free me from this captivity." She tied the letter to the little dog's neck and waved him off with her white hand. The little dog climbed among the logs with which the serpent had blocked up the entrance into his lair, ran straight to the royal chambers and brought the tsar the needed information.

The tsar ordered that Nikita the Tanner be found and he himself went with the tsaritsa to ask him to cleanse their land of the fierce serpent and cannibal and free the tsarevna. Just at that time Nikita the Tanner (he always kept twelve hides in his hand), when he found out that the tsar and grand prince himself had come to his household, became timid and started shaking from fright, and his hands shook, so he took and ripped those twelve hides up at one time and no matter how much the tsar and his tsaritsa begged him, he would not go forth against that serpent. "You see," he said to the most illustrious prince, "I am a peaceable man, timid. I cannot fight against that serpent, that's no task for a peasant."

So the tsar summoned his counselors and order them to think up a way to convince Nikita to go against the serpent because he could really defeat him—the serpent himself had spoken of that. And they decided to summon five thousand children and send them to beg Nikita the Tanner, thinking he would take pity on their tears. And so the children in an uncountable crowd came to the household of Nikita the Tanner and they all got down on their knees and started begging him with tears to go out against the serpent. All the little girls cried and said, "Uncle Nikita, save us, don't let us grow up just to perish; while we're still young, let us stroll and run about, and know no woe; not so that when each of us grows up, it will be not for the joy of our parents but to our destruction, to a fierce death from the pagan serpent and cannibal." The little boys also cried and shouted, "Uncle Nikita, we shall not get up from here, we won't budge from this place, we won't leave your broad courtyard until you tell us you will go out and defeat that fierce monster. We all have little sisters and will all want to have brides when we grow up, but they won't be for our own joy or that of our parents: they'll be in tears and misfortune for devouring by that serpent and cannibal."

So the peasant Nikita the Tanner was filled with tears himself, while looking at their tears. "Well," he said, "let it swallow me then, if it doesn't choke. Maybe if I get back skillfully enough, I can be like a stake in his throat! But looking at you makes me so sad. You can go now, and I'll go out against the serpent."

So Nikita the Tanner took three hundred poods of hemp and wove it into a great braided thong and he smeared it with pitch and the hemp soaked up three hundred poods of pitch. Then he wrapped the thong around himself so that the serpent couldn't eat him, couldn't gobble him up in a single bite, and he set off against him.

So Nikita the Tanner came up to the serpent's lair, and the serpent saw him, and he curled up his tail and locked himself in and he wouldn't go out to meet him. "Come out, brother, the better into the open steppe," shouted Nikita the Tanner. "And if you don't, I'll scatter your lair to the wind, all of it!" And he started to work, dragging log after log, like kindling, and throwing them behind him. The serpent saw the unavoidable catastrophe, that it would be worse for Nikita to smother him in his lair, so he went out into the open steppe.

Nikita struggled with him for long time, or a short time, but he finally got him down in hand-to-hand fighting. The serpent then started imploring him: "Don't beat me to death, Nikitushka, there's no one stronger than we are in the whole world. Let me live with you, doing nothing but good and never even seeing the bad. You and I will divide the whole earth, the entire world equally. You can live in one half and I'll live in the other, and neither of us will be disgraced by it."

"Very well," said Nikita the Tanner. "But first we'll have to plow a furrow across the land as a marker. Can you pull a plow?"

"I can plow," said the serpent. So Nikita made a plow bottom weighing three hundred poods and put a plow to it, and he harnessed up the serpent and they started to plow a furrow out near Kiev, and they made the furrow from Kiev right to the edge of the sea.

The serpent panted and got worn out. He was glad his service had come to an end. "Well," he said to Nikitushka, "Now we have divided the entire earth between us, so which half is mine and which is yours?"

"We've divided the earth," said Nikita, but he wouldn't let the serpent out of his harness, "but we still haven't divided the sea. Now pull that plow through the sea and let's mark it off, otherwise you'll say afterward that I'm taking your water."

There was nothing for the serpent to do. The serpent dragged the plow through the deep blue sea, he was swimming, keeping his jagged head above water, looking all around to see when he'd be coming to the end of the sea. When they'd gotten out to the middle of the sea, Nikita the Tanner killed that serpent and drowned him in the sea.

There's nothing to be said about the tsar's daughter. She was freed and started living and prospering in her father's chambers.

But that furrow remained and is there even now. It was two *sazhens* deep and the height above the ground was the same. No matter how many centuries have passed, you can still make that furrow out, it's only a little filled in. And they plow around it, on both sides, but they don't touch it. Those who don't know about it call the furrow a wall, but for what purpose and by whom this "wall" was built, they don't say.

Nikita the Tanner, having done his holy deed, took nothing for his labor. He went back once again to tanning skins, as before.

15. Ivan the Mare's Son

From Riazan district. One of the most popular versions of the type "The Three Underground Tsardoms," widely known throughout the East Slavic world. The Grimms' tale "The Gnome" is partially analogous, as is "Strong Hans." SUS 301 A, B.

There lived an old man and old woman in great poverty. Then the old woman said to the old man: "Old man, you just lie around on the stove. You'd better go into the woods and collect some bast and weave some boots and go into town and sell them."

So the old man set off and he collected the bast and he wove twelve boots, and he set off for town and he sold them for twelve kopecks cash: they were cheap then. He was coming back and he saw twelve brothers dragging a mare downhill. The old man said: "Brothers, sell me that little mother!"

"Give us twelve kopecks' cash." So he gave for the little mother what he had taken for the bast boots.

This little mother gave herself a shake downhill and her tail turned into pearls, her mane gold, and she said to the old man: "Well, old man, mount up, and don't catch your head in the clouds!"

He mounted and rode on her to the old woman. The old woman rejoiced, she grabbed a sickle and ran about the rows and furrows with it, she cut the grass and fed it to the little mare. This little mare became a dam in the first hour, and in the second she foaled. The colt grew not by the day but by the hour.

The little peasant rode out on his little mare to plow near the main road. The colt ran about and played in the plowed field, sinking up to its knees in the earth. Some gentlemen were riding along the main road and they saw the colt and took an extreme fancy to him. These gentlemen said: "Peasant, sell us the colt!"

"Buy it."

"What do you want for it?"

"Give me five hundred rubles." One landowner didn't quibble about it and gave him five hundred rubles and he tied up the colt and rode off.

Then the old man returned to the old woman with the money. The old woman rejoiced at it. They hired a laborer and became rich. They gave a ball and completely forgot about the little mare. They didn't give her any fodder. She came up to a window. "Peasant! Why are you drinking and carousing when you have forgotten about me?" The old man immediately sent his laborer out with the bast mat to cover it with oats, as many as she would eat. Then the little mare reared up, rose into the air and flew away.

She flew into the open steppe, and there she began to think to herself: "Who will feed me and give me anything to drink here?" And then she said, "In the first hour I shall be pregnant and in the second I will give birth to Ivan the Mare's Son!" So Ivan was born to her, the Mare's Son, and he grew not by the day but by the hour. He dug a well, he fixed it with a pump, he cut a rick full of hay and fenced it, and he said: "Here's hay for you, mother, and water for you, and now I'm off: a twelve-headed serpent has carried away our tsar's daughter and I am going to rescue her." And off he went.

He walked along and he met up with Mount-bogatyr. "Oh," he says, "Ivan Mare's Son, there had been no sound of you and now God has brought you before my very eyes." So they went on together. Wherever there was a mountain, Mount leaned into it with his side and moved the mountain: there would just be a flat space.

Whether they walked little or much, they met up with Oak-bogatyr. "Oh," he said, "Ivan Mare's Son, there had been no sound of you and now God has brought you before my very eyes."

"Greetings," he said. "Where are you going?"

"We are going to rescue the tsar's daughter."

"Take me along as a companion," he said.

"Very well." They set off. Wherever there was a forest, Oak leaned into it with his side and moved the trees. There would just be a flat space.

So they came to the serpent's lair and it was necessary to be lowered into that lair. They wove a hawser and lowered Oak-bogatyr. They let him halfway down into the lair. Oak swung by the hawser. They pulled him back out. Ivan Mare's Son asked him, "What's the matter, brother?"

"It's scary, brother, really! You go yourself!"

So Ivan Mare's Son got on and was lowered into the lair. He saw a serpent lying there on the tsar's daughter's knees. She was looking [for lice] on all twelve heads. She was very glad to see him and showed him a bench: "Over there," she said, "on the right side is strength, you move it to the left! And on the left side is weakness, you put it on the right!" He moved them.

Suddenly the serpent awoke. "Phoo, phoo, phoo! It smells of a Russian spirit." He rushed over onto the right side to drink weakness, while Ivan Mare's Son drank strength on the right. They took their sabers and began to fight.

Ivan the Mare's Son had already worn himself out and he said, "Cursed serpent! Look back! Your kingdom is on fire!" He looked over his shoulder and Ivan Mare's Son chopped off all twelve of his heads. The tsar's daughter rejoiced, removed a diamond ring from her hand and put it on his right hand. And he put her on the hawser on which he had been lowered. Mount and Oak bogatyrs pulled her out. Then they lowered the hawser for him. But he knew their intention, which was that they wanted to kill him, so he took and tied on a stone. They raised it halfway up and then cut through the hawser and the stone fell. Tsarevich Ivan began crying bitterly for he had saved the tsar's daughter and ruined himself.

He remained in the serpent's kingdom alone. Suddenly out of nowhere there appeared twelve doves, all natural sisters. "Oh," they said, "Ivan Mare's Son, there had been no sound of you and now you have appeared before our very eyes. How did you get here?" So then he told them all his adventures. "Well, you probably want to go back to your Rus."

"Yes, that wouldn't be bad, if it were possible," he said.

"And why not? Only you have to do what we tell you."

"Whatever is possible, I'll fulfill," he said.

"You have to kill twelve bullocks, bake twelve batches of bread, cut them into little bits, and do it all by a certain time." He prepared it all. At whatever time they had indicated they came flying into the serpent's kingdom. He put out everything that he had readied on their wings and got on himself. They flew for twelve days and twelve nights and then there appeared a light, moonlight. They had no more provisions and the bird on which he was riding was exhausted. "Ivan Mare's Son, we are going to abandon you!" But Ivan Mare's Son immediately took his penknife out of his pocket and cut out the tendon from his right leg, divided it into twelve portions, and threw it to them and fed them all at once, and at that very moment they tossed him onto the earth. The birds coughed up the tendon and it again became part of his leg.

Then he saw that his mother had run up and killed herself, falling on a stone, and the ravens were already pecking at her bones. He caught a young raven. The old raven asked him to release the young raven and said, "Whatever you desire, Ivan Mare's Son, I will fulfill it."

"When you have fulfilled it, I will release the young raven." Within three days the raven returned and he had brought some living and dead water. He gathered his mother's bones for Ivan Mare's Son, sprinkled them with the dead water, and covered them over with her hide. He sprinkled them with the living water and the little mare shook herself as if nothing had ever happened.

Ivan Mare's Son said farewell to her and sent her where she had been before. "But I'm going to a wedding—on such and such a day there'll be a wedding at our tsar's."

So just at that time they were marrying the tsar's daughter to Oak. Ivan Mare's Son met up with a beggar. He took the beggar's old worn-out clothing, put it on, and gave him his own. He came into the palace. He stood in the entry hall and asked for alms for Ivan Mare's Son. The bride was sitting with the groom at a table and she heard him ask for alms for Ivan Mare's Son, and she asked her father and mother to give her alms for the beggar from their own pocket. That the tsar ordered done. The bride offered the alms. Ivan Mare's Son took them in his right hand. The bride saw her own diamond ring and suddenly called out in a strange voice: "Oh, Oak bogatyr is not my fiancé, it's this one, Ivan Mare's Son!" And then she told the tsar everything. The tsar ordered Oak scattered to the four winds in the steppe and he married her to Ivan Mare's Son and entrusted the entire tsardom to him.

16. Maria Morevna

Provenance unknown. The various episodes are widely known throughout the world, but this particular combination of tale types is rather unusual. Especially unusual are the episodes where Tsarevich Ivan earns his hero's horse and the final episode where this same horse is the downfall of Koshchei the Deathless. It has been argued that this latter episode reflects the pre-Christian belief in a god of the underworld. This tale is one of the most popular Russian wonder-tales of the past century. SUS 552A + 400$_1$ + 554 + 302$_2$.

In a certain tsardom, in a certain country, there lived and dwelt Ivan Tsarevich. He had three sisters: one was Maria Tsarevna, the next was Olga Tsarevna, and the third was Anna Tsarevna. Their father and mother died. And as they were dying, they instructed their son: "Whoever first starts courting your sisters, give them up to him. Don't keep your sisters long about you." The tsarevich buried his parents and in grief went off with his sisters to take a walk in a green garden. Suddenly there appeared in the sky a dark storm cloud, a terrible thunderstorm was getting up. "Sisters, let's go home," said Ivan Tsarevich. They had just got back into the palace when there was a clap of thunder, the ceiling split open, and into the room flew a bright falcon. The falcon threw himself onto the floor and became a fine young lad, and he said, "Greetings, Ivan Tsarevich. I used to come as a guest but now I've come as a matchmaker. I want to court your sister, Maria Tsarevna."

"If my sister is pleased by you, I won't stop her. Let her go with God's blessing." Maria Tsarevna agreed. The falcon was married and he carried her off to his own tsardom.

Days passed after days, the hours ran after the hours, the whole year as if it had never been. Ivan Tsarevich went off with his two sisters to take a walk in a green garden. Again there was a storm cloud with a whirlwind and lightning. "Let's go home, sisters," said the tsarevich. They had just got into the palace when there was a clap of thunder, the roof fell in, the ceiling split, and in flew an eagle. He threw himself on the floor and became a fine young lad. "Greetings, Ivan Tsarevich. I used to come as a guest but now I've come as a matchmaker. I want to court your sister Olga Tsarevna." Ivan Tsarevich answered: "If my sister is pleased by you, then let her marry you. I certainly won't stand against her will." Olga Tsarevna agreed and married the eagle. The eagle picked her up and carried her off to his own tsardom.

Another year passed and Ivan Tsarevich said to his youngest sister: "Let's go for a walk in the green garden." They walked for a little while. Once more there was a storm cloud, with a whirlwind and lightning. "Let's return home, sister." So they returned home. They didn't have time to sit down when there was a clap of thunder, the ceiling parted, and in flew a raven. The raven threw himself against the floor and became a fine young lad. The earlier young lads had been handsome, but this one was finest of all. "Well, Ivan Tsarevich, I used to come as a guest but now I've come to court. Give me Anna Tsarevna!"

"I'll not stand in my sister's way. If you are attractive to her, then let her marry you." Anna Tsarevna married the raven, and he carried her off to his own tsardom.

Ivan Tsarevich was left alone. For a whole year he lived without his sisters and became bored. "I'll go looking for my sisters." So he got ready for the trip. He walked and walked and saw lying in the steppe a beaten force and army. Ivan Tsarevich asked, "If any man is alive, call out. Who killed this great force?"

The one living man responded, "Maria Morevna, the beautiful princess, killed off this great army." And so Ivan Tsarevich went on further. He rode up to some white tents and Maria Morevna came out to greet him. "Greetings, tsarevich, where is God taking you? Are you free or no?"

Ivan Tsarevich answered her, "Fine young lads don't go riding around if they aren't free."

"Well, if there's no rush, come and be my guest in these tents." Ivan Tsarevich was pleased at that. He spent two nights in the tents, fell in love with Maria Morevna and married her.

Maria Morevna, the beautiful daughter of the king, took him with her to her own country. They lived there together for a certain amount of time, and then the princess thought of going to war. She gave Ivan Tsarevich all the estate and ordered him: "You can go anywhere, look after everything, only you may not look in this closet."

He just couldn't stand that and as soon as Maria Morevna had ridden away, he rushed to the closet, opened the door, and looked. Koshchei the Deathless was hanging there, fettered by twelve chains. Koshchei the Deathless said to Ivan Tsarevich, "Have pity on me! Let me have a drink. For ten years I have been tormented here. I haven't eaten, I haven't drunk, my throat is completely dried out." The tsarevich gave him a whole bucket of water. He drank it and asked, "You can't slake my thirst with just one bucket. Give me another." The tsarevich gave him a second bucket. Koshchei drank that and asked for a third. When he had drunk the third bucket, he got back his former strength. He yanked on the chains and broke all twelve at once. "Thanks, Ivan Tsarevich," said Koshchei the Deathless, "Now you will never see Maria Morevna any more than you'll see your ears." And in a terrifying whirlwind he flew out the window. Along the road he caught up to Maria Morevna, the beautiful princess, he grabbed her and carried her off to his place.

Ivan Tsarevich started weeping bitterly, equipped himself, and set off on the road, the way. "Whatever happens, I'll find Maria Morevna."

One day passed, another day passed, at sunset of the third day he saw a palace even better than the first and next to the palace there stood an oak, and on the oak there sat a falcon. The falcon flew down from the oak, threw himself against the ground, turned into a fine young lad and shouted: "Oh, my dear brother-in-law! How has the Lord been treating you?" Out ran Maria Tsarevna, she greeted Ivan Tsarevich joyfully, began asking after his health and began telling him about her own way of life. The tsarevich was their guest for three days and then said, "I cannot remain your guest for long, I am going to search for my wife, Maria Morevna, the beautiful princess."

"It will be difficult for you to find her," answered the falcon. "Leave your silver spoon in any case. We shall look at it and remember you." Ivan Tsarevich left his silver spoon with the falcon and set off along the road.

He walked for a day, he walked for a second, at sunset on the third day he saw a palace still better than the first. And next to the palace an oak was standing and on the oak an eagle was perched. The eagle flew down from the tree, threw himself against the ground and turned into a fine young lad and he shouted, "Get up, Olga Tsarevna. Our dear brother has come." Olga Tsarevna immediately came running to meet him, and started kissing and embracing him, asking after his health and telling him about her own way of life.

Ivan Tsarevich was their guest for three days, but then he said, "I have no more time to be your guest. I am going to find my wife, Maria Morevna, the beautiful princess."

The eagle answered, "You'll have difficulty finding her. Leave your silver fork with us. We shall look at it and remember you." He left the silver fork and set off along the road.

He walked for a day, he walked for a second and at sunset on the third day he saw a palace better than the first two, and next to the palace stood an oak and on that oak a raven was perched. The raven flew down from the oak, threw himself against the ground, turned into a fine young lad, and shouted, "Anna Tsarevna, come out quickly, our brother is coming!" Anna Tsarevna ran out, she greeted him joyfully, she began to kiss and embrace him, to ask after his health and tell him about her own way of life.

Ivan Tsarevich was their guest for three days and then he said, "Farewell, I am going to search for my wife, Maria Morevna, the beautiful princess."

The raven answered, "You'll have difficulty finding her. Leave your silver snuff box with us. We shall look at it and remember you." Ivan Tsarevich gave them his silver snuff box, took his leave, and set off along the road.

He walked for a day, he walked for a second, and at sunset on the third day he got to Maria Morevna. She caught sight of her dear one, threw herself around his neck, burst into tears and said, "Oh, Ivan Tsarevich! Why didn't you listen to me? You looked into that closet and let Koshchei the Deathless out!"

"Forgive me, Maria Morevna. Let's not bring up the past. It would be better for you to come riding with me before Koshchei the Deathless sees us, before he can catch up to us." So they got ready and rode away. Now Koshchei was out hunting. Toward evening he turned back toward home and his good horse stumbled. "Why are you stumbling, you hay-burning nag? Or do you sense some disaster?"

The horse answered, "Ivan Tsarevich has come and taken away Maria Morevna."

"And can we catch up to them?"

"You can sow wheat, wait for it to grow, cut it and mill it, turn it into flour, make five ovens of bread, eat the bread, and riding at a fast clip we will still have time to catch them." Koshchei started galloping and caught up to Ivan Tsarevich. "Well," he said, "I'll let you go the first time on account of your kindness in giving me the water to drink. And a second time I'll forgive you, but watch out the third time—I'll hack you to bits." He took Maria Morevna away from him and carried her off. Ivan Tsarevich sat down on a stone and wept. He cried and he cried and then he once more returned for Maria Morevna. Koshchei the Deathless wasn't at home. "Let us go, Maria Morevna."

"Oh, Ivan Tsarevich. He will catch us!" But they got ready and rode away. Koshchei the Deathless was returning home when his good horse stumbled beneath him. "Why are you stumbling, you hay-burning nag? Or do you sense some disaster?"

"Ivan Tsarevich has come and taken Maria Morevna away with him."

"And can we catch up to them?"

"You can sow barley, wait for it to grow, cut and mill it, brew beer, drink yourself drunk, sleep it off, and then riding at a fast clip, we'll still have time to catch them."

Koshchei galloped off and caught up to Ivan Tsarevich. "I told you that you were not to see Maria Morevna any more than your ears." He took her and carried her off.

Ivan Tsarevich remained alone. He cried and he cried and then returned for Maria Morevna once more. Just then Koshchei was not at home. "Let's go, Maria Morevna!"

"Oh, Ivan Tsarevich, he'll catch up to us and cut you into pieces."

"Let him cut. I cannot live without you." So they got ready and they set off.

Koshchei the Deathless was coming home when his good horse stumbled beneath him. "Why are you stumbling? Or do you sense some disaster?"

"Ivan Tsarevich has come and taken Maria Morevna away with him." Koshchei galloped off, caught up to Ivan Tsarevich, cut him into tiny pieces, put the pieces in a pitch barrel, took the barrel and fitted it with iron hoops, and threw it in the deep blue sea. Then he took Maria Morevna away to his own place.

At that very same time, at Ivan Tsarevich's brothers-in-law, the silver darkened. "Oh," they said, "it's apparent that a misfortune has taken place." The eagle threw himself into the deep blue sea, grabbed hold of and dragged the barrel to the shore, the falcon flew after the living water and the raven after the dead water. They all flew together in one place, broke open the barrel and took out the pieces of Ivan Tsarevich. They washed them and put them together as they were supposed to be. The raven sprinkled them with the dead water and the body grew together, became one piece. The falcon sprinkled it with living water and Ivan Tsarevich shuddered, stood up, and said, "Oh, I've been asleep so long!"

"You would have slept a lot longer, if it hadn't been for us," the brothers-in-law answered. "Now, let's go visit someone."

"No, brothers, I'll go search for Maria Morevna." He came to her and said, "Find out from Koshchei the Deathless where he got such a fine horse."

So Maria Morevna seized the opportunity to ask Koshchei about it. Koshchei said, "Beyond the thrice-nine tsardom in the thrice-ten tsardom, beyond the fiery river, there lives Baba Yaga. She has this mare on which she circles the earth every day. And she has lots of other fine mares. I was a herder for her for three days, and I didn't lose a single mare, and so Baba Yaga gave me a little colt."

"And how did you get across the fiery river?"

"I have this kerchief and I wave it to the right side three times and a high, high bridge appears that the fire can't reach." Maria Morevna listened and told all of this to Ivan Tsarevich and she took the kerchief and gave it to him.

So Ivan Tsarevich crossed the fiery river and went to Baba Yaga's. He walked for a long time, without drinking or eating. And he chanced to encounter a strange bird with her little ones. Ivan Tsarevich said, "I shall eat one of the chicks."

"Don't eat any, Ivan Tsarevich," the strange bird begged, "sometime I'll be useful to you." He went on further and saw in the forest a beehive. "I'll take a little bit of honey," he said. The queen bee responded, "Don't touch my honey, Ivan Tsarevich, and sometime I'll be useful to you." So he didn't touch it and went on further. Then he chanced to meet a lioness with a lion cub. "I'll just eat this lion cub. I want to eat so much that I'm getting sick from it."

"Don't touch it, Ivan Tsarevich," begged the lioness, "sometime I'll be useful to you."

"Alright, let it be as you say."

The hungry man set out. He walked and he walked and there stood the house of Baba Yaga. Around the house were twelve stakes and on eleven of them a human head. Only one was unoccupied. "Good day, granny."

"Good day, Ivan Tsarevich! Why have you come? On your own account or by force?"

"I came to earn a hero's horse from you."

"Go right ahead, tsarevich. And with me you don't have to serve a whole year, just three days. If you herd my young mares, I'll give you a hero's horse. If not, well, don't get angry, your head will stick out on that last stake." Ivan Tsarevich agreed. Baba Yaga fed him and gave him a drink and then she ordered him to start to work on the task. He had just driven the mares out into the field when the mares raised up their tails and they scattered themselves throughout the meadows. The tsarevich didn't manage to get a good look at them when they had all disappeared. So right then he started crying and became very sad, and he sat down on a stone and went to sleep.

The sun had already set when a little bird from beyond the seas flew up and woke him up. "Get up, Ivan Tsarevich, your mares are already at home." The tsarevich got up and returned home and Baba Yaga was making a noise and shouting at her mares, "Why did you come back?"

"Why should we not return? Birds from all over the earth flew up and nearly pecked out our eyes."

"Well, tomorrow don't go out into the meadows, go into the deep and dreamy forests."

So Ivan Tsarevich slept through the night and in the morning Baba Yaga said to him, "Now see here, tsarevich, if you don't herd my mares, if you lose even one, your wild little head shall be on that stake." So he drove the horses into the field. They immediately raised up their tails and scattered themselves throughout the deep forests. Again he sat down on the stone and he cried and cried and fell asleep. The sun sat behind the forest. The lioness ran up. "Get up, Ivan Tsarevich, the mares are already gathered up." Ivan Tsarevich got up and went home. Baba Yaga was making more noise than before and she shouted at her mares, "Why did you come back?"

"Why should we not return? All sorts of wild beasts from around the whole world came and just about tore us to pieces."

"Well, tomorrow, you run off into the deep blue sea."

Once more Ivan Tsarevich slept through the night. In the morning Baba Yaga sent him off to herd her mares. "If you don't herd the mares, your wild little head will be on that stake." He drove the horses into the field. They immediately raised up their tails, disappeared from view and ran into the deep blue sea. They stood in water up to their necks. Ivan Tsarevich sat down on the stone, started crying, and fell asleep. The sun set beyond the forest and a bee flew up and said, "Get up, Tsarevich! All the mares are gathered up. But when you get back home, don't show yourself to Baba Yaga. Go straight to the stables and hide behind the mangers. There is a mangy little colt, lying in the dung heap. You steal him and in the middle of the night you go away from the house with him."

Ivan Tsarevich got up, made his way to the stables and lay down behind the manger. Baba Yaga made a noise and shouted at her mares. "Why have you come back?"

"Why should we not come back? An innumerable host of bees came flying up from all over the world and started stinging us from all sides until we bled."

Baba Yaga fell asleep and at darkest midnight Ivan Tsarevich stole the mangy little colt, saddled him, got on, and galloped to the river of fire. He rode right up to the river, waved the kerchief three times to the right side and suddenly out of nowhere there appeared a high and fine bridge hanging over the river. Ivan Tsarevich crossed over the bridge and waved just twice with the kerchief on the left side. A thin, thin bridge remained over the river. In the morning Baba Yaga woke up. Her mangy little colt was nowhere to be seen. She rushed off in pursuit. She galloped at full speed in her iron mortar, directing it with the pestle, and erasing the traces with a mop. She galloped up to the fiery river, glanced at it and thought: "The bridge is a good one." She set off over the bridge, got to the middle, and then the bridge broke and Baba Yaga went tumbling into the river. That's where her fierce death finally took place!

Ivan Tsarevich fed the colt out in the green meadows and he became a wonderful horse. The tsarevich came to Maria Morevna. She came running out and threw herself around his neck. "How did God resurrect you?"

"Just so," he said, "come with me."

"I am afraid, Ivan Tsarevich! If Koshchei catches up, you'll be chopped up again."

"Well, he won't catch up. Now I have a fine hero's horse, he flies like a bird." So they mounted the horse and rode off.

Koshchei the Deathless was returning home when his horse stumbled beneath him. "What's this, you hay-burning nag, why are you stumbling? Or do you sense some disaster?"

"Ivan Tsarevich has come, he has taken Maria Morevna away."

"And can we catch up to them?"

"God only knows. Now Ivan Tsarevich has a hero's horse better than I."

"No, I won't stand for that," said Koshchei the Deathless. "I'll chase after them." In a long time or a short time he caught up to Ivan Tsarevich, jumped down onto the earth and tried to slash him with his sharp saber. At that very moment Ivan Tsarevich's horse kicked Koshchei the Deathless with his hoof with all his might and he knocked out his brains, and the tsarevich finished him off with his mace. After that the tsarevich made a heap of firewood, lit it, burned Koshchei on the bonfire, and scattered his ashes in the wind.

Maria Morevna got on Koshchei's horse, and Ivan Tsarevich on his own and they rode off. First they visited the raven, then the eagle, and finally the falcon. Wherever they went they were met with joy. "Oh, Ivan Tsarevich, we had never dared hope to see you again. And you weren't wrong when you put so much in it, truly you'll never find another like Maria Morevna anywhere in the world. So they visited there, they feasted, and then they went back to their own tsardom. They got there and began living and prospering, earning well and drinking mead.

17. The Witch and the Sun's Sister

This is a rare tale, met only in a retelling in Russian (Smirnov 324) and in one Hungarian version. SUS 313J*.

In a kingdom, in a far-away land, there lived, there were a tsar and his tsaritsa. They had a son, Tsarevich Ivan, who was mute from birth. One day when he was about twelve years old, he went to the stables to see his favorite stable hand. That stable hand always told him stories, and this time Ivan came to hear stories too, but that is not what he heard. "Tsarevich Ivan!" said the stable hand.

"Your mother will soon give birth to a daughter, a sister for you. She will be a hideous witch, eat your father and mother and all of the servants, so go and ask your father for the best possible horse, as if you were just going for a ride, and ride away from here whichever way your eyes point, if you want to be spared this misfortune." Tsarevich Ivan ran to his father and spoke to him for the first time in his life. The tsar was so happy at this that he didn't even ask why he needed a good steed. He immediately ordered the best mount from his herds to be saddled for the tsarevich. Tsarevich Ivan mounted and rode wherever his eyes took him.

For a long, long time he rode. He came upon two old seamstresses and asked that they take him in to live with them. The old women answered. "We would be happy to take you in, Tsarevich Ivan, but we have not long to live. When we break up this chest of needles and use up this chest of thread, then death will come right away!"

Tsarevich Ivan started to cry and rode on. For a long, long time he rode and came up to Oak-turner and asked: "Take me in!"

"I would be happy to take you in, Tsarevich Ivan, but I haven't long to live. As soon as I tear out all of these oaks by their roots, then it will be my death!"

The tsarevich cried more than before and rode still further and further. He came up to Mountain-turner and started to ask him, but he answered: "I would be happy to take you in, Ivan, but I haven't long to live myself. You see, I've been put here to twist out mountains. As soon as I manage with these last ones, then here is my death!" Tsarevich Ivan broke into bitter tears and rode on still further.

For a long, long time he rode. Finally he arrived at the home of Sun's sister. She took him in, wined him, dined him, cared for him as if he were her own son. The tsarevich lived well, but still from time to time he would get a little depressed: he would want to find out what was going on at home. Once in a while he would go up on a tall mountain, look at his palace, and see that everything had been eaten, only the walls were left! He would sigh and cry!

Once he looked and cried a little and then went back, and Sun's sister asked: "Why have you been crying, Tsarevich Ivan?"

He said: "The wind blew in my eyes." Another time it was the same, so Sun's sister forbade the wind to blow. The third time Tsarevich Ivan came home teary-eyed and there was nothing else to do—he had to tell all, and he asked Sun's sister to let him, good lad that he was, visit his homeland.

She wouldn't let him go and yet he begged. Finally his pleas met with success and she let him go to visit his homeland and she gave him, for the road, a brush, a comb, and two apples of youth: no matter how old a person might be, if he eats an apple, he becomes younger in an instant!

When Tsarevich Ivan came up to Mountain-turner, only one mountain was left. He took his brush and threw it into an open field. Suddenly, from nowhere, there grew out of the ground tall, tall mountains whose peaks pressed against the sky. And how many there were, seen and unseen! Mountain-turner was overjoyed and merrily started to work.

For a long time or a short time he rode. When Tsarevich Ivan came up to Oak-turner, only three oak trees remained. He took his comb and threw it into an open field. Suddenly, from nowhere, there noisily rose from the ground dense oak forests, one tree wider than the next! Oak-turner was overjoyed, was thankful to the tsarevich, and went to tear out the age-old oaks. For a long time or a short time he rode. When Tsarevich Ivan came up to the old women, he gave them each an apple. They ate them and in an instant grew younger; they gave him a piece of cloth: whenever you wave the cloth, a whole lake will appear!

And so Tsarevich Ivan returned home. His sister ran out, greeted him, and took care of him: "Sit down brother," she said. "play the gusli, and I'll go prepare dinner." The tsarevich sat down and badly strummed the gusli.

A mouse crawled out of its hole and said to him in a human voice: "Save yourself, tsarevich, run quickly! Your sister went to sharpen her teeth." Tsarevich Ivan went out of the chamber, mounted his horse, and galloped away; and the mouse ran along the strings. The gusli sounded bad and the sister didn't know that her brother had gone. Having sharpened her teeth, she rushed into the chamber, but there was not a soul there, only a mouse slipping into its hole. The witch became angry, gnashed her teeth, and set out in pursuit.

Tsarevich Ivan heard some noise and looked around. His sister was almost upon him. He waved his cloth and there appeared a deep lake. While the witch was getting across the lake, Tsarevich Ivan rode far away. She took off even faster . . . she was really close! Oak-turner guessed that the tsarevich was escaping from his sister and started tearing out oaks and piling them onto the road. He piled up a whole mountain! There was no path for the witch! She started clearing the way; she chewed and chewed and barely broke through, but Tsarevich Ivan was already far away. She rushed to catch up: she sped and sped, only a little more . . . he can't get away! Mountain-turner saw the witch, took hold of the tallest mountain and turned it right onto the road, and on that mountain he placed another. While the witch was clambering and climbing, Tsarevich Ivan rode and rode and ended up far away.

The witch made it across the mountains and again launched after her brother. She glimpsed him and said, "Now you won't get away from me!" She was close, she was catching up!

At the same time, Tsarevich Ivan galloped up to the chambers of Sun's sister and yelled, "Sun! Sun! Open the window." Sun's sister opened the window and Tsarevich Ivan jumped through it along with his horse. The witch started to plead that they give her back her brother with his head, but Sun's sister did not obey her and did not give him up.

Then the witch said: "Let Tsarevich Ivan go with me to the scales and see who outweighs whom! If I outweigh him, then I will get to eat him, if he weighs more, then let him kill me!" They went. First Tsarevich Ivan sat on the scales, then the witch started to climb on. She had only started to put her first foot up when Tsarevich Ivan was thrown up into the air, and with such force that he landed right up in the sky and in the chambers of Sun's sister. And the witch-serpent remained on the ground.

18. The Milk of Wild Beasts

Apparently collected in Orel district by P.I. Iakushkin for P.V. Kireevskii, from whose collection it made its way to Afanas'ev. One of the more popular tales and therefore often printed in children's collections, it has also been collected frequently in all three branches of East Slavic. It is well known throughout Europe and the Near East. SUS 314A* + 315.

In a certain tsardom, but not in our country, there lived and dwelt a tsar in his tsardom, a king in his kingdom, and they had these children: a son Ivan Tsarevich and a daughter Elena the Beautiful. There appeared in his tsardom a bear with iron fur who began eating all his subjects. . . .The bear ate people, and the tsar sat and thought about how he was to save his children. He ordered a high tower built and in it he put Ivan Tsarevich and Elena the Beautiful, and he laid in provisions for them for five years.

So the bear ate up all the people, and then he ran to the tsar's palace and in vexation began to gnaw on a broom. "Don't gnaw on me, bear of the iron fur!" said the broom. "You ought to go into the steppe and there you'll see this tower, and in the tower sit Ivan Tsarevich and Elena the Beautiful." So the bear ran to the tower and began rocking it. Ivan Tsarevich became frightened and threw food at him, and when the bear had eaten what he wanted, he fell asleep.

The bear slept but Ivan Tsarevich and Elena the Beautiful ran without a glance backward. In the road there stood a horse. "Horse, oh horse! Save us!" they said. They had no sooner mounted up on the horse, than the bear caught up to them. He tore the horse into pieces, put them into his mouth, and carried them to the tower. They gave him some food, he ate his fill, and again fell asleep.

The bear slept, and Ivan Tsarevich and Elena the Beautiful ran without a glance backward. On the road there were some geese walking. "Geese, oh geese! Save us!" they said. They got on the geese and flew off, but the bear woke up, scorched the geese with flames, and brought them to the tower. Once more they gave him food. He ate his fill and fell asleep again.

The bear slept but Ivan Tsarevich and Elena the Beautiful ran without a glance backward. In the road there stood a three-year-old bullock. "Bullock, bullock! Save us!" they said. "The bear with the iron fur is after us."

"Climb on my back. You, Ivan Tsarevich, sit with your rear to the front and when you see the bear, tell me." As soon as the bear caught up to him the bullock let fly a stream at him and plastered his eyes shut. Three times the bear caught up to them and three times the bullock plastered his eyes shut. They started crossing a river with the bear after them—and he drowned.

They felt like something to eat, so then the bullock said, "Butcher me and eat me, and collect my bones, and strike them. And out of them a little man like a fist about the size of a nail but with a beard a cubit long will appear. He will do everything for you."

Time went by and they ate up the bullock and wanted something else to eat. They tapped gently on the bones and out came the little man the size of a fist. So they went into the forest and in that forest stood a house, and it was a robbers' house. Little Fist killed the robbers and their headman and locked them up in one room. But he ordered Elena not to go in there. She couldn't stay out, though, and looked in and fell in love with the headman's head.

She asked Ivan Tsarevich to get some living and dead water for her. When he had got the living and the dead waters, the tsarevna brought the headman back to life, and they agreed to get rid of Ivan Tsarevich.

First she agreed to send him after some wolf's milk. So Ivan Tsarevich and Little Fist set off. They found a mother wolf. "Give us some milk!" She asked them to take her wolf pup, too, because he just farted and fooled around, and ate other folk's bread. So they took the milk and the wolf pup, and they went back to Elena the Beautiful. They gave her the milk, but they kept the wolf pup for themselves. With him they wouldn't be able to get rid of Ivan.

So then she sent them after bear's milk. So Ivan and Little Fist went to get some bear's milk and they found a sow-bear. "Give us some milk." She asked them to take a bear cub because he just farted around and ate other folk's bread. Again, having taken the milk and the bear cub, they went to Elena the Beautiful. They gave her the milk, but they kept the bear cub. Without the bear cub she wouldn't be likely to get rid of Ivan Tsarevich.

So then she sent him after lion's milk. Ivan Tsarevich and Little Fist set off and they found a lioness. They took some milk, but she asked them to take a lion cub because he just farted around and ate other folk's bread. They returned to Elena the Beautiful, gave her the milk, but they kept the lion cub for themselves.

Afterward the headman and Elena the Beautiful saw that there was no way for them to be rid of Ivan Tsarevich. They sent him to get the eggs of the firebird. So Ivan Tsarevich and Little Fist set out to get the eggs. They found the firebird and wanted to get the eggs, but she got angry and swallowed up Little Fist. So Ivan Tsarevich went home without any eggs. He came to Elena the Beautiful and told her that he had been unable to get the eggs and that the firebird had swallowed up Little Fist. Elena the Beautiful and the headman were overjoyed and said that now Ivan Tsarevich would be unable to do anything without Little Fist. They ordered him killed, but Ivan Tsarevich overheard this and begged his sister to let him bathe in the bathhouse before his death.

Elena the Beautiful ordered the bathhouse heated and Ivan Tsarevich went into the bathhouse. But Elena the Beautiful sent someone to say to him that he should bathe quickly. Ivan Tsarevich paid no attention to her, but washed without any hurry. Suddenly the little wolf, the little bear, and the little lion came running in to him and told him that Little Fist had been rescued from the firebird and would soon come to him. Ivan Tsarevich told them to lie near the threshold of the bathhouse and he went on washing. Elena the Beautiful once more sent word to him that he should wash more quickly and that if he didn't soon come out, she would come in after him. Ivan Tsarevich paid no attention to her, nor did he come out of the bathhouse. Elena the Beautiful waited and waited, and when she could wait no more, she and the headman went to see what he was doing in there.

She came there and saw that he was washing and paying no attention to her orders. This angered her, and she gave him a blow. Out of nowhere, Little Fist ordered the little wolf, little bear, and little lion to tear the headman to little bits, and he took Elena and tied her naked to a tree so that the gnats and mosquitoes could eat up her body. Then he and Ivan Tsarevich set off down the highway and byway.

They saw some large palaces and Little Fist said, "Wouldn't you like to get married, Ivan Tsarevich? In that house there lives a warrior-maiden and she's looking for just such a young man as you to overcome her." So they went into the house and they had hardly gotten into the house when Ivan Tsarevich mounted a horse with Little Fist behind him and he called out the warrior-maiden to fight. They fought and fought, but then the warrior-maiden struck Ivan Tsarevich in the chest and Ivan Tsarevich very nearly fell, but his Little Fist held him up. Finally, Ivan Tsarevich struck the warrior-maiden with his spear, and she immediately fell from her horse.

When Ivan Tsarevich had knocked her down, the warrior-maiden said to him, "Well, Ivan Tsarevich, now you can marry me."

Soon a tale is told, but not so soon is the deed done. Ivan Tsarevich married the warrior-maiden. "Well, Ivan Tsarevich," said Little Fist, "If on the first night you don't feel right, come outside to me. I'll help you in your misfortune." So Ivan Tsarevich lay down to sleep with the warrior-maiden. Suddenly the warrior-maiden placed a hand on his chest. This made Ivan Tsarevich feel ill and he asked to go outside. When he had gone out, he called for Little Fist, who told him that the warrior-maiden was trying to smother him. Little Fist went to the warrior-maiden and started beating her, all the while intoning, "Respect your husband, respect your husband." After that they began to live and prosper and become wealthy.

But then the warrior-maiden asked Ivan Tsarevich to untie Elena the Beautiful and bring her to live with them. He immediately sent someone to untie her and bring her to them. Elena the Beautiful lived with them for a long time. Once she said to Ivan Tsarevich, "Brother, let me search for lice in your hair." She started looking and stuck a dead tooth into his head. Ivan Tsarevich began dying. The little lion saw that he was dying and pulled out the dead tooth. The tsarevich began coming back to life, but the lion cub was dying. So the little bear pulled out the tooth and the lion cub began coming to life as the bear cub died. A fox saw he was dying, pulled out the tooth, and since she was more clever than the rest, she threw the tooth into a frying pan, which caused it to break into pieces. But then Ivan Tsarevich ordered Elena the Beautiful tied to the tail of a warrior's horse and she was scattered throughout the steppe. I was there, I drank mead, it ran through my moustaches, but none got into my mouth.

19. Baba Yaga and the Nimble Youth

Taken down in Shadrin district of Perm province by A.N. Zyrianov. Recorded frequently throughout Europe. SUS 327C.

There lived this tomcat, sparrow, and a third was a nimble youth. The tomcat and the sparrow went out to cut wood, and they said to the nimble youth, "Take care of the house and watch out: if Baba Yaga comes here to count the spoons, you don't say a word; just be silent."

"Alright," answered the nimble youth. The tomcat and the sparrow went away, and the nimble youth sat down on the stove behind the chimney.

Suddenly Baba Yaga appeared, took the spoons, and started counting them: "This is tomcat's spoon, this is sparrow's spoon, and this third one is the nimble youth's spoon."

The nimble youth couldn't hold back and he shouted, "Don't touch my spoon, Baba Yaga!" She grabbed the nimble youth, got in her mortar, and set off. She rode in her mortar, steering with the pestle and sweeping her traces away with a broom.

The nimble youth called out, "Tomcat, run! Sparrow, fly!" They heard him and came as fast as they could. The cat scratched Baba Yaga and the sparrow pecked her, and they took back the nimble youth.

The next day they got ready to go into the forest to chop wood again, and they instructed the nimble youth, "Look here, if that Baba Yaga comes here, don't you say a thing; we are going far away this time."

So the nimble youth just sat down on the stove behind the chimney. Suddenly Baba Yaga came and started counting the spoons: "This one's tomcat's spoon, this one's sparrow's spoon, and this one's the nimble youth's."

The nimble youth couldn't hold back and he shouted, "Don't touch my spoon, Baba Yaga." Baba Yaga grabbed the nimble youth and was dragging him away, but the nimble youth shouted out, "Tomcat, run! Sparrow, fly!" They heard him and came running. The tomcat scratched, the sparrow pecked Baba Yaga. They took back the nimble youth and went home.

On the third day they were getting ready to go into the forest to cut wood, and they said to the nimble youth, "Listen, if Baba Yaga comes, be silent. We are going very far away." So the tomcat and the sparrow went away and the third of them, the nimble youth, got comfortable on the stove behind the chimney.

Suddenly that Baba Yaga came and took the spoons, and started counting, "This is tomcat's spoon, and this is sparrow's spoon, and this third one is the nimble youth's." The nimble youth was silent. Baba Yaga counted them out a second time: "This is tomcat's spoon, this is sparrow's spoon, and this is the nimble youth's spoon." The nimble youth was silent. Baba Yaga counted for a third time. "This is tomcat's spoon, this is the sparrow's, and this is the nimble youth's spoon."

The nimble youth couldn't remain still and he bellowed, "Don't touch my spoon, you slut." Baba Yaga grabbed the nimble youth and dragged him away. The nimble youth shouted, "Tomcat, run! Sparrow, fly!" But his brothers didn't hear him.

Baba Yaga dragged the nimble youth home, put him in the cellar box, heated up the stove herself, and said to her eldest daughter, "Maiden! I am going to Rus. You roast that nimble youth for my dinner."

"Very good," she said. The oven was hot and the maid ordered the nimble youth to come out. He did so. "Lie down on that pan," said the maid. The youth lay down, but he stuck one foot up to the ceiling and the other on the floor. The maid said, "Not like that, not like that!"

The nimble youth said, "Then how? Teach me how then!"

The maid lay down on the pan. The nimble youth was not shy—he grabbed the oven glove and popped the pan with Baba Yaga's daughter on it into the oven. Then he went back to sit in the cellar box, and he sat there waiting for Baba Yaga.

Suddenly in Baba Yaga came running: "I'm about to go riding, I'm about to go sliding, all on the nimble youth's bones."

And the nimble youth replied to her, "Go riding and go sliding on your own daughter's bones!"

Baba Yaga gasped and then she looked: her daughter was roasted. She shrieked, "Oh, you rascal, just you wait!"

So her middle daughter heated up the oven and told the nimble youth to come out. He came out, lay down on the pan, put one leg in the ceiling and the other on the floor. The maid said, "Not like that, not like that!"

"Show me how, then!" The maid lay down on the pan. The nimble youth took it and popped it into the oven. Then he went back to the cellar box where he sat.

Suddenly the Baba Yaga came in: "I'm about to go riding, I'm about to go sliding, all on the nimble youth's bones."

But the nimble youth replied to her, "Go riding, go sliding on your daughter's bones."

The Yagishna became furious. "Wait," she said, "you won't succeed at this." She ordered her youngest daughter to roast him. But that was not to be, and the nimble youth roasted her, too.

Baba Yaga was madder than ever before. "Wait," she said, "you won't succeed at this!" She heated up the oven and shouted, "Come out, nimble youth! Lie down on this pan." The nimble youth lay down, but he placed one foot in the ceiling and the other against the floor, and he wouldn't fit into the oven. Baba Yaga said, "Not like that, not like that!"

But the nimble youth pretended he didn't know how. "I don't know how," he said, "Teach me."

So then Baba Yaga shrank herself up and lay down on the pan. The nimble youth wasn't a bit timid. He popped her into the oven and set off home. He came running in and said to his brothers, "That's what I did with Baba Yaga!"

20. Ivan Tsarevich and the Gray Wolf

Told by E.I. Sorokovikov (Magai), seventy years old, a hunter from Tunkin aimak, in 1938, who was one of the best-known narrators of the twentieth century. This is the only Russian version of 328, although it is known in Ukrainian and Belarusian. The combination is apparently also unique. SUS 550 + 328.

Beyond the thrice-nine land, in the thrice-ten tsardom, in a glorious maiden country, there lived a tsar, Arkhipat. He had three sons. The oldest son was called Lopai, the middle one Krutin, and the third was called Ivan Tsarevich. He had a splendid garden, the sort you can't tell about in a tale or describe with a pen. And in that splendid garden there was a marvelous apple tree with golden apples. But someone was creeping into this garden to take down the apples and carry them off. Tsar Arkhipat came every morning to the garden and every morning he counted several apples fewer. Then he called his sons and had a conversation with them.

"Well, my dear children, you mighty, glorious warriors! Can you help me in my despair?"

"What is your despair?" asked the sons. "We are glad to try to do you a great, true and honorable favor."

So then he began telling them about losing his apples and the brothers began thinking and guessing how to go about catching the thief. First in line was the oldest brother, Lopai, and the second was Krutin. The third in line was Ivan Tsarevich. And so off went the oldest brother to guard the apple tree and he boasted to his brother, "If that thief dares to come, he won't get out of my hands!" So then he went into the garden and flopped down beneath the apple tree on the green grass, and there he fell into a warrior's deep sleep. He got up in the morning and examined the apple tree. About ten apples were missing. "What shall I tell father? If I tell him that I saw the thief, but didn't catch him, then I am no warrior. But if I tell him I slept through it all, that will be still worse for me."

But he went and told his father, "Dear papa. No matter how I sat, no matter how I guarded, I don't know how, but some apples disappeared."

"That's bad," said Tsar Arkhipat. "I was counting on you as my eldest son."

The next time it got dark, it was time for the middle brother, Krutin, to go. When night had fallen, Krutin went into the garden. He looked around in the darkness of the night, and drowsiness began to overcome him. No matter how he struggled, how he sat there, nonetheless he lay down under the apple tree and slept a warrior's deep sleep. He slept through until morning. Then he looked at the apple tree and an innumerable number of apples had disappeared. "What will I say to my father?" he thought. He thought of something and went to his father.

Tsar Arkhipat asked his son, "Well, my dear little Krutinushka, what did you see?"

Then Krutin hung his head and said to his father, "I had such a terrible headache that I lay there without moving."

"That's bad," said Tsar Arkhipat. "I was counting on you."

The third evening approached and Ivan Tsarevich came and asked his father's blessing. He said to his father, "I'll need to take a rope. This night is going to be an unlucky one for that thief. Just as easily as a jug is filled with water, I'll twist off his head!" And then he left the palace and set off for the precious garden.

He sat down beneath the precious apple tree and observed the night: he couldn't see a thing. Drowsiness began to come over him and Ivan Tsarevich resisted. And just then he caught sight of an unfamiliar light. This light came closer and closer to him. It blinded his sight entirely, but he resisted and saw the firebird, which sat on the precious apple tree and picked the golden apples. Now, Ivan Tsarevich thought to himself, I'll certainly catch that thief now! He stood up and crept on his tiptoes forward, but the firebird was extremely lively and tore himself out of the tsarevich's hands and away. All that remained was a single feather from the firebird in Ivan Tsarevich's hand.

Ivan Tsarevich began looking at the feather and he was sorry for the firebird. Then he went into the royal palace and bowed to his father. "So now, dear father, the thief came and quick as lightning he was away. But as a souvenir I have this feather here in my hands."

His father was very satisfied because Ivan Tsarevich had found out who the thief was and with proof right there in his hands. Then the tsar said to his children, "Now, my dear children, if only you could catch that firebird! That would truly be fine."

The two older brothers envied Ivan Tsarevich: "Ivan Tsarevich only managed to get that firebird's feather; we'll go and get the firebird itself."

Then they gave the tsar their promise to do so, saddled their warhorses, and put on their warrior's armor. With their father's blessing, they mounted their good horses and rode out into the open steppe to search for that firebird. And then Ivan Tsarevich came in and said to his father, "Why, dear father, did you send my older brothers off to search for the firebird? Give me your blessing, too. Am I worse than my brothers? I will go in search of the firebird, too."

His father begged him and tried to persuade him not to abandon him. "You are now the only one left with me, and I am old; I have one foot in the grave."

But Ivan Tsarevich insisted on his right and his father released him. He went into the stables to pick out a good horse, and he chose one and saddled him with a Turkish saddle. Then he asked his father's blessing. As he said farewell to his last son, his father wept bitterly.

Ivan Tsarevich got on his good horse and rode out into the steppe, into the vast emptiness. He rode for a day, then for a second, and on the third he rode up to where a stone was lying. There was an inscription on the stone: "Whoever goes straight on will suffer cold and hunger; whoever goes to the right will be alive but his horse will be killed; whoever goes to the left will be killed but his horse will be alive."

He thought about it for a long time before he finally thought it out: "Even if I lose my horse, I'll still be able to pursue the firebird." So he turned to the right and rode on. He had been riding for some time when he came to a deep forest. Outside it was dark and he was gazing about in the darkness of the night when suddenly there appeared out of nowhere a gray wolf. He grabbed Ivan Tsarevich's horse right out from under him and then disappeared right into the earth, as if he'd descended into the pits of Hell. Ivan Tsarevich grabbed for his weapons, which he had with him, but he could see no one anywhere around.

What should he do now? He went on, on foot. He walked for a day, then a second, and then a third. Finally his hunger began to get the best of him. He walked on for a full ten days and on the eleventh his strength gave out and a terrible debility overcame him. Death was staring him in the face, and then he stumbled and was about to fall to the ground when suddenly out of nowhere the gray wolf appeared.

"Good health, Ivan Tsarevich! Forgive me for devouring your horse, but you saw the inscription. You ought not to have ridden to the right. But there's nothing more to be done. I want only the good, and I'll teach only wisdom." Then he asked him where his journey was taking him.

And Ivan told him, "I have come from my own tsardom where I gave a promise to my father to search out the firebird that has been carrying off our golden apples."

"Oh, Ivan Tsarevich, it will be difficult for you to get hold of the firebird, but I will help you. Now get onto my back and hold tightly to my fur."

So Ivan Tsarevich got onto the gray wolf and that gray wolf sprang forward, he flew along faster than the whirlwind and hurricane, like a tempered arrow let loose from a tautly drawn bow. And they flew right into the tsardom of Tsar Dalmat. The gray wolf stopped and said to Ivan Tsarevich. "Now you hop over that fence and into the garden where you'll see your treasure. Take the firebird but don't take the cage. If you take the cage, you'll surely perish together with your head."

So then Ivan Tsarevich hopped across the fence and into the garden where he saw his treasure. He fell to admiring the firebird as he took her out of the cage, and he thought to himself, "What shall I show her to my father in? That is a very expensive cage, all covered with diamonds. No, I'll take the cage, too, and let be what will be!"

But when he touched the cage, the alarm was sounded, and all the guards came running and took Ivan Tsarevich by his white hands. They led him to Tsar Dalmat. Tsar Dalmat looked at him sternly, and he spoke to him even more sternly: "So you think you've got two heads! You, young man, came to steal my firebird, didn't you? Now I shall order your punishment."

Ivan Tsarevich bowed to him. "Don't chop off my head. It would be better to give me some task to perform for you."

So then, Tsar Dalmat said, "All right, my dear young man, you go to Raflet's tsardom and obtain from Tsar Raflet his golden-maned horse. If you don't get it, then you'll never see the firebird again, and I'll chop off your head."

So then Ivan Tsarevich wept bitterly and left Dalmat's tsardom. He walked for a day, then a second, and then he walked for a third. And thus much time passed. His legs began to give way beneath him and he wept bitterly; he wanted to fall through the earth. Then out of nowhere, as if out of the earth, the gray wolf rose up before him and reproached him. "Why are you feeling so sorry for yourself? I told you not to take that cage."

So Ivan Tsarevich began to apologize to the gray wolf. "All right then. Get on my back and hold onto the fur even more tightly." And the gray wolf flew with more spirit than the whirlwind or the hurricane. He was like a tempered arrow loosed from a tautly strung bow. They came to Raflet's tsardom and now the gray wolf spoke to Ivan Tsarevich: "Climb through that wall and go into the stables. All the guards will be asleep. Then you can take the horse with the golden mane, but you must not take his bridle, which is covered with the finest diamonds. If you covet them and take them, you'll surely perish together with your head!"

Ivan Tsarevich climbed over the wall and went into the stables where he saw the golden-maned horse, and there on a peg was hanging the finest stamped bridle. "Well," he thought to himself, "what will I use to lead the horse if I don't have that fine bridle? I'll chance it and take the bridle anyway." When he started taking it down, such an alarm was sounded that Tsar Raflet's servants came running from all sides. They seized Ivan Tsarevich and bound his hands, and then they led him to Tsar Raflet. Tsar Raflet looked at him sternly, but he spoke more sternly still. "You think you've got two heads, don't you, young man, coming here to steal my horse? Well, what do we have to say to you? Take this rascal and execute him!"

So Ivan Tsarevich began bowing and fervently begging Tsar Raflet not to execute him but to give him some mighty task. And then Tsar Raflet said to Ivan Tsarevich, "If you want to get your hands on my horse, then ride out beyond the thrice-nine seas and the thrice-nine lands to the thrice-ten tsardom, to that famous maiden country, where lives Tsarevna Iakuta the Beautiful. If you bring her back to me, I'll give you the golden-maned horse and its fine bridle. But if you don't, I'll order you executed." And he chased him out of his chambers.

So Ivan Tsarevich went out into the steppe and cried. And then he thought, "How unlucky I am to have been born in this world. Why didn't I go to the left? It would have been better to leave my horse alive." And at the very moment of these tears, there appeared the gray wolf.

"Why are you so sad and sorrowful, Ivan Tsarevich, with hot tears pouring down over your face?"

"Why should I not weep and be sorrowful when Tsar Raflet has given me such an order? If I don't fulfill it, I'll perish."

"There's nothing for you to be sad about, Ivan Tsarevich; just get on my back and hold on tight."

And off the gray wolf flew. Mountains and rivers passed between his feet, and he dusted the steppes with his tail. Then they came to the maidens' country. And then the gray wolf said to Ivan Tsarevich: "Now then, brother, I'll get Iakuta the Beautiful and not you. You stay here in the steppe." And then he ran through a wall into the garden and up to Iakuta the Beautiful, and he hid in the bushes.

In the morning Iakuta the Beautiful came out with her nannies and her mummies into the green garden to walk and breathe in the fresh air. Suddenly out jumped the gray wolf, caught her in his teeth, and hopped back over the wall and away. He ran out into the open steppe where Ivan Tsarevich was waiting for him. "Now, Ivan Tsarevich, get on now and hold on even tighter to my fur."

Ivan Tsarevich took Iakuta the Beautiful into his arms, got onto the gray wolf, and they flew off to Raflet's tsardom. The gray wolf stopped and Ivan Tsarevich and Iakuta the Beautiful got off the gray wolf. She was half dead. Along the way, as he was holding her in his arms, Ivan Tsarevich had thought, "Oh, what indescribable beauty! How can I avoid giving her up to Tsar Raflet, to divert his eyes from her?" The gray wolf guessed his thought.

"Now then, Ivan Tsarevich, we shall leave Iakuta the Beautiful in this tent and you will take me along instead of Iakuta the Beautiful," said the gray wolf.

And then he threw himself upon the ground and turned into Iakuta. Ivan Tsarevich took the false Iakuta the Beautiful and led him to Tsar Raflet. And when Tsar Raflet saw her, he couldn't sit on his royal throne. He went up and praised Ivan Tsarevich, "Well done, Ivan Tsarevich! Now you can have my horse."

He ordered his grooms to give his horse with the gold bridle to Ivan. Ivan mounted the horse and rode away out of Raflet's tsardom.

Then Tsar Raflet ordered Iakuta the Beautiful to go into his bedroom, where he kissed and caressed her, and grasped her by her full breasts. But suddenly a wolf's muzzle was stuck in his face, grinding its teeth. Raflet was terribly frightened and he called his faithful servants, but the gray wolf was out the window, and all trace of him turned cold.

He came running up to Ivan Tsarevich and put Iakuta the Beautiful on the golden-maned horse, while Ivan Tsarevich got on the gray wolf and off they rode to Tsar Dalmat's tsardom.

They had to ride for a very long time, and meanwhile Ivan Tsarevich thought in his mind about diverting Tsar Dalmat's attention and not giving up the golden-maned horse. When they got to Tsar Dalmat's tsardom, the gray wolf stopped and said to Ivan Tsarevich, "We'll leave Iakuta the Beautiful here in this tent with the golden-maned horse, and you can lead me before Tsar Dalmat."

The gray wolf did a somersault and somersaulted himself into a horse, he became a golden-maned horse. Ivan Tsarevich took him and led him to Tsar Dalmat.

When Tsar Dalmat saw the beautiful golden-maned horse, he couldn't remain seated on his royal throne. He met Ivan Tsarevich, brought out the firebird with its fine cage and with other expensive gifts. "Yes, Ivan Tsarevich, you have served me faithfully in this faithful task." He presented him the cage with the firebird and then he took the reins of the golden-maned horse and led him into his best stable. But Ivan Tsarevich carried the firebird out into the open steppe to where Iakuta the Beautiful was.

Tsar Dalmat decided to go for a ride on the golden-maned horse and he started harnessing him in his finest tack. He got into a cart and rode out into the open steppe. The horse was proud, with his arched neck. Tsar Dalmat couldn't look at this golden-maned horse enough! Then, the dear horse started kicking in the traces and striking out with his hooves, and he ruined all the expensive tack before turning into the gray wolf again. Tsar Dalmat didn't even try to control him; he just looked around for some weapons, but the gray wolf in any case had vanished into thin air.

He came running up to Ivan Tsarevich. "Well, brother, get on my back and hold tight to my fur. Time's passing." And the beautiful Iakuta got on the golden-maned horse and then rode for a long time until they came to the place where the wolf had killed Ivan's horse before. Here the gray wolf stopped. "Well, Ivan Tsarevich, I can't go any further now because this is the border. Even though I did something bad to you, eating your horse, I nonetheless got you the firebird, the golden-maned horse, and a bride for you, Iakuta the Beautiful." As he said farewell, the gray wolf said, "I hope we'll meet again perhaps."

But when he had said farewell to Ivan Tsarevich, the gray wolf disappeared into the earth, into the very depths of hell. And Ivan Tsarevich got on the golden-maned horse and took Iakuta the Beautiful into his arms, and he took the firebird, and he rode off to his dear father in Arkhipat's tsardom.

He rode for a day, then for a second, and on the third day he began to get sleepy, so he spread his fine tent and they lay down to rest in the tent, and Ivan Tsarevich fell into a warrior's slumber.

Just at that time, his brothers Lopai and Krutin came riding up. They saw the sleeping pair and admired the beauty of Iakuta the Beautiful and they recognized their brother, Ivan Tsarevich. They were overcome by envy—they hadn't managed to get anything, but Ivan Tsarevich had the firebird, the golden-maned horse, and also a bride, an indescribable beauty. They decided to kill their blood brother. They chopped off his head, and then they started dividing up the booty.

The older brother took Iakuta the Beautiful and Krutin took the golden-maned horse and the firebird. Then they rode off toward their own tsardom. They had not ridden half the day when Tsar Koshchei the Deathless attacked them. He killed both brothers and threw them to the wolves to eat, and he took Iakuta the Beautiful and the golden-maned horse, and rode off to his own enchanted tsardom.

For two days Ivan Tsarevich lay in the open steppe, but on the third day a wonder-working raven flew up with two little ravens intending to peck out his eyes. Suddenly, out of nowhere, the gray wolf appeared and he grabbed the raven by the tail. The raven cawed and struggled, but it couldn't get out of the hands of the gray wolf. The raven begged the gray wolf to leave it alive, and then the gray wolf said to the raven, "If you fetch the living and dead water, I'll leave you alive, but if you don't, I'll kill you and your little ones, too. Now leave your little ravens here with me as hostages and you fly off and look for the living water."

The raven gave its children over to the gray wolf and flapped its wings before flying off wherever its nose might take it. It was gone more than three days, but on the fourth the raven came flying back carrying two little bags, and it said, "Here in this one is the living water, and in the other is the dead."

So the gray wolf took the one little bag and sprinkled the little raven, the one he had torn in two, and then he sprinkled him with the water from the second bag, and the little raven grew back together and flew off. So then the gray wolf said to the raven, "Enough, I don't need you any more. Fly wherever you want."

So then the raven and the little ravens flapped their wings and the gray wolf went up to Ivan Tsarevich and sprinkled him with some water from the first bag in which the living water was, and immediately his head grew together with his body, and then he sprinkled him a second time, and Ivan Tsarevich sighed, so then he sprinkled him a third time and this time Ivan Tsarevich sat up on his butt and said, "Oh, how long I've slept!"

Then the gray wolf said to him, "Yes, Ivan Tsarevich, you would have had to sleep forever if not for me. After our parting, your two brothers came upon you while you were sleeping, and out of envy they killed you and divided up the booty, and then they went off home to be welcomed with great glory. But they hadn't been traveling for more than half a day when Koshchei the Deathless Tsar attacked them, and he killed them and left them to be eaten by wolves and crows. And Koshchei the Deathless Tsar carried off Iakuta the Beautiful, the golden-maned horse, and the firebird into his enchanted tsardom.

"I would go with you to get back your treasure, but I am not permitted to go further than here. This is my legal limit. I wish only good for you and will instruct you only with sound counsel: go along this path and when three days have passed, you will find a little hut on cock's legs. Say to this hut: 'Turn, little hut, with your butt to the forest, and your front to me.' And when the little hut has turned, go into it and you will see in the hut Baba Yaga, with one bony leg and a lead eye. She travels about in a mortar, steering it with a pestle, and sweeping her tracks away with a broom.

"At first she'll be angry with you and seek even to eat you up. But you tell her that gray wolf has sent you. She knows me and will teach you how to bring about the death of Koshchei."

So the gray wolf and Ivan Tsarevich said farewell and he was gone. But Ivan Tsarevich went along the path as he had been told. He walked for a day, then for a second day, and on the third day he heard a noise and crashing, and roaring. The roar was soul destroying. He approached the roar. He came out onto a small meadow and in that meadow two forest spirits were fighting. They had torn to shreds everything they had on.

He began shouting at them to stop, he questioned them. Finally they had had enough of their fight and they stopped. Ivan Tsarevich interrogated them. "What ought this to mean, what are you fighting about?"

And then the two forest spirits said, "Ivan Tsarevich, we have found our grandfather's buried treasure. We don't know how to divide it, and therefore we were fighting and the winner was to take all."

"What sort of treasure is this?" asked Ivan Tsarevich.

"One of them said, "The first treasure is a fighting club, the second a tablecloth that sets out a meal itself, and the third is a hat that makes the wearer invisible."

"Oh, my!" said Ivan Tsarevich, "I can understand fighting over such a trove."

So then they grasped hold of each other and started fighting with each other again, and they struck and they howled. Then they had had enough and they stopped again.

Ivan Tsarevich offered them a proposal: "Why should you fight on and on and waste your strength? I would give you some good advice."

The forest spirits were very happy at that and they asked about the advice, which he then proceeded to give them. "Here on this path, in about three versts, there stands a large gnarly oak, and I'll line you up and say 'One! Two! Three!' and then you race off and whoever runs there first should take the trove."

The *leshii* were amazed at that sage counsel and they agreed to run. So then Ivan Tsarevich lined them up and when they were even, "One! Two! Three!" The *leshii* tore off with just a glimpse of their heels. Then Ivan Tsarevich thought to himself, "I've little time to waste hanging around here." He put on the invisible cap, put the fighting stick under his arm, took the self-laying tablecloth, and set off further.

When the *leshii* had run to the place and there was nobody there, they knew they had been tricked, and they started darting about in all directions. They went to the right and then to the left, sniffing out the tracks. They would run in a circle and then turn back, but finally they recognized that they weren't going to find him and so they exchanged glances and then, howling like wolves, they went off.

But Ivan Tsarevich had also set off further. He walked and walked, and whether near or far, or low or high, a tale is soon told, but the deed is not so quickly done. He spread out the self-laying tablecloth and out of nowhere there appeared all sorts of drinks and things to eat, and various wines. So Ivan Tsarevich had a good drink and a good meal, and rested superbly. Afterward he got up and went on further until he came to that clearing. And there in the clearing he saw this hut on cock's legs, and it could turn around. He spoke to the hut: "Turn, little hut, with your rear to the forest and your front to me." The little hut turned its rear to the forest and its front to him. Then Ivan Tsarevich opened the door and went into the little hut, and there he saw, riding around, Baba Yaga, with the skeletal leg, the lead eye, riding in her mortar, which she drove with her pestle, and sweeping the tracks with a broom.

"Phoo, phoo! The Russian Bone! Never before heard, never before seen, and now come right into my yard." And she wanted to devour him.

"What are you—?" said Ivan Tsarevich, "What are you doing? Why, the gray wolf sent me here."

The old woman stopped immediately and said, "Gray wolf? I know him. He is my friend and relation."

And Ivan Tsarevich said, "The gray wolf is my good friend."

And so then the old woman farted, knocked over the table, got down on her hands and knees, fetched some teacakes, and began to treat Ivan Tsarevich.

"And for what purpose have you deigned to come to me?"

So then he told her about his misfortune. "And so the gray wolf sent me to you," he said, "because 'granny knows where Koshchei's death is located.'"

"Oh, I know it," she said, "I know," said Baba Yaga, "but obtaining it is difficult. I have a horse, and he knows the road, but you'll have to obtain Koshchei's death by yourself."

"Very well, granny, just point me in the direction and tell me."

The old woman went outside and gave this tumultuous whistle, and she shouted in a warrior's voice, "Sivka-burka, Magic Kaurka, stand ready here to go!"

Sivka-burka came running, and stood at the ready as if fixed to the ground. Then she gave the reins to Ivan Tsarevich. He started saddling the good horse, and when he had saddled the good horse, the old woman said to him, "When he takes you to the ocean-sea, in the ocean-sea there is an island, Buian. And on that island of Buian there stands an oak, and beneath that oak there is a trunk, and in that trunk there is a hare, and in that hare there is a duck, and in that duck there is an egg. And that is Koshcheii's death."

So Ivan Tsarevich said farewell to Baba Yaga with the skeletal leg and rode away, and he flew higher than the standing forest, and below the strolling clouds, and they came to the ocean-sea. On the shore next to the ocean-sea a net was cast and in the net a pike was thrashing about. He wanted to get hold of this pike for his dinner, but the pike started talking to him in a human voice. "Ivan Tsarevich, let me free; perhaps I will be of use to you."

And Ivan Tsarevich said, "How can you be of use? You're just a fish and not a man."

And the fish said, "The impossible is sometimes possible." So Ivan Tsarevich thought about it for a little while and then he released the pike back into the water, and the pike swam away.

Ivan Tsarevich rode off a little and then he said, "Well, Sivka-burka, Magic Kaurka! Let's gallop off to the island of Buian."

So he leapt halfway there and then swam the other halfway and came out on the shore. And there on the island of Buian he saw an oak standing, and he went up to the oak and began examining it. It was a very mighty oak. "How am I to fell this oak?" he thought. And suddenly he remembered that he had his beating club. "Well, beating club, take out this oak by the roots!" And the beating club was pleased to try. It started striking at the roots and it cut through all of them and then started on the trunk. Soon the oak fell. And there beneath the oak there was a trunk.

So now he gave the order to the beating club to strike the trunk, and it soon broke the trunk apart. When the trunk was broken apart, a hare tried to fly out of it, but Ivan cut it in two with his sharp sword. When he had done that, out flew a duck and it started to fly away, but Ivan Tsarevich took his bow and shot the duck, and his arrow struck right in the duck's eager heart, and the duck was brought down, and out of it flew an egg, which fell and rolled toward the sea. But no matter how Ivan Tsarevich tried, catch that egg he could not. It rolled into the sea, and Ivan Tsarevich threw up his hands. "Well, farewell Koshchei's death; I'll never get Iakuta the Beautiful, nor see Koshchei dead."

He sat down on the ground to weep and be sorrowful. And just at that moment there was a flash of scales in the water and he thought it was his tears falling from his eyes, but then the pike came up out of the water, holding the egg in its mouth, and it said to Ivan Tsarevich, "Remember, Ivan Tsarevich, that a debt repaid is beautiful."

Ivan Tsarevich took the egg, turned it over, and put it in his bag, and then he went up to Sivka-burka the Magic Kaurka and said, "Well, Sivka-burka, Magic Kaurka, carry me back to land."

But Sivka-burka leapt only half the way, and then he swam the other half and they came to Koshchei's tsardom. The horse said to him, "Well, Ivan Tsarevich, I will carry you only as far as Koshchei's palace, but further than that I can't. And why can't I go further? Next to Koshchei's palace, at the gates, there is a twelve-headed serpent tethered. Nobody could get past that. The serpent would grab and eat up anyone who tried."

So then they rode up, and Ivan Tsarevich saw that six of the serpent's heads were sleeping, and the other six were standing guard. Ivan Tsarevich dismounted from his Sivka-burka, from his Magic Kaurka. And the Sivka-burka said farewell to Ivan Tsarevich and flew back to Baba Yaga of the bony leg, and Ivan Tsarevich put on his invisible cap and thought, "How shall I get by? Even if I can't in fact be seen, maybe this serpent has his own ways of finding out. If he strikes me, then it's goodbye to Koshchei's death and Iakuta the Beautiful."

He thought and thought, but he couldn't think up anything, and then suddenly he thought of it and he said, "Heh, beating club, get rid of that serpent!" And the beating club started in with the heads that weren't asleep. It beat them into powder and dust. And then the other six heads, which were now awake, six terrifying, evil heads, came darting out in all directions, but they couldn't see anything. So then Ivan Tsarevich said, "Now, beating club, beat those other six heads."

And the beating club started on the remaining six heads and in quick time they were finished.

So now Ivan Tsarevich took his beating club, put it in a bag, and started to go up into the enchanted palace, and there he saw a splendid garden.

"I'll just go into that garden and enjoy it a little." In the garden he saw an exquisite gazebo, and as he approached the gazebo, he heard these quiet moans, quiet sobs. Iakuta the Beautiful was crying and weeping, pitying her own fate.

"Why was I born on this earth, I am so miserable! I am separated from my Ivan Tsarevich, and evil people have killed Ivan Tsarevich, and now they are killed and fierce beasts rip them up, and I am in this terrible torture at the hands of the evil Koshchei the Deathless, who gives me no rest, trying to force me to marry him and be his faithful wife. But I do not wish to be his faithful wife and would rather accept a certain death."

Ivan Tsarevich went up to the gazebo and spoke these words, "I see your tears and hear your sighs, oh beautiful Iakuta." And he immediately removed his invisible hat. She saw him and recognized him and was about to throw herself into his embrace when she stopped. "No. Ivan Tsarevich is not alive; he was killed that day by his brothers; you only resemble Ivan Tsarevich."

Ivan Tsarevich began explaining to her how he had lain beneath the open skies for three days and then the gray wolf had seen him and guarded him for three days, waiting for the magician raven who had tried to peck out his eyes but the wolf had caught him by the tail. So then that magician raven handed over the young ravens as hostages and went off to fetch the living water. And so it flew away and it flew for three days before it brought back the living and the dead waters, and with that the gray wolf had brought Ivan Tsarevich back to life.

Iakuta the Beautiful couldn't help but believe him. She knew very well that the gray wolf had great ability, that he could have brought him back to life. She jumped up and hugged and kissed him.

Just then Tsar Koshchei the Deathless was approaching and Ivan Tsarevich ordered her to sit in a chair. She sat down in a golden chair and Koshchei the Deathless entered the gazebo and saw her happy and cheerful. He said to her, "You are my happiness! Today I see you as quite different from how you have been before. Why have you been so sad and crying, longing for that little boy, Ivan Tsarevich? Even if there were three Ivan Tsareviches, they could not save you; I would still possess you!"

He went up to Iakuta the Beautiful and was about to embrace her. But then Ivan Tsarevich pulled out his beating club and said, "Now, club, whack him on the legs and on the arms and on his cheekbones!" And the club began beating him. Koshchei the Deathless jumped back, somersaulted, and whirled around like a ten-year-old child, squealing.

And Ivan Tsarevich added, "Beat him, whack him, beating club, on his legs, and on the arms, and on his cheek bones."

So just then Koshchei said to him, "Who are you? Show yourself to me!"

Ivan Tsarevich couldn't resist any longer and he took off his invisible cap. "I am that same Ivan Tsarevich you were just now abusing."

So then Koshchei the Deathless stretched out his hand to him. "Why should we quarrel? Give me your hand and we'll make peace."

But Ivan Tsarevich knew very well that he was deathless. He pulled the egg out of his bag and said, "Here. Take this!" Then he threw it against a stone and broke it into tiny pieces, and Koshchei the Deathless, in a terrible death struggle, gave up the ghost. Now Ivan Tsarevich took his Iakuta the Beautiful and they went into the royal palace.

There were many important people, and boyars, and princes there, and they all said, "You have done a fine thing; you have killed that tsar. Now you shall be our tsar."

And he said, "I have no intention of living in your tsardom; I intend to stroll through the open steppe."

So he put on his invisible cap and ordered his beating club to whack them. They broke many an arm and legs, and heads, and then he stopped his beating club, put it away, and began collecting the treasures of that deathless tsar.

He collected many precious stones and rough diamonds and polished diamonds, and turquoises, and emeralds, and pearls. Then he took Koshchei's horse. He put Iakuta on the golden-maned horse, took the firebird, and rode back to his homeland.

As he rode along, there was no end to his happiness. His father thought he was childless, that he would die without seeing his sons. And then Ivan Tsarevich told his father about his journey, the whole story of his obtaining the firebird and the golden-maned horse, and Iakuta the Beautiful, and how his brothers had killed him, and then how Koshchei the Deathless had taken possession of their treasure and carried it off to his enchanted tsardom, and how the gray wolf had got the living water and brought him back to life.

"I killed Koshchei the Deathless, got the firebird, the golden-maned horse, and Iakuta the Beautiful, and now I have come back to your tsardom."

They organized a wedding. The feast lasted for an entire week. Wine flowed like a river. I even had a drink, but it flowed over my moustache and none went into my mouth.

21. The Maiden Tsar

From Orenburg province. Although similar tales are known throughout Eurasia, none of them is really like this one. The closest version to this text is one from Perm, Afanas'ev 233. Note the appearance of a merchant's son as hero. SUS 400$_2$.

In a certain tsardom, in a certain land, there was a merchant; his wife had died. He was left with just a son, Ivan. He appointed an uncle and mentor for his son, and then after a little while he got married for a second time. Since Ivan the merchant's son was already of an age and was very handsome, his stepmother fell in love with him. Once Ivan the merchant's son set off on a raft with his uncle to go hunting in the sea. Suddenly they saw thirty ships sailing toward them. On these thirty ships was a maiden tsar with thirty other maids, all her sworn sisters. When the little raft came up next to the ships, all thirty of the ships dropped anchor. Ivan the merchant's son and his uncle were summoned on board the very best ship. There the tsar maiden welcomed them with thirty maids, her sworn sisters, and she said to Ivan the merchant's son that she loved him madly and had come to see him from afar. Right there they were engaged.

The maiden tsar told Ivan the merchant's son to come to the same place at the same time in the morning, and then she said farewell to him and sailed away. And then Ivan the merchant's son went home, had his supper, and lay down to sleep. His stepmother led his uncle into her room, got him drunk, and began asking him whether something hadn't happened while they were out hunting. The uncle told her everything. When she heard it, she gave him a pin and said, "Tomorrow when those ships are sailing up to you, stick this pin in the clothing of Ivan the merchant's son." The uncle promised to do as she had ordered.

In the morning Ivan the merchant's son got up and set off hunting. When the uncle caught sight of the ships sailing toward them, he immediately stuck the pin in the clothes of the merchant's son. "Oh, how I want to sleep!" said the merchant's son. "Listen, uncle, I'm going to take a nap now, and when the ships come up close, please wake me up."

"Fine. Why should I not wake you up?" And then the ships sailed up and dropped anchor. The maiden tsar sent for Ivan the merchant's son, requesting his presence quickly. But he was sound asleep. They tried to awaken him; they poked and pushed him, but no matter what they did, they couldn't wake him up. So they left him.

The maiden tsar commanded the uncle to direct Ivan the merchant's son to appear there the next morning, and then she ordered anchors raised to set sail. When the ships had sailed off a little way, the uncle pulled out the pin, and Ivan the merchant's son woke up, jumped up, and started shouting for the maiden tsar to turn back. But no, she was already far away and didn't hear him. He came home very sad, mournful. His stepmother led the uncle into her room, got him drunk, and questioned him about everything that had taken place, and then she ordered him to stick the pin in again the next day.

The next day Ivan the merchant's son went out hunting, but again he slept the entire time, and didn't see the maiden tsar. Once more she ordered him to appear before her.

On the third day he intended to go hunting with his uncle. As they were approaching the old place, they saw the ships were sailing there in the distance. Immediately the uncle stuck in the pin and Ivan the merchant's son fell into a deep sleep. The ships sailed up and dropped anchor. The maiden tsar sent after the one she intended to be her groom, ordering him to appear on the ship. They tried to wake him up in every way possible, but no matter what they did, they couldn't wake him up. But the maiden tsar suspected the wiles of the stepmother and the treachery of the uncle. She wrote Ivan the merchant's son to cut off the uncle's head and then, if he loved his bride to be, to search for her in the thrice-nine land, in the thrice-ten tsardom. As soon as the ships had unfurled their sails and sailed off into the deep blue sea, the uncle pulled the pin out of the clothing of the merchant's son. He woke up and began shouting and calling to the tsar maiden, but she was far away and didn't hear anything. The uncle gave him the letter from the maiden tsar. Ivan the merchant's son read it, took out his sharp saber and cut off the evil uncle's head. Then he made his way quickly to the shore, then he went home quickly, took leave of his father, and set off on his route and way to look for the thrice-ten tsardom.

He was walking along, wherever his eyes might take him, for a long time or a short time, for soon is a tale told, but not so soon is the deed done, and he came to this hut. The hut stood in the open steppe, on cock's knees, and it could turn about. He went into the hut and there was Baba Yaga of the bony leg. "Phoo, phoo!" she said. "No Russian soul has been heard here, nor seen here, and then in you come walking! Do you come out of choice or by force, my good lad?"

"Pretty much out of choice, but twice as much by force. Do you know where the thrice-ten tsardom is?"

"No, I don't know," she answered. But then she told him to go to her middle sister, who perhaps might know.

So Ivan the merchant's son thanked her and set out again. He walked and walked whether near or far, whether for a long time or a short time, and he came to exactly the same kind of little hut. He went in and there was a Baba Yaga. "Phoo, phoo!" she said, "No Russian soul has been heard here, nor seen here, and you come walking in yourself. Have you come out of choice or by force, my good lad?"

"Pretty much out of choice, but twice as much by force. Do you know where the thrice-ten tsardom is?"

"No, I don't know," answered the Yaga, and she ordered him to go to the youngest sister. Perhaps she might know. "If she gets angry with you and wants to devour you, take her three horns and ask to play on them. Play the first horn quietly, the second a little louder, and the third louder still." So Ivan the merchant's son thanked the Yaga and set off further.

He walked and walked for a long time or a short time, whether near or far, and finally he saw a hut, standing in the open steppe, on cock's knees, and it could turn. He went in and there was Baba Yaga. "Phoo, phoo! No Russian soul has been heard here, nor seen here, and you come walking in yourself," said Baba Yaga, and she ran off to sharpen her teeth in order to eat her uninvited guest. Ivan the merchant's son asked her for the three horns, and he played the first softly, then the second a little louder, and the third louder still.

Suddenly from all sides all sorts of birds flew up, and among them was a firebird. "Sit yourself down on my back," said the firebird, "and we'll fly wherever you need to go. Otherwise Baba Yaga will eat you." So he managed to scramble onto her back just as Baba Yaga came running up. She grabbed the firebird by the tail and pulled out a few feathers.

The firebird flew off with Ivan the merchant's son. For a long time she carried him through the sky and finally she flew to the wide sea. "Well, Ivan the merchant's son, the thrice-ten tsardom lies beyond that sea, but I don't have the strength to carry you to that side. You'll have to make your own way there!" Ivan the merchant's son got down from the firebird, thanked her, and set off along the shore.

He walked and walked and there stood a little hut. He entered. An old, old woman met him. She gave him drinks and something to eat, and then questioned him about where he was going, why he was on such a journey. He told her that he was going to the thrice-ten tsardom in search of the tsar maiden, his future bride. "Oh," said the old woman, "She doesn't love you anymore. If you get in her sight, the tsar maiden will tear you up. Her love is hidden far away."

"How can I obtain it?"

"Wait a little bit. My own daughter lives with the tsar maiden and today she has promised to come and visit me. Perhaps we can find out something through her."

So then the old woman turned Ivan the merchant's son into a pin and stuck it into the wall. In the evening her daughter came flying by. Her mother questioned her, whether she knew where the tsar maiden's love was hidden. "I don't know," the daughter responded, but she promised to try to get it out of the tsar maiden herself. The next day she came back again and told her mother, "On the other side of the ocean-sea there stands an oak, and in the oak is a trunk, and in the trunk a hare, and in the hare a duck, and in the duck an egg, and in the egg is the tsar maiden's love."

Ivan the merchant's son took some bread and set off for the indicated place. He found the oak, took the trunk out of it, took the hare out of the trunk, the duck out of the hare, the egg out of the duck, and returned with the egg to the old woman. It was the old woman's name day. She invited the tsar maiden and thirty maidens, her sworn sisters, to be her guests. Then she baked the egg and she decked out Ivan the merchant's son in fancy clothes and hid him.

Suddenly at midday the tsar maiden and the thirty other maidens flew up, sat down at the table, and began dining. After dinner the old woman gave each of them an ordinary egg, but she gave the tsar maiden the egg that Ivan the merchant's son had obtained. The tsar maiden ate it and at that moment fell deeply, deeply in love with Ivan the merchant's son. The old woman immediately led him out and there was so much joy, so much happiness! The tsar maiden went away with her groom, the merchant's son, to her own tsardom. There they were married and they lived and became prosperous.

22. Elena the Wise

Of unknown provenance. The combination with A–T 306 "Nocturnal Dances" makes this tale somewhat unusual. It is much better known in Western Europe than among the Slavs, however. SUS 401₁ + 306.

In a certain tsardom, in a certain country, this tsar had a golden regiment, and in this regiment there served a soldier by the name of Ivan who was a very fine young man. The ruler was very fond of him and began to reward him with ranks. In a short time he made him colonel. The senior officers envied him. "Why have we served for thirty years to reach our ranks and he has taken all the ranks at once? We need to take him down a little, or else he will outrank us." So the generals and councillor boyars went strolling by the sea and they fitted out a ship and then they invited Ivan the colonel to join them. They went out into the open sea and they sailed until late evening. Ivan grew tired and lay down on a cot and fell into a very deep sleep. The boyars and the generals had been waiting for this very thing. They took him and placed him in a sloop and let it loose on the sea, and then they all returned back. A little bit later, heavy clouds came up and a storm arose. The waves came up and carried the sloop to some unknown place, it was carried far, far away and tossed up on an island.

There Ivan woke up and saw that the place was deserted and that there were no signs of the ship, and the sea was fearfully agitated. "Obviously the ship was broken up by the storm and all my comrades have drowned. Thank God that I have some-how survived!" He set off to explore the island. He walked and walked. He didn't see a single wild beast or passing bird, nor was there a human dwelling.

Whether after a long time or a short time, Ivan happened upon an underground entrance. He went down by this entrance into a deep abyss and came to an under-ground tsardom where a six-headed serpent ruled. He saw the white-stone palaces and went in. The first one was empty, in the second there wasn't a soul, but in the third, in the deep sleep of a warrior, slept the six-headed serpent. Alongside him stood a table and on that table lay an enormous book. Ivan opened up the book and read and read and he read up to that page where it said that the tsar could not give birth to a tsar, that a tsar could only be born of a tsaritsa. He went and scratched out these words with a pocket knife and in their place he wrote that a tsaritsa could not give birth to a tsar, that only a tsar could give birth to a tsar.

After an hour the serpent turned onto his other side and farted so loudly that he woke himself up. Ivan just gasped. "Listen, father," he said to the serpent, "it's time for you to get up."

The serpent heard this human voice, cast his eyes over his guest, and asked, "And where have you come from? As many years as I have lived on earth, up to now I have never seen a single human in my tsardom."

"What do you mean, where am I from? Why, I am your son! Just now you turned over on your side and you made such a bang that I jumped out. . . ."

"Well," said the serpent, "let me look in the book to see whether a tsar can give birth to a tsar." He opened up the book and read through to where it said that and he was convinced. "That's true, my son!" He took Ivan by the hand and led him through all the storerooms and showed him all the innumerable riches and they began to live and dwell together.

Some time passed and the six-headed serpent said, "Well, son, here are the keys to all my palaces. Go everywhere, you can go into anything you like, only you dare not glance into this one palace that is locked with a double lock, one gold and the other silver. I am going to fly around the world, take a look at people, and amuse myself." So he handed over the keys and flew away from the underground tsardom to wander around the whole, wide world. Ivan remained all alone. He lived there a month, then a second, and a third, and a year was nearly up. He was bored now and thought about looking around the palaces. He walked and walked and turned up by the forbidden chamber. The young man couldn't endure it. He pulled out a key, unlocked both locks—the gold and the silver—and he opened the oaken door.

In the room there sat two maidens both fettered in chains. One was the tsarevna Elena the Wise and the other was her servant. The tsarevna had little golden wings, her servant had little silver ones. Elena the Wise said, "Greetings, young man! Do us just a little favor and give us each a little glass of spring water to drink." Ivan, looking at her indescribable beauty, forgot all about the serpent. He felt sorry for the poor prisoners and he poured out two glasses of spring water and gave them to the beautiful maidens. They drank, they shuddered, the iron rings of the bonds snapped, their heavy chains fell off, the beautiful maidens flapped their wings and flew out an open window. Then Ivan came to his senses and locked the empty room, went out onto the porch, and sat on a step. He hung his unruly head lower than his mighty shoulders and was deeply, deeply saddened. What sort of answer could he give?

Suddenly the winds whistled, a strong storm came up and in flew the six-headed serpent. "Greetings, my son!" Ivan couldn't answer a word. "Why are you so silent? Or has some misfortune taken place?"

"It's bad, father! I did not observe your commandment and I looked in that room where the two maidens were sitting fettered in their chains. I gave them some spring water to drink. They drank it, they shuddered, they flapped their wings, and they flew away through the open window."

The serpent was extremely angry. He began to curse and swear at Ivan in every way. Then he took an iron rod, heated it red-hot, and weighed in with three blows across his back. "Now then, it's just lucky for you that you are my son. Otherwise, I would eat you alive." As soon as Ivan's back had healed up, he asked the serpent, "Father, permit me to go out into the world and search for Elena the Wise."

"Get along with you! I tried to catch her for thirty-three years and barely managed to catch her by trickery."

"Oh, let me father! Let me try my luck!"

"Oh alright, as you wish then. Here is a flying carpet for you. If you desire, it will carry you out of here. But I feel sorry for you because Elena the Wise is really clever. If you catch her, she will still get around you and deceive you."

Ivan sat down on the flying carpet and flew out of the underworld tsardom. He hardly had time to wink before he turned up in a splendid garden. He went up to a pond, sat down beneath a broom bush, and began viewing and admiring how little gold and silver fishes were playing in the clear water. Not five minutes had passed when Elena the Wise came flying up with her servant girl. They took off their wings, put them down near the broom bush, undressed completely, and rushed into the water to bathe. Ivan stole their wings away quietly, came out from under the broom, and shouted in a loud voice, "Oh, now you are in my hands!" The beautiful maidens leapt out of the pond, threw their clothes on and approached the long man to plead and appeal to him to return their wings. "No," answered Ivan, "I won't give them back for anything. I've taken a liking to you, Elena the Wise, more than the bright sun. Now I shall take you to my father and mother and I will marry you and you will be my wife and I will be your husband."

So then the tsarevna's servant spoke, "Listen, young man! You want to marry Elena the Wise, but why are you holding me here? It would be better to give me my wings. At some time I will be of use to you." Ivan thought and thought and then he gave her the silver wings. She quickly tied them on, shook herself, and flew far, far away.

After that Ivan made a chest, put the golden wings in it, and locked it tightly with a lock. He sat down on his flying carpet, took Elena the Wise with him and flew away to his own country. He flew to his father and mother and he introduced his promised wife to them. He asked them to love her and accept her. Then they had a celebration such as no one had ever seen. The next day Ivan gave his mother the key to the chest. "Watch over it," he asked her, "until the right time, and don't give the key to anybody. I will go and appear before the tsar and summon him to a wedding."

The moment he was gone, Elena the Wise came running in, "Mother, give me the key to the chest. I need to get a dress to get prepared for the wedding." His mother, who knew nothing about it, gave her the key without any fear. Elena the Wise rushed to the chest, opened the top, took out her wings, tied them on, flapped them a time or two, and she was out of sight! The groom returned home: "Mother, Where is my bride? It is time to get ready for the wedding."

"Oh, my son, she has flown away."

The young man sighed deeply, said farewell to his mother and father, sat down on his flying carpet, and flew off to the underground tsardom and the six-headed serpent. The serpent saw him and said, "Well, my daring fellow! It wasn't for nothing that I told you that you wouldn't acquire Elena the Wise for yourself, and that if you did, she would deceive you."

"You are right, father! But nevertheless, I am going to try. I am going to court her."

"Oh, you are irrepressible! You see, she has this rule laid down: everybody who courts her has to hide three times, and if she finds him, then she will immediately chop off his head. Many fine warriors have come to court her, and every single one of them has lost his head. The same is prepared for you. Listen to me. Here, take this flint and steel. When Elena the Wise makes you hide, strike the flint against the steel, make a spark, and light some feather grass. At that moment a gray-winged eagle will appear and lift you up to the third layer of clouds. If that doesn't work, strike the flint again and put it in the deep blue sea. An enormous pike fish will swim to shore and take you and carry you into the abyss of the sea. If Elena the Wise finds you there, then there's no place else to hide from her." So Ivan took the flint and steel, thanked the six-headed serpent, and flew off on the flying carpet.

Whether long or short, whether near or far, he flew well beyond the thrice-nine land into the thrice-ten country where Elena the Wise lived. Her palace shone as if it were on fire, for it was made of pure silver and gold. At the gates on iron palings were stuck eleven warriors' heads. Ivan, the young man, started thinking, "Eleven heads are already raised up on these palings. Mine is sure to be the twelfth." He landed in the broad courtyard, went up to a high porch, and went right into the room.

Elena the Wise met him. "Why have you dared to come here?" she said. "I want to marry you," he said.

"Just try it! If you can manage to hide from me, I will marry you. If you don't, you will pay for it with your head."

Ivan went out into the empty steppe, took his flint and steel, made a little fire, and burned some feather grass. Suddenly out of nowhere up flew a gray-winged eagle and spoke in a human voice: "Quickly, young man, mount up and hold tight, or else you'll fall off."

Ivan got on the eagle, grabbed tightly with both hands, and the eagle flapped its wings and soared high up and went beyond the third bank of clouds. It looked like he was well hidden, that no one would find him, but Elena the Wise had this mirror. She only had to look into it and all the universe would open to her. In an instant you can see what is going on throughout the whole wide world. So she went up to this mirror and gazed at it and she immediately saw the whole truth. "That's enough of that, my clever one!" shouted Elena in a loud voice. "I see that you have flown beyond the third cloud bank, that the gray-winged eagle has carried you there, and now it is time to come back to earth."

So Ivan returned to earth, got down from the eagle, and went up to the seashore. He struck the flint and steel, started a little fire and let it go out on the deep blue sea. Suddenly out of nowhere an enormous pike fish came swimming up to the shore. "Well, young man," said the pike, "climb into my mouth and I will hide you on the bottom of the sea." The fish stretched open its jaws, swallowed the young man, and together with him it descended into the abyss of the sea and covered itself all over with sand.

"Well," thought Ivan, "I just hope this turns out all right!"

But not quite! Elena the Wise just had to look into her mirror and she immediately knew everything. "That's enough, my clever one! I see that you have managed to get yourself inside that enormous pike fish and you are now sitting in the abyss of the sea, covered over with the shifting sands. It is time to come out onto dry land." The pike fish swam out onto the shore, cast the young man out of it, and once more went away into the sea. Ivan returned to Elena the Wise and her broad courtyard, sat on her porch, and fell into deep thought and sadness.

Just then Elena the Wise's servant girl came running up the steps. "Why are you so sad, young man?"

"How can I be happy? If I don't hide on this third try, I will have to part with the whole, wide world. So I am sitting here waiting for death."

"Don't grieve, don't think bad things for your unruly head! There was once a time when I promised to be of use to you. I did not speak empty words. Come on, I'll hide you." She took him by the hand and led him into the palace and put him behind the mirror.

A little later Elena the Wise came running in and looked in the mirror, but she could not see her groom! The time passed and she was angry. She struck the mirror out of vexation and smashed the glass into bits, and then the young man, Ivan, appeared to her. There was nothing else to do, she had to submit. But at the home of Elena the Wise there was no one to brew meads, no one to cure the wines. But there was a fine feast and a fine little wedding. They were married and began to live and dwell and even prosper.

23. The Frog Tsarevna

Recorded in Shadrinsk district by A. Zyrianov. The tale in this combination is known throughout the world, and it is especially popular in modern times among Russian children. SUS 402 + 400$_1$.

In a certain tsardom, in a certain land, there lived and dwelt a tsar with his tsaritsa. He had three sons and all were young, unmarried, such stout lads as you can't tell about in a tale or describe with a pen. The youngest was called Ivan Tsarevich. The tsar made this speech to them, "Dear children, each of you take an arrow, pull back your taut bow string, and let the arrows go in various directions. On whomever's court your arrow falls, you will go courting." The oldest brother let fly his arrow and it fell on a boyar's court, right opposite the maidens' quarters. The middle brother let go his and it flew to a merchant's court and stopped next to a beautiful porch, and on that porch stood a beautiful maiden, the merchant's daughter. Then the youngest brother let his arrow go and it fell into a filthy swamp where a croaker frog picked it up.

Ivan Tsarevich said, "How am I supposed to take this old croaker frog? A frog's no equal to me!"

"Take her!" said his father. "That is your fate."

So the tsareviches were all married: the eldest to the boyar's daughter, the middle one to the merchant's daughter, and Ivan Tsarevich to the croaking frog. The tsar summoned them and gave them this command: "Your wives are to bake me by tomorrow morning a fine white loaf of bread."

Ivan Tsarevich came back to his chambers very unhappy, his proud head was hanging lower than his shoulders. "Croak! Croak! Ivan Tsarevich! Why are you so unhappy?" the frog asked him. "Or have you perhaps heard something unpleasant from your father?"

"How should I not be unhappy? My lord and father has ordered you to bake him a fine, white loaf of bread by tomorrow."

"Don't grieve, tsarevich! Go lie down to sleep and rest. The morning is wiser than the evening." So she put the tsarevich to sleep and threw off her frog's skin and turned into a lovely maiden, Vasilisa the Most Wise. She went out onto the beautiful porch and shouted in a loud voice, "Mummies and nannies! Come here, get yourselves ready! Make a soft white bread like I used to eat, like I ate at my dear father's table!"

The next morning Ivan Tsarevich woke up and the frog's loaf was long since ready. And it was so fine that you can neither imagine such, nor envision such, just describe it in a tale! The bread was decorated with various intricacies. On the sides you could see the royal cities with their battlements. The tsar expressed his thanks to Ivan Tsarevich for the bread and at the same time issued a command to his three sons: "Let your wives each weave a carpet for me in one night." Ivan Tsarevich returned very unhappy, his proud head was hanging lower than his shoulders. "Why are you so unhappy? Or have you perhaps heard something unpleasant from your father?"

"How should I not be unhappy? My lord and father has ordered you to weave a silk carpet for him in one night."

"Don't grieve, tsarevich! Go to sleep and rest. The morning is wiser than the evening!" She put him to sleep, then threw off her frog's skin and turned into a lovely maiden, Vasilisa the Most Wise. She went out onto the beautiful porch and shouted in a loud voice, "Mummies and nannies! Come here, get yourselves ready to weave a silk carpet, just like the one I sat upon at my dear father's house."

No sooner said than done. In the morning Ivan Tsarevich woke up and the frog had the carpet long since ready. It was simply amazing, such as you can neither imagine or envision, but perhaps tell about in a tale. The carpet was decorated with gold and silver in intricate patterns. The tsar expressed his thanks to Ivan Tsarevich for the carpet, but at the same time he issued a new command to his three sons: "Let each of your wives appear before me with you for an inspection."

Again he returned very unhappy, his proud head was hanging lower than his shoulders. "Croak, croak! Ivan Tsarevich! Why are you so sad? Or has your father perhaps heard some unpleasant word?"

"How should I not be sad? My lord and father has ordered that you come before him for inspection. How can I show you off among people?"

"Don't grieve, tsarevich! You go to the tsar by yourself and I'll come along after you. As soon as you hear a bang and thunder, say, 'That's my little frog coming along in her little box.'"

So the older brothers appeared for the inspection with their wives, all decked out and beautifully done up. They stood alongside Ivan Tsarevich and laughed, "Well, brother, why did you come without your wife? You could have brought her in a kerchief. And where did you ever find such a beauty? Perhaps you brought her out of some swamp!"

Suddenly there was a great bang and thunder, and the entire palace shook. The guests were terrified and all jumped up from their places, not knowing what to do. But Ivan Tsarevich said, "Don't be afraid, ladies and gentlemen! It's just my little frog coming along in her little box." A golden carriage flew up to the royal porch with six horses hitched to it, and out stepped Vasilisa the Most Wise, and such a beauty as you can't imagine or envision, but perhaps you could tell of it in a tale. She took Ivan Tsarevich by the arm and led him to the oaken tables and pressed table linens.

All the guests began to eat and drink and enjoy themselves. Vasilisa the Most Wise finished her goblet and poured the remnants into her left sleeve. She tasted the swan and hid the bones in her right sleeve. The wives of the older brothers saw what she was doing and did the same thing. Afterward when Vasilisa the Most Wise went to dance with Ivan Tsarevich, she waved her left hand and made a beautiful lake. Then she waved with her right hand and there were white swans swimming on the water. The tsar and his guests were utterly amazed. When the older daughters-in-law went to dance, they waved with their left hands and splashed water everywhere; when they waved with their right hands, bones went flying right into the tsar's eye! The tsar got angry and dismissed them dishonorably.

At the same time, Ivan Tsarevich took the opportunity to run home, where he found the frog's skin. He burned it in a big fire. When Vasilisa the Most Wise came home, she reached for it, but there was no frog's skin and she was saddened, she wept, and she said to the tsarevich, "Oh, Ivan Tsarevich! What have you done? If you had only waited for a little while, I would have been yours forever, but now—farewell! Look for me beyond the thrice-nine land in the thrice-ten tsardom, with Koshchei the Deathless." She turned into a swan and flew away out the window.

Ivan Tsarevich wept bitterly, and he prayed to God in all four directions, and then he set off wherever his eyes might lead him. He walked near or far, for a long time or a short time, and then he happened to encounter a little old man. "Good health, my fine young man," the old man said. "What are you looking for, what is your destination?" The tsarevich told him of his misfortune. "Oh, Ivan Tsarevich, why did you burn up that frog's skin? You had never worn it and it was not for you to cast it away. Vasilisa the Most Wise was born more clever and wiser than her father. For that he was spiteful toward her and ordered that for three years she should be a frog. Here's a ball for you. Wherever it rolls, you step lively after it."

Ivan Tsarevich expressed this thanks to the old man and set out after the ball. He went through the open steppe, and he encountered a bear. "Let me kill this beast," he said.

But the bear implored him, "Don't kill me, Ivan Tsarevich. Sometime I'll be of use to you."

He went on further and saw a drake flying toward him. The tsarevich aimed with his rifle and was about to shoot the bird when suddenly it implored him in a human voice, "Don't kill me, Ivan Tsarevich. Sometime I'll be of use to you."

So Ivan Tsarevich spared it and went on further, and toward the deep blue sea he saw a pike fish lying there on the sands. "Oh, Ivan Tsarevich," the pike implored him. "Take pity on me and let me go back into the sea." He threw her into the sea and went on along the shore.

Whether in a short time or a long time, the little ball rolled up to a little hut. The little hut stood on cock's legs, and it could turn around and around. Ivan Tsarevich said, "Little hut, little hut! Stand as you were, as your mother commanded, with your front to me and your rear to the sea." The little hut turned its rear to the sea and the tsarevich entered her and saw lying on the stove, on the ninth brick, Baba Yaga of the bony leg, and her nose had grown into the ceiling, and her snot was spread over the threshold, and her teats were twisted over a hook, and she was sharpening her teeth. "Welcome, youth, why have you deigned to pay your respects to me?" Baba Yaga asked Ivan Tsarevich.

"Oh, you old slut! You should first have fed me and given me a drink, let me steam in the bath, and then you should interrogate me."

So Baba Yaga fed him, gave him a drink, steamed him in the bath, and then the tsarevich told her that he was seeking his wife, Vasilisa the Most Wise. "Oh, I know," she said. "Right now she is with Koshchei the Deathless. It will be difficult to obtain her. It's difficult to deal with Koshchei. His death is on the end of a needle, and the needle's in an egg, and the egg's in a duck, and the duck is in a hare, and the hare is in a trunk, and the trunk stands high in an oak tree, and Koshchei watches that oak as he does his own eyes."

The Yaga showed him the place where the oak tree grew and Ivan Tsarevich went there, but he didn't know what to do, how to obtain the trunk. Suddenly out of nowhere up ran the bear and pulled the oak up by its roots. The trunk fell and broke into smithereens. The hare ran out of the trunk and fled from the place as fast as its legs could carry it. But the second hare ran after him, caught up to him, grabbed him, and tore him into bits. The duck flew out of her, and the duck dropped the egg, which fell into the sea. Ivan Tsarevich saw his inevitable misfortune and broke into tears. Suddenly the pike swam up to the shore holding the egg in its teeth. He broke it and got the needle, and he then broke off the tip.

No matter how Koshchei struggled, no matter how he dashed to all sides, he was forced to die! Ivan Tsarevich went into Koshchei's house, took Vasilisa the Most Wise, and returned home. After that they lived together for a long time and happily.

24. The Petrified Tsarevna

Collected in 1948 by a teacher, Maia Pervushina, from E. Nogina, fifty-four, of the village of Lesnoi. This is the well-known "Sleeping Beauty" in a Russian form. SUS 410 + 405.

In a certain tsardom, in a certain country, there lived and dwelt Tsar Gromoboi, the thunderfighter. He had a son, Viacheslav Gromoboevich, who was very handsome. And in this city, there was a merchant's daughter, Svetlana, who was very beautiful. And he once glimpsed this Svetlana and then every evening he would ride out on his fine horse past her window so that she could get a glimpse of him. But Svetlana didn't like anybody. And so one beautiful day our Viacheslav set out on his good horse for a ride to the seashore. And he looked and saw an old woman standing there and she asked Viacheslav, "Why are you, Viacheslav, the tsar's son, so sad? What sadness and boredom eats at you? With what are you dissatisfied or who has attacked you?"

"No, granny, no one has attacked me, but hurt me, yes, you guessed it. You see, granny, in this city we have one maiden who is very beautiful and she once even let me get a glimpse of her, but she won't even look at me."

"Now then, my good man, I shall help you in this misfortune. Come with me to my hut and there I'll fix everything up for you myself."

So Viacheslav tethered his horse and went into the hut with the old woman. "Sit down, Viacheslav. Here's what I'm going to tell you to do at home: go home and when you get up in the morning, massage your face with whatever medicine I give you, and you will be very handsome and then this Svetlana will love you."

Viacheslav thanked the old woman, went out, got on his horse, and rode off to his home in the city, and he thought: "So now Svetlana will love me." He arrived home, locked himself in his bedroom, but all night he could not fall asleep. It was scarcely light and Viacheslav took the old woman's medicine and started massaging his face. He looked in the mirror—he had become truly beautiful. He went out to the stables, took his horse and went for a ride in the early morning about the city, alongside Svetlana's window. At that time she was sewing at the window and she saw the royal son riding on horseback, his whole face in lard! And she started laughing at him so much that Viacheslav grew angry and rode straight to the old woman's house without stopping in at home. "Why was Svetlana laughing at him?" Viacheslav wondered.

He rode up to the hut, dismounted, and knocked on the door, but the old woman already knew that Viacheslav had come. She answered: "Welcome, royal son!"

Viacheslav went into the hut, threw a purse full of money onto the table, and shouted: "You old crone, what have you done? Svetlana doesn't love me, even today she laughed at me. What am I to do now?"

"Now then, good young man, sit down on the bench and don't scold me, I'm old and perhaps I'll help you in your misfortune. Now take this little ball and wherever it rolls, you go after it. It will lead you to my brother." Viacheslav thanked the old woman, paid her the money, and rode home.

He arrived home and told his mother: "Dear mama, make me some dried biscuits, I am going to go throughout the whole world, I'm going to go and look at people, show myself, and take a look at a bride."

So Viacheslav arose early in the morning, saddled his horse, and rode off down the road on his journey. He let the ball roll. Wherever it rolled, that's where Viacheslav rode. He rode up to a certain coaching inn and knocked at the gates. The master came out and asked what sort of guest he was and from where he had come to grace his table. The guest was shown into the hut and the horse given some spring wheat. The guest was seated at an oaken table and they began to treat him to expensive wines and snacks. Then they put him to bed in a separate little room on a soft eiderdown. And Viacheslav heard some music on the other side of the wall, and the words, "Viacheslav, save me! . . .Viacheslav, save me!"

In the morning Viacheslav arose and asked his host. "What was that music on the other side of the wall here?"

"Now then, Viacheslav Gromoboevich, if you want to know, then I'll tell you. One hundred years ago there was a city here and in it there lived a tsar with his tsaritsa and they had one daughter, very beautiful she was, a hundred times more beautiful than her mother. And then one beautiful day the father rode off to war with his armies and left his wife with this favorite daughter. Now the mother disliked her daughter because everybody said, 'Your daughter is very beautiful.' Once the tsaritsa sent her suite of servants for a walk in the woods. At that same time that same old woman from the seashore called in on the tsaritsa. And the old woman said, 'Why are you sad, little mother tsaritsa?' 'How should I not be sad? I have a daughter. All say that she is more beautiful than I. Help me in my woe. How can I get rid of her?' And the old woman answered: 'I will be able to help you but only if you do as I order. Come to me this evening. I will give you some of a substance, then you will be rid of your daughter.' The old woman took her leave of the tsaritsa and went to her home on the seashore. When the tsaritsa had returned home, she had decided to do this unkind thing with her daughter. When everything was quiet and without saying anything to anybody, the tsaritsa set off for the old woman-sorceress's. When the tsaritsa arrived at the sorceress's, the old woman had already prepared a magic potion. She gave a little pot of it to her and said to the tsaritsa: 'When you reach home, ask your daughter to let you search in her hair [for lice]. When she sits down, then pour this magic potion on her, unnoticed. She will then be petrified for one hundred years.' The tsaritsa thanked the sorceress and went back to her palace. As soon as the tsaritsa arrived back at the palace, she called her daughter into her chamber. 'Dear Daughter, let me search in your hair, let me finger your russet locks.' Now the young tsarevna sensed no misfortune. She humbly came and sat on a chair. At that moment her evil mother the tsaritsa poured the magic potion on her, unnoticed. Then the tsaritsa saw that her daughter had been turned into stone for one hundred years. In a short time the war ended, and the tsar and father returned home and asked where his favorite daughter, Natasha, was. The tsaritsa answered: 'Natasha died five years ago!' But Natasha had a favorite nanny and she disclosed the entire secret to the tsar, that his favorite daughter Natasha had been turned into stone and was sitting in her room. When the tsar went into the room, he wanted to destroy the magic bonds, but his sword flew apart on them. Then the tsar went into the bedroom, cut off the tsaritsa's head and decided on suicide. Since then the beautiful Natasha has been sitting within these walls, awaiting her rescuer."

Viacheslav spent another night, got up in the morning, harnessed his good horse, and placed the little ball on the road. The little ball started rolling and Viacheslav went after it. It rolled and rolled and rolled up to an underground entrance. Our Viacheslav began to descend along a marble staircase, he came up to some doors and knocked. And a sorcerer answered. "Welcome, Viacheslav Gromboevich! I've long been expecting you." He sat him at a table and treated him to various wines and foods. In one goblet was a strong wine, in the other a weak one. And the old man offered Viacheslav the weak wine in the silver goblet, but took the strong wine in the gold goblet for himself.

At that moment Viacheslav guessed it—something was going wrong for him. "Old man, at home I drink from a golden goblet and as your guest I ought to drink at your house from the golden goblet." The old man and sorcerer could not dissuade him but was forced to concede him the gold goblet. Then Viacheslav felt in himself a great strength. And he asked the sorcerer for a magic sword in order to break the magic bonds and free Natasha.

The old man gave him the sword, wished him a happy journey, told him to stop by again, and said, "I will aid you in your every misfortune."

As soon as Viacheslav had arrived at the coaching inn, he struck with his sword the wall in which Natasha was sitting. The wall crumbled and Natasha rushed to him, threw herself on his neck, kissed him and said, "You are my savior! Were it not for you, I would still be sitting in that dungeon."

And she was just as she had been when she was enchanted. Such a beauty she was! When the host learned that the affair had been concluded, he immediately organized a party. They spent the night and then Viacheslav came to an agreement with the host and hostess and carried them off to the city together with his young and most beautiful bride. They came home and were married in the church. Then they had the celebration. The whole city was there, and I was there, too. I drank mead and beer, the beer was warm, it flowed over my moustaches, but never got into my mouth.

25. Fenist the Bright Falcon Feather

From Riazan. Recorded from the eighteenth century until after World War II, from the Russian north and from the south, from the Urals and Western Siberia. Known sporadically throughout Europe. The A–T index gives the wrong number for the Afanas'ev analogue: it should be 234/235. SUS 432.

There lived and dwelt a merchant and this merchant had three daughters. The merchant was getting ready for the fair and he asked his daughters, "What should I buy you?"

The eldest said, "Buy me some material for a dress."

The second said, "Buy me a scarf."

The third one said, "Buy me Fenist the Bright Falcon Feather." The merchant traveled for a long time or a short time, and then he was returning home. He brought those two daughters their gifts, but he forgot about the third one. She started to cry. "Don't cry," he said, "I'll soon be going to the fair again and I'll bring it to you. I'll console you!"

Soon he was getting ready to go to the fair once more and he asked his daughters, "What should I buy you?"

The first said, "bracelets," the second said "earrings," and the third said, "Fenist the Bright Falcon Feather." He traveled for a long time or a short time, he returned and he brought those two daughters their gifts, but he again forgot about the youngest. She started crying and again he consoled her, "I'll bring it to you," he said. "Soon I'll be going again."

He got ready to go to the fair once more and he asked his daughters, "What shall I buy you?" The first said, "satin slippers," the second, "a ring," and the third "Fenist the Bright Falcon Feather." He traveled for a long time or a short time, then he returned home and he brought gifts for all three daughters.

So then the youngest began to sit all the time with that feather in her bedroom. Her sisters talked between themselves: "What can this mean? What is she talking about in there? Let's listen in," they said. That feather was magic: it was a tsar's son. "Let's have a party," the sisters said, "we'll invite her and ply her with drinks, with wine." So they invited her and got her drunk. She went into her bedroom and fell into a deep sleep. Her sisters went into her bedroom up to the window where Fenist the Bright Falcon Feather flew in and stuck knives in it.

He came flying to her, cut himself on the knives, and saw that she was asleep. He wrote in his own blood, "If you love me, seek me beyond the thrice-nine land in the thrice-ten tsardom."

She woke up, saw the note, and began crying bitterly and then she started asking her father to let her go search for Fenist the Bright Falcon Feather. For a long time he would not let her go, but she pleaded with him. He let her go. She went to the smithy, ordered three pairs of iron boots, three iron rods, and three iron loaves. The smith made her the three pairs of iron boots, three iron rods, and three iron loaves, and she set off.

She walked and she walked and she walked. She wore out the boots, she broke a rod, she ate up a loaf. She came to a hut and the hut stood on cock's legs and could turn around. "Hut, little hut! Stand with your rear to the forest and your front to me!" The hut turned.

So she went into the hut and there was Baba Yaga thrashing about from corner to corner: with one lip she was wiping the floor and with her nose she was blocking up the chimney. (Her nose was about the size of the Perevitskii Bridge!) "Phoo, phoo, phoo," she said, "it used to be that you couldn't hear the sound of a Russian or catch a glimpse of one, but now a Russian spirit is sitting right down on my spoon and taking a ride right into my mouth. Well, beautiful maiden, are you trying to do something or are you getting out of something?"

"Oh, granny, it's not that I'm trying to get out of something; it's that I'm trying to do something."

"Why have you come here?" she asked.

"Here's why, granny. I had this Feather of Fenist the Bright Falcon, but it flew away."

"Oh, that's a relative of mine. Here, take this little silver dish and this golden apple; it goes by itself. Go now until you come to my cousin's hut. She'll show you the way. I'm nasty, but she is much nastier than I am. Farewell! Don't tarry."

She set off and she walked and walked and walked. She wore out the boots, she broke a rod, and ate up a loaf. She approached and saw a hut standing there on cock's legs and it could turn about. "Hut, little hut! Stand with your rear to the forest and your front to me!"

The hut turned. She went in. There Baba Yaga was flinging herself from corner to corner, with one breast she was wiping down the stove and with the other stopping up the chimney. She hissed through her teeth, "Phoo, phoo, phoo. It used to be that you couldn't hear the sound of a Russian or catch a glimpse of one, but now a Russian spirit is sitting right down on my spoon and taking a ride right into my mouth." The girl was terribly frightened and bowed very low. "Well, beautiful maiden, are you trying to do something or are you getting out of something?"

"Oh, granny, it's not that I'm trying to get out of something; it's that I'm trying to do something."

"Don't tell me about it, I already know." She gave her a golden comb, a silver tow, and a golden spindle that spun by itself. "You'll get there with these, farewell! My cousin is there; I'm nasty but she's much nastier than I."

She set off and she walked and walked and walked. She wore out the boots, she broke a rod, and ate up a loaf. She approached and saw a hut standing there on cock's legs and it could turn about. "Hut, little hut! Stand with your rear to the forest and your front to me!"

The hut turned and she went in. Baba Yaga was in the hut, her leg of bone, her iron nose grown into the ceiling, she was lying there, puffing and panting away. "Phoo, phoo, phoo. It used to be that you couldn't hear the sound of a Russian or catch a glimpse of one, but now a Russian spirit is sitting right down on my spoon and tumbling right into my mouth. Well, beautiful maiden, are you trying to do something or are you getting out of something?"

"Oh, granny, it's not that I'm trying to get out of something; it's that I'm trying to do something. I had this Feather of Fenist the Bright Falcon, but it flew away from me."

"It's too bad you thought of him. He's my nephew." She gave her some golden lace frames and a silver needle that sews by itself. "With these you'll reach him. Go now! That tsardom isn't very far off now. There are some bushes. You lie down next to the bushes and he will go off hunting with his hunters. The dogs will run up to you and you'll be in his kingdom." So she thanked her and set off.

She walked and walked and walked, she wore out her boots, she broke the last rod and ate the last loaf. Then she saw some bushes in sight. "Those are probably the ones." She went up to the bushes, lay down next to them, and heard the terrible barking of the dogs. The hunters thought it was probably some beast and galloped. They galloped up and saw the beautiful maiden and reported it to the tsar, Fenist the Bright Falcon Feather. "Where do you order that she be sent?" The tsar said, "To the backyard, to the old woman." And so they sent her off there.

At the old woman's she asked about everything. Fenist the Bright Falcon Feather had married. She went up to a pond and saw that a dark-haired girl was washing the shirt in which Fenist the Bright Falcon Feather had been cut, but no way could she wash the blood out. She noted that it was the same shirt and said, "Here, miss, I'll wash it for you." She took the shirt and started to weep over it. She wept and wept until she had washed away all but one little drop. The dark-haired maiden took the shirt and went to the tsaritsa to praise her. And the tsaritsa praised her.

And then she asked to search for Fenist the Bright Falcon Feather, and received the tsaritsa's permission to sit opposite the court with her treasures and she brought out a little table and set it up opposite the court and then she brought out the dish and the golden apple, which rolled along by itself. The tsaritsa sent the dark-haired maid out to ask, "Are those for sale or will you bargain, and if so, what is the condition?"

"They are for bargaining and the bargain is to sleep one night with Fenist the Bright Falcon Feather." She agreed. The tsar came riding in, the tsaritsa plied him with drink until he was drunk and then put him in the study. She let the maid in to him and she wept over him, she wept and pinched him and told him all. But because he was drunk he heard nothing. The hours passed and she sent the maiden out.

On the next day the tsar got up and rode off to hunt. Once again she took the golden comb, the silver tow, and the golden spindle that spins of itself. She set them up opposite the court. The tsaritsa fell for it and once again sent the dark-haired maid out to ask, "Are those for sale or will you bargain, and if so, what is the condition?"

"They are for bargaining and the bargain is to sleep one night with Fenist the Bright Falcon Feather." The tsaritsa agreed. The tsar came home from the hunt, and once again the tsaritsa gave him refreshment.

The tsar was surprised, "There is some reason for my body's aching." He didn't drink so much as let it flow through him. The hour arrived and the tsar went to the study, but he didn't want to sleep and yet fell asleep. They let the girl in to him. Once more she wept, pinched him, but he didn't hear, he slept the sleep of the dead. In the morning they sent her away.

On the third day the tsar once more set off to hunt. And she carried out the golden lace frames and the silver needle that sews by itself and set them up opposite the palace. The tsaritsa fell for it and again sent out the black-haired maiden: "Go and ask whether those are for sale or for bargaining."

She said, "They're for bargaining and the condition is to sleep the night with Fenist the Bright Falcon Feather." The tsaritsa agreed.

The tsar came back and the tsaritsa began to give him refreshment, and he pretended that he was asleep. He started waiting to see what would happen. "What is this, my body aches and the tsaritsa is always plying me with drinks?" They let the girl in to him. They were overjoyed to see each other. He heard everything from her and cried just as she did. Before morning he again pretended to be asleep. At that time they sent her out again.

So in the morning the tsar got up and rode off to hunt, but at the same time he ordered that all the tsars and bogatyrs be summoned to a ball. All came riding in for the ball, but the tsaritsa knew nothing about the purpose of the ball. They all rode up and sat down at the table. And then the tsar says, "Listen, my dear guests! Which is the truer wife for me? The one who would sell me for treasure or the one who walked looking for me, wore out three pairs of boots, broke three rods, and gnawed at three iron loaves?" And then he ordered the precious things put in the hall. And all in one voice shouted that it was the wife who had worked until she had sweated blood. So then he ordered the other tied to the tail of a gray stallion and ordered it to roam throughout the steppe. And with the other he put on a wedding. And then he went to her father's land, to her father, and the tsar rejoiced that she was alive and had married such a one.

26. How the Tsar's Daughter Came to Know Need

From Vereiskii district of Moscow region, 1897. This is a common tale type among the Ukrainians, but it is recorded only three times among the Russians. Uncommon in Western Europe. SUS 437.

The workers were working. The tsar's daughter heard that there was need in the world and she wanted to find out what need was. So she took along her servants—a coachman, a maid, and her nanny—she gathered them together and set off looking for need. She traveled with them a long time, but they found no need. The maid said, "I can't go any further." With that word the tsar's daughter sent her away, but they still didn't see any need.

She rode on for a long time, but they found no need, no need anywhere. Then the nanny also refused to go any further, saying, "I can't go on."

She was left alone with her coachman but they didn't see any need; they didn't find it. The coachman begged her to "let me go; I can't go any further." And so she went on alone.

She walked and walked, but she found no need. From far off she saw a beautiful estate, really fine, and she said, "I'll go there. I've been in all these tsardoms, but what is that beautiful village over there?" So that's where she went. She came up to it and there was a large, splendid garden with such flowers as you could never see anywhere else. In the garden there was a royal palace, and it was wondrously built, very ornate. All around the building was a wrought-iron fence and then there were the gates. At the gates were fierce lions, terrifying lions. But she still didn't find any need.

Opposite the gates was the parade ground. And at the parade ground stood more lions. But she still didn't find any need. She went up to the parade ground and the lions bowed to her. Again, she didn't see any need. She went up to the entrance, and the entrance opened. It wasn't clear who opened it. She went up and into the palace and she wanted to drink a little tea. It wasn't clear who set the table, but the tea was ready. And yet she didn't find any need. She sipped her tea, as one is supposed to. She walked about the palace and then she came to one big hall. There hung a coffin on twelve chains, and next to the coffin was a portrait on the wall of a handsome young man (it was an enchanted tsarevich).

On the table lay a book in which it was written: "Whoever reads this book will receive him as groom." She picked up the book and read. And then every morning breakfast and tea were set out on the table for her, but she didn't know who did it. And she still didn't see any need. And she read on for a long time.

Then one day she was bored, so she went to the sea for a walk. Some sailors had kidnapped a little girl. She took pity and so she helped rescue the little girl. She shouted to some other people to help her. So then she took the little girl in because she wanted to, and she also had lots of money, and everything was ready for her, too. She raised the little girl and taught her to read and write. Then she helped her read that book. But she still didn't see any need.

They read for a long time. Only a little was left to read in the book. The tsar's daughter was feeling like dropping off to sleep. She said to the girl from the sea, "You read to such and such a place, but don't read any further." The little girl from the sea didn't obey her—she was, of course, just curious. She couldn't understand what these pages were that she was not to read. "I'll just go on and read them," she thought. So she read the rest of them and the coffin fell down. It fell down and shattered, and out came a tsar's son—he got out of the coffin. She obviously had "read him out of the coffin."

He stood up and asked, "Who are you?"

And she answered him, "I am a tsar's daughter."

He said, "Do you live here alone?"

"No, I have this girl from the sea here, too." (She'll soon know need!)

He soon tried to persuade her to get married, but the girl from the sea, the princess, would let nothing pass, so she sat in her room and said, "Now I've come to know need! I've always heard the peasants talking about need." He paced by the room and asked his bride, "Why does that girl from the sea keep talking about need?"

"You see, peasants carried her away and I rescued her when I was out for a walk. So now she always talks about need."

So the tsar's son had all his wedding preparations made and he was ready to get married. But then he remembered that girl: "I'll have to give her some clothes," he thought.

So he arranged it, but his wife said, "Why bother clothing her? She is a simple girl of the sea. I even taught her to read and write."

But with what God sent they gave her clothes and shoes, and then the wedding was ready. He invited all their friends and all the royal family. They were performing the wedding ceremonies, but the maiden was still sitting with need.

Then at a certain time the enchanted tsar's son thought of putting on a ball. He invited all the tsars, and for the tsaritsa he had the most splendid dress prepared—and one for the girl from the sea, too. Then he could see that the tsaritsa was no royal daughter and the girl from the sea was really a tsar's daughter. So he called them together and treated them exactly the same. His wife spoke very coarsely: "Why have you dressed out that girl from the sea?"

He replied, "I wanted to because I wanted there to be a maiden at the ball who had not been offended by me."

The dances began. The real tsar's daughter danced beautifully; the other was like a drooping bag. In his ardent excitement he went up to some of his friends and asked them, took counsel with them. "Which of them is the royal daughter?" (He will soon sort it out and shoot the one for her false lies.)

Then his friends pointed to the royal daughter and said, "That one is the royal daughter." Then they said, "That one is not a tsar's daughter."

So he asked them, "What am I to do with her for her lies?"

They all advised him to shoot her. So he took her to a large chair and fed her. "Sit down in the chair," he said. Then he took out a revolver and shot her, and that was that. No more sea girl. He apologized to the tsar's daughter, took her by the hand, and pronounced her his bride. And coins were distributed to the pleasure of all.

They were married, and all the people were amazed. I was there and drank mead. It flowed over my moustaches, but none got into my mouth and all my work's in vain.

27. Go Where You Know Not Where, Bring Back You Know Not What

This is a typical combination of the two tale types in East Slavic, Baltic, and Turkic. Provenance unknown. The first type is well known as the "Swan Maidens." SUS 465A + 465C.

This retired soldier Tarabanov set out to see the world. He walked for a week, then a second, and then a third. He walked for a whole year and got beyond the thrice-nine lands into the thrice-ten country. He was in such a dense forest that other than the sky and the trees he could see nothing. After a long or a short time, he made his way out into an open clearing, and in the clearing a huge palace had been built. He looked at the palace and was amazed. At such wealth one could only be astonished, not imagine or guess. It's only to be found in a folktale! He walked all around the palace but there were no gates, no entrance, no way in at all. How could that be? He looked and saw a long pole lying there. He raised it up and leaned it up to the balcony. He took on some daring and climbed up the pole. Then he climbed onto the balcony and opened some glass doors. He went through all the rooms but everywhere it was empty. He didn't encounter a soul.

He went into a large hall where there stood a round table, and on the table were twelve different dishes with various kinds of food and twelve decanters with sweet wines. He felt like sating his hunger so from each dish he took a little bite and from each decanter just a single shot. He drank and he ate, and then he climbed up onto the stove, put his knapsack under his head, and went to sleep. He really hadn't had time to start dreaming properly when twelve swans suddenly flew in the window, threw themselves upon the ground, and turned into beautiful maidens, each one more beautiful than the others. They placed their wings upon the stove, sat down at the table, and began eating—each from her own plate and each drinking from her own decanter. "Listen, sisters," one of them said, "Something's not quite right here. It appears a little of our wine's been drunk and some of the food already sampled."

"That's enough talk, sister! You always know more than the rest of us."

The soldier noted where they had put down their wings. He stealthily got up and took a pair of wings from that very maiden who was the most perspicacious. Then he hid them.

The beautiful maidens finished eating, got up from the table, and ran to the stove to collect their wings. They all selected their wings but those of the one maiden were missing. "Oh, sisters! My wings aren't here!"

"What of it? It's because you are too clever." So the eleven sisters threw themselves on the floor, turned into white swans, and flew out the windows. The twelfth remained there as she was, and she began weeping bitterly.

The soldier climbed down from the stove. The beautiful maiden saw him and begged him piteously to return her wings to her. The soldier said to her, "No matter how much you beg, no matter how much you cry, I'm not going to give you back your wings. It would be better for you to agree to be my wife and live together with me." So they came to an understanding, embraced, and kissed fervently.

The beautiful maiden led him, her intended husband, into some deep cellars. There she opened a big chest that was belted with iron, and she said, "Take some gold, as much as you can carry, so that we'll have something to live on. Not having enough will mean not having a proper household." So the soldier filled his pockets full of gold, threw the old, worn-out shirts out of his knapsack, and stuffed it full of gold, too. Then they got ready and set off together along the long highways and byways.

After a long time or a short time, they came to a fine capital city, where they rented rooms and settled into married life. One day his wife spoke to the soldier, "Here are a hundred rubles. Go into the shops and, wherever they have it, buy a hundred rubles worth of silk for me.

The soldier set off for the shops, but along the way there was this tavern. He thought, "Oughtn't I be able to have just one *grivennik* of drink out of a hundred rubles? I'll go in!" So he went into the tavern, drank a pint of vodka, paid his *grivennik*, and set about getting the silk. He bought a large roll of silk, brought it home, and gave it to his wife.

"How much did you pay for this?" she asked.

"A hundred rubles," he responded.

"That's not true. You bought this for a hundred rubles less one *grivennik*. Where did you spend that *grivennik*? You most likely drank it up in a tavern."

"Oh, what a clever one," the soldier thought to himself. "She knows the ins and outs of everything." From the silk the soldier's wife made three wonderful carpets for three thousand and then she sent her husband out to sell them.

A rich merchant gave three thousand for each of them. He waited for a big feast day and took them to the king himself as a gift. The king looked at them and gasped with astonishment. "What talented hands have made these!"

"These were made by a simple soldier's wife," the merchant said.

"That cannot be. Where does she live? I will go to see her myself."

The next day he got ready and set off to order some new work from her. When he got there, he saw the beautiful lady and fell head over heels in love with her. He returned to the palace and there he thought an evil thought about getting rid of her living husband. He summoned his favorite general. "Think up a way to get rid of that soldier and I'll reward you with ranks and villages, and a gold treasure."

"Your highness! You should give him a difficult task: let him go to the end of the world and fetch back the Servant Saura. That Servant Saura can live in your pocket, and whatever you order it to do, it will quickly do it."

The king sent for the soldier, and they soon brought him to the palace, where he started right in attacking him. "Oh, you utter fool! You go around bars and taverns all the while boasting that fetching the Servant Saura would be a trifling thing. Why didn't you come to me before? Why didn't you tell me about this earlier? My doors are never closed to anybody."

"Your highness! I never dreamed of boasting of any such thing!"

"Now, brother Tarabanov. You can't get out of it. Go to the end of the earth and fetch me the Servant Saura. If you don't bring him back, then it will be capital punishment for you."

The soldier ran off to his wife and told her of his woe. She took out a ring. "Here's this ring," she said, "Wherever it rolls, you follow along after it. Don't be afraid of anything!" She left him to collect his thoughts and then she sent him off down the road.

The ring rolled and rolled along, and it rolled up to a little hut, hopped up onto a porch, through the door, and under the stove. The soldier went into the hut, climbed beneath the stove, and sat there waiting. Suddenly in came an old man, the size of a fingernail, with a beard a yard long, and he shouted, "Heh, Saura! Feed me!" He had no sooner given the order than at that very minute a roast steer appeared, with a well-honed knife in its side, garlic stuffed up his rear, and a forty-bucket barrel of an excellent beer. The old man the size of a fingernail, with a beard a yard long, sat down next to the steer, pulled out the well-honed knife, and started slicing the meat, nibbling at the garlic, and eating and praising the dish. He worked the steer over down to the last bones, drank the entire barrel of beer, and stated, "Thanks, Saura! Your food is fine. I'll come to visit you again in three years." He said his farewells, and went away.

The soldier climbed out from under the stove, gave himself a dash of daring, and shouted, "Heh, Saura! Are you here?"

"I'm here, soldier."

"Feed me too, brother." Saura gave him a roast steer and a forty-bucket barrel of beer. The soldier was frightened. "Why did you give me so much, Saura? I couldn't eat or drink this in a whole year." He ate a couple of bites and drank about a bottle, thanked Saura for his dinner, and asked, "Would you like to serve me, Saura?"

"If you'll take me, I'll go with pleasure. My old man is such a glutton that you wear yourself out trying to satisfy him."

"Let's go then! Climb into my pocket."

"I've long since been there, master."

Tarabanov left the hut, and the ring rolled along, showing him the way, and after a long time or a short time, it brought him home. He went straight to the ruler, shouted out, "Saura," and left him there to serve at the king's court.

Once more the king summoned the general. "You told me that the soldier Tarabanov would perish and fail to obtain that Saura. Well, he's returned hale and hearty, and he's brought Saura."

"Your highness! Let me search out a more difficult task for him. Order him to go to the other world and find out how your deceased father is getting along there."

The king didn't have to think long about this. He immediately ordered a courier to bring in the soldier Tarabanov. The courier galloped to him and said, "Heh, soldier, get dressed. The king requires you."

The soldier shined the buttons on his greatcoat, got dressed, got on the courier's horse, and rode to the palace. He appeared before the king. The king said to him, "Listen, you utter fool! So you've been going about the taverns and the bars boasting, and, without reporting it to me, that you can go to the other world and find out how my deceased father is getting along there!"

"Forgive me, your highness! It would never enter into my head to make such a boast—to go to the other world. Outside of death, I swear to God I don't know any other way to get there."

"Do as you wish, but go immediately and find out about my father. Otherwise, it's my sword, and your head from your shoulders!"

Tarabanov returned home, hung his reckless head lower than his mighty shoulders and was extremely sad. His wife asked him, "Why are you so despondent, my dearest friend? Tell me the whole story."

So he told her everything just as it had happened. "Never mind, don't be sad! Lie down and sleep. The morning is wiser than the evening."

In the morning of the next day as soon as the soldier had awakened, his wife sent him off. "Go to the ruler and ask him to let you take as your companion that same general who puts the king up to these things."

Tarabanov got dressed and went to the king. He asked him, "Your royal highness! Give me that general as a companion. Let him be a witness to my actually being in the other world finding out about your parent without any deceit."

"That's a good idea, brother. Go on home and get ready, and I'll send him to you." Tarabanov returned home and prepared for the trip. Then the king summoned the general to appear before him. "You go with that soldier," he said, "otherwise I can't believe just him by himself." The general shuddered, but there was nothing he could do. He could not disobey the king's command. Unwillingly he set off for the soldier's residence.

Tarabanov put some hard tack in his knapsack, poured some water in his flask, said goodbye to his wife, took her ring, and said to the general, "So with God's will we're off!" They went outside and next to the porch was a coach and four, all harnessed. "Who's that for?" asked the soldier.

"What do you mean 'who's it for?' It's for us to ride in."

"No, your excellency. We require no coach. We'll walk to the other world." So then the ring began rolling with the soldier following, and the general dragging along after him. It was a long journey, and if the soldier wanted something to eat, he would soak some hard tack in water and eat it. But his companion could only watch and gnash his teeth. If the soldier would give him some hard tack, that would be fine. If not, he would just have to go on.

Sooner or later, further or nearer—the deed is not so quickly done as the tale is told—they came to a dense and dreamy forest and descended into a deep, deep ravine. There the ring stopped. The soldier and the general sat down on the ground and started eating hard tack. They hadn't managed to finish when they looked up and saw two devils riding on the old king and pulling a load of wood. And it was a big cart, too. They drove the king with clubs, one from the right side and the other from the left. "Look, your excellency! Could that be the old king?"

"You're right," said the general. "That's him all right."

"Heh, you unclean ones!" shouted the soldier. "Free that dead man to me for a while. I need to ask him about a thing or two."

"We have time to wait. While you're talking with him, we won't have to haul wood."

"Why should you work? Here, take this fresh man of mine in his place!"

The devils quickly unhitched the old king and put the general in his place in the cart, and then they began whipping him from both sides. He struggled but he pulled.

The soldier asked the old king about his life and circumstances in the other world. "Oh, soldier, I've a very poor life indeed. Give my greeting to my son and ask him to have a memorial service said for me. Then perhaps the Lord will forgive me and free me from these eternal torments. And say this firmly to him in my name that he never abuse the common folk or his troops. God will give no reward for that!"

"But he likely won't believe what I tell him. Can you give me some sort of sign for him?"

"Here's a key. As soon as he sees it, he will believe you." They had only just managed to conclude their conversation when the devils came riding back. The soldier said farewell to the old king, took the general from the devils, and they set off on their journey back home.

They came back to their own kingdom and appeared at the palace. "Your highness!" the soldier said to the king, "I saw your dead parent, and he lives very poorly in that world. He sends his regards to you and asks you to have a memorial service said for him so that God will forgive him and free him from the eternal torments. And he ordered me to insist on this: let my son not abuse the common folk or the troops. For the Lord will punish you dearly if you do."

"But is it true that you went to the other world and saw my father?"

The general said, "On my back the signs are still visible. The devils beat me there with their clubs as they drove me along."

Then the soldier brought out the key and the king glanced at it. "Why, that's the very key from the secret chest. When they buried my father, they forgot to take it out of his pocket." So the king was convinced that the soldier was speaking the whole truth, and then he made him a general and stopped thinking about his beautiful wife.

28. The Mare's Head

Recorded in Kuibyshev region, Kaluga oblast in 1977, from E.P. Mitrosheikova. The A–T–U 480/SUS 480 and related types are among the most popular in the Russian tradition. SUS 480.

There lived this peasant and woman and they had a daughter. The wife died and he took a stepmother and her daughter. She hated the girl.

"Take your daughter away," she said, "into the forest."

"Oh, how could I! She'll get frightened there and she'll start crying."

"Take her!"

But there was a little guard hut there. He drove her to the hut, made her a knocker to go "tap-tap" for her. "I'll be cutting firewood, and you listen," he said to her. If the knocker went "tap-tap," she'd say: "My father's cutting firewood."

She sat there, dreaming, and it was cold in the hut, but then the knocker went "tap-tap," the maple went "rap-rap." Then she figured it out that the doorknocker was hanging there. She goes out and says, "Doorknocker tap-tap, maple knocker rap-rap, whoever's in the woods, whoever's in the dark, come in and spend the night with me."

A bear came: "I'm in the woods, I'm in the dark. Let me in to spend the night with you."

"No, you're not my father, I won't open up for you," she said. The bear went away. Then she spoke again: "Door knocker tap-tap, maple knocker rap-rap, whoever's in the woods, whoever's in the dark, come in and spend the night with me."

A wolf came: "I'm in the woods, I'm in the dark. Let me in to spend the night with you."

"No, you're not my father."

So she didn't open up for the wolf either. And a hare was walking by, she came up, and a fox at the same time, and they asked to come in and spend the night. She decided to open up to no one. Once more she went out: "Door knocker tap-tap, maple knocker rap-rap, whoever's in the woods, whoever's in the dark, come in and spend the night with me."

Up rolled a mare's head: "I'm in the woods, I'm in the dark. Let me in to spend the night with you."

"And who are you?"

"Why, I'm a head, open up for me."

She opened the door. "Close it."

She closed it, it came in. "Crawl in my right ear and out my left ear."

The little girl crawled in. And when she had crawled out again, she was beautiful, nicely dressed, a perfect young lady.

Morning came and the stepmother sent the old man into the woods.

"Go after your slut!" She thought the girl would already have died in the hut. The grandfather readied the sleigh, harnessed the horse, and set off. Her father came and there sat the girl—pretty, beautiful, dressed in fine clothes, and all sorts of good things before her! The stepmother was already preparing the funeral. The dog barked: "Woof, woof! The stepmother's sits there like a scullery maid, the old man's is coming like a young lady."

"Phooey, the stepmother's sits like a young lady, the old man's coming like a scullery maid."

The old man drove up into the yard. She came out [of the hut] and looked around—she was a perfect young lady, and there were many fine things. "Take my daughter into the woods!"

He got ready and drove her off. He did the same for her: he attached a door-knocker and told her to listen. The knocker would rap: "That old so and so is coming for me, he's cutting wood; and he's not my real father."

She got bored. "Doorknocker tap-tap, maple knocker rap-rap. Come spend the night with me, whoever's in the woods."

The bear came. "I'm in the woods, I'm in the dark, let me in to spend the night."

She got frightened, she locked herself in, she didn't let him in. She sat there. She didn't go out again. The head comes rolling up.

"Beautiful maiden, open the door."

"I won't open the door."

"Open the door. I'm out here, I'm a head, open up!" She opened the door and in rolled the head. "Beautiful maiden, give me a drink, feed me."

"You're no fine lady."

"Beautiful maiden, make up the bed for me!"

"You're no fine lady."

"Climb in my left ear, crawl out the right (the wrong way around, it was).

So she crawled in: it's the old witch woman, the Yaga, her teeth filed sharp, horrible, disheveled, mangy.

The stepmother gave no peace to the old man and before dawn: "Go after my daughter."

He set off. And she was back there, getting ready: "My daughter will come, we'll have a feast. There'll be pancakes and porridge and everything on earth."

The little dog ran up: "Bow, wow! The old man's fine young lady strolls about, but the stepmother's is being brought like a tigress."

"Oh, phooey, the old man's is like a scullery maid, sitting behind the stove, and they're bringing the stepmother's as a fine young lady."

So he brought her to her and she climbed out, all messed up, with long teeth and huge eyes.

And that's all, that's the story at an end, finally.

29. Baba Yaga

Recorded by Afanas'ev in his home district of Bobrov, this is a very common combination of tale types. SUS 480A* + 313H.

There lived this old man and his woman; the old man was widowed and he got married to another wife, but from his first wife he still had this little girl. The evil stepmother didn't like her. She beat her and wondered how to get rid of her entirely. Once her father went away somewhere and the stepmother said to the little girl, "Go visit your aunt and my sister, and ask her for a needle and thread—to sew a shirt for you." Now this aunt was Baba Yaga of the bony leg.

This little girl was no fool, however, and first she dropped in on her own aunt. "Good health to you, auntie!"

"Good health to you, my own dear niece. Why have you come here?"

"Mother has sent me to her sister's for a needle and thread, to sew a shirt for me."

So then the aunt spoke to her, "There, my niece, you'll find a birch that will lash you in the face, and you must tie it back with a ribbon. Then the gates will squeak and bang, and you must pour some oil on the hinges. Next dogs will try to tear at you, and you must throw them some bread. Finally, a tomcat will want to claw your eyes out, and you must give him some ham." So off went the little girl and she walked and she walked and then she was there.

There stood a little hut and in it Baba Yaga of the bony leg was sitting, weaving. "Good health to you, auntie!"

"Good health to you, my own dear one!"

"Mother has sent me to ask for a needle and thread of you, to sew me a shirt."

"Very good. Sit and weave a while." So the girl sat down at the loom and Baba Yaga went out and said to her maid-servant, "Quickly, heat the bath and wash my niece. Then watch her carefully; I intend to have her for breakfast."

The girl sat there neither dead nor alive, completely terrified, and she asked the maid-servant, "Dear cousin, don't put so much wood on the fire and pour more water on it, and bring the water here in a sieve." Then she gave her a kerchief.

So Baba Yaga was waiting for this. She went up to the window and asked, "Are you weaving, little niece? Are you weaving, my dear?"

"I am weaving, auntie, I am weaving, my dear." So Baba Yaga walked off a little way, and the girl gave the tomcat some ham and asked him, "Isn't there some way of getting away from here?"

"Here's a comb and here's a towel," said the tomcat. "Take them and run. Baba Yaga will chase after you. Put your ear to the ground and when you know that she is close by, first throw down the towel and it will make a wide, wide river; then if Baba Yaga crosses that river and is catching up to you, throw down the comb and it will make a deep, dense forest; she won't be able to get through that."

So the little girl took the towel and the comb and ran. The dogs wanted to tear her up, so she threw them some bread, and they let her go through. The gates wanted to slam and squeak, so she poured a little oil on their hinges, and they let her pass. The birch tried to scratch at her eyes, but she tied it up with ribbon, and it let her pass through. Then the cat sat down at the loom and wove, but it wasn't really weaving—it tangled all the skeins. So then Baba Yaga came up to the window and asked, "Are you weaving, my niece; are you weaving, my very own darling?"

"I am weaving, auntie; I am weaving, my dear," the tomcat answered rudely.

Baba Yaga rushed into the hut and saw that the young girl had gone away, so she started beating the cat and cursing. Why hadn't the tomcat scratched out her eyes? "I've served you so much," said the cat, "and you don't give me even a bone. She gave me ham."

Baba Yaga threw herself on the dogs, on the gate, on the birch tree, on the maid-servant, and she cursed them all and struck them.

The dogs said, "We have served you so much and you haven't even thrown us burnt crusts, but she gave us real bread."

The gate said, "We've served you so much but you never gave us any oil for our hinges."

The birch tree said, "I've served you, but you never bound me up with a thread, and she tied me with a ribbon."

The maid-servant said, "I've served you so much but you never gave me even a rag, and she gave me a kerchief."

Baba Yaga of the bony leg quickly sat down in her mortar, and driving it with the pestle, and with her broom sweeping the tracks away, chased after the little girl. The little girl put her ear to the earth and heard Baba Yaga chasing after her, and when she was already close, she threw down the towel. It made a broad, broad river. Baba Yaga came up to the river and started grinding her teeth in her spite. Then she went back home, took her bullocks, and drove them to the river. The bullocks drank that river dry! Baba Yaga set off once more in pursuit. The little girl put her ear to the earth and heard Baba Yaga already close. She threw down the comb and it formed such a deep and terrible forest! Baba Yaga started chewing on it, but no matter how she tried, she couldn't chew through it, so she returned home.

The old man had already come home, and he asked, "Where's my daughter?"

"She went to auntie," said the stepmother. A little while later the girl came running home.

"Where have you been?" her father asked.

"Oh, father," she said, "It was like this: mother sent me to auntie to ask for a needle and thread to sew me a shirt, but that auntie, that Baba Yaga, wanted to eat me up."

"How did you get away, daughter?"

"Well, it was like this." And the daughter told him. The old man found out everything and got angry with his wife and he shot her. Then he and his daughter began living and prospering. I was there. I drank the mead and beer, and it flowed through my moustaches and none got into my mouth.

30. The Swan-Geese

One of the most popular children's tales in Russia, although this version from Kursk is not entirely typical. Not well known beyond the East Slavic territories. SUS 480A*.

There lived this old man with this old woman and they had a daughter and a little son. "Daughter, daughter!" said the mother, "We are going to work. We'll bring you a bun, make you a dress, and buy you a kerchief. Be clever and watch your brother; don't go out of the yard." The old folks went away and the daughter forgot what they had told her to do. She put her little brother on the grass beneath the window and ran out of the yard to play and amuse herself. Then the swan-geese flew up and seized the little boy, and carried him away on their wings.

The girl came back and looked—her brother was gone! She gasped and dashed about here and there, but no, he wasn't there. She called out, burst out in tears, and recited the bad things that were to come from her father and mother—her brother didn't respond. She ran into the steppe and there she caught sight of the swan-geese, far away, and then they disappeared beyond the dark forest.

For a long time the swan-geese had been earning a bad reputation, doing a lot of mischief, kidnapping little children. The little girl guessed that they had carried away her little brother and rushed off to pursue them.

She ran and ran and came to a stove. "Stove, stove, tell me where the geese have flown!"

"Eat one of my rye pies and I'll tell you."

"Oh, at my father's they don't even eat wheat pies!" So the stove didn't tell her.

She ran on further and there was an apple tree. "Apple tree, apple tree, tell me where the geese have flown!"

"Eat one of my wild apples and I'll tell you."

"Oh, at my father's they don't even eat the orchard apples."

She ran on further and there met a river of milk with banks of honey custard. "River of milk with banks of honey custard! Where did the geese fly?"

"Eat some of my plain custard and milk and I will tell you."

"Oh, at my father's they don't even eat the cream."

She'd have run a long time through the steppe and wandered a long time through the forest, but fortunately she encountered a hedgehog. She was about to kick him out of the way, fearing he would prick her. She asked him, "Hedgehog, hedgehog! Where did the geese fly?"

"That way," the hedgehog pointed.

She ran along and came to a little hut on cock's legs. It was standing there, but it could turn around. In the hut sat Baba Yaga, with her wrinkled face and one leg of clay, and there sat her little brother on a bench playing with golden apples. His sister saw him, crept up, grabbed him, and carried him off. But the geese were flying right after her. The evil geese would catch her! Where should she hide? She came to the river of milk with banks of honey custard flowing along. "Oh, mother river, hide me!"

"Eat this simple custard." There was nothing else to do—she ate it. The river hid her beneath its banks and the geese flew on by.

She came out, said "Thank you," and ran on with her little brother. But the geese returned and flew right by. She came out and said "Thank you," and ran on with her little brother. But the geese turned back and flew straight at them. What should she do? What a misfortune! There stood the apple tree. "Apple tree, oh little mother apple tree! Hide me!"

"Eat my wild apple." She quickly ate it. The apple tree bent its branches over them and covered them with her leaves. The geese flew right by. She came out and ran on with her little brother, but the geese saw them and were after her. They were just about to attack—they were striking with their wings and it looked bad—but they tore themselves away!

Happily, on the road they met the stove. "Oh madam stove, hide me!"

"Eat this rye pie." She quickly popped it in her mouth, popped into the stove, and sat in the oven. The geese flew and flew, they shrieked and shrieked, but then they flew away with nothing at all. And she ran home, and just in time, too. She ran home just as her mother and father returned.

31. Vasilisa the Beautiful

Recorded in the Urals in the 1850s, perhaps from Perm or Solikamsk. Rarely recorded except in Ukrainian and Hungarian. This is widely regarded as a cautionary tale. SUS 480B*.

There lived an old man and old woman. Of children they had but one daughter. Once in the evening the old woman accidentally put out the fire and then her daughter set off for the next village to get some fire. Going along the road she met this man who was riding on a red horse and he was dressed in red. He asked her, "Where are you off to?"

And she said, "I'm after some fire."

But the man said to her, "Don't go, the lout will eat you up."

The girl said, "No, he wouldn't dare."

Having gone on she met another man on a white horse and he was all dressed in white. Again, this man asked the girl where she was going. She said to him: "After fire."

"No, don't go, the lout will eat you up," said the man.

She said, "No, he won't eat me." She set off and chanced to meet a third man on a brown horse all dressed in brown. And this man asked the girl where she was going. She said, "After fire."

"Don't go, the lout will eat you," said the man.

"No, he won't eat me," said the girl and she set off again. She came up to a watering trough, then went on a bit further and she saw a human arm and leg. She went into the hut and saw human heads. Here's where the lout lives. The lout asked the girl what she saw on the way. She said, "A man on a red horse dressed in red."

And the lout said to her, "That's my sun. What else?"

"I saw another man, on a white horse, all dressed in white."

The lout said to her, "That's my moon. And what else?"

The girl said, "Also a third man on a brown horse, all dressed in brown."

"That's my son," said the lout. "What else did you see?"

"I saw human arms and legs lying about on the street!"

"Those are my rakes and forks," said the lout. "What else did you see, girl?"

"I saw human heads."

"Those are my cooking pots!" Then there was a bang, slap, slam . . . and he ate up the girl.

Tales of Magic

The Russian tales of magic, as they are known, are among the most popular in the tradition. There are no clear boundaries between some of these tales and the tales of heroes, however. In this group, one encounters tales with magic helpers, familiar to Western readers as fairy godmothers, sometimes witches or trolls, or magic horses or wands. The Russian tales of magic know these and many other helpers as well. Here one meets Burenushka the little red cow, the Russian Cinderella and her golden slipper, and the internationally known Armless Maiden. Even a wolf can serve as a helper in the tales of magic. There are also magic objects including loaves of bread that are never diminished no matter how much the hero eats, and magic fiddles and fifes that cause all who hear them (including pigs!) to dance. Supernatural strength is also a feature of some tales of magic, and a host of other motifs appear in these tales that are part of every Russian child's upbringing. For more on these wondertales, see Haney, *CRF,* vol. 4.

32. A Prince and His "Uncle"

Of unknown provenance. This is a very common tale in all branches of East Slavic. It has also been recorded throughout Europe and in North and South America. It is typologically related to the classical myths of Silenus and the biblical myth of Solomon and Asmodeus, but equally obvious are the ties to the old Norse Heimskringla and the Gesta Danorum of Saxo Grammaticus. In recent times, the American Robert Bly has attempted to create a "masculine mythology" from the Grimms' version of this tale. SUS 502.

There lived and dwelt this king, and he had an adolescent son. The prince was excellent in every way: handsome and well mannered, he caused his father no pain, for the king was tormented by greed, by a desire to squeeze even more profits and increase his quit rents a little. Once he saw an old man with sables and martens and beavers and foxes.

"Halt, old man! Where are you from?"

"By birth I'm from such-and-such a village, father, but now I'm serving the forest spirit [*leshii*]."

"And how do you catch these beasts?"

"Well, the forest spirit sets out snares and the beast is stupid and gets caught."

"Now, listen, old man! I shall supply you with wine and give you some money, then will show me where to put out these snares?" The old man was tempted and showed him. The king immediately ordered the forest spirit caught and fettered to an iron post, and then he put out the snares in his own forest preserves.

So the forest spirit sat there at the iron post and looked in a window because that post was standing in a garden. The prince came out with some women and nannies and with some trusty servant girls to walk about the garden. He walked by the post and the forest spirit shouted at him: "Oh princely child! Release me! I shall be of service to you."

"But how should I release you?"

"Go to your mother and tell her this: 'Dear Mother of mine, look for some lice on my head!' Then you lay your head on her knees and she will start searching around on your head. You seize the moment to pull the key out of your mother's pocket and then let me free!" So that's what the prince did. He pulled the key out of his mother's pocket and ran into the garden, then he made himself an arrow, placed it on a taut bow, and let it go far, far away, and then he shouted to the women and nannies to go fetch the arrow. The women and nannies all ran away and at that moment the prince unlocked the iron post and freed the forest spirit.

The forest spirit set off to tear up the royal snares! The king saw that he wasn't snaring any more beasts, he got angry and attacked his wife; why had she given out the key and let the forest spirit loose? And then he called his boyars, his generals, and his councilors so that they might judge: should her head be removed on the block or should she be sent into exile? Things were bad for the prince. He pitied his own mother and so he admitted to his father that it was his fault. "It was this way and that way and that's how it happened." The king was sorely aggrieved and what should he do with his son? He could not execute him, so it was decided to send him out into the four corners of the world to the four winds of the summer, to all the winter blizzards, to all the autumn whirlwinds. They gave him a pack and an old "uncle" as a servant.

So the prince and his "uncle" went out into the open steppe. They walked near or far, high or low, and then they saw a well. The prince said to the "uncle": "Go get some water!"

"I won't do it!" answered the "uncle."

They went on further, they walked and walked, and there was another well. "Go fetch some water! I feel like a drink," the prince asked the "uncle" a second time.

"I won't go," said the "uncle."

So on and on they walked, and then they encountered a third well and the "uncle" again would not go, so the prince went after the water himself. He let himself down into the well and the "uncle" banged the top onto it and said, "I won't let you out. You be the servant and I'll be the prince." There was nothing to be done so the prince agreed and gave him a note to that effect in his own blood. Then they exchanged clothes and set off further.

So they came to another country. They went to the tsar in his palace, the "uncle" in front, and the prince behind him. The "uncle" began living at that tsar's as a guest, and he ate and drank with him at the same table. He said to him: "Your royal highness! Take my servant into the kitchen, at least." So they took the prince into the kitchen and made him fetch wood and scour the pots and pans. A little time passed and the prince had learned to prepare food better than the tsar's cooks. His lordship found out about this, befriended him, and began giving him gold. The cooks were offended by this and they began seeking a way to be rid of him.

Once the prince made a pie and put it in the oven, and the cooks got hold of some poison, took it and put it in the pie. The tsar sat down to eat and they handed him the pie. The tsar was about to take his knife to it when the chief cook ran in: "Your highness! Please don't eat it!" And he said a lot of nasty things against the prince.

The tsar did not spare even his favorite dog. He cut off a piece of pie and threw it onto the ground. The dog ate it and died right then and there. The king summoned the prince and shouted at him in a loud voice: "How did you dare to prepare a pie for me with poison in it? I order you to be executed immediately!"

"I know nothing, your highness, I know nothing of it at all!" the prince answered.

"It is obvious that your cooks were offended when you favored me, they have brought me down on purpose." The tsar forgave him and ordered him to be his groom.

The prince led the horses off to be watered. On the way he encountered the forest spirit. "Greetings, royal son! Come visit me!"

"I'm afraid the horses would run away."

"Never mind, come on!" Then a hut appeared on the spot. The forest spirit had three daughters. He asked the first one: "And what will we reward the king's son with for having freed me from the iron post?"

The daughter said: "Give him the self-setting tablecloth." The prince left the forest spirit with the gift and looked: all the horses were there. He spread the cloth: "Whatever you want, you just ask for it—food and drinks!"

The next day he herded the tsar's horses to water and the forest spirit again appeared: "Come visit me!" He brought him and asked his second daughter: "And what will we reward the king's son with?"

"I will give him a mirror: whatever you like you can see in this mirror."

On the third day the forest spirit again encountered the prince, took him into his home, and asked the youngest daughter: "And what will we reward the king's son with?"

"I will give him a fife. Just press it to your lips and musicians and singers will immediately appear." So the king's son began to live happily. He ate and drank well, he knew and found out about everything, and music resounded the whole day long. What could be better? And the horses?! It was a miracle purely and simply: they were happy and handsome and quick off the mark.

The tsar began to boast to his favorite daughter how the lord had sent him this fabulous groom. But the beautiful tsarevna had long since taken notice herself of the groom—why should a beautiful maiden not note a handsome lad! The tsarevna became curious. Why were the new groom's horses faster and more stately than those of the others? "I think I'll just go into his chambers," she thought, "and take a look at how he's living, poor fellow." Well it's a well-known fact: what a woman wants to do she does. She awaited a time when the prince had herded the horses out to be watered, then she went into his chambers and stole a glance in his mirror. Immediately she understood everything, and she carried away with her his self-setting tablecloth, his mirror, and the fife.

At that very moment a misfortune struck the tsar. The seven-headed monster Idolishche attacked his kingdom and demanded a tsarevna for his wife. "And if they won't give her to me, I'll take her by force!" he said, and he arrayed his troops, which were thousands upon thousands. It looked bad for the tsar. He sent a clarion call throughout the entire tsardom, he summoned the princes and the bogatyrs. Whoever should defeat Idolishche of the Seven Heads would receive half the kingdom and in addition a daughter in marriage. So the princes and the bogatyrs gathered and rode off to do battle against Idolishche, and "uncle" set off together with the tsar's army. And our groom mounted his gray mare and dragged along behind all the rest.

He rode along and then he met up with the forest spirit. "Where are you going, royal son?"

"To fight."

"You won't go far on that nag! And a groom at that! Come pay me a visit!"

He brought him into his hut and poured him a glass of vodka. The prince drank it. "Do you feel much strength in yourself now?" asked the forest spirit.

"If I had a cudgel of fifty poods, I'd throw it up into the air and let it fall on my head and I wouldn't even feel the blow!"

He gave him another glass to drink. "And now do you have much strength?"

"Why, if I had a cudgel of a hundred poods, I could throw it beyond the clouds!"

So he poured him a third glass. "And now how's your strength?"

"Why, if you could place a column from the earth to heaven, I could turn over the entire universe!" The forest spirit filtrated some vodka from another tap and gave it to the prince. The prince drank it and his strength was diminished to one-seventh.

Afterward the forest spirit led him onto the porch and whistled a hero's whistle. Out of nowhere there came running a jet-black horse and the earth shook and flames came from its nostrils and smoke poured out of its ears in a column and sparks showered from under its hooves. It ran up to the porch and fell on its knees. "Now there's a horse for you!" He also gave him a fighting cudgel and a silk lash. The prince rode out on his jet-black horse against the hostile force. He looked and there was his "uncle" who had climbed up in a birch and was sitting there shaking from fear. The prince lashed him a time or two with his lash and flew off at the enemy force. He slashed down many of the foe with his sword, still more he trampled with his horse, and he carried off all seven heads of Idolishche.

And the tsarevna saw the whole thing. She couldn't wait to look in the mirror to see how it would turn out. So she immediately rode out and asked the prince: "With what do you order us to show our gratitude?"

"Kiss me, beautiful maiden!" The tsarevna was not embarrassed, she pressed him to her ardent heart and kissed him loudly and soundly so that the entire army might hear.

The prince struck his horse—and was off! He returned home and sat in his misery as if he had never been at the battle. But his "uncle" was boasting to everyone, saying to them all: "It was I who defeated Idolishche."

The tsar greeted him with great honor and betrothed him to his daughter and gave a great feast. Only the tsarevna was no fool, suddenly right out of the blue she had a headache, her heart burned. What will happen, what is to be done for the promised son-in-law? "Father," he says to the tsar, "give me a ship and I will go for medicines for my bride. Only let that groom go with me. You see, I've really grown very used to him. . . ." The tsar listened to him, gave him the ship and the groom.

So they set off, near or far away they sailed, and the "uncle" ordered a sack sewn. And he put the groom in it and threw it into the water. The princess looked in the mirror and saw the misfortune! She got into her carriage and rushed to the sea, but the forest spirit was already sitting there, knitting a net. "Little man, help me in my great sorrow, an evil 'uncle' is drowning the prince!"

"Allow me, beautiful maiden, the net is already ready. Stretch out your white hands to it!" So the princess let the net out into the deep sea and she hauled in the prince and took him with her. And at home she told her father the whole story.

So now there was a happy little feast and then a little wedding. The tsar didn't need to brew any mead or distill fine wines—there was plenty! And "uncle" bought up various supplies and went back. He came into the palace and they seized him right there. He pleaded, but it was too late. They shot him in a flash at the gates. The prince's wedding was happy. All the taverns and public houses were opened for a whole week to all the people for free. And I was there, and drank mead and wine, it flowed over my moustache, but none got into my mouth.

33. The Golden Slipper

Originally recorded in Shenkursk of Arkhangelsk province. This version is closer to the internationally known Cinderella than 510B (Cap o' Rushes), which is not known outside of Europe. SUS 510A.

There lived and dwelt this old man with this old woman. The old man and the old woman had two daughters. Once the old man rode into town and there he bought one sister a little fish and the other sister a little fish, too. The older daughter ate her fish but the younger one went to the well and said, "Oh, Little Mother Fish, shall I eat you or not?"

"Don't eat me," said the little fish; "let me go into the water; I will be of use to you." She let the little fish go in the well and went home. The old woman really disliked her younger daughter. She dressed her sister in the very best clothing and went with her to the liturgy in the church, but she left the younger one at home with two measures of rye and ordered her to clean all the chaff out of it before she came back from church.

The girl went after some water and sat down by the well, crying. The little fish swam up to the surface and asked her, "What are you crying about, beautiful maiden?"

"How should I not cry?" the beautiful maiden answered. "Mother dressed my sister in the very best clothing and went away with her to the liturgy, and she left me at home and ordered me to clean all the chaff out of two measures of rye before she comes back from church!"

The little fish said, "Don't cry. Go and get dressed, and go to church; the rye will be cleaned." She got dressed and went to the liturgy. Her mother didn't recognize her. The liturgy was ending and the girl came home. Her mother also came home and asked, "Well, you little fool, did you clean the chaff out of the rye?"

"I cleaned it all," she answered.

"There was such a beautiful maiden at liturgy!" her mother said. "The priest couldn't chant or read—he just kept looking at her. And you, fool, just look at yourself, how you go around."

"Even though I wasn't there, I know," said the maiden.

"How could you know?" her mother said.

The next time the mother dressed the older sister in the very best clothing and set off with her to liturgy. She left the younger daughter three measures of grain and said, "While I am praying to God, you get the chaff out of that grain."

So then she went to liturgy and the daughter went for some water from the well. She sat by the well and wept. The little fish swam up to the surface and asked, "Why are you weeping, beautiful maiden?"

"How should I not weep? My mother dressed my sister in the very best clothing and went with her to liturgy, and she left me at home and ordered me to clean the chaff out of three measures of grain before she comes home from church."

The little fish said, "Don't cry! Go home and get dressed, then go after her to church; the grain will be cleaned!"

She got dressed and went to church and began praying to God. The priest couldn't chant or read—he just kept looking at her. The liturgy was finishing. There happened to be at that liturgy a tsarevich from some distant place. Our beautiful maiden was most attractive to him. He wanted to find out who she was. He threw some pitch under one of her slippers. The slipper got stuck and she went home. "I'll marry whoever's slipper this is!" The slipper was all stitched in gold.

So then the old woman came home. "Oh, what a beautiful maiden there was there!" she said. "The priest couldn't chant or read—he just kept looking at her, and you, fool, just look at yourself: you're a ragamuffin!"

So after that the tsarevich sought the maiden who had lost her slipper through all the districts, but he couldn't find anyone whom the slipper fit. He came to the old woman and asked her, "Show me your maiden. Perhaps the slipper will fit her."

"My daughter would soil that slipper," the old woman answered. The beautiful maiden came out and the tsarevich tried the slipper on her foot. It fit her perfectly. He married her and they began to live and prosper and acquired wealth. I was there, I drank beer. It flowed over my lips but none got into my mouth. They gave me a blue *kaftan*, but a crow flew by shouting, "Blue *kaftan*, blue *kaftan*!" I thought it was saying "Off with the *kaftan*," so I took off the *kaftan*. Then they gave me a top hat and started putting it down over my neck. Then they gave me some red slippers, and the crow came flying and shouted, "Red slippers, red slippers!" I thought it was saying, "Stolen slippers," so I took them and tossed them.

34. Burenushka the Little Red Cow

Recorded in Arkhangelsk province. This is a typical combination of types among the East Slavs, although it is not limited to them. The most ancient written version of this tale type is to be found in the *Mahabharata*. Yagishna is an alternative name for the Russian witch. SUS 511 + 403.

In no certain tsardom, in no certain land, there lived and dwelt a tsar with his tsaritsa, and they had a single daughter, Tsarevna Maria. When the tsaritsa died, the tsar took another wife, Yagishna. This Yagishna gave birth to two daughters: one had two eyes, but the other had three eyes. The stepmother didn't like Tsarevna Maria and she sent her out to herd the little red cow and she gave her just a dry crust of bread.

The tsarevna set off into the steppe, and she bowed to the little red cow's right leg, and then she ate and drank her fill, and then she got herself all pretty and spent the whole day walking after the little red cow just like a landlord's wife. The day passed and again she bowed to the right leg, removed her pretty clothes, and came home, bringing back the crust of bread, which she placed upon the table. "How's that bitch keeping alive?" wondered Yagishna. The next day she gave Tsarevna Maria the same old crust of bread, but she sent her older daughter out with her. "Watch carefully and find out what Maria Tsarevna is finding to eat."

They came into the steppe and Maria Tsarevna said, "Let me look for lice on your head." She started looking while at the same time mumbling, "Sleep, sleep, sister! Sleep, sleep, my very own! Sleep, sleep little eye! Sleep, sleep, the other one, too." The sister went fast asleep and Maria Tsarevna got up, went up to the little red cow, and bowed to her right leg. Then she ate and drank, dressed herself up, and walked around all day like a landlord's wife. Evening came; Maria Tsarevna changed clothes and said, "Get up, sister, get up, my dear. Let's go home."

"Oh, no," said the sister sorrowfully. "I've slept all day and seen nothing; mother will scold me now."

They came home and her mother asked her, "What did Maria Tsarevna drink? What did she eat?"

"I didn't see anything." Yagishna cursed her and in the morning she sent her three-eyed daughter out. "Go and watch what that bitch eats and drinks." So the maidens came into the steppe to herd the little red cow. Tsarevna Maria said, "Sister, let me search for lice on your head."

"Go right ahead, sister, go ahead, my dear." Maria Tsarevna began looking and mumbling, "Sleep, sleep, sister! Sleep, sleep, my very own! Sleep, sleep little eye! Sleep, the other one too!" But she forgot the third eye and that third eye watched and watched what Maria Tsarevna was doing. She ran up to the little red cow, bowed to the right leg, drank and ate her fill, and got dressed in fine clothes. When the sun began to set, she again bowed to the right leg and changed her clothes and then woke up the three-eyed one: "Wake up sister, wake up, my dear! Let's go home."

So Maria Tsarevna came home, and she put the dry crust of bread on the table.

Her mother asked her daughter, "What did she drink and eat?" The three-eyed daughter told her everything. Yagishna demanded, "Old man, slaughter the little red cow." The old man slaughtered the cow and Maria Tsarevna begged him to give her the lower intestine at least. The old man gave her the lower intestine. She took it and planted it on the gatepost, and a willow bush grew up with all sorts of beautiful berries flourishing, and on it various kinds of little birds sat and sang the songs both of tsars and peasants.

Ivan Tsarevich heard about Maria Tsarevna and he came to her stepmother. He put a platter on the table and said, "Whichever maiden can pick me a full platter of berries I will marry." Yagishna sent her elder daughter to pick berries, but the little birds wouldn't let her come close. When she tried, they tried to peck out her eyes. So then she sent her second daughter, but they wouldn't let her come close either. Finally she let Maria Tsarevna go. Maria Tsarevna took the platter and set off to pick the berries. She picked and the tiny birds added twice or three times as many to the platter. She came back and put the platter on the table, and then she bowed to the tsarevich. Then came a happy feast and the wedding as Ivan Tsarevich took Maria Tsarevna for himself and they began to live and prosper, and acquired wealth.

Whether they lived for a long time or a short time, Maria Tsarevna gave birth to a son. She wanted to visit her father. She went to visit him with her husband. Her stepmother turned her into a goose and she arranged for Ivan Tsarevich to marry her older daughter. Then Ivan Tsarevich went back home.

An old man who was his tutor got up early in the morning, washed himself white as snow, took the infant into his arms, and went out into the steppe to a little bush. Some geese were flying, gray geese were flying. "Oh, geese, gray geese! Where have you seen the mother of this infant?"

"In the next flock," they answered.

Another flock came flying. "Oh geese, gray geese! Where have you seen the mother of this infant?"

The mother of the infant flew down to earth, removed her skin and put on another, took the infant into her arms and began feeding it at her breasts, crying, "Today I shall feed you, tomorrow I shall feed you, but day after tomorrow I shall fly away beyond the dark forests, beyond the high mountains."

The old man set off home. The little lad slept until morning without waking while the substitute wife scolded the old man for going off into the steppe and for having nearly starved her son. In the morning the old man once more got up early, washed himself as white as snow, and went with the child into the steppe and Ivan Tsarevich got up, set off unseen after the old man, and climbed into the bush.

Some geese were flying, gray geese were flying. "Oh, geese, gray geese! Where have you seen the mother of this infant?"

"In the next flock."

Another flock came flying. "Oh geese, gray geese! Where have you seen the mother of this infant?"

The infant's mother leapt to the ground, pulled off her skin, pulled off another, threw it on the bush, and began feeding the infant at her breast. As she was saying farewell to him, she said, "Tomorrow I will fly away beyond the dark forests, over the high mountains!"

She gave the infant back to the old man. "What is that awful smell?" she said. She was about to put her skins back on. She reached for them but they were not to be found. Ivan Tsarevich had burned them. He grabbed Maria Tsarevna and she turned into a frog, then into a lizard and every sort of reptile, and then afterward into a spindle. Ivan Tsarevich broke the spindle in two, threw the top of it over his head and the bottom in front of him, and then she appeared as a beautiful young woman.

They set off home together. Yagishna's daughter shrieked and yelled, "The destroyer is coming, the murderess is coming!"

Ivan Tsarevich summoned the princes and boyars and asked them, "With which wife do you want me to live?"

They said, "With the first."

"Well, gentlemen, I'll live with whichever wife first leaps to the top of the gates." Yagishna's daughter went right up to the top of the gates, but Maria Tsarevich grasped it tightly and did not climb up. So Ivan Tsarevich took his rifle and shot the false wife, and lived with Maria Tsarevna as before, happily and prosperously.

35. Sivko-Burko

Recorded in Perm province of the Urals. Known throughout Europe and carried to the Americas in English, French, and Spanish. Also known in Turkish, Caucasian, and various languages of India. SUS 530.

There lived and dwelt an old man, and he had three sons. The third was Ivan the Fool, who did nothing but sit on the stove in a corner and sniffle. The father was dying and he said, "Children, when I die, you are to take turns coming to my grave to sleep for three nights." Then he died. They buried the old man and then night fell. It was time for the oldest brother to go spend the night on the grave, but he— whether he was lazy or afraid—said to his little brother, "Ivan the Fool! You go to our father's grave and sleep there instead of me. You don't do anything anyway."

So Ivan the Fool got ready and went to the grave. He lay down and at midnight the grave suddenly opened, the old man came out, and he asked, "Who are you? Are you my oldest son?"

"No, father, I am Ivan the Fool."

The old man recognized him and asked, "Why didn't my oldest son come?"

"He sent me, father."

"Well, that's your good fortune." The old man whistled and shouted in a warrior's voice: "Sivko-Burko, Magic Black Steed!" Sivko ran and the earth shook, sparks flew out of his eyes, and from his nostrils a pillar of smoke! "Here's a good warhorse for you, my son. And you, horse, serve him as you have served me." When the old man had finished saying that, he lay down in his grave.

Ivan the Fool stroked and petted his Sivko and then released him. He himself went home.

At home his brothers asked him, "Well, Ivan the Fool, did you spend the night well?"

"Very well, brothers."

The second night came and the middle brother also didn't want to spend the night on the grave. He said, "Ivan the Fool! Go to the grave of our father and spend the night there instead of me."

Ivan the Fool without saying a word got ready and went off to the grave. He lay down and waited for midnight. At midnight the grave opened and his father came. He asked, "You, are you my middle son?"

"No," said Ivan the Fool. "It's me again, father." The old man shouted with his warrior's voice, he whistled with a young man's whistle: "Sivko-Burko, Magic Black Steed!" Burko ran and the earth shook, flames came out of his eyes, and from his nostrils a pillar of smoke. "Well, Burko, as you have served me, now serve my son. Now be gone!" And Burko ran away. The old man lay down in his grave, and Ivan the Fool went home.

Again his brothers asked him, "How did you sleep, Ivan the Fool?"

"Very well, brothers!" The third night it was Ivan's turn. He could scarcely wait. He got ready and set off. He lay down on the grave and at midnight the old man came out again. He already knew it was Ivan the Fool. He shouted with the warrior's voice and whistled with a young man's whistle. "Sivko-Burko, Magic Black Steed!" The black steed ran and the earth shook, from his eyes flames burst, and from his nostrils a pillar of smoke. "Well, Black Steed! As you have served me, now serve my son." When the old man had said this, he said farewell to Ivan the Fool, and lay down in his grave. Ivan the Fool stroked his black steed, looked him over, and released him. Then he went home.

Again his brothers asked him, "How did you spend the night, Ivan the Fool?"

"Very well, brothers."

They went on living. Two of the brothers worked, but Ivan the Fool did nothing. Suddenly the tsar sent out a proclamation: he would marry his daughter to the person who could tear down the tsarevna's portrait from high up on the house. The brothers got ready to watch someone try to tear down the portrait. Ivan the Fool sat on the stove behind the chimney and begged, "Brothers, give me a horse and I'll go and have a look, too."

His brothers ridiculed him: "You sit there, Fool, on the stove. Why should you go? Just to make people laugh?" But Ivan the Fool would not be denied. His brothers couldn't put him off. "All right, Fool, you take that three-legged mare there."

So they all rode off. Ivan the Fool rode with them into the open steppe, into the wide expanses. He got down from his little mare, killed her, skinned her, and hung the skin on the corral. He just threw the flesh away. Then he whistled with a young man's whistle and shouted with a warrior's cry: "Sivko-Burko, Magic Black Steed!" Sivko ran and the earth shook, out of his eyes flames burst, and from his nostrils came a pillar of smoke. Ivan the Fool climbed in one ear and ate and drank his fill, then he climbed out the other, dressed and became a handsome young man, such that his brothers would not recognize him. He got on Sivko and went to tear down the portrait.

There was a huge crowd of people. When they saw the young man, they all started staring. Ivan the Fool started his horse with a wave. His horse leapt but missed the portrait by three logs. They had all seen from where he came, but no one saw him go away. He released his horse and went home, back to the stove. Soon his brothers came back and told their wives, "Well, wives, there was this young man there whom no one had ever seen before. He only missed taking the portrait by three logs. We saw where he came from but we don't know where he went. He'll probably come again."

Ivan the Fool sat on the stove and said, "Brothers, wasn't I there?"

"How in the devil could you be there? Sit, fool, on the stove and wipe your nose."

Time passed. Another proclamation from the tsar. Again the brothers got ready to go and Ivan the Fool said, "Brothers, give me some horse or other."

They answered, "Sit there, you fool, stay at home. You'd just ruin another horse." But they couldn't put him off, so they gave him another lame mare. Ivan the Fool dispatched her, too. He killed her, hung up her skin on the corral, and threw away the flesh. Then he whistled with a young man's whistle and shouted with a warrior's cry.

"Sivko-Burko, Magic Black Steed!" Burko ran and the earth shook, from his nose flames burst, and from his nostrils a pillar of smoke. Ivan the Fool climbed in the right ear and dressed, and then he climbed out the left. He had become a handsome young man. He leapt onto his horse and rode off. This time he was only two logs short of the portrait. They all saw where he came from but no one saw where he went. He released Burko and walked home. He sat down on the stove, waiting for his brothers.

His brothers came and said, "Women, that same young man came again. He only missed the portrait by two logs."

Ivan the Fool said to them, "Brothers, wasn't I there?"

"Sit there, fool! You might as well have been with the devil."

Not long after this there was another proclamation from the tsar. The brothers got ready, and Ivan the Fool asked, "Give me, brothers, some sort of horse. I'll go and have a look too."

"You sit at home, fool. Why should we waste a horse on you?"

But they couldn't deny him. They argued and argued and then they gave him a poor old mare. They rode off. Ivan the Fool went off, killed her, and threw away the flesh. Then he whistled with his young man's whistle and shouted with a warrior's cry: "Sivko-Burko, Magic Black Steed!" The black steed ran and the earth shook, and from its eyes flames burst, and from its nostrils a pillar of smoke. Ivan the Fool went in one ear and ate and drank his fill, then he climbed out the other and was dressed as a young man. He got on his horse and set off. When they got to the tsar's apartments, he tore down the portrait and bunting around it. They saw where he came from but they didn't see where he went. He released his black steed and went home.

He sat down on the stove and waited for his brothers. His brothers came and said, "Well, mistresses, that same young man jumped so high today that he tore down the portrait."

Ivan the Fool was sitting behind the chimney and he spoke up, "Brothers, wasn't I there?"

"Go on sitting there, you fool. You might as well have been with the devil."

After a little time the tsar held a ball and he summoned all the boyars, *voevodas*, princes, councilors, senators, merchants, traders, and peasants. And Ivan's brothers went. Ivan wasn't left behind. He went and sat there behind the chimney on the stove, watching, and with his mouth open. The tsarevna greeted her guests, bringing beer to each of them and wondering whether one of them wouldn't wipe his brow with that bunting. That would be her groom. But no one did. And she didn't see Ivan the Fool on the stove.

The guests all left. The next day the tsar held another ball, but again they couldn't find the one with the cloth. On the third day the tsarevna was once again offering beer to the guests. She had served them all, but no one had wiped himself with the cloth. "My intended one is just not here!" she thought to herself. Then she glanced behind the chimney and saw Ivan the Fool. He was dressed poorly, he was covered in soot, his hair was unkempt. She poured him a glass of beer and his brothers watched, thinking, "the tsarevna is offering beer to that fool!" Ivan the Fool drank some of the beer and wiped himself with the cloth. The tsarevna rejoiced and took him by the hand. She led him to her father and said, "Father, this is my intended!"

The brothers felt as if they had been stabbed in the heart with a knife. "What is the tsarevna doing? Has she gone mad? She's made that fool her intended groom."

Conversations were short. There was a happy feast and then the wedding. Our Ivan is no longer Ivan the Fool; now he is Ivan the Tsar's son-in-law. He got ready, he bathed, and he became that young man such that people couldn't recognize him. Thus, the brothers found out what it means to go to the grave of one's father.

36. The Pig with the Golden Bristles

From Bobrov district of Voronezh province and probably recorded by Afanas'ev himself. This version lacks the usual opening episode of the three brothers guarding their deceased father's grave. Known in Persian as well. SUS 530A.

There lived and dwelt this tsar, and he had a daughter, Incomparable Beauty, and you can't tell about her in a tale or describe her with a pen. The tsar made an announcement throughout all the towns that whoever should kiss the tsarevna through twelve panes of glass, should, regardless of his birth, have the tsarevna as his bride and receive half the tsardom. Now in this tsardom there lived a merchant who had three sons. Two—the oldest and the middle—were intelligent, but the third was a fool. The two oldest sons said, "Father, we are going to win the tsarevna!"

"Go with God," the merchant said.

They took for themselves the very best horses and got ready for the journey, the trip, and the fool also made preparations. "Why are you going, fool?" the brothers said, "Where would you kiss the tsarevna?" and they laughed hysterically at him.

So off they rode, and the fool dragged along behind them on a mangy, poor old nag. He rode out into the steppe and shouted in a loud voice, "Heh, Sivka-Burka, Magical Steed! Stand before me as a leaf before the grass." Suddenly out of nowhere there appeared an outstanding steed. As it ran, the earth shook. The fool climbed in one ear and out the other and became a handsome young man such has never been seen nor heard of. He got on the horse and rode to the tsar's court. There he let fly and he broke six panes of glass. Everybody gasped and shouted, "Who is he?" or "Hold him!" or "Catch him!" But by then all trace had gone. He rode off into the steppe, climbed in one ear and out the other of his horse, and became once more the fool. He got on his nag and rode home. Then he sat down on the stove. When his brothers returned, they told the story.

"There was this young man, father, and he broke through six panes of glass at once."

And from the stove the fool shouted, "Brothers, oh brothers! Wasn't that me you saw?"

"What are you on about, you fool? Should you love the tsarevna? You aren't even worth her fingernails."

The next day the brothers once more got ready to ride to the tsar's court, and the fool also made his preparations. "What for, fool?" the brothers laughed. "Didn't you get enough the last time?"

The fool rode out on his mangy, poor old horse into the steppe again and shouted in a loud voice, "Heh, Sivka-Burka, Magical Steed! Stand before me as a leaf before the grass." The horse ran, the earth shook. Once more he climbed into one ear and out the other, and he became a handsome young man such has never been seen nor heard of.

He flew off to the tsar's court where he broke all twelve panes of glass and kissed the tsarevna, Incomparable Beauty, and she put a stamp right in the middle of his forehead. Everybody gasped and shouted, "Who is that?" "Catch him, hold him!" But all trace of him was long gone. He rode off alone into the steppe, once more climbed into one ear of his horse and then out the other, and thus became the same fool he had been before. He came home, tied up his forehead with a rag, pretending that he had a headache, and lay down on the stove.

His brothers returned and told the story, "Oh, father, there was this young man, and he broke through all twelve panes at once and kissed the tsarevich."

And from the stove the fool responded, "Brothers, dear brothers! Wasn't that me you saw?"

"What do you mean, you fool!"

All this time the tsarevna was wondering who her husband was to be. She came to the tsar and said, "Let me gather all the tsareviches and princes, nobles and merchants, and all the peasants to a feast, a council, and find out who kissed me." The tsar permitted it. So all the baptized world came together. The tsarevna herself made the rounds, treating all to wine and looking carefully to see who might have a mark on the forehead. She went around to all, and at the end she brought some wine to the fool. "What's that you're hiding with that bandage?" the tsarevna asked.

"Oh, it's nothing. My head aches," answered the fool.

"Well, untie it."

So the fool untied his head and the tsarevna recognized the mark—and fainted. The tsar said, "It's too late as we've given our word: that's how it must be. You shall be his bride."

So the fool and the tsarevna were married. She wept most bitterly, and the other two tsarevnas, her sisters, who got married to tsareviches, laughed at her. "You got married to a fool!"

Once the tsar summoned his sons-in-law, and he said to them, "My most amicable sons-in-law! I have heard that in a certain tsardom, in a certain land, there is a marvelous creature: a pig with golden bristles. Could you not obtain one? Try!" So the two clever sons-in-law saddled the very best horses there were, mounted them, and rode away. "Well," the tsar said to the fool, "You go, too."

So the fool took the very worst horse there was in the stables and set off after the tsareviches. He rode out into the open steppe and shouted in a loud voice, "Heh, Sivka-Burka, Magical Steed! Stand before me like the leaf before the grass." Out of nowhere there appeared a wonderful horse. When he snorted, he pawed the earth with a hoof. The fool climbed in one ear and out the other. When he jumped out, there stood before him two young men and they asked him, "What do you want? What do you desire?"

"That there should be a tent set up with a bed in it, and near it a pig grazing with golden bristles."

It all appeared within a minute. The tent was set up, a bed was in the tent, on the bed the fool was stretched out, and such a handsome young man that no one could recognize him! And in a nearby meadow a pig with golden bristles was grazing. The other sons-in-law rode and rode but they never saw a pig with golden bristles and they had to return home. They rode up to the tent and there they saw the marvelous creature. "Oh, there's a pig with golden bristles strolling around here! Let's go and whatever it takes, we'll give. We'll buy the pig with golden bristles and please our father-in-law."

They rode up to the tent and exchanged greetings. The fool asked them, "Where are you going? What are you looking for?"

"Won't you sell us your pig with the golden bristles? We've been looking for one for such a long time."

"No, it's not for sale. I need it for myself."

"Take whatever you want, only sell it to us." They offered a thousand for the pig, and even two, then three thousand and more.

But the fool wouldn't agree. "I wouldn't take even a hundred thousand."

"Oh, please, give it to us. Take what you want."

"Well, if it's so much needed by you, I'll give it to you, and I won't take much for it. Just the *mizinets* or little toe from your foot."

They thought and thought about it, but then they took off their boots and cut off a little toe. The fool took the toes and hid them on himself, and then he gave them the pig with the golden bristles.

The brothers-in-law came riding home, bringing with them the pig with the golden bristles. The tsar was overjoyed and didn't know how to address them, where to seat them at the table, or what to treat them to. "You didn't see the fool anywhere?" the tsar asked them.

"We didn't see hide or hair of him, nor did we hear him at all."

But the fool climbed in one of his horse's ears and out the other, and now he was the same fool as before. He killed his nag, skinned her, and put the skin on himself. Then he caught some magpies, ravens, daws, and sparrows, pinned them inside his skin, and set off home. He came into the court and let all the birds go. They flew around to various places and broke out all the windows. Tsarevna Incomparable Beauty broke out into tears when she saw this, while her sisters laughed at her. "Our husbands have brought the pig with the golden bristles, but your fool, just look at him, your fool is dressed as an utter imbecile."

The tsar shouted at the fool, "You ignoramus!"

Another time the tsar summoned his sons-in-law and said to them, "My amicable sons-in-law! I have heard that in such and such a tsardom, in such a land, there is this marvelous creature: A deer with golden antlers and a golden tail. Could you not obtain it for me somehow?"

"We could, your royal highness." So the two clever sons-in-law saddled up the best horses that there were and set off.

"Well," said the tsar to the fool, "you had better go, too."

So the fool took the worst nag there was in the stables and rode out after the clever sons-in-law. He rode into the steppe, shouted in a loud voice, "Heh Sivka-Burka, Magical Steed! Stand before me like a leaf before grass." Out of nowhere there appeared a wonderful steed. When he snorted, he pawed the earth with a hoof. So the fool climbed in one ear and out the other, and then out of somewhere there leapt two young men. They asked him, "What do you want, what do you desire?"

"That there be a tent set up here, with a bed in the tent, and nearby be grazing a deer with golden antlers and a golden tail." And in just one minute the tent was set up, there was a bed inside it, on that bed the fool was stretched out, and so handsome he was that you wouldn't recognize him! And in a nearby meadow grazed a deer with golden antlers and a golden tail.

The clever sons-in-law rode and rode but they never saw such a deer and were returning home. They rode up to the tent and saw the marvelous creature. "There's where that deer with the golden horns and golden tail is grazing! Let's go! Whatever it takes, we'll give for it. We'll buy the deer and please our father-in-law."

They rode up and exchanged greetings. The fool asked them, "Where are you going? What are you looking for?"

"Won't you sell us that deer with the golden horns and golden tail?"

"No, it's not for sale. I need it myself."

"Take whatever you want for it," and they would give a thousand, two, or three thousand, even more. The fool didn't want to hear of it; he wouldn't take the money.

"If you need my deer so much, then I'll just take something of little value for it: the finger from one hand." They thought and thought about, but then they agreed. They removed their gloves and cut off the little fingers from one hand. The fool hid the fingers on himself and gave them the deer.

The sons-in-law came home, bringing the golden-horned and golden-tailed deer; the tsar was overjoyed. He didn't know how to address them, where to seat them at the table, or what to treat them to. "You didn't see the fool, did you?" asked the tsar.

"We didn't see hide or hair of him, nor did we hear him at all." But the fool climbed in one ear of his horse and out the other and became just the same fool as he had been. Then he killed his mare, skinned her, and put the skin on himself. He caught all sorts of daws and crows, and magpies and sparrows, and he pinned them in the skin around himself, and he went home. He came into the courtyard and let the birds go in various directions.

His wife, the tsarevna, wept and her sisters laughed at her. "Our husbands brought home the deer with the golden horns and golden tail, and your fool—just look what he's done."

The tsar shouted at the fool, "You are an ignoramus," and then he gave half his tsardom to the clever sons-in-law.

For the third time the tsar summoned his sons-in-law and said, "Well, my amicable sons-in-law, I will give you all my tsardom if you can obtain for me the golden-maned and golden-tailed horse, which I have heard is in a certain tsardom, in a certain land." So the two clever sons-in-law saddled the very finest horses there were, just as before, and rode off on the highway and byway. The tsar sent the fool, too. "Well? You go, too."

So the fool took the very worst nag from the stables, got on her, and rode out after the clever ones. He rode out into the steppe and shouted with a very loud voice, "Sivka-Burka, Magical Steed! Stand before me like a leaf before the grass." Out of somewhere the marvelous horse appeared. It snorted and pawed at the ground with its hoof. So then he climbed in one ear and out the other and became such a handsome young man that you wouldn't have recognized him. And then out of nowhere there appeared two young men who asked him, "What do you want? What do you desire?"

"That a tent should stand here, and in the tent a bed, and nearby a golden-maned and golden-tailed horse should graze."

Immediately a tent was set up and in the tent was a bed and on the bed lay stretched out the fool, while nearby in the meadow there grazed the golden-maned and golden-tailed horse. The clever sons-in-law rode and rode but nowhere did they see a golden-maned and golden-tailed horse. They were returning home and then they rode up to the tent and saw the miraculous creature. "So that's where the golden-maned and golden-tailed horse roams and grazes. Let's go and give whatever it takes, and we'll purchase that golden-maned and golden-tailed horse."

The fool said, "Where are you going? What are you looking for?"

"Sell us that golden-maned and golden-tailed horse."

"No, he's not for sale. I need him myself."

"Whatever you want, we'll give you, but sell him to us." And they offered for the horse, a thousand, then two, three, and even more.

"I won't take even a hundred thousand," said the fool. "But if the horse is so necessary for you, I'll give him to you and take nothing much of value. Let me cut a strip off your back the size of a strap." They thought and thought, they turned it over and over. They really wanted the horse, but they felt sorry for themselves. Finally they decided. They stripped off their clothes, removing their shirts, and the fool cut a strip the size of a strap from their backs. He hid the strips on himself and gave them the horse.

The sons-in-law came home and brought forth the golden-maned and golden-tailed horse. The tsar was overjoyed and didn't know how to address them, or where to seat them at the table, and what to treat them with. But he gave them the other half of his tsardom. And once more the fool climbed in one ear of his horse and out the other, and thus became what he had been before. Then he killed his old nag, skinned her, and put the skin on himself. He caught daws, magpies, crows, and sparrows, and pinned them up in the skin. He went into the courtyard and let the birds go on all sides. They flew off in all directions and broke nearly all the windows. The tsarevna, his wife, wept, and her sisters laughed at her. "Our husbands have brought home the horse with the golden mane and the golden tail, and your fool, just look at him, what an imbecile he is!"

The tsar shouted at the fool, "What an ignoramus! I shall have you shot."

And then the fool asked, "What are you going to reward me with?"

"And why should I reward you, you fool?"

"If the truth be known, I was the one who acquired for you the pig with the golden bristles, the deer with the golden horns, and the horse with the golden mane and tail."

"How can you prove that?" asked the tsar.

The fool said, "Order my brothers-in-law to take off their boots." The sons-in-law began protesting; they didn't want to remove their boots.

"Take off your boots," the tsar insisted. "There's no harm in that." So they took off their boots and the tsar noticed that the little toe was missing from one of their feet.

"Here they are," said the fool. "Now order them to take off their gloves." They took off their gloves, and there was no little finger on one hand. "Here they are," said the fool. "Now order them to take off their shirts." The tsar saw that the truth was coming out, and he ordered them to undress. They removed their shirts and the tsar saw on each of them a strip of skin had been cut out the size of a strap, about a finger or two wide. "Here are the strips!" said the fool, and then he told how it had all happened. The tsar didn't know how to treat him or reward him. He gave him the entire tsardom, and the other sons-in-law who had deceived him—he ordered them shot. The fool went out into the steppe, and shouted in a loud voice, "Heh you, Sivka-Burka, Magical Steed! Stand before me like a leaf before the grass." The horse ran, the ground shook. The fool climbed in one ear and out the other, became a young man and handsome too, returned home and began living happily and prosperously with his tsarevna.

37. Dirty Face

Dorogobuzh area, Kokoshkanskaia province. Taken down from a fifty-year-old peasant, Ustin. Recorded in Ukrainian and Belarusian as well as Russian. SUS 533**.

This merchant had a young daughter. She didn't have a woe in the world. Then she said, "What is woe in the world? I think I'll go and find out what woe in the world really is." So she selected some clothing for herself, and lots of money, and all sorts of provisions—whatever she might need. Then she went out onto the highway. And there stood a pillar, and on the pillar was an inscription that read: "If you go in this direction you'll find riches; if in the second direction, you'll have plenty to eat; if in the third direction, you'll find woe." So she chose the third way. She went through the forest, through swamps, and she ripped her clothing up, and she ate all the food she had with her, her provisions, and she had nothing left at all. She had some money, but there was nowhere to buy anything. But anyway the Lord brought her through and she came out into a clearing where there stood a house. She knocked on the door, but there was no answer. She sat there almost until sundown and then she went up to the back porch and looked, and the door opened. She went into the house. A chest of drawers was standing there. She looked in the chest of drawers and there was some women's clothing, and also some men's. So here every sort of provision was prepared for her. She could eat something—everything. In the light she saw a book lying there—a psalter. Then she said, "I'll go along into the hall" (this was from the entrance). She went into the hall and there stood a coffin with iron bands. There was a man in the coffin, and on it was the inscription: "If only someone will read the psalter over me for three years and if it be a male of my age, he will be my brother. If an older man, then my father. If it be a woman who reads and who is my age, then she shall be my wife, and if she is older, then she will be my sister."

Then in the morning she prayed to God and took the psalter to read. She read it for one year and not a single bird came by, so she read it a second year. . . . Two women were leading a dirty girl to sell her in the town. She asked them, "Where are you going?"

"We are going to town," they said.

"And for what good reason?"

"We are taking this dirty-faced girl to sell her."

"Sell her to me in my boredom. I am so alone here!"

"Please, go ahead and buy her!" they said.

"Would I have to pay a lot for her?"

"Oh, and how much would you give for her?"

"Maybe I'd give you a ruble."

"You can give us thirty rubles, miss." So she took out the money, handed it over to them, and prepared a bath for the girl. She washed her, and dressed her as was appropriate.

So then the young lady had been reading the psalter book for two and a half years now, and she was worn out by it. She said, "I'll lie down, I'll just lie down. I just don't care. I am exhausted. You, dirty face, go out for a walk. Only don't touch this book lying here." She lay down, of course, and rested, and then she went to sleep for just about half a year. She was exhausted after the year and a half. But she had taken precaution to wake up. That's how interested she was in what would happen!

So then the dirty-faced maiden walked and walked. She tried to wake up the mistress, but she wouldn't get up. So she took the book, opened it up, and started tearing pages out of it (because she was illiterate). She tore them out and threw them around. She got up to the very last page and then she tore it out. The iron bands snapped and the coffin opened. A body rose up in it. Then it spoke: "Well, was it you who read the psalter over me?"

"Yes," she said, "it was me."

"So it was really you?"

"Yes, it was me."

Then he asked her for the third time, "Was that you who read?"

"Yes," she said. But this time her mistress got up, although she was silent.

"Well, if it was you, then you must be my bride," he said. "But who is that there?"

"That is my servant!"

"Well, if that is your servant, then ask her how I should thank her."

So the dirty-faced girl came and asked, "What do you need? My groom wants to thank you, so what trinket would you like?"

"Why thank me? I don't need anything at all. I need only three dolls and three plates, and three forks, three knives, and three spoons."

Of course, she prepared something for them to eat and gave them dinner. Then she arranged her dolls around the kitchen workbench, and she placed the knives, forks, and plates out, too. This was the ruler's son on whom a witch had cast her spell (there used to be these wizards in olden times!). She thought for a little time: "Why is it that I don't need anything? I need three dolls, three plates, three knives, three forks, and three spoons! I should have taken a little money for some occasion."

Then having thought and pondered all this, she got up from the table and ran into the kitchen to see what could be done with the dolls. And she told the dolls, "You, little dolls, eat and hear my woe. I went out to find woe. I came out onto the highway, and there stood a pillar, and on the pillar was an inscription that read (but go on eating, dolls, hear my woe): 'If you go in this direction you'll find riches; if in the second direction, you'll know no hunger; if in the third direction, you'll find woe.' (But eat, my dolls, and listen to my woe.) So in fact I went through the forest and the swamps, and I tore all my clothes. I had money, but there was no place to buy anything. I could have starved (but you, my dolls, keep on eating and listen to my woe). I came to a clearing and there stood a house. (You eat, my dolls, and listen to my woe.) I sat there from morning until evening and thought. I wondered what would happen to me—only God alone could know! So then I went up to it, but the doors were all locked. (Eat, my dolls, and listen to my woe.) So I went into the house, and there stood a chest of drawers, and in it hung some clothing, both men's and women's. Of course, I had something to eat, and I rested. (And you, my dolls, eat and listen to my woe.) So then I went down and into a hall. I came into the hall and there stood a coffin with iron bands. (Now you eat, my dolls, and listen to my woe.) There was an inscription on the coffin. I read the inscription, which said that whoever read the psalter for three years over the corpse should be rewarded. (But you eat, my dolls, and listen to my woe.) I read the psalter over it a year. Then these two women were leading this girl with the dirty face to sell her. (But you, dolls, eat and listen to my woe.) They brought her up to me. I asked them, 'Where is God taking you?'

"'Mistress, we are going to sell this dirty-faced girl.'

"'Perhaps you will sell her to me?'

"'If you want to buy her, buy her!' (But you, dolls, eat and hear my woe.)

"'How much are you asking?'

"'Thirty rubles.' (And you, my dolls, eat and listen to my woe.)

"So I paid thirty rubles, and I prepared a bath, and I washed away her village filth, clothed her, and gave her shoes. (You, my dolls, eat and listen to my woe.) Then I read the psalter a year over this corpse, and then two and a half years, before I became exhausted and I lay down to rest. I said, 'Don't take up this book, don't handle it at all.' (You, dolls, eat, and listen to my woe.) After I had slept much or a little time, she took the book and handled it, and she tore out the pages and threw them on the ground. (But you, dolls, eat and listen to my woe.) She got to the last page and ripped it out, too. (And you, dolls, eat and listen to my woe.) Then the iron bands broke, the coffin lid rose up, and the body got up. 'Oh, how soundly I have slept!' he said. 'Yes,' she said, 'you have really slept soundly.'

"He said, 'Why are you sitting there on the divan so silently, mistress?' (But you, dolls, eat and listen to my woe.) Then the body asked, 'Are you the one who read the psalter over me?' 'Yes,' she said. And he asked her three times, and she answered, 'Yes, it was me.' (But you eat, dolls, and listen to my woe.)"

So then the tsar's son came in to her in the kitchen. "So, was it you, then, who read the psalter?"

"It certainly was." And he asked her three times.

"Then you shall be my bride. And you, dirty face, acted improperly. I shall tie you to a horse's tail and let you go into the steppe so that your bones will never be seen in this world again. You can't act according to the rules, you went against the law."

38. Ivan Tsarevich, the Gray Wolf, and Elena the Most Beautiful

Despite the popularity of this tale among the reading public of the twentieth century, it is not a common tale, and its popularity likely derives from the versions of the early nineteenth-century poets, Iazykov and Zhukovskii, in themselves derived from the block-print, *lubki*. This variant was related before 1915 to Azadovskii by N.O. Vinokurova, a famed narrator who lived on the Upper Lena River in Eastern Siberia. SUS 550.

There lived and dwelt Prince Enislav Andreich. And he had three sons: Kolia, Mitia, and Vania, who was youngest of all. So then all these children grew up to be big and they needed to be married. And he had a splendid garden. Saints alive, what a splendid garden it was! But then someone started thieving, started stealing his precious apples. And thus the prince very much regretted spending the labor on the garden, which was still being raided. No guards seemed to be able to catch the thief. So the tsar stopped drinking and eating, and was really grieving over it. And his children also stopped playing.

"Dear papa, why have you become so sad? Dear papa, we had better pursue the thief, but please don't grieve so."

Their father rejoiced that the children promised to guard the garden. This is what the oldest son promised:

"Papa, today it will be my turn. I will go and stand watch in the garden."

So Kolia went out to stand watch in the garden. From evening on he walked and walked around, but he saw no one. He sat down on the soft grass, put his head down, and went to sleep. In the morning his father sent a messenger to summon him back. "Well, did you see anything good out there? Can't you bring some joy to me with something? Did you see the thief perhaps?"

"No, my dear father and parent. I didn't sleep all night, I didn't take my eyes off the tree, and I saw no one."

The tsar thought deeply about this.

In short, the same thing happened with Mitia. He responded with the same experience. And he also had slept all night. And now it was the youngest son's turn to go into the garden. Ivan Tsarevich, the youngest son, set off to stand watch in his father's garden. He was even afraid to sit down, let alone lie down. When he got sleepy, he washed himself with dew from the grass, but he didn't lie down—he kept watch over the garden.

Halfway through the night, or so it seemed to him, something suddenly lit up the garden. It got lighter and lighter in the garden, and then he saw the firebird fly in and perch on the golden apple tree. So Vania quietly stole up and then crawled to the tree stealthily and grabbed the bird by the tail. The bird was powerful and tore away, leaving just a single feather in his hand.

So the youngest son came back to his father, without any messengers, and his father asked him, "Well, my dear Vania, did you perhaps see any of the thieves?"

"Well, my dear father, I didn't manage to catch him quite, but I did find out who is devastating your garden. Father, it isn't an old woman and it isn't an old man. Here, father, I brought a remembrance of the thief for you: it's the firebird."

The tsar rejoiced; all his sadness and grief disappeared. From then on he ate and drank, and he knew no sadness, and the garden ceased being raided. But then one splendid day the tsar had this premonition about this firebird.

"Now, my dear sons, you ought to catch a good horse for yourselves and go out riding, look around the territory, and see whether you can come upon that firebird."

The children thanked their father and set off on the road and way, all three of them. So then the youngest son, rode whether for a long or short time, and he came to a crossroads. On a pillar there was an inscription. Ivan Tsarevich read the inscription:

"Whoever goes to the right shall die. Whoever goes along the middle way will have his horse stolen, and then a gray wolf will devour it. If you go to the left you will yourself be hungry and cold."

So Ivan Tsarevich stood there for a whole hour, thinking. "Which road should I decide to take? I guess I'll take the middle road, even though my horse will be eaten by a gray wolf."

So he went off down the middle road and then out of nowhere a gray wolf was running alongside. "Well, Ivan Tsarevich, get off your good horse. There's no point in fussing about it: you read the inscription on the pillar."

So Ivan Tsarevich was forced to dismount his good horse and then in front of his very eyes the gray wolf tore him into tiny pieces. Ivan Tsarevich was deeply saddened by this and he set off on foot. Sooner or longer, or shorter, he walked until he was tired. He wasn't used to walking on foot and he sat down on the soft grass. He sat there sadly thinking: "What am I going to do now?"

Then suddenly out of nowhere the gray wolf came running up to him. "Well now, Ivan Tsarevich, why are you sitting here feeling so sad?"

"How should I not feel sadness when I've been left without my good horse?"

"Where were you going on your good horse? Tell me the whole truth!" So then he told him everything in detail. "Oh, phooey! You would never have found the firebird in all your lifetime on your good horse! That's why I tore your horse up into bits. I will serve you in faith and truth. You'd have ridden for three years on your good horse to get to the firebird, but I'll get you there in just three hours," the wolf said. "I won't abandon you, Ivan Tsarevich, I will serve you in faith and in truth. Get on my back and hang on tightly."

Well, quicker to say, he ran up to the fortress where the firebird was sitting. "Now, Ivan Tsarevich, listen to the instructions I have for you. Hear me, and don't forget. There's that very high fortress. You get into that fortress and the firebird will be sitting there. This is an excellent time—the sentries are all asleep. But hear me: don't take the cage."

So Ivan Tsarevich climbed into the fortress, and took the firebird, and to his good fortune the sentries were asleep. He took the firebird and then he gazed at the cage. His heart caught fire. "Oh, that's purest gold! Why should I not take it too?"

So he forgot the wolf's instructions. As soon as he touched the cage, a noise resounded: strings were strummed, drums beaten, and all the courtiers jumped into action. They caught Ivan Tsarevich right there. They brought him before Tsar Afron for questioning.

"Who are you and where are you from?"

"I am Ivan Tsarevich."

"Oh, how embarrassing. A tsar's son and he's come thieving. What stupid things to do! Like a simple peasant."

"But your bird was flying into our garden."

"Since I know your father, you should have come to me and asked me in good conscience, and I'd have given you the bird out of respect for your father. But now I'll send out bad reports about you to all the towns and all the Moscows. Although you could do me a favor and I would forgive you. In such and such a town in such and such a land there is a Tsar Kusman with a golden-maned horse. Bring me the horse and I'll give you the firebird and its cage." (Now he's sending him off to be a thief.)

Ivan Tsarevich was very sad as he went to the gray wolf. "I told you not to touch that cage. Why didn't you listen to my orders? Oh well, get on my back." They went up to the fortress where the golden-maned horse was stabled, to Prince Kusman. They rode right up to it. "Well, crawl into the fortress while all the court is asleep. But watch out: don't touch the bridle."

So he entered the fortress and he caught the golden-maned horse. Then Ivan Tsarevich spied the bridle and it was all decorated in diamonds. Oh, how fine it would be to walk that horse in it! He had no sooner touched the bridle when a sound went throughout the fortress. It carried right to the prince, and all the court woke up. They brought Ivan Tsarevich in for questioning.

"Who are you and where are you from?"

"I am Ivan Tsarevich."

"Oh what stupid things you've got yourself into, Ivan Tsarevich! Horse stealing—not even a simple peasant would agree to do that. Well, maybe I can forgive you. Prince Dalmat has this Elena the Beautiful. You bring her to me. I'll give you the horse and the bridle too."

So Ivan Tsarevich was very sad. He set off back to the gray wolf. "Oh, Ivan Tsarevich, you didn't heed my instructions. You make so much trouble for me, the gray wolf, and you just mess everything up."

"Oh, forgive me, forgive me, gray wolf. For God's sake!"

"Alright, you are forgiven. Get on my back. In for a penny, in for a pound!"

They made their way to that prince, that Dalmat. They went up to the Prince Dalmat's fortress and into his garden. And there was no one in the garden but Elena the Beautiful with her nannies and her mummies, who were all strolling around.

"I don't think I'll let you into that garden," said the gray wolf. "I'd better go myself. You had better go on back and somewhere I'll catch up to you."

So Ivan Tsarevich set off back and the gray wolf went into the fortress and into the garden. He wouldn't let the tsarevich go with him. The gray wolf sat down behind a bush and watched. Elena the Beautiful came out with her maids to stroll in the garden. The gray wolf watched her. And then, when she had wandered a little to one side of her nannies, the gray wolf grabbed Elena the Beautiful and threw her onto his back. He caught up with Ivan Tsarevich and Ivan Tsarevich was overjoyed that the gray wolf and Elena the Beautiful had caught up with him.

"Well, get on, Ivan Tsarevich, you act as if there's no one pursuing us."

But Ivan Tsarevich thought to himself. "Why should I part with such a beautiful maiden? Why should I exchange her for a horse?"

The gray wolf asked him, "Why are you so sorrowful now, Ivan Tsarevich?"

"Why should I not be sad, gray wolf? How can I part with such a treasure?"

The gray wolf answered, "But I won't abandon you, I won't be parted from such beauty!"

So they went back to Prince Kusman because they had to deliver Elena the Beautiful to him and he had to take the horse.

"So now, Ivan Tsarevich, we'll hide Elena the Beautiful here somewhere, and I'll turn inside out and then become an Elena the Beautiful, and you can take me and we'll obtain the horse."

So the gray wolf turned round and round and turned into an exact Elena the Beautiful. Ivan Tsarevich led him in and Prince Kusman was overjoyed that they had brought Elena the Beautiful to him. He took her and gave the horse with its bridle to Ivan Tsarevich, and he also thanked him.

So Ivan Tsarevich led the golden-maned horse with its bridle out and he and

Elena the Beautiful got on it and set off. They rode for a long time or a short time.

"What are you thinking about, Ivan Tsarevich?"

"I'm just thinking how sad it will be to part with this treasure, this golden-maned horse. But what would Elena the Beautiful and I ride on?"

"Don't be sad. I'll help you."

So they came to Prince Afron. The gray wolf said, "This time I'll turn myself into a golden-maned horse, and you hide this horse with Elena the Beautiful, and take me to Afron."

So Ivan Tsarevich led him to Prince Afron. When the prince had received the golden-maned horse, he thanked him and gave him the cage together with the firebird. So then he and Elena the Beautiful got on the golden-maned horse together with the firebird and they set off down the road.

They rode for a long or a short time. Then the gray wolf caught up to them.

"So, Ivan Tsarevich, let's say farewell now. You are just about to ride up to the borders of your own land."

So Ivan Tsarevich got off his horse and bowed three times to the earth before the gray wolf. He thanked the gray one with deep respect. And the gray wolf said, "Don't be so quick to say farewell; I'll still be of use to you."

But he thought to himself, "How can you still be of use to me? All my desires have been fulfilled."

They were not far from his homeland. It occurred to him to rest. He set up his tent and they lay down to rest. Ivan Tsarevich fell soundly asleep. Then his brothers rode up to him. They had been riding around different lands looking for the firebird. They made one firm decision: "Let us kill our brother and all his treasures will be ours. Otherwise, if we go to our father, we will have nothing, and he will have the firebird, the golden-maned horse, and Elena the Beautiful."

So having decided this, they killed their brother and tore him into bits. Then they got on the fine horse, took the firebird, and set Elena the Beautiful on the horse. They threatened her, "Don't you say anything to anyone at home!"

Out of nowhere the gray wolf came running to the bits and pieces they had torn up. And some ravens were flying overhead. The gray wolf caught a little raven. "Send this little raven of yours! Let him fetch the living and the dead waters. And if you don't send him, I'll destroy your entire family of ravens!"

So the raven flew away. And the gray wolf started putting together all the pieces of Ivan Tsarevich. The raven flew back with the living and dead water. When the gray wolf sprinkled Ivan Tsarevich with this water, he once more became alive.

"How could I have slept so long?"

"You slept very well," said the gray wolf. "You were completely torn to bits. If I hadn't come along, you'd have remained like that forever. Your own dear brothers did you in and then took away all your treasures. Well, get on my back."

So Ivan Tsarevich got on the wolf's back and they caught up with his brothers and took away his treasures. The gray wolf put Ivan Tsarevich on the golden-maned horse with all his treasures and then he asked Ivan Tsarevich, "Well, shall I devour your brothers, tear them to bits, or will you forgive them?"

"Oh, gray wolf! I will forgive them, but will you also forgive them?"

So he thanked the gray wolf and they parted forever. And Ivan Tsarevich rode off home to his father.

His father was overjoyed when he welcomed Ivan Tsarevich, and they had a great feast, and there was much merrymaking, and then a wedding. And Ivan Tsarevich and Elena the Beautiful were married. He became tsar when the tsar gave him his tsardom for his services.

39. The Rejuvenating Apples

Collected in 1964 from Iosif Fedorovich Kozhin, fifty-five years old, of Olenitsa. The earliest versions of this tale in Russian date to the eighteenth century. Common in Russian, less so in Ukrainian and Belarusian. Quite common throughout Western Europe. SUS 551 + 300A.

There was a poor peasant who had three sons. The oldest had already turned twenty. The parents had become old, and they felt like becoming young, like getting hold of some rejuvenating apples. The father sent the eldest son, who got ready to go:

"Well, father, bless me as I'm off to show myself, to see people!"

"Well, my child, off you go, and God be with you!"

The father and mother blessed him, mother got some provisions together for the journey, and our Egor set off on his journey, on the long road. This son came to a road junction. There were three roads: one to the right, one straight on, and one to the left, and at the junction of the roads there was written: "If you go by the right, it's to die; if you go straight, it's to prison; if you go by the left, you'll find nothing." Well, he had no longing to be killed. . . . Our Egor thought and thought, and set off along the left road.

For a long while, for a short while, soon he encountered a little house that was no little house, but simply a palace surrounded by paling, a fence, and gates. They took him in, he steamed in the bathhouse. The mistress was young. Whether she was a tsaritsa there or a grand duchess is your business, but let's say the tsaritsa had ordered the bathhouse heated. They washed him, fed him, and gave him sweet wine to drink. Then she tricked him: "Now, please, onto the cot!" He plopped down and plunged into a pit.

Whether a year or perhaps two passed in time, no news, and the old man kept withering away, and he sent his second son. Whether long or short, soon the tale is told, not so soon the deed is done. So he rode, and rode up to the same junction. He thought and thought and then he chose the same, he rode out along the same road. And the same thing happened. They gave him something to drink, fed him, and let him steam in the bathhouse. They gave him sweet wine, and then the tsaritsa tricked him: "Now, please, onto the cot!" He plopped onto the bed and rolled off beneath a mountain.

Next came Ivan's turn. "Go, Ivanushko, search for your brothers, and see whether you can't find some such apples, only three apples are needed." So that was that. Ivanushko did not protest, he was glad to be riding out. Our Ivanushko went by the road, the path, and a hare hopped out to meet him. Ivanushko removed his bow from behind his back, arrow to bow, intending to shoot the hare. But the hare said to him in a human voice: "Don't shoot, Ivanushko, I'll be of use to you!" So that was that. Our Ivanushko didn't shoot. "Off you run," he said, "If you're of use, fine; if you're of no use, it's also alright."

He went further by the road, the path. Near or far, low or high, a bear happened to meet him. Ivan wanted to shoot him, but the bear spoke with a human voice. "Don't shoot, Ivanushko, I'll be of use to you."

So then our Ivan came out to the blue sea. And there on the sand beside the sea lay a pike, its mouth gaping, it was intending to die. "Oh, Ivanushko, peasant's son, throw me back into the sea; I'll be of use to you."

Well, Ivanushko threw the pike into the sea, and set off further. He came up to a hut on cock's legs, with a rooster's head. "Hut, little hut! Turn with your rear to the woods, with your front to me, so that I, a youth, might come in and then leave." The hut turned. Ivan the Peasant's Son entered the hut, and in that hut was an old woman.

"Phoo, phoo, it smells of a Russian soul! Whosoever are you, young lad, where would you be from?"

"And you, granny, first give your guest a drink, feed him, and put him to sleep. Then ask." So granny heated up the bathhouse and steamed our Ivan, then put him to bed, and began to question him.

"So now, granny, and now so. . . . I am Ivan the Peasant's Son. I have set out to seek my brothers and to look for some apples for my father in order to rejuvenate him."

"Oh, Ivanushko, Ivanushko! You will have to endure much misfortune. Well, sleep on. Morning is wiser than evening." In the morning the granny gave him a drink, fed him, and outfitted him for the road. "Here's a little ball," she says, "Wherever the little ball rolls, you follow after it!"

So Ivan set out after the ball. The ball rolled and Ivan went on and came to the junction where his brothers had been. Our Ivan thought a great deal and set off where it was written: "Go to the right and you'll find death." And he came into a town. He stopped at an old granny's who lived alone on the edge of town and he saw how the people all go around sad, and he asked the old granny, the one who lives alone on the edge of town, "Why is it so sad in your town? The people go about so sad and despondent."

"Oh, don't speak of it, my child. Each day," she says, "we pay a tribute. A serpent takes a maiden, a beautiful maiden, and tonight it is the turn of the tsar's daughter. Therefore, my child, we have such mourning. And the tsar says 'Whoever saves my daughter . . . ' and to that one he promises half the kingdom and his daughter in marriage."

Our Ivan ate and listened to the granny, then set off for the palace, to the tsar. "Forge me," he said, "three cudgels of ten, fifteen, and twenty poods." Well, at the tsar's a deed is soon done, smiths forged him the first cudgel. Our Ivan took that cudgel, his arms didn't even feel its weight. "And now forge me one of fifteen poods." They forged him a cudgel of fifteen poods. "Oh, this one's just fine. Now forge one of twenty and one of twenty-five poods." They were added to his others. He inquired where they took away the girls, went there earlier, and hid among the bushes. The time came, they brought the girl and left her on shore alone. But our Ivan didn't show himself, he sat. The morning star appeared, a serpent of three heads flies up, smoke pours from its nostrils, fire flies from its ears.

"Phoo, phoo, breakfast is ready!"

Our Ivan jumps out. "Won't you choke on that breakfast?"

"Ooh, a second for starters!" the serpent shouted. It flew at our Ivan, but Ivan was there with his cudgel, the fifteen-pood one. They fought and fought, he chopped off one head and planted his cudgel in the ground. Grasp, grab, but his arms couldn't reach the second cudgel, and the serpent was overcoming Ivan. Suddenly, out of nowhere, the hare came dragging the cudgel to within arm's reach. Again they fought and fought, he chopped off the second head and shoved the second cudgel into the ground. His hands couldn't reach the third and the serpent was overcoming him. Well now, the hare has little strength, and out of nowhere came the bear. The bear dragged the third cudgel to him, and Ivan over-came the serpent. But the tsarevna was barely alive. He went up to that tsarevna and kissed her sugary lips. "Well, let's go to your father. What is promised we'll let him deliver."

They rode, they came to town. The tsar was joyful, delighted, with a happy little feast for the wedding. They played out the wedding, entertained everyone. But Ivan kept thinking just one thing, that he had to ride back to the junction, to take the second road. He left his young bride there and set off alone. He came again to the junction. He thought and thought: "Where to now?" He set off where it was written: "Go straight and you'll land in jail." He walked and walked and walked—near or far, low or high—he came up to a little hut on a cock's legs, with a rooster's head.

"Little hut, little hut, turn with your rear to the forest, with your front to me so that I, a good lad, can go in and come out again."

The little hut turned. Ivan the Peasant's Son went in and in that hut sat an old woman. "Phoo, phoo, phoo," she said, "it smells of a Russian soul. Whose are you, good lad, and where would you be from?"

"And you, granny, first of all, give a guest a drink, feed him, put him to bed, and then you ask."

Well, granny heated up the bathhouse, steamed our Ivan the Peasant's Son, put him to bed and then began to question him. "This is this, granny, and that is that. I am Ivan, the son of a peasant, and I've come to search for my brothers, and for apples for my father to rejuvenate him. I went to the right and found a wife, but now I don't know where to go."

"Sleep," she said, "morning is wiser than the evening." In the morning the old woman directed him: "Go and come to a tower. Don't go close, don't show yourself, and when night falls, you'll get through the paling." And she gave him an amulet. "Put this on that paling and then you'll see how to go in and come out."

So our Ivan set out further on his journey. He came to the town. He looked from afar, he couldn't walk round it, ride round, or jump over it. He waited for darkest night. He approached the paling, hung the amulet on the paling, stretched and pulled, and at that spot a passageway was formed. And granny had instructed him: "When you come back, don't forget to take it back."

He made his way to the passage. And you won't believe the plants there: apples trees, pears, and plums, like in the garden of Paradise. Ivan walked about the garden, and saw three apple trees. He picked one apple from each tree and then went back by the same path and road. He removed the amulet from the paling and the hole was gone, the gates were gone.

So he came back to the junction. "Well, now I'll go by this road, by the left." He came to a tower, the beauty there gave him a drink, fed him, and led him to a bed to sleep, she wanted to put him down. He grabbed her by her white hand and thrust her head onto the bed, and the mistress of the bed rolled ahead, underground. He dragged back the bed, and there was a pit. And you could hear the mistress shouting: "Ivan the Peasant's Son, don't destroy us! Take those keys there and unlock the door!"

He collected the keys and opened the door in the cellar, and there were more or less twenty people and his two brothers among them. He led them out, Ivan set them free. "Well, what shall you do with the mistress? Now it's up to you."

"Hack off her head!"

"Hack it off, chop it off, and send her house up in smoke." That's what they did. Then they all departed, each on his own way.

"Well, brothers, you go with me now." They came to the junction. Now which way? They can't go home. And he says nothing of the apples. "So let's go that way," he said, "to the tsar's. My wife is there." The tsar entertained them, equipped them for the road, as many goods as they could grasp, and they went home to their father and mother. They put a wedding together, it isn't said whether mother and father were rejuvenated or not. Probably they became young on account of the apples. And that's all.

My speech wasn't, as they say, like pouring out melted butter—one word from another, but now it has all come out. So much about tsar and serpent, and what of the hero? Ivan the Russian peasant comes out smelling like a rose!

40. The Three Sons-in-Law

Told by P.N. Bol'shedvorskaia, who lived on the Kulenga River in Eastern Siberia. SUS 552A + 302.

Not in an unknown tsardom, not in an unknown land, but in fact in the one in which we live, there lived and dwelt this ruler. And the ruler had three daughters and one son. They called him Ivan Tsarevich. When the ruler was dying, he instructed his son, "Dearest son, listen and you will know to whom you are to marry my daughters, your sisters."

"I am listening, papa."

Suddenly a storm came up, with the most terrible earthquakes. An eagle flew up, struck itself against the earth, turned into a young man, and went into the palace. "Good health, Ivan Tsarevich!"

"Come in, young man. Why has God brought you here?"

"I heard that you have an eligible bride. Do you wish to marry off your oldest sister?"

"I'd like to know to whom I'm marrying her."

"In three years you'll find out."

The tsar hardly had time to brew the beer and make the wine. They were married and off to bed!

In the morning Ivan Tsarevich got up to congratulate the newlyweds, to see how they were. "So that's it. I somehow didn't think that the eagle would carry off my sister! Now how will I marry off my middle sister?"

A terrible storm arose and there was an earthquake, and up flew a falcon. It struck itself against the earth, became a young man, and went into the palace. "I wish you good health, Ivan Tsarevich. I have heard that you have a sister and I wish to take her in marriage."

"I'd like to know to whom I am giving her."

"You'll find out in three years."

Well, the tsar hardly had time to brew the beer and make the wine. They were married and off to bed! In the morning Ivan Tsarevich got up, but the falcon had carried off his middle sister. And soon he had given the third to a raven.

Three years passed, and Ivan Tsarevich remembered that he needed to visit his sisters, to search them out. So he set off to search for them. He saw a woman warrior approaching, Maria Tsarevna, the Princess with the Pouch. They rode together to do battle, but then they agreed to conditions: "If I knock you off your horse, you will live in my tsardom; if you knock me off mine, I'll live in yours."

So they rode at each other, she came out first. At her attack he didn't move on his horse. When he knocked her off her horse, she fell, and his horse stepped onto her breast. Then she got up and they became acquainted. She said to him, "First let's go to my tsardom as I need to put things in order there."

So when they arrived, she paid visits to her regiments. She left him with the keys to twelve rooms, but to a thirteenth there was no key. It was tied with a little string and sealed. He walked and walked. "What was this? He could walk through all the rooms except that one. He went there and saw Kashshei* the Immortal hanging on twelve chains.

"Why are you here?"

"I was sewing your wife some slippers and I tricked her. She put me in here and desires to starve me to death. Oh, Ivan Tsarevich, bring me a glass of water, give me a drink. You will live two lifetimes."

He drank a glass of water and flexed his muscles—three chains flew off him. "No, Ivan Tsarevich, bring me a second glass of water, and you'll live three lifetimes." He drank. When he flexed himself, the rest of the chains flew off and off flew Kashshei the Immortal.

He went out on the upper balcony and saw all the regiments in mourning. He asked why this was so, why the soldiers were in mourning. "Because you let Kashshei the Immortal free. He has carried away Maria Tsarevna, the Princess with the Pouch."

"Beyond how many towns and how many lands?"

"What does it matter? Whoever goes there loses his head."

But he rode off to look for her. First he went to his sisters. He came out on a fine little porch. He whistled and shouted a command: "Sivka-Burka, magic horse. Stand before me like a leaf before the grass." And Sivka came running, Mother Moist Earth trembled, fire came out of its backside, from its nostrils a pillar of smoke, coals flying from its ears. He began putting on the saddle blankets, and on top of the blankets a Circassian saddle. "I shall stand like steel, sit in my Circassian saddle, and whip my horse's sides." His horse became angry, flew right off the earth, higher even than the forest, but lower than the clouds it went.

He rode near or far, low or high, then there stood a palace in the steppe. His sister sat on the balcony and she shouted out to him. She met her brother and kissed his sweet lips, she led him to the table, laid with a tablecloth. Mead drinks were ready.

"Well, my dear brother, drink, feast, be merry. But soon my kind husband and your kind brother-in-law will come flying here. We shall have to hide you or he'll eat you."

Her husband came flying up, threw himself on the ground, and became a good young man. He entered the palace. "Good health, kind wife. Who is visiting you? Unseen and unheard, but Russian bones have come by themselves!"

"You have flown by way of Russian towns and through Siberian lands, and you have picked up that Russian scent, you can safely say."

---

*Kashshei (also known as Koshchei or Kashchei) is usually regarded as a personification of death and depicted as a skeleton.

"No, tell me who is here. It's your brother and my kind brother-in-law. And I know where he's going."

So Ivan Tsarevich came out and they celebrated and they drank and they made merry. They spent the night. And then he set off to visit the second sister. Again, a palace stood in the steppe. His sister sat on the balcony. She caught sight of him and shouted. She met her brother, kissed his sweet lips, led him to the table, laid with a tablecloth, with mead drinks. "Well, my own dear brother! Drink, feast, and be merry. Soon my kind husband and your kind brother-in-law will arrive. We shall have to hide you or he'll eat you."

Her husband came, threw himself upon the ground, became a good young man, and entered the palace. "Good health, kind wife! Who is visiting you? Unseen and unheard, but Russian bones have come by themselves!"

"Oh, that's because you have flown by way of Russian towns and through Siberian lands, and you have picked up that Russian scent, you can safely say."

"Tell me who is here. It's your brother, my kind brother-in-law. And I know where he is going."

He came out, they drank and they made merry. They spent the night and in the morning he set off for the third sister.

Once more a palace stood in the steppe. His sister was sitting on the balcony. She caught sight of him and shouted. She met her brother. She kissed his sweet lips, led him to the table, laid with a tablecloth and with mead drinks. "Well, dear brother, drink, feast, and be merry. Soon my kind husband and your kind brother-in-law will arrive. We will have to hide you or he'll eat you."

Her husband arrived, threw himself upon the ground, turned himself into a good young man, and entered the palace. "Unseen and unheard, but Russian bones have come by themselves. Tell me who is visiting you?"

"Oh, you have been flying through Russian towns and Siberian lands, and you have picked up that Russian scent."

"I know who it is. It is your own brother, my kind brother-in-law. And I know where he is going." So he came out and they drank, feasted, made merry. Then he spent the night with his youngest sister. He was ready to go on when his two brothers-in-law, the eagle and the falcon, came. "Leave us something to look for you with."

To the oldest he left a sword. "If I should be ill, this sword will become dull, and if I should die, it will blacken." He gave the falcon a ring in the same way: "If I should be ill, this ring with become dull, and if I should die, it will blacken." To the third he gave half a glass of water. "If I should be ill, it will be full, but if I die, it will turn to blood."

Then he rode off. When he had arrived at Kashshei the Immortal's, there were lions standing at the gates of the palace. Maria Tsarevna met him. She shouted, "Nannies, mummies, servants! Take those lions a chunk of meat so they won't walk on the steps."

She gave the lions the chunks and then set off with him. "Well," he thought, "I'll carry you away."

Kashshei the Immortal came flying home and he asked his servants where Maria Tsarevna was. "Ivan Tsarevich has carried her off," they said.

"Go and ask my good horse when we need to set off in pursuit."

The horse said, "Do your plowing, plant your grain, brew the beer, bake the pies, and we'll still catch up to them halfway there."

So Kashshei the Immortal drank a barrel of wine, nibbled on half a beef, slept such that the ground shook. All this passed, then he set out in pursuit. They caught up to them on the road, he took Maria Tsarevna, and said to Ivan Tsarevich, "Here's one glass of water, Ivan Tsarevich, and you still have two lives to live."

But he went after her again in the same tracks. And the same thing happened. The horse told him to wait, but they caught up to them. Kashshei took a little barrel with him, opened it, and put Ivan Tsarevich in it. Then he let it go out to sea.

Soon the eagle flew to the falcon. The brothers-in-law were becoming uneasy. "What's happening with you?"

"The ring has started to blacken."

They flew to the youngest one. "What's happening with you?"

"There is blood in the glass."

They flew off looking for him, through the mountains and valleys, over the broad steppes, the forests and the seas. Then they saw a little barrel floating in the sea. The eagle made the falcon pick it up. "Fly up higher, then go down and pick up that little barrel. Let it down so that it breaks open and we'll see what's in it."

The falcon said, "No, eagle, you are stronger. You lift it and knock it open."

The eagle soared above him, then lifted up the little barrel, and put it down. When they had broken it open, Ivan Tsarevich lay inside. The eagle said, "I'll put him together again. Falcon, you fly for the living water, and you, raven, for the dead water."

When he had barely managed to put Ivan together again, they brought the water. The eagle got him all together and then sprinkled him with the dead, then the living waters. He said, "Come ride with us."

"No, I must search for her. Although I'm now on foot, I'll go."

"But here's what you have to ask. Let Maria Marevna ask Kashshei how to fly across fiery rivers and how he got his horse from Yega Yegishna,* and let her ask him where his death is to be found."

So once more he came to the palace of Maria Marevna. She met him, she rejoiced, and she hid him. Kashshei came flying in, drank a barrel of wine, nibbled on half a beef. Having eaten and drunk, he lay down to sleep. She sat down on the bed beside him.

"Oh, my dear friend, now that you have stolen Ivan Tsarevich from me, tell me: where is your death?"

---

*Also Baba Yaga, the Russian witch.

"My death is in the horns of a bull." She made them bring that bull in and she decorated its horns with precious stones, and she wept, sitting beside it. Kashshei saw it. "Oh, you woman, foolish woman! A woman's hair is long, but her wit is short. Here is where my death is: in the sea, in the ocean, there stands an oak, and beneath the oak is a trunk, and in the trunk is a hare, and in the hare is a duck, and in the duck is an egg, and there is my death."

"Oh, my dear friend, now I am calm. And where did you acquire your horse?"

"I acquired this horse from Yega Yegishna. She has his brother who is much more lively than mine. You would have to be clever to get him."

"What did you have to do to get your horse?"

"I had to herd twelve mares and these mares are her daughters. Finally, it's hard to get away from her."

"And how did you get away from her?"

"I have this kerchief. I wave it and out comes a fiery river. She can't cross the fiery river. Then you also have to count poppy seeds."

"Are there many?"

"Three zillion forty thousand poppy seeds in all."

Then she said, "Is that all there is to tell about it?"

"That's all."

"Then sleep, my friend."

He fell asleep, and as he slept, the earth shook. She took his kerchief and gave it to Ivan Tsarevich.

"Go to Yega Yegishna, most cunning of all, with one bony leg." She baked him some tasty snacks to have along the way. As he walked, he ate them, and finally he sat down hungry. He was sitting beside a path and he saw a bear. He aimed at her to shoot her for food.

"Don't shoot me, Ivan Tsarevich, I'll be useful to you in the future. Sit on that old rotten log. Gnaw it and you'll be satisfied.

He sat down and gnawed it, and his hunger was somewhat eased. He went through the steppe and he saw some wasps with their honeycombs. He wanted to eat some honey, but a wasp said to him, "Don't ruin me, Ivan Tsarevich. Swallow some spit instead and you'll be satisfied. Then in the future I'll be of use to you."

He walked on, he walked along the sea, and there lay a pike. He decided to eat it. "Don't eat me. Push me back into the sea with your foot. I'll be useful to you later on."

He walked along, and he came to a palace surrounded by pickets, and on every picket was a head.

Only one picket was without a head. "Well," he said, "there'll be no getting by that for this good lad either! One picket without a head means that will be my own unruly one!"

So then he came to a hut in which the Yegishna was lying, most cunning of all, she of the bony leg, with one leg in one corner and the other in the other corner. She raised her head and asked, "Where are you going, young man, Ivan Tsarevich?"

"So, you old whore. You haven't fed me or given me a drink and yet you question me."

She raised her head, opened the cellar, got on her knees, and got some cake. She wet it with a little cabbage soup and fed him. But then she went back to asking him questions, where was he going?

"I have heard, Yega Yegishna, that you have a warhorse."

"I have much work: herding my mares and counting poppy seeds."

In the morning she got up and fed him, and then she drove out the twelve mares. The mares tore off for the forest. They simply raised their tails and were gone. He went over to the hemp barn, wove himself a knout, put it beneath his head, and went to sleep. There was nothing more to be done as the mares had gone away.

He slept very soundly until the bear came running to him and slapped him on a cheek. "Get up, Ivan Tsarevich. Take charge of the mares now for your service to me." So she led them to him and he controlled them with his knout so that they could scarcely run. He herded them into the yard and Yega Yegishna came out.

"For shame, for shame, Ivan Tsarevich! You didn't feed them but let them roam more than usual."

She gave him something to eat and then she went and took three brass rods, three iron rods, and three lead rods. While he was eating, she went into the yard, and he listened to everything. She was lambasting them. "Oh, you so-and-sos! Don't you know that your mother hasn't eaten Russian flesh in such a long time? And you couldn't even run away from him."

"But there was no way for us to run away in the forest. There were beasts everywhere tormenting us." The next day they were herded out again. Once more they raised their tails and disappeared into the forest. And he went up to the hemp and lay down to sleep. When it was time to go home, a wasp flew up and stung him on the cheek.

"Ivan Tsarevich, get up! That's for your service to us." So he led them back, he herded them. And he fed them better than the day before. He herded them home. "For shame, for shame, Ivan Tsarevich! Yesterday you fed them well, but today still better, such that they are scarcely alive."

So then he said, "I myself have had enough of roaming."

But she went and got three iron rods, three brass rods, and three lead rods. And she began letting them have it, "Oh, you so-and-sos! You know I haven't eaten Russian flesh for so long, and you couldn't run away from him."

The next day he herded them out again. And again they raised their tails and disappeared into the sea. He went to the hemp and lay down to sleep. Then the sea became agitated and the pike hit him in the forehead with its tail. "Get up, Ivan Tsarevich! Take this for your service to me." The pike led the mares to him and he let them have it with the knout more than before. They were hardly alive as he drove them home. He drove them into the yard and Yega Yegishna came out.

"Well, Ivan Tsarevich, you are no herder! You are killing my mares."

But he drove them in, and she gave him something to eat, and then she took three iron rods and three rods of brass and three lead rods, and did she let them have it! "Oh, you so-and-sos! Don't you know that your mother has not eaten Russian flesh for a long time? Why couldn't you run away from him? Alright. Ivan Tsarevich, you have one more task. Now you must count these poppy seeds, and then you may take a horse for your work. But he's a poor horse; he's in the root cellar."

He took the poppy seeds and tossed them from hand to hand. "Three zillion forty thousand."

"You guessed it." Then at night she curried her mares, just as smooth as silk, and then she led out that warhorse. "Choose any one," she said.

He took the warhorse and led it off. But it was frightening to mount it. "Well," it said, "let me go, Ivan Tsarevich. I'll roam for three dawns and three dusks."

So Ivan Tsarevich set off on foot. When the horse had finished roaming, he ran up and said, "Let me go back, Ivan Tsarevich, to my old mistress. When I arrive, she'll be overjoyed. And when she is so happy, she'll put my warhorse armor on me and tie me to a white oak pillar with a silver ring. Then she'll sit down with her daughters to drink tea and I'll break loose and run away."

He came running up to her and whinnied. The mistress was overjoyed, made her daughters bring out the warrior's saddle and all the warrior's armor. Then she tied him to a white oak pillar with a silver ring. They all sat down to drink tea and admire him. "So, Ivan Tsarevich, it was never for you to possess my horse."

Then the horse whinnied, stamped his legs, and set off to catch up to Ivan Tsarevich. She got into her mortar and chased after him with her pestle. The horse got there first. "Well, Ivan Tsarevich, a rumor is spreading throughout the land that Yega Yegishna is after you. Wave your kerchief."

He waved the kerchief and a fiery river appeared. He managed to get away. "Now, where, Ivan Tsarevich? What is our destination?"

"We are headed for the ocean-sea. In the sea and in the ocean there is an oak, and beneath that oak is a trunk, and in the trunk is a hare, and in the hare a duck, and in the duck an egg. We must obtain that egg."

By the time he had managed to say all that, they had appeared there. The good horse tore out the oak and Ivan Tsarevich broke open the trunk. But the long ears ran away into the forest. Suddenly out of nowhere appeared the bear—she had caught it and she brought it to him. So he killed the hare and took out the duck. He slaughtered the duck and took out the egg. He started rinsing it in the sea, but it slipped away. So the pike brought it back to him.

He wrapped it in his kerchief and said, "Now, take me to such and such a place."

He hadn't had time to turn about when he was there. Maria Marevna, the Princess with the Pouch, met him. There was no point in their talking at length, so they got on the horse and rode away. Kashshei the Immortal came flying after them.

"Where is Maria Marevna, the Princess with the Pouch?"

"Ivan Tsarevich has carried her away."

"Oh, those sons of bitches, those brothers-in-law have brought him to life. Go and ask my good horse when I need to set off to catch up to them."

His good horse said, "Quickly, get on and we'll see what we can do."

They chased after them, and the horse said, "Well, Ivan Tsareavich, only a little time remains. Kashshei the Immortal is nearby. It is time to hoist the egg."

As Kashshei came nearer, Ivan Tsarevich raised the egg, and Kashshei began to die. One brother horse said to the other, "Wait, stop!" But Ivan Tsarevich took the egg, got up, and crushed it. Kashshei fell from his horse. So Ivan Tsarevich burned him, scattered the ashes, it all went up in smoke, and our tale resolved itself with that.

41. The Everlasting Piece

Recorded from a certain Kalmykov in the village of Logachevka, Buzulukskii district. Only one other version from Siberia, is known in East Slavic. SUS 613D*.

A soldier was leaving the service. He walked all day until evening. Night came. The soldier climbed up into a tall oak. Soon he saw an old man beneath the oak with hair as white as the moon and a big white beard. The old man went up to the oak where the soldier was sitting and sounded a horn. Out jumped twelve wolves. The old man took a loaf from his bag, divided it into thirteen parts, and gave one piece to each wolf. The remaining piece he gave to the soldier. The soldier took the piece of bread and began eating it greedily. But however much he ate, the piece was not diminished. At dawn the old man once more sounded his horn and the wolves ran away. The soldier climbed down from the oak and walked on. Soon he came to a village and he asked a rich peasant to spend the night. The soldier went into the hut, sat down at the table, and decided to eat after his journey. He took out the piece of bread and ate. The peasant saw that the piece was not diminished. "Soldier, sell me that piece," said the peasant.

"I won't sell it," answered the soldier, "it's an everlasting piece; with it I'll never be in want; I'll always be full."

The peasant began questioning the soldier as to where he had acquired the everlasting piece, and the soldier told him. Having spent the night, the soldier left.

Then that evening the rich peasant went into the forest, climbed up into the oak, and waited for the old man. Soon the old man came, went up to the oak, and sounded his horn. The twelve wolves came running. The old man drew a loaf out of his bag, divided it into eleven parts, and gave them to the wolves. For one wolf there was no bread. The old man pointed at the peasant with his finger. The wolf leapt into the oak and tore up the rich peasant.

42. Little Boy Green

A variant of the legend "Eruslan Lazarevich," common in Russian and Belarusian and somewhat known in Ukrainian. Boasting at a feast is common cause for a command to the hero to go into action in both the folktale and the folk epic. SUS 650B*.

This took place in the city in Kiev at the prince's, at Vladimir's, where he was holding a feast. It was a most honorable feast and it was a joyful feast. All at the feast drank too much and all at the feast ate too much and all at the feast did begin boasting. The foolish man boasted of his good wife, the wise man boasted of his golden treasure, but there sat Little Boy Green, and he boasted of his fine horse. So then Prince Vladimir spoke, "If you have such a horse, I will assign you a task. You are to ride far, far away through the open steppes, to the meadows along the seas, and bring me from there a man who knows the tsar's thought, the ruler's thought."

So everyone went home from the happy feast to their own homes, but the little boy went home with his reckless head hung lower than his mighty shoulders. His mother and father met him and spoke these words to him, "Oh, our dear child, our beloved child, everyone has come away from the feast happy but you are walking along unhappy, with your head hung low."

And he spoke such words to them as these: "How am I supposed to be happy, mother and father, when the tsar has put upon me a very heavy, a very difficult task? He has ordered me to ride far, far away through the open steppes, to the meadows along the seas, and bring from there a man who knows the tsar's thought, the ruler's thought."

He saddled and bridled his good horse and rode off, did Little Boy Green. He rode one full day, then another, and finally a third. His horse became tired and wanted to eat, but they came upon a great military force, a defeated army. So many men had been killed that a black raven could not encircle them in a full day, nor could a fine young man ride round them on his horse. He went among the troops and found one living person, and he asked that living person, "Who fought this army and slaughtered it?"

"It was Ivan, the Russian warrior."

"And why did he fight and kill?"

"He fought that army and destroyed it because he needs to get married in our king's land and he would take the king's daughter by force because she will not marry him and her father won't give her away. So he came for her and beat that army." So the boy went away from that army and he rode a full day, then a second day, and finally a third, and he came upon a great military force, a defeated army. A black raven could not encircle them in a full day, nor could a fine young man ride round them on his horse—so many had been killed!

Once more he found a single living man and he asked that living person, "Who has defeated this army and killed everybody?" The living person said that it was Ivan the Russian warrior who had defeated the army and killed everybody. "And why did he fight and kill everyone?"

"He fought and killed everyone because he has to take our king's beautiful daughter by force because she won't go of her own free will and her father won't give her away."

So then Little Boy Green rode on for a full day, then a second, finally a third. He rode upon a great army, a vast force that had been defeated, and in the steppe he saw a white canvas tent standing there, and there was a pillar next to the tent, and there was a gold ring by the pillar with a fine horse attached, and a white banner unfurled. The horse had been given spring wheat. Little Boy Green got down from his good horse and let it go to the feed bag, and it pushed away Ivan the warrior's horse and the little boy's horse munched the spring wheat and Ivan the Russian warrior's horse had to wander over the green meadows nibbling the green grass.

The little boy went into the white tent and in the white tent Ivan the Russian warrior was sleeping a warrior's sleep. Little Boy Green saw a white oak barrel with some strong drink, with vodka, and in the barrel a gold goblet was floating upside down and there was an inscription on it: "This goblet is one and a half buckets." He decanted the first goblet and drank to the strong drink. He decanted a second goblet and drank to health, then he decanted a third and drank to foolishness. And now the little child was drunk, and he smashed up that white oak barrel with the strong drink, with the vodka, and he smashed the golden goblet and then he ruined the white oak tables with their various sweet dishes and more drinks, and he smashed the icon of the Savior, and he extinguished the candles of fine wax, and then he tumbled off to sleep.

Then Ivan the Russian warrior woke up and he was absolutely amazed: "What sort of idiot has ridden up here? He's let his horse in to my horse's fodder, opened up my white oak barrel with strong drink in it, smashed my golden goblet, ruined the white oak tables with the various sweet dishes and more drinks. He smashed the icons of the Savior and extinguished the fine wax candles." And he raised his sharp sword and got ready to cut off his reckless head, thinking that "It's the same thing to kill someone sleeping as the dead. He won't get out of my hands in any case."

But just then Little Boy Green woke up and sat on the bed. "Oh, Ivan the Russian warrior, I am now your guest. Give me something to drink!"

In response Ivan said to him, "You are not worth my wasting my drink on."

"How can that be? I am your guest!"

"You are no more a guest here than a bone from the open steppe. You're just worth nothing to a warrior."

And in reply he spoke these words, "You may be a warrior in your tent, but you are a useless hound in the steppe." So now Ivan saw that an unforeseen misfortune had arrived at his white tent. He took a goblet and ladled some water and then he took it to the little boy to drink. And when they had both drunk, the two warriors went into the open steppe to test each other's strength.

Little Boy Green set off at a fair pace and Ivan the Russian warrior at a full gallop, and they rode apart about a verst, and then they rode at each other and struck each other, but they didn't wound each other seriously, and so they rode apart two versts and rode at each other and struck each other again, but they didn't wound each other seriously. So the third time they rode three versts apart and then they came at each other, and Little Boy Green knocked the Russian warrior right out of his saddle and his horse pinned Ivan the Russian warrior down by his armor. So then Little Boy Green spoke these words, "God aided me to pin Ivan the Russian warrior with this dull lance." So then he asked him, "Which do you want, death or life?"

"Oh, little boy, formerly we had no quarrel with you and in the future there shall be none." Then Little Boy Green got down from his horse and took Ivan the Russian warrior by his white hands and raised him up on his shaky legs, kissed him on his sugary lips, and they called each other brothers. Little Boy Green was called the big brother, and Ivan the Russian warrior was the little brother, and then they rode to the white canvas tent, and there they began drinking and eating and making merry.

So Ivan the Russian warrior went to the king to get married and he invited his brother Little Boy Green to go along, and the king received them as good folk and they spent whole days feasting. Then Ivan the Russian warrior got married at the court of that king and Little Boy Green asked the king, "Would you happen to know someone who knows the thoughts of the tsar, his royal thoughts?"

The king found such a person beneath the red banner, and this person knew the tsar's thoughts. So then Little Boy Green took this person with him and conducted him to Prince Vladimir.

Then Prince Vladimir said, "You have served me in a great task and earned my friendship. For that friendship you will now take some towns and suburbs, and various districts." He did not stint himself the towns or suburbs or various districts.

And Prince Vladimir had a beautiful daughter, a princess, and so he said to Vladimir, "Give her to me in marriage, and then at your very end, give me your position!"

So then Prince Vladimir agreed to give his daughter to Little Boy Green and at his death his kingdom to his son-in-law.

43. The Fiddler in Hell

From Tver province. Related to the medieval Novgorod tale about the *posadnik* (mayor), Shchil. Common in Russian and Belarusian. SUS 677** + 761A*.

There lived and dwelt a peasant who had three sons. He lived richly, he collected two pots full of money and one of them he buried in the threshing barn, the other beneath the gates. Then this peasant died, not having told anybody about the money. Once there was a festival in the village and a fiddler was walking about when he suddenly fell right through the ground. He fell through the earth and found himself in hell right at the very spot where the rich peasant was being tormented. "Good health to you, my friend," said the fiddler.

The peasant answered him, "Bad luck to you for falling into this place. This is hell, and I am sitting here in hell."

"So, uncle, what did you do to get yourself here?"

"I'm here on account of my money. I had a whole lot of money, I gave nothing to beggars, and I buried two pots full in the ground. And now I'm being tormented, beaten with sticks, torn with claws."

"Could that happen to me? Maybe they're going to torment me too!"

"Go and sit behind the chimney for three years without eating, and you'll remain whole."

So the fiddler hid himself behind the chimney, but then the devils came and started beating the rich merchant and repeating, "This is for you, moneybags! You got masses and masses of money, but you didn't know how to hide it very well; you buried it where it's hard to watch over it. People are always riding over it at those gates and the horses' hooves pound our heads, while in the threshing barn we're always being thrashed with those flails."

As soon as the devils had gone away, the peasant said to the fiddler: "If you get out of here, tell my children to take the money. One pot is buried by the gates and the other beneath the threshing floor, and make sure they give it to the poor."

Just then a horde of devils came running in and they asked the rich peasant, "Why does this place stink of Russians here?"

The peasant said, "It's because you've been wandering about Russia and you picked up the scent there."

"What nonsense!" They started searching and they found the fiddler and shouted "Ho, ho, ho! There's a fiddler here!"

They dragged him from the stove and made him play on the fiddle. He played for three years, although it seemed like only three days to him. He was exhausted and said, "How amazing! Sometimes I've been playing and I've broken all my strings in one evening, but now I've been playing for three days and they are still good. Blessed be the Lord!" No sooner had he spoken when all the strings burst. "Well, brothers," said the fiddler, "see for yourself. The strings have broken and I've nothing to play on."

"Wait," said one of the unclean ones. "I've two bunches of strings and I'll bring them to you." He ran and got them. The fiddler took the strings, stretched them out, and once more said, "Blessed be the Lord!" and both bunches burst. "No, brothers, your strings are of no use to me. I have my own at home. If you let me, I'll go get them."

But the devils wouldn't release him. "You're not getting away," they said.

"If you don't believe it, then send someone from among you to accompany me." So the devils chose one of their own and sent him with the fiddler.

The fiddler came to the village. In a distant hut he heard a wedding being celebrated. "Let's go to the wedding!"

"Alright, let's."

So they went into the hut and there they recognized the fiddler and asked him, "Where have you spent these past three years, brother?"

"I've been in the other world."

They sat for a while, they walked about for a while, and then the devil called the fiddler. "It's time to go."

But the fiddler said, "Wait just a little while. Let me play my fiddle a bit, to amuse the young folk." So they all sat there until the cocks crowed and then the devil disappeared and the fiddler told the rich peasant's sons, "Your father orders you to take the money. There is one pot buried next to the gates and one in the threshing barn. And you are to give all this money to the beggars." So they dug up both pots and gave the money away to the beggarly brotherhood, but the more they gave away, the more there was.

So then they took the pots to the crossroads. Whoever passed by could take as much money as he could grasp in his hand, but still there was no diminishing of the money. They sent a petition to the ruler reporting that in a certain town there was this twisting road about fifty versts long, but if it were straightened, it would be about five versts. The ruler gave orders to build a straight bridge. So they built the straight bridge of five versts and with that they used up both pots of money.

At that time some maiden gave birth to a son and abandoned him in his infancy. For three years this little boy neither ate nor drank, but the angel of God always walked beside him. Then the little boy came to the bridge and said, "Oh, what a fine bridge. Let God grant the kingdom of heaven to the one whose money built this bridge." The Lord heard this prayer and ordered his angels to let the rich peasant out of the inferno of Hell.

44. The Snow Maiden

First published in 1845 by M.A. Maksimovich, who has added much to the story to make it more "literary." This is a common tale among Russians but it is less common among Ukrainians and Belarusians. Thompson lists only versions in Lithuanian and Serbian in addition to the Russian. SUS 703*.

There lived and dwelt this peasant Ivan and he had a wife Maria, but they didn't have any children. Ivan and Maria lived in love and harmony; and so they grew old but they still didn't have any children. They were greatly saddened by this and only looking at the children of other folks brought them any comfort. But there was nothing to be done! So, apparently, that was what the Lord had allotted them. Everything on earth happens not by our will but by the Lord's design.

Then once when winter had come and much new snow had fallen up to the knee, all the little children went outside to play and our old folks sat up next to the window to watch them. The children ran, they raced about, and they started making a snow woman* out of the snow. Ivan and Maria watched silently, deep in thought. Suddenly Ivan started laughing and said, "They should come over here, wife, and make a snow woman for us."

A cheerful moment apparently also struck Maria at that same time. "Well," she said, "let's go and have some fun in our old age. Only why do you need to make a snow woman? Neither of us needs that. Instead, we'd better make a child out of snow, since God didn't give us a live one."

"That's right, that's right . . . ," said Ivan, and he took his hat and went off into the garden with the old woman.

And in fact they did start in making a doll out of snow. They put the body together with the arms, then the legs, and on top they put a little round heap of snow and smoothed a head out of it.

"God help you!" said someone, walking by.

"Thank you, we are most grateful!" answered Ivan. "God's help is always good in anything," he added.

"And what are you making there?"

"Well, you see," answered Ivan. "A snow maiden," Maria said, laughing.

And they sculpted a little nose and beard (!) and then two little pits on the face, and just as Ivan had finished sketching a mouth, a warm breath of air came out of it! Ivan quickly raised a hand and looked as the little pits on the face began bulging out and out of them little blue eyes began peering, and then the raspberry lips started smiling. "Oh my gosh," said Ivan, "is this some sort of a ghost?" And he crossed himself. But the doll bowed her head to him, as if she were alive, and began moving her arms and legs in the snow, just like a newborn infant in diapers.

"Oh, Ivan, Ivan!" Maria shouted, shivering from delight. "The Lord has given us a child," and she rushed to embrace Snow Maiden and then all the snow tumbled off Snow Maiden like the shell from an egg, and in Maria's arms there was a real, live girl. "Oh you are my very dear Snow Maiden!" the old woman exclaimed, hugging her long-desired and unexpected child, and they all ran into the hut. After seeing such a miracle Ivan came to his senses with great difficulty, but Maria was wild with joy.

Now, Snow Maiden grew not by the days but by the hours, and each day was better than the last. Ivan and Maria could not have been more overjoyed with her. And everything about the house was joyful. The girls from the village were constantly in and out, they amused themselves and always selected granny's daughter to play, just like a doll, and they talked with her, they sang her songs, they played all sorts of games,

---

*The figure made from snow is invariably a "snow woman" in Russian.

and they taught her to do all the things they did. And Snow Maiden was very clever. She took note of everything and took everything in. And over that winter she became just like a maiden of very nearly thirteen years, and she understood everything, and she could talk about everything, and with such a sweet voice, that they all listened, spellbound. And she was so kind, so obedient, and so outgoing to all. And she was as white as snow, her eyes were like forget-me-nots, her blond hair came down to her waist, but she didn't have any red on her cheeks, as if she didn't have any real blood in her body. . . . Despite this she was most attractive and pretty as a picture. And when she would ever start playing, she was so considerate and pleasant that the heart was overjoyed. People just couldn't admire Snow Maiden enough.

The old woman Maria could find no fault with her. "Ivan," she said to her husband, "God has given us this joy for our old age! And my heartsick sadness has passed!"

But Ivan said, "It is a thanksgiving to the Lord! Here joy is not eternal, nor is sadness without end. . . ."

Winter passed. The spring sun began playing about in the heavens and it started warming the earth. In the melted spots the grass began to show green, and the lark began to sing. The beautiful maidens began to gather in the processions through the villages, singing:

> *Beautiful Spring!*
> *How did you come here?*
> *How did you arrive?*
> *On the plow, on the harrow!*

But the Snow Maiden became somehow bored. "What is the matter with you, my child?" Maria said so often to her, drawing her close. "You are not ill, are you? You are so unhappy, so out of sorts, has some evil man cast a spell on you?"

But the Snow Maiden would always answer, "Never mind, granny, I am healthy. . . ."

Then one day the spring with those beautiful days drove away the last snow. Gardens and meadows burst into bloom, the nightingale started singing, as did the other birds, and everything in God's world became more alive and more cheerful. And Snow Maiden, the dear, began to pine away even more and more. She avoided her girlfriends and kept hiding from the sun in the shade, just like a lily of the valley beneath a tree. She only liked it splashing in the icy spring beneath the green willow tree. Snow Maiden stayed in the shade and cold, or even better, the frequent showers. In a shower or in twilight she would become happier. And then once a big gray cloud moved over them and spattered them with big hailstones. Snow Maiden was as overjoyed by this as another would have been by precious pearls. When the sun once more began to bake and the hail had turned into water, Snow Maiden broke into tears over it, as if she herself would begin weeping like a sister weeps for her very own brother.

Then the end of spring came and St. John's Day arrived.* The village girls gathered for their walk to the groves and they dropped in to take Snow Maiden with them. They went up to granny Maria. "Let her, let Snow Maiden come with us!"

Maria was afraid to let her go and Snow Maiden did not want to go, but there was just no way of talking them out of it. Besides, Maria thought, it would be good for her Snow Maiden to get out and enjoy herself. So she dressed her, kissed her and said, "Now go, my child, have a good time with your girlfriends! And you, girls, see that you look after my Snow Maiden. She's my heart's own joy, as you know."

"Good, good!" they all shouted happily, and they grabbed Snow Maiden and went off in a group to the grove.

There they wove wreaths for themselves, braiding in bunches of flowers, and they sang their sad and glad songs. Snow Maiden would not be parted from them.

When the sun was going down, the girls made a bonfire from grasses and brush, lit it and got in a long line one behind the other in their wreaths. They placed Snow Maiden at the end of the line. "Look," they said, "when we start running, you come running behind us, and don't fall behind." So drawing out their long Midsummer song, they leapt through the fire.

Suddenly behind them there was a great noise and pitiful groaning. "Oh, ah . . . !" They looked around in fright, but there was no one there. They looked at each other and saw that Snow Maiden wasn't there. "She is probably hiding, the naughty thing," they said, and they ran off to look for her. But nowhere could they find her. They shouted, called out, but there was no response at all. "Where could she have got to?" the girls said. "It is obvious that she ran home," they said and went back into the village. But Snow Maiden wasn't there either.

They looked for her all the next day, and they looked for her the third. They covered the entire grove—bush by bush, sapling by sapling—but Snow Maiden was still not there, any trace of her was lost.

For a long time Ivan and Maria were bitter and they wept for their Snow Maiden. Every day for a long time the poor old woman went into the thickets to look for her, and she always called out for her just like a hapless cuckoo.

"Ai, ai, little Snow Maiden! Oh, oh, my little dove!"

Frequently it seemed to her that she heard Snow Maiden's voice calling back to her: "Oh . . ." but there was no sign of Snow Maiden.

What had happened to Snow Maiden? Had a fierce beast carried her off into the deep forest, or a cruel bird carried her off to the deep blue sea? When Snow Maiden ran off after her girlfriends and leapt into the fire, she had suddenly been carried upward by a light breath of air, wrapped in a thin little cloud . . . and she flew up into the ethereal heights.

---

*June, Midsummer. An important holiday in rural Russia. The village girls went to birch groves to cut a birch tree to decorate in the village.

45. The Armless Maiden

Recorded in Orlov province. A very common tale, known throughout Europe and apparently related to the tale of the maid with the chopped-off arms in the "Thousand and One Nights." SUS 706.

In a certain tsardom, not in our country, there lived a rich merchant; and he had two children, a son and a daughter. Both the father and the mother died. The brother said to his sister, "Come, sister, let's leave this town. I'll open a shop and we'll start trading, and I'll rent some lodgings for you, and that's how we'll live." So then they set off for another province, and they came to that province, and the brother registered himself, and rented a shop with fine goods. The brother decided to get married, and so he got married. He took a sorceress as his wife.

The brother got ready to start trading in his shop, and he ordered his sister, "Sister, you look after the house." His wife found what he ordered his sister to do offensive. To get back at him she broke up all the furniture, and when he returned, she was waiting for him. She met him and said, "See what kind of sister you have, she has broken up all the furniture in the pantry!"

"Oh well," he answered, "that happens from time to time."

So then the next day he set off for the shop, and he said goodbye to his wife and sister, and he said to his sister, "Sister, please look after the house as best you can."

So then his wife watched for a time when her husband wasn't there and she went into the stables and cut off the head of his favorite horse with his saber. She stood on the porch and waited for him. "Look what sort of sister you have," she said. "She's cut off the head of your favorite horse!"

"Let the dogs eat what's for dogs!" her husband answered.

On the third day her husband went once more to the shop. He said goodbye and spoke to his sister, "Please look after the mistress so that she doesn't hurt herself or the baby, if she should happen to give birth to one." When she gave birth to a baby, she cut off its head. Then she sat there and wept over the baby.

So then in came the husband. "Oh, what a sister you have! I hardly had managed to give birth to the child, when she came and cut off its head with a saber." The husband said nothing; he burst into tears and left them immediately.

Night came. At precisely midnight he got up and said, "Dear sister! Get ready. You and I are going to liturgy."

"But brother, my dear," she said, "I don't think there's any holiday now."

"No, sister, there is a holiday. Let's go."

"It's early," she said, "too early to be going, brother."

"It's just like you young maidens, to take time over getting ready. Hurry and get dressed," he said. So his dear sister began getting ready. But she couldn't get ready because her hands fell off. Her brother came and said, "Faster, sister, get dressed faster."

"But it's still early, brother!"

"No, sister, its not early—it's time."

Finally the sister was ready. They sat down in the carriage and rode off to liturgy. Whether they rode for a long time or short, they came to a forest. The sister said, "What forest is this?" He answered, "This is a hedge around the church." Their carriage got caught up in some brush. The brother said, "Get out, sister, and untangle the carriage."

"Oh brother, my dear, I can't, I'll soil my dress."

"But, sister, I'll buy you a new dress, better than that one."

So she got out of the carriage and started untangling it, but her brother chopped off her arms at the elbow, whipped up each of his horses and rode away from her.

So the sister was left there, weeping tears, and then she set out through the forest. But no matter how much she walked, whether for a long time or a short time, she walked about the forest, she got all scratched up but could find no sign that would lead her out of the forest. Then there was this little path that went out and led her out of the forest, after several years. So then she got out of this forest and came to a trading town and she went up to the window of the richest merchant to beg for alms. This merchant had a son, an only son, and the apple of his father's eye, and he fell in love with the beggar girl. He said, "Papa and mama, marry me!"

"And to whom should we marry you?"

"To that beggar girl."

"Oh, my friend, can it be than in this city of merchants there are no fine daughters?"

"Marry me to her! And if you won't marry me to her, I'll do something to myself," he said. So though they were ashamed of their favorite son, they gathered all the merchants together, and the clergy, and they asked them to judge: should he be married to the beggar girl or not? Then the priests said, "It appears that it is his fate, that it is God's will that he marry the beggar girl."

So then they lived together for a year, and then another, and then he set off for another province where her brother, you see, was still sitting in his shop. As he was saying farewell, he asked, "Papa and mama, do not abandon my wife! When she is giving birth, write me the news immediately, at that very instant." As soon as their son had left, after two or three months his wife gave birth to a child up to its elbows all gold and both sides studded with many stars, while on his forehead was a crescent moon and opposite his heart a beautiful sun. When the grandparents looked at the child, they were delighted and set out to write their dear son about it immediately. They sent an old man with this express note.

But the sorceress daughter-in-law found out about it and called in the old man. "Come here, old man, and rest."

"No, I have no time, they are sending me in haste."

"Oh, come, old man, rest and dine."

So she sat him down to eat, and took his letter pouch away, took out the note, read it, tore it into tiny bits, and wrote another saying that "Your wife gave birth, and it was half dog and half bear, which she conceived living in the forest with the beasts."

Then the old man went to the merchant's son and gave him the letter. He read it and burst into tears. Then he wrote a letter saying not to touch anything until he returned home. "I'll come and find out what sort of child has been born."

So then the sorceress called the old man in again. "Come and sit and rest," she said. So he came in and again she enchanted him, took the note away from him, read it, tore it up, and wrote another saying that when the letter was received, she was to be chased away from the court.

The old man delivered the letter, the father and mother read it and grieved. "Why is it that he has brought us this loss? We married him off, and then, apparently, he no longer needs this wife!" They weren't so sorry for the wife as they were for the infant. They blessed both her and the infant, tied it to its mother's breast, and sent them from the courtyard.

So she set off, weeping bitter tears, and she walked for a long time or a short time through the steppe. There was no forest, nor was there a village. Then she came up to a hollow, and she felt like having something to drink. She glanced to the right and there was a well. So even though she wanted something to drink, she was afraid to bend over for fear of dropping the infant. But then it seemed to her that water was somehow closer to her. She bent over and the child fell out of its wrapping and into the well. She walked around the well and cried. How should she get the child out of the well? An old man came up and said, "Why are you crying, maid?"

"Why should I not cry? I bent over the well to get a drink of water and my infant fell into it."

"Go, bend over, and take him out."

"No, little father, I have no arms—just these stumps."

"Go, bend over, and take the infant!" So she went up to the well, stretched out her arms, and the lord favored her—her whole arms appeared. She bent over, got her child, and began praying to God in all four directions.

When she had prayed to God, she set off and came to the court where her brother and husband were, and she begged to spend the night. Her husband said, "Brother, let that beggar woman in. Beggar women can tell folktales and preambles to folktales, and they can also utter some real truths."

Then the bride said, "We have no place for her to sleep; it's already tight here."

"No, brother, let her in, please. I love how beggar women tell tales and stories more than anything else." So they let her in. She sat down on the stove with her infant.

Her husband said, "Well, my dear, tell us a little tale now, at least tell us a yarn."

She said, "I don't know how to tell tales or stories, but I do know how to tell the truth. Listen," she said, "and I'll tell you some truth, ladies and gentlemen." And she began to talk. 'In a certain tsardom, but not in our country, there lived a rich merchant and he had two children, a son and a daughter. The father and mother both died. The brother said to his sister, 'let's leave this town, sister.' And so they came to another province. The brother got himself situated. He rented a shop with fine goods. Then it occurred to him to get married. He got married, he married a sorceress. . . ."

At this point the brother's wife blurted out, "This bitch has just come here to bore us!"

But her husband said, "Go on, go on, little mother. I just love stories like this one."

"So then the brother got ready to trade in his shop and he said to his sister, 'Sister, you look after things at home!' And his wife was offended that he gave such an order to his sister. And in her anger she broke up all the furniture. . . ."

And when she had told how he had taken her to liturgy, then chopped off her arms, and how she had given birth, how her brother's wife had summoned the old man, the sorceress again shouted out, "Now she's talking plain gibberish!"

But her husband said, "Brother, make your wife be quiet. This is really a fine story!" So then she went on talking and told how her husband had written that they should keep the child until he arrived home.

Here her brother's wife shouted out, "What nonsense she prates!" Then she told how she had come to this house, and her brother's wife again shouted, "See how the bitch babbles on!" Then her husband said, "Brother, tell her to shut up. Why does she keep interrupting?" So then she told them how they had let her into the hut and how she had told them the true story. She pointed to them and said, "You are my husband, you are my brother, and you are my sister-in-law."

Then her husband jumped up to her on the stove and said, "Oh, my friend, show me the child. Is it true what my father and mother wrote?" They took the baby and took off the blankets and underclothes—and the whole room lit up! "It's true, it's the truth what you've told in the story. This is my wife and this is my son—golden up to his elbow, with stars scattered on his sides, a crescent moon on his forehead, and opposite his heart a beautiful sun."

Then her brother took his very best mare out of the stables, tied his wife to her tail, and let her loose in the steppe. She galloped away and returned with just one braid. The rest of her was scattered in the steppe. Then they harnessed a troika of horses and set off home to his father and mother, and they began living and prospering. I was there and drank mead and wine and it flowed through my moustache and none got into my mouth.

Legends

There is no general agreement about classifying legends and the Russians now follow the ATU system, which puts some legendary tales in other categories. I have followed this ATU/SUS system, although tales involving historical figures are occasionally therefore found in other groupings (see nos. 65, 75, 77, 78, 85). Many legends in the Russian tradition involve ecclesiastical themes: Christ and his apostles, saints, stories about hermits or seekers after a better life. There are also a number about truly impressive sinners! Some legends are mere anecdotes (nos. 51 and 53). One included in this collection is a novella in its own right (no. 58). This latter tale, "The Skomorokh Vavilo," portrays the pagan *skomorokh* in a very sympathetic light. For more on the legends, see Haney, *CRF*, vol. 5.

46. The Poor Widow

There are a number of closely related tales in Ukrainian and Belarusian but this is the only one in Russian. A number of versions have been recorded in the Balkans and one from the Saami. SUS 750B****.

It was a long time ago—Christ still wandered about the earth with his twelve apostles. Once they were walking along, as if they were just simple people—you couldn't recognize that this was Christ with the apostles. So they entered this village and asked a rich peasant to take them in for the night. But the rich peasant wouldn't admit them. "There's a widow who lives over there. She takes in beggars. Go to her place."

So they asked the widow to let them spend the night, and the widow was poor, she was really destitute! She didn't have a thing. There was only a small crust of bread and about a fistful of flour. She had a cow but the cow was dry and she still hadn't calved. "I have only a little hut," she said, "and there's no room for you all to lie down."

"Never mind, we'll manage to settle in somehow." So the widow took the travelers in but she didn't know what to feed them with.

"What shall I feed you with, my dears?" said the widow. "All that I have is this small crust of bread and about a fistful of flour. And the cow still hasn't delivered her calf and there's no milk. I keep waiting for her to calve. Don't think badly of me for my hospitality."

"Oh, granny," the Savior said, "do not be troubled. We shall be satisfied. Give us what there is and we shall eat the loaf. Everything, granny, is from God. . . ."

So they sat down at the table and began having supper, and with that one little loaf all were satisfied and there were several chunks left over. "So, granny, you said that you had nothing to feed us with," said the Savior. "Just look at how we are satisfied and there are chunks of bread left over. Granny, everything comes from God."

So Christ and His apostles spent the night at the poor widow's. In the morning the widow said to the girl, "Go and scrape the flour in the granary bin. Maybe there'll be a fistful for some *bliny* to feed the travelers. The girl went and brought flour, a full clay pot. The old woman couldn't believe her eyes, she couldn't fathom where so much had come from. There'd been only a tiny bit but now there was enough for *bliny*, and the girl then said, "There's enough left in the granary bin for next time!"

So the widow baked some *bliny* and served them to the Savior and apostles: "Eat, my dear ones, what God has sent. . . ."

"Thanks, granny, thanks."

So they ate and took their leave of the poor widow and then they set off on their journey. They were going along the road when off to the side of them on a little knoll sat a gray wolf. He bowed to Christ and asked him for something to eat. "Lord," he howled, "I want to eat!"

"Go to that poor widow and eat her cow and calf," said the Savior.

The apostles were doubtful of this and said, "Lord, why did you tell him to kill that old widow's cow? She received us so warmly and fed us. She was so happy waiting for the cow's calf. She would have milk, food for her whole family."

"This is how it should be," the Savior replied, and they walked on. The wolf ran and killed the poor widow's cow. When the old woman found out about it, she sighed and said, "God gave, and God took away. All is His holy will."

So then as Christ and His apostles were walking along they met on the road a barrel of money rolling along. The Savior said, "Barrel, roll up to that rich peasant's courtyard."

And the apostles were once more surprised. "Lord, it would be better to order that barrel to roll into the poor widow's courtyard. The rich man already has so much."

"But that is the way it's supposed to be," answered the Savior Himself, and they set off further. So the barrel of money rolled straight to the rich merchant's courtyard. The peasant took it, hid all the money, but he was still dissatisfied.

"If only the Lord Himself had sent so much!" he thought to himself. Christ and the apostles just went on and on.

But then at midday it was really hot and the apostles wanted to drink something. "Jesus, we want to drink," they said to the Savior.

"Go along," the Savior said, "Further along this road, you'll find a well, and there you can drink as much as you like."

So the apostles set out and they walked and walked and they saw a well. They glanced into it. In it there was such muck and filth—toads, snakes, and frogs—every sort of vile thing. Without drinking, the apostles hurried back to the Savior. "Did you get some water?" Christ asked them.

"No, Lord."

"Why not?"

"You pointed out this well to us, Savior, but it's really horrible even to look in." Christ didn't reply to them and they just went on down the road.

They walked and they walked and then the apostles again said to the Savior, "Jesus, we want to drink something."

The Savior sent them in the opposite direction. "Over there you'll see this well; go there and drink." So the apostles went to the other well and it was really fine! Wondrous trees were growing there, and birds from paradise were singing as if they'd never left there. The apostles drank their fill, and the water was so pure, cold, and sweet, and then they returned. The Savior asked them, "Why were you away so long?"

"We just drank our fill and then stayed there for three minutes," they answered.

"But that wasn't three minutes; that was three whole years," said the Lord. "It will be as bad for the rich peasant in the other world as it was at the first well, and for the poor widow it will be as good in the other world as it was at the second well."

47. The Serpent

Recorded in the village of Maega, Vologda province, in about 1890. This is the only version known in the Russian tradition. The tale reflects a common belief about serpents taking milk from spiteful women, cows, and so on. SUS 751B.

In a certain village there was this married peasant and his old mother lived with him. He and his bride didn't like the old woman and often cursed her and scolded her. Once on Christ's very day they left the liturgy and sat down at the table to break the fast. For some reason the son became angry with his mother and said, "I would rather see a serpent at the table than you!"

A little while later his wife went to the cellar for some milk and saw on a vat an enormous serpent. As soon as the serpent saw the woman, it leapt on her and wrapped itself around her neck. No amount of effort could tear that serpent away from the woman's neck. And so the serpent lived with her, nourished by milk from her breast. If the woman went to the bathhouse to wash, the serpent crawled off her and perched on the ceiling near the doors, and when the woman left, it would once more leap upon her neck. And so the woman died with that serpent.

48. The Hermit and the Devil

This is an unusual combination of two tale types. The tale was originally collected by Vladimir Dal'. The wreathing (holding a wreath or crown) over the heads of the bride and groom is an important part of the Orthodox wedding ceremony. According to tradition, Judas hanged himself from an aspen tree; it is thus the gallows tree of Russian peasant lore. SUS 753* + 839A.

There was this hermit who had prayed thirty years to God. Devils often ran by him. One of them, a cripple, fell far behind his comrades. The hermit stopped the crippled one and said, "Where do you devils run?"

The crippled one said, "We run to the tsar for dinner."

"When you're running back, bring me a saltcellar from the tsar. Then I'll believe that you dine there." He brought him the saltcellar. The hermit then said, "When next you run by to the tsar's for dinner, stop by here and return the saltcellar." In the meantime, he wrote on the saltcellar: "You, oh Tsar, are eating without grace. Devils are eating with you."

The lord tsar ordered that all at the table stand and bless themselves. After that the devils came running in to dinner but they couldn't approach the table that had been blessed. It burned them, so they ran back and started asking the crippled one. "You stayed behind with that hermit. You probably talked to him and told him that we go to dinner, didn't you?"

He said, "I just brought him a single saltcellar from the tsar." They started beating up that crippled devil for that, for telling anything to the hermit. So in revenge the crippled one built a smithy opposite the hermit's cell and started turning old men into young men in his forge.

The hermit saw this and wanted to be transformed himself. He went to the smithy, to the little devil, and he said, "Would it be possible to turn me into a young man?"

"Of course," said the crippled one, and he threw the hermit into the fire. He cooked him and cooked him and turned him into a youth. Then he placed him before a mirror. "Look now, is this you?"

The hermit just couldn't look at himself enough. Then he liked the idea of getting married. The crippled one presented him with a bride. Neither could gaze at the other enough, neither could stop admiring the other! So it was time to go to the wreathing and the little devil said to the hermit, "Look, when they are about to place the wreaths over you, don't cross yourself."

The hermit thought, "Why should I not cross myself when they are holding the wreaths over us?" He disobeyed and crossed himself, and when he had crossed himself, he saw an aspen bent over them, and from it hung a noose. If he hadn't crossed himself, he would have been hanging from that tree, but God led him away from eternal destruction.

49. The Proud Rich Man

This tale is based on the Gospel text, 2 Corinthians 8:9, but its theme has circulated in the written tradition from the seventeenth century in a variety of forms, all of which are dissimilar from this one, however. SUS 757.

I don't know where, but there lived and dwelt this *pan*, so rich that he measured rubles by the boxful, gold in quarters, and he didn't even know the number of copper coins he possessed. He had so many serfs, so much land and forests and hayfields that it's impossible to take them all in, you could never count them all up. But, oh my! What a misfortune befell him! From a rich man he became poorer than all us sinners. And for what reason? Because he forgot God and worked for the Unclean Force only. It used to be that good folk heard the matins in God's church but at his place they played music and he squatted down, warming himself. He never went to church and didn't know why people go there. But once he thought of going there to take a look at what was occurring, and so on the Lord's holiday the *pan* set off with his wife to attend liturgy. All Orthodox Christians were praying to God, but the *pan* and his wife stood by themselves, looked around at all sides, and chuckled. The deacon began reading "And the rich shall become poor and hunger after . . ." and then the *pan* ran up to him, tore the book out of his hands, and grabbed at his bald spot.

"How do you dare, you fool, to say such words in my presence? Is it possible that I will become poor and crave something? Oh, you coffin chaser, just you wait. I'll show you how to laugh at me! If you ever dare to speak such words, I'll banish you to the stables and you won't forget it for a month of Sundays. Give me some ink!" The deacon was more dead than alive but with all his strength he got the inkwell and a pen. And the priest at the altar hid himself and shook, the poor thing, as if he had a fever. The deacon brought the inkwell and the pen. "Look here, you ignoramus," said the *pan*, "what I write down here will not be read during my lifetime nor after." Suddenly a storm came up with lightning constantly flashing, and with thunder more and more strong, and then with every strike—and this be the Lord's will—all who were in the church fell down onto the floor. Only the *pan* and his wife stood there chuckling.

The verger came running in: "Oh, misfortune!" he said, "A gentleman's house is on fire." They tried to put out the fire but couldn't, you just can't argue with God. Everything burned up completely, as if this nobleman's house had never existed. But the rich man just spat on that and soon there appeared new rooms even better than the others. But since that time whenever the deacon began to read in the church and got to that place where it is written that the rich shall become poor and hunger after this and that, every time, no matter what happened, it would begin to thunder throughout the heavens.

So then once the *pan* decided to go hunting. People got together, about two hundred it must have been, and about the same number of dogs. They mounted their horses, sounded the horns, and galloped into the forest. There they hunted down hares and foxes and wolves and bears, when suddenly a splendid deer ran out, such as you've never seen before. The *pan* struck out after the deer. His horse flew like a bird, but the animal was still faster.

He was close! He was catching up! But then it was gone. Midday had already passed and the sun was already low. It was already getting dark but he kept on chasing after the splendid animal. Deepest night fell, and no matter what, you couldn't seen anything in the forest. Finally our *pan* stopped his horse. What was to be done? He sounded his horn to see whether his other hunters would respond. He listened carefully but nothing could be heard except the noise of the wood. He sounded the horn a second and a third time, but no one responded. Just the far-off forest called out, "*tru, tru, tru*" and so the *pan* rode on further.

It seemed to him that a village was nearby, that horses were neighing and dogs were barking. But he still couldn't see any dwellings—just the earth and the sky and the wavy spruces swirling in their crowns. Already his horse had stopped and was barely moving its legs and he himself could scarcely sit on the steed. Suddenly a light flashed. Once more the *pan* blew his trumpet, hoping that if there were people there, they would come out to meet him. It happened as he wished. About twelve men jumped out of the trees, met him, but not as a *pan* should be met. One grabbed him by the back of the head, so that the *pan* fell to the earth like a sheaf of grain. When he came to, he was completely naked, just as when his mother had given birth to him. He wanted to turn over, but there was no way! His hands were bound tightly. He looked about, and around a fire sat bandits and with them their ataman in a red *kaftan*. "Why is it, you sons-of-bitches, that you don't cover up the landlord," he shouted at his lads. Immediately about ten of them rushed at the *pan* and began to "entertain" him with their rods. "That's enough," the ataman bellowed again. "Take him to Wolf Gulch and tie him up to a tree. He's no use to us any more, but he will be helpful to the wolves: they'll have a tasty morsel for breakfast!"

They grabbed the *pan* by the legs and dragged him into Wolf Gulch and tied him firmly to a spruce. The *pan* stood there for an entire day, then he stood a second full day, and he had no strength to endure any more. Inside he was burning with fire, his mouth was dried out, and his soul was nearly ready to part from his body. But he never thought of confessing. Only one thing was on his mind: "As soon as I get home, I'll get my peasants together and go and kill these cursed wood bandits."

But not far from Wolf Gulch in a clearing a herd was grazing. At midday it was quite hot so the shepherds drove their sheep and cows into the gulch to rest just beneath that very spruce, there to weave *lapti*. How surprised they were! There beneath the spruce stood a naked man with his hands and feet tied. "Heh Gritsko!" said one shepherd. "That man is dressed as his mother bore him! And he's been beaten all over, he's covered in blood. Let's go and untie him. Perhaps he's still alive."

"Why not? Let's untie him," said the other. With these words they went up to the spruce and untied the ropes.

The *pan* was silent, but as soon as they had taken the ropes off him, then he began to shout: "Oh lads, take off your cloak and give it to me. Though your dress is poor, it's still better than being naked. Then take me to the landlord's manor. Don't you know, you useless chaps, who I am? I am your landlord."

"Oh, do you see, Gritsko, what sort of bird this is? It's our landlord. Ha, ha, ha! But there's no denying it: he does look like the landlord. Such a fine *kaftan* he's wearing, all covered in that fine pattern. No, man, God knows you, knows what sort of man you are. I'll tell you that our *pan* lives in the best of quarters and dresses in gold clothing."

"Oh, you louts, how do you dare insult your master? I'll get you, just wait until I get home." And the *pan* rushed at them, intending to drag off the cloak of one of the shepherds.

"So that's what you're like," said a shepherd, "we untie your bound hands and feet and you come running to bite. This is for you, you tramp, this is for you, you bandit!" And they started letting the *pan* have it with their whips. The *pan* ran from them but they were after him. Whack! Whack! Whack! Whack! Then the *pan* ran to one side as fast as his legs would take him. He ran for a long time, until he ran out of strength and fell down stretched out on the road. Fortunately some elders were coming his way. One of them took pity on him and gave him his garment. The *pan* wrapped it round him and set off with them, surviving on alms. Along the road he told them everything that had happened to him. He said he would pay back those who had insulted him and reward the elders because they had given him clothing and taken him with them. The elders were already preparing new baskets to fill with the *pan*'s money. When they came into the village, they went right into the lord's chambers. The servants shouted at them, "Where are you going? Get out of here!"

The *pan* said, "Don't you see, you fools, that I'm your lord!"

"What lord? We had this *pan*, but he disappeared."

"You lie, you beasts! I am the *pan*!"

"Well, brother, just wait a moment."

The *pan* was about to start fighting when suddenly they grabbed him by the arms and led him to his wife. When she heard that such an abused and ragged person was her husband, she grew angry and ordered that he be whipped and buried alive in the earth. In the church once more they sang the fateful words. And the rich shall become poor and hunger after . . . and after the reading by the deacon this time no more claps of thunder were heard.

50. The Bigamist

Cherepovetskii area, village of Bol'shoi Dvor, Dmitrievsk district. From a peasant woman, Avdotia Gladysheva, 1900. This is a rare tale in East Slavic and it is not common in Europe. SUS 767*.

In a certain town there lived an officer with his wife. Once they sent him on business to another town for a long period of time. Living there he became acquainted with a widow who had a beautiful daughter. The girl was most pleasing to him and he started courting her, and he tried to persuade her to begin a love affair with him. She wouldn't agree. Then he began trying to get her to marry him. Before she would marry him, she asked whether he wasn't already married. He answered in the negative. She obliged him to swear to it. He swore in the name of some three saints. The wedding took place in one of the town churches. The young people visited her mother. The whole business affair was ended and the officer had to return home. He took his leave of his mother-in-law, took his young wife, and rode away. On the way he confessed to her that he was married. The young thing burst into tears and reproached him for his deceit. He offered her a condition: if she wanted to ride on with him, he would call her his servant. Despite the insult, she agreed out of her love. They arrive home. His legal wife greeted the officer joyfully, but she was amazed when she saw the young girl from far away. He explained that on the road, he had hired this servant, and the second wife confirmed this. And so they began living.

But then the first wife began noticing that between her husband and the servant there were some relations and she became really jealous. The guesses turned into the obvious when the servant one bright and beautiful day gave birth to a child. After this the situation for all of them became impossible. Soon the first wife found an undetectable means to poison her rival's child. When the infant already lay in his little coffin, he started foaming at the mouth. His mother, that is, the second wife, took this foam from his lips and put it in a tea cup. They buried the child the very same day. The first wife poured herself some tea in the tea cup containing the foam taken from the infant's lips, and thus she was poisoned and died. By this deed the second wife became unintentionally guilty of the death of the first wife of her husband. Her husband was furious and threatened to hand her over to the courts for the poisoning, which he in fact did. Formerly in the courts there was the custom of judging one soul against the other and thus for the poisoning she was condemned to death by being buried alive.

So it turned out that the two women were buried in the same grave, one dead and one alive, and they were covered up with earth. The first night the living corpse called out in her prayers to the three saints to whom her husband had made his oath. Suddenly the grave opened, she came out, and by some unseen force she was carried into a church, where the verger, who saw the woman, was frightened and ran to the priest. The two of them came and asked from a distance, "What sort of woman are you?"

And she answered them, "I can't hear you, come closer." Then she told the priest everything that had happened with her and he discovered that it was she whom he had married to the officer. So then she went to her mother and told her everything and began living with her. Some time later the officer was again sent on business to that same town. He went to his mother-in-law. His wife knew that he had come because she had the powers of insight and she hid herself. He, in no way embarrassed, started saying to his mother-in-law that her daughter was well, had given birth to a healthy child, and he hadn't brought her with him because she had to look after the household. Suddenly from another room his second wife came out. He caught sight of her, shrieked, and immediately was deprived of his reason.

51. The Old Woman in Church

Written down in the *Pismovnik* of N. Kurganov in 1769, this amusing tale is widely known throughout Europe but it is less common in Russia, where there is only one additional recording. SUS 778A*.

A rather silly old woman, being once in church, purchased two candles. One she placed before the image of St Michael, the other without looking before the icon "The Devil Vanquished." A deacon, seeing this, said to her, "Oh, what are you doing, granny? You have placed that candle before the devil."

She replied, "Don't fret, father. It's not bad to have friends everywhere, in heaven or in hell. We still don't know where we will be!"

52. The Golden Saucer and the Silver Apple

This is a very popular tale throughout Europe. In the Grimms' collection it is called "The Singing Bone." This version was collected by Mitropol'skaia among the Russians living in Lithuania. SUS 780.

There lived and dwelt an old man and an old woman, and they had three daughters. He was a successful merchant, and two of the daughters were always very elegant but they showed off before the youngest and forced her to work. She fed the ducks and hens, she split the kindling, and they made fun of her, but her father still loved her most. Well, so he got ready to go to the bazaar with his goods, and the eldest asked, "Papa, buy me a golden ring."

And the second asked, "Papa, buy me a crimson blouse to go with my *sarafan*."

But the youngest was silent and gazed into his eyes. The father said, "Well, and you, my hard-working daughter, what should I bring you?" And she requested, "Papa, if you think about me, then buy me a little golden saucer and a little silver apple."

The sisters laughed, "What will she do with a little golden saucer and a little silver apple?"

So the merchant rode off to sell his goods in the town. He rode and rode and finally arrived there. He traded everything, he sold up and bought all his daughters presents. Then he readied himself to go home. He came home and gave them all their presents.

"Well, and for you, my smart one, I have brought the little golden saucer and the little silver apple." But her sisters mocked her: they were interested to know what she would do. She took the little golden saucer and the little silver apple and she chanted:

> Roll 'round, roll 'round, little apple!
> Around this little golden saucer!
> Show me cities and towns,
> And the beauty of the heavens,
> And the heights of the mountains.

Her father went up to her to look, and she asked, "Papa, do you want to see everything?" Her father agreed and then she began to chant again:

> Roll 'round, roll 'round, little apple!
> Around this little golden saucer!
> Show me cities and towns,
> And the beauty of the heavens
> And the heights of the mountains.

Her father loved her more than ever. Her sisters were envious, and decided to steal the little golden saucer and the little silver apple. They enticed the youngest one into the wood, after berries. In the wood they killed her, buried her in a pit, and made a little mound. They told their father that wolves had eaten her.

In time, rushes grew up in the wood and a herder began to pasture his cows there. He herded them and he made a fife out of a reed. The fife played and sang out:

> Play, play, fife!
> Comfort father, my beloved,
> And her own dear mother,
> But do not awaken me
> From my heavy sleep,
> Until you get some of the water of life
> From the tsar's well.

The people gathered, the father ran up, and the fife played:

> My evil sisters murdered me
> For my little golden saucer,
> For my little silver apple.

The old father dug up the mound, found his daughter, and sprinkled her with his hands, and then they brought some living water from the tsar's well and sprinkled her. And she came alive! Then the tsar said, "Let her be my wife." Now the sisters took fright. She would kill them.

But the youngest one said, "Let my sisters follow behind me, I forgive them everything."

They brought her the little golden saucer and the little silver apple. She began to show the tsar the sea, mountains, cities, and towns. And she chanted:

> Roll 'round, roll 'round, little apple!
> Around this little golden saucer!
> Show me cities and towns,
> And the beauty of the heavens
> And the heights of the mountains.

She showed the tsar his own royal regiments. Then came the wedding. They began the feasting, the rites. I was there, drank tea and mead. It flowed over my lips, but none got into my mouth.

53. Kas'ian and Nikolai

Recorded in the Orel district by P.I. Iakushkin and published by Afanas'ev in his *Legends*. The tale has clear reminiscences of ancient, pre-Christian beliefs. Uncommon in Russian and Belarusian, unknown in Ukrainian. SUS 790**.

Once in the autumn a peasant got his cart stuck along the road. It is well known what sort of roads we have; and it was autumn, so there's nothing more to say. And then Kas'ian the Gracious came walking by. The peasant didn't recognize him and asked him, "Help me, fellow countryman, to drag out my cart!"

"Go on, you!" Kas'ian the Gracious said to him. "I've no time at all to waste with you." And so he went on his own way.

A little while later along came Nikola the Gracious. "Father," wailed the peasant again, "Father, help me to drag my cart out of the mud." And so Nikola the Gracious helped him.

So then Kas'ian the Gracious and Nikola the Gracious came to God in paradise. "Where have you been, Kas'ian?" asked God.

"I've been on earth," he answered. "I chanced to go past a peasant whose cart had got stuck. He asked me to help him pull it out. But I didn't want to soil my heavenly clothing."

"And where did you get so soiled?" God asked Nikola the Gracious.

"I was on earth. I was walking along the same road and I helped the peasant pull out his cart," answered Nikola the Gracious.

"Listen, Kas'ian!" said God then, "You didn't help the peasant and therefore a prayer service in your name will be sung only once in four years. But for you, Nikola the Gracious, because you helped the peasant pull out his cart, they will offer services to you twice a year." And since that time that is what has happened: a service to Kas'ian is sung only in leap year, but there are two for Nikola each year.

54. Why Women Lost Their Rights

This topical tale was recorded by R.P. Arefev in 1969 in the village of Varfolomeevka in the maritime region. The narrator was M.F. Litvinenko, then seventy-two. The fact that Litvinenko was of Ukrainian stock and that the tale is especially common in Ukrainian suggests a tie. But how different it is from the Afanas'ev tale published in his *Legends, 1*! SUS 791.

When Jesus Christ and Peter were walking the earth, women were in charge. Once they dropped into a village to a certain man's house and asked him to let them in to spend the night. "I would let you in, but I'm afraid of my wife."

They persuaded him and the man was weak: he was persuaded. "Lie down over there beneath that bench," he said. (There used to be benches but now we have chairs and couches, but then there were just benches.)

So they lay down to sleep. Jesus Christ was beneath the bench and Peter was on the edge. The mistress came home. "Who are you? What are you doing here?"

"These are some passersby who asked to spend the night, and I let them in."

"Who gave you permission? Why did you let them in?"

And then she started in. The mistress beat them and beat them, then beat them some more, as much as she could. She was exhausted and sat down to rest. She took

Peter and started to let Peter have it. She beat him and beat him, as she wished. She again sat down to rest. Peter thought, "Wait, she won't get me underneath the bench. I'll hide beneath a bench and push Jesus Christ out and He can get his share."

When she was well rested, she started to give the second one his. She knew she had beaten the one on the edge, and the other one was underneath the bench, so she got him out and started beating Peter again. But Jesus Christ was asleep and heard nothing at all.

In the morning they left, Jesus Christ was walking with Peter, and Peter turned to Jesus Christ: "Oh Lord, take away women's rights," and only in these years of the Revolution has the woman won her rights, neither above nor below her husband, but as his equal.

55. A Tale of a Drunkard

From Afanas'ev's collection of legends, no. 22. Afanas'ev took the tale from an eighteenth-century manuscript. He noted that the tale existed in several versions throughout Russia. SUS 800*.

On a certain day the Lord sent his angels to take away the soul of a drunkard, and he ordered them to put it at the gates of the Most Perfect Paradise. The drunkard knocked at the gates of paradise and Peter the apostle came and said, "Who is knocking at the gates of paradise?"

And the drunkard answered him, "I am the drunkard and I wish to come and live in paradise."

Then the apostle Peter said, "Go away from here, man. Drunkards are not permitted to reside here, for them are the everlasting torments prepared, together with the fornicators."

And the drunkard said, "Oh Master, I hear your voice but I do not see your face and I do not know your name."

"I am Peter the apostle, the one who has the keys of the kingdom of glory."

"Do you remember, master Peter, when the Jews brought our Lord Jesus Christ before Caiaphas (Matthew: 26) for judgment and they asked you 'Are you a disciple of Jesus of Nazareth' and three times you denied Him. If it had not been for your tears and repentance, you would not have gone to paradise either. Even though I am a drunkard, and have drunk on all of God's days, I have always praised the name of the Lord at every tankard, and I have never denied Him."

Peter heard the drunkard's answer, stepped away from the heavenly gates, and fell into doubt about the man who was a drunkard.

A second time the drunkard knocked at the gates of the Most Perfect Paradise and the tsar and the prophet David went to the gates and said, "Who is knocking at the gates of the heavenly paradise?"

And the voice spoke to him, "I am the drunkard and I wish to live with you in paradise."

And Tsar David said to him, "Go away, man. Go away! Drunkards do not reside here. For them a place is prepared in the timeless torments together with the fornicators."

And the drunkard replied, "My lord, I hear your voice, but I do not see your face, nor do I know your name."

And Tsar David said to him, "I am the tsar and prophet who is sitting with Abraham and Isaac in the bosom of this tsardom, and I compiled the *Psalter* and composed the songs of the Trinity."

And then came the drunkard's reply, "Do you remember, Tsar David, your fight with Goliath when you sent your servant Uriah away to war, condemning him to death, and taking his wife in adultery? Had it not been for your tears and repentance, you would not be in paradise."

Having heard this, David went away and fell into doubt about this man.

Then for the third time the drunkard began knocking at the gates of the Most Perfect Paradise. And John the Theologian came to the gates and said, "Who is knocking at the gates of the Most Perfect Paradise?"

And the drunkard answered, "I am a drunkard and I wish to live in paradise together with you."

And John the Theologian said, "Go away from here, man; drunkards do not reside here. For them is a place prepared in everlasting fire together with debauchers."

And the drunkard answered, "Sir, your voice I hear, but I don't see your face, nor do I know your name."

"I am John the Theologian, friend of Christ, confidant, beloved, and virgin."

"Oh, Sir John the Theologian, did you not write in your gospel to love one another, but you hate me and will not let me dwell in paradise. Or do you deny what your own hand has written or will you tear that page out of the book that you yourself wrote?

John the Theologian stepped aside and thought about this man and then he ordered the apostle Peter to admit him into the heavenly kingdom.

---

56. Who Brought Vodka to Rus

The consequences of drinking are made abundantly clear in this little tale, well known among Ukrainians and Belarusians but otherwise not recorded among Russians. First published in 1863, the tale was one of many collected by school-teachers from Tula province as part of the "To the People" campaign. Not included in *CRF*. SUS 810A.

There lived and dwelt this peasant and his wife. They had seven children. The peasant was getting ready to go into the field to plow. When he was ready, he hitched up his horse and then ran into his hut to grab a bit of bread. He went into the hut, went up to the table, and on the table lay a crust of bread. He took the crust of bread and rode off.

He came to the field and started plowing. He plowed up half the field and then he unhitched his horse and let her go to the grass, while he began eating the bread. Then he fell to thinking: "Why didn't I leave that crust of bread for the children?" Having thought about it, he lay the bit of bread to one side.

An imp stole up and carried off the bread. The peasant looked for it but the bread was gone, and so he said, "God be with whoever carried it off!"

The imp ran up to the devil: "Grandfather! I stole some bread from Uncle Sidor."

"What did he say?"

"He said, 'God be with whoever carried it off!'"

"Go then and hire on as a laborer with him for three years."

The imp ran up to the peasant. "Uncle Sidor, hire me on as a worker."

"I have no bread, nothing to feed you with. What would you eat?"

"You'll get along without eating, and so will I."

"Will you need a lot?"

"Forty *altyns*."

"Forty is a lot. Take thirty." So they agreed on thirty *altyns* for the year.

"Well," said the peasant, "go on, plow." The imp started plowing and he worked so hard that all the fields, the meadows and the uplands—all were plowed over. And he sowed the grain, and so much came up that there was no one to harvest it.

Then the imp said, "Uncle Sidor, rather than waste that grain, let's make some vodka."

"What is this vodka anyhow?"

"I know how, I'll make it." They gathered the grain and the imp made the vodka. He poured out a shot and brought it over: "Uncle Sidor, go on, drink up!" Sidor drank it. "Well, how do you feel?"

Sidor said, "It's as if I'm twenty years younger!" The imp brought him a second shot. He drank the second. "It's like seventeen years younger!" He poured out a third and Sidor drank it, too.

"I'm drunk," he said, and lay down. The imp tried to wake him up, but Sidor said, "Go to the devil; let me sleep." The imp disappeared.

So Uncle Sidor learned to make vodka, and from him others learned; and since then everyone in Rus has started drinking vodka.

57. The Forest Spirit

Published in 1941. The narrator was a sixty-two-year-old peasant who was semiliterate and lived in Kianda. Stories featuring the forest spirit, the *leshii,* are uncommon. The belief that he or a *koldun* not invited to a traditional wedding would appear anyway and in some way function as a spoiler was widespread even well into the twentieth century. SUS 810C*.

In a certain village there lived a peasant. He had a good farm, and raised lots of grain. So he thought he would haul all the grain onto the threshing floor and then thresh it all at once. So he loaded the first load into the drying shed and when he came to thresh, it had all been threshed. So he brought in another load and in the morning when he came it was all threshed. And then the third was threshed and so was the fourth. It was all threshed. There was no straw, no chaff left anywhere. All was clean. He thought, "Someone is doing the threshing for me."

He talked about it with his old woman, and the old woman said, "Go, go 'round to the witch. She'll find out who is doing the threshing."

So he went to her and this is what she said, "It's the Forest Spirit who is threshing your grain, but I'll help you, I'll tell you what you have to do. Before midnight come to the threshing floor and sit down facing the little hut, facing the doors, and have a cross with you. The Forest Spirit will carry all the straw out of the hut in three armfuls. When he brings the third armful, he will drop three sheaves and when he bends over for these three sheaves, you hurry over and put this cross around his neck and he will be your servant."

So that's what the old man did. Toward midnight he went to the threshing floor, sat down facing the hut, holding the little cross. He was sitting there when at twelve o'clock a terrible noise broke out, a wind. It was the Forest Spirit. So then he came and immediately started hauling out the straw, a third of it in each armful. He carried out the first armload, then he carried out the second, and he started carrying out the third when he dropped three sheaves next to the doors. He bent over these sheaves and when he had bent his head, the old man slipped the little cross around his neck.

The Forest Spirit pleaded with the old man: "Please, let me go, I've never bothered you. I'll give everything back to you. Make a large slip* so that it will all go in one load and I'll help you and we'll drag it all home for you. I've got everything stacked up here. There's lumber behind the drying shed. I carried it all into that wood and stored it in a pit."

So the old man made a big slip and all the straw that had been threshed they put on the slip. Then he harnessed up the Forest Spirit and brought everything to the old man right then and there. The old man put the grain in the barn and the straw in the shed. Again the Forest Spirit began pleading: "Let me go, please, take off this little cross."

But the old man said, "I won't take it off just yet. I don't have any firewood. Let's go and cut some firewood."

So they set off for the forest. The Forest Spirit cut the thickest oak—an *arshin* thick and thirty *sazhens* long—in just two strokes and then he hoisted the oak onto his shoulder and started carrying it off. The old man sat down on the end of the oak and the Forest Spirit carried the wood and the old man together. He brought the oak home and the old man got down. Then he threw the oak down and once more he said, " Old man, take off the little cross and let me go free."

---

*A flat-bottomed carrier without wheels.

"No, I won't let you go. Cut up this wood for me, chop it into lengths, and lay a bonfire."

Well, in an instant he cut it up, chopped it into lengths, and laid a bonfire. It was big enough to be three bonfires! And then once more he asked, "Take off the cross, let me go free."

"No, be my guest a little longer. Work for another week. This next week my niece is getting married. You and I will go to the wedding together."

"Well, there's nothing to be done."

So they started in on the wedding. They came to summon the old man to the Inspection* and he dragged the Forest Spirit along with him. "Come along with me." So off they went and when they got there, the old man led him to the main corner as if he were an important relative, and the Forest Spirit said to him, "I'll stand there by the doors and watch the wedding party. And I don't want anything to eat or drink." You see, nobody could see him.

So then they started bringing out the last of the dishes. A maid brought out the porridge; another maid—very pretty—brought the soured milk in a cup. The Forest Spirit took this maid and spun her around and she fell and spilled the milk. The Forest Spirit clapped his hands and laughed at the top of his voice. He thought it was all so funny that the girl had fallen!

And thus it was that they found out that the Forest Spirit was at the wedding. All the wedding guests were very annoyed with the old man for bringing such a guest along.

The feast was finished and all departed, and the old man went too, leading away his guest. He came home and once more the Forest Spirit pleaded with him, "Old man, take off the little cross and let me go free."

Then the old man let him go and the Forest Spirit went away into the forest and he never came back to the old man. The old man lived as he had before.

(In olden times they believed this, but now they don't believe anything.)

---

*To inspect the dowry, which was accompanied by a list. In the seventeenth century the inspection of the physical conditions of the bride was undertaken by the future mother-in-law. The forest spirit was regarded as a bachelor and to be avoided at all costs.

---

58. The Skomorokh Vavilo

Sadovnikov recorded this tale from one Vasilii Avdeev in the Samara province in the 1870s. It is believed that the *skomorokhi* continued the tradition of the pagan priests of Rus. Their tradition survived in the remote north and Urals until the eighteenth century. The story of Vavilo is particularly well told and the sympathetic portrayal of Vavilo is evidence of the tale's antiquity. Although there are other Russian versions, there are none recorded in Ukrainian or Belarusian. SUS 845A*.

This father had three sons and once he thought of toiling for God. "Children," he said, "twenty-four versts from this village build me a cell, take some food there, and there I shall toil." So they built him his cell and every day they took provisions to him. He would drink his fill, eat his fill, and then go out onto the surrounding bank to sleep. Once St. Nicholas came by. "Peace be to that well-fed boar lying there."

The old man replied, "I'm a hermit, and I pray to God."

"No, you're not managing any labors. You eat and drink and then lie there sleeping. Get up! In a certain town there's this *skomorokh* named Vavilo. If you can outdo his deed, you shall go to the kingdom of heaven."

"And what sort of deed does he do, grandfather?"

"I don't know," he said, "I've only heard about him: that a bell rings far away."

So he went off to that town and searched out Vavilo the Skomorokh. He went up to his window and there were his two wives with him. "Is Vavilo the Skomorokh here?"

"He's here." He went into the hut.

"Where is he?"

"He's playing at the games."

"At which games?"

"He was at the governor's, hopping and dancing."

"Will he be coming back soon?"

"He'll be back when the first cocks crow, or when they cart him home."

The first cocks crowed, Vavilo came, and he asked his wives, the twin sisters, "Who is this old man?"

"He's laboring for God."

"And where have you been?"

"In the forest. My children built me this cell there. An old man came to me and said I should toil and he sent me here."

"Oh! And what is my labor?" said Vavilo the Skomorokh, "I only hop about and dance."

"I wanted to ask you," said the old man, "what kind of food do you eat?"

"My food is just dry crusts and plain water. These wives, twin sisters, bring me drink and feed me and lay me on my bed."

"I want to experience your feat, Vavilo," he said.

"You won't manage, it's too difficult. You are a well-fed old man, and I'm lean." So in the morning a man came looking for Vavilo.

"Is Vavilo at home?"

"Yes, he's at home."

"We ask that he come to a name day celebration for someone."

"Go with God. I'll come on foot. Only first I'll wash and then I'll pray.

So then they sat down together and had breakfast. The women gave a hunk of dry bread to him and to the visitor. "Well, friend, let's go to the name day," Vavilo said.

"Let's go. Tell me, Vavilo, what feat do you perform?"

"My feat is just to put on my boots." The old man put on the boots and found out that there were nail points sticking up. The old man stayed with Vavilo in the house and the boots were soon full of blood. Then Vavilo sent a horse for him. They tossed a fed-out boar on it to take to the name day. When they seated them at the table, the old man remained there until the cock's cry. Vavilo the Skomorokh made it to the courtyard. "Let's go, fellow laborer, to spend the night at my hut. (But Vavilo the Skomorokh only hopped and danced—he didn't eat anything.) The old man was starved and couldn't move from his place. He set off with him into the hut. They got halfway there and the old man could go no farther. Vavilo asked a man to carry him to the courtyard.

They arrived at the home of Vavilo the Skomorokh. "Well," he said, "is my task not a worthy one?"

"It is very good."

"And what of yours?"

"Mine's no good. My boots are filled with blood. But I'll test it some more. I'll spend the night and see what your other feat is." So they sat down at the table and had supper: they were given dry crusts and a little warm water.

"Now, women, take off our shoes." And they removed them. Then Vavilo the Skomorokh said to his wives, "I want to sleep. Place me on the couch. Some others will also come after me." Vavilo's couch was in the passageway, in the fresh air. His wives took him by the arms and legs and swung him and then they threw him on the bed. The old man, still at the table, watched. "And I've got to manage such a feat as that and my heels hurt!" So they took Vavilo and put him down and covered him with a linen blanket. The old man said, "Put me down like that, women!" So they took him by the arms and legs and threw him and he was pierced all over with nail points! He lay there through the night and he was covered all over with blood, but Vavilo lay there as if nothing had happened.

They came for Vavilo before dawn. He said to the sisters, "Carry that visitor from my couch. He lay there like a stone through the night." So the wives picked him up and brought him into the hut. "Well, grandfather, are you going with me?"

"No," he said.

"Why not?"

"Well, Vavilo, your feat is great indeed! The Lord has commanded you to endure and endure, but I cannot endure it. I lost so much blood that I sense that I couldn't walk the ten versts to my children's yard."

The old man went away and said, "Farewell!"

"Farewell, but if you like, you can come with me!"

Then Vavilo was the guest of a soldier. And a holy angel came to him and said, "Vavilo the Skomorokh," he said, "They've come for your soul."

"Who has?"

"The holy angels."

"I don't know any holy angels. I just hop and dance. What kind of angels?"

"Come! Your wives have made you a coffin, and when you get home, you will die."

When he got home, a coffin was standing there. The sisters were frightened and crying.

"Vavilo, lie down in the coffin," they said. And then a dove flew to him with a holy angel. "Are you a dove?" he asked.

"Yes, I'm a dove."

"What kind of dove are you?

"I'm your holy angel. God has rewarded you. Vavilo the Skomorokh, you will be Vavilo the Skomorokh, the Dove God." And thus he died.

Tales of Love and Life

Although current Russian research suggests that tales we term "of love and life" were originally derived from early agricultural dances, songs, rituals, and so on. The majority of these tales, in the form we have them, are no older than the seventeenth century and most are more recent than that. (See M.A. Vavilova, Russkaia *bytovaia skazka* (Vologda, 1984), pp. 18–21.) In many of them there is an obvious satirical bent, while others not infrequently play on erotic themes deemed by censors too risky to be presented to the general reading public. The cast of characters is much larger than in the wondertales, and the roles are often reversed. The virtuous maidens of the wondertale are often singularly lacking in virtue in the tales of love and life, and their suitors and husbands lack even the barest outlines of the heroic Ivan of the tales of heroes. One frequently encounters soldiers and their adversaries, the generals, in these tales. Some border on the category of anecdote and are little more than jokes, while others approach the oral novella, in Thompson's term, and are thus quite sophisticated, oral short stories. For more on these tales, see Haney, *CRF,* vol. 6.

59. The Self-Playing *Gusli*

From Perm province. The version published by Afanas'ev is truncated. A more complete version was published in Geneva in 1872 (see "Selected Bibliography of Works in English" under Afanasiev, *Russian Secret Tales*). This is a popular tale among the Russians and Ukrainians, but not among the Belarusians. It is popular among the Baltic peoples and has been collected sporadically throughout Europe. The fullest version consists of two movements. In the first the youth acquires the self-playing *gusli* that can make various animals dance, or return to him if the instrument is a fife or whistle. This attracts a young lady, who desires one of the animals. The youth agrees to give her one if he can see her naked (see her mark). She lets him and then he wins her with that knowledge. There may be a further test involving the lass's choice of partner after she spends the night with several. Invariably she chooses the original youth. SUS 850.

In a certain tsardom, in a certain land, there lived and dwelt a peasant who had a son. The peasant's name was Alexei and the son's Vanka. When summer came, Alexei ploughed his land and planted turnips and the turnips grew so big and sweet—oh Lord, what a joy it was to look at them!

The peasant was glad; he went to his field every morning, admired his turnips, and gave thanks to God. But one day he noticed that someone was stealing his turnips and so he began watching the field; he watched and watched, but saw no one.

Then he sent Vanka to the field, saying: "Go watch the turnips." Vanka went to the field and saw a boy digging up the turnips and filling two enormous bags with them; he slung them over his back and began dragging them along with great difficulty. His legs were bent under him; his back creaked! The boy dragged and dragged the bags until his strength failed him; then he threw the bags on the ground and suddenly he saw Vanka standing before him.

"Do me a favor, my good man," said the boy. "Help me carry these bags home; grandfather will reward you for it."

When Vanka saw the boy, he stood petrified, staring at him with wide eyes. Then he came to and said, "Alright, I'll help you!"

He slung the two bags of turnips over his shoulders and carried them after the boy, who skipped ahead, saying: "Grandfather sends me for turnips every day. If you bring them to him, he will give you much silver and gold. But don't take it. Ask him for the self-playing *gusli* instead."

After a while they came to the boy's house. In a corner sat a gray-haired man with horns. Vanka bowed to him. The old man offered him a nugget of gold for his troubles. Vanka's eyes began to gleam but the boy whispered to him: "Don't take it." Vanka said, "I don't want gold. Give me the self-playing *gusli*, and all the turnips will be yours."

When he mentioned the self-playing *gusli*, the old man's eyes popped out an inch, his mouth opened to his ears, and the horns on his forehead began jumping. Vanka was seized with fear, but the boy said, "Give it to him, grandfather."

"You want a great deal! But so be it. Take the *gusli*, and in return give me whatever is dearest to you in your own house."

Vanka thought to himself: "Our little hut barely sticks out of the ground; surely there is nothing precious in it." So he said aloud, "I agree." And he took the self-playing *gusli* and went home.

When he arrived, he found that his father had died on the threshold. He wept and mourned for him, buried him, and went forth to seek his fortune. He came to a large city, the capital of a great ruler. In front of the ruler's palace was a meadow in which some pigs were grazing. Vanka went to the swineherd, bought the pigs from him, and began tending them. Whenever he strummed the self-playing *gusli*, his whole herd began dancing. One day when the tsar was away, his daughter was sitting by the window and she saw Vanka sitting on a tree stump, strumming his self-playing *gusli* while his pigs danced in front of him. The tsarevna sent her maid to ask this swineherd to sell her at least one of the dancing pigs. Vanka said, "Let her come herself!" The tsarevna came and said, "Swineherd, sell me one of your pigs."

"My pigs are not for sale, they are already promised."

"And what is their price?"

"Well, tsarevna, if you wish to have one of my pigs, show me your white body up to your knees."

The tsarevna thought and thought, looked all around her to make sure that no one was watching, and raised her dress up to her knees, revealing a little birthmark on her right leg. Vanka gave her a pig. The tsarevna ordered them to lead it to her palace, called the musicians, and made them play. She wanted to see how the pig would dance to their music, but it only hid in the corners, squealing and grunting.

The tsar returned and decided to marry off his daughter. He summoned all the boyars and lords and merchants and peasants; kings and princes and people of all kinds came from foreign lands and gathered in his palace. The tsar said, "He who guesses what mark there is on my daughter shall be married to her!" None of them could guess; and no matter how they tried, they could not find out where the mark was. Finally Vanka stepped forth and said that the tsarevna had a little birthmark on her right leg. "You have guessed right," said the tsar. He married Vanka to his daughter and gave a great feast for all the people. Vanka was now the tsar's son-in-law and began living a sweet and carefree life.

60. About Ivan the Fool

This rare tale was collected near Voronezh sometime before 1937. The narrator was well known and Novikov and Ossovetsskii collected some seventy tales from her. SUS 853.

The tsar's daughter, Princess Mar'ia, had always been at the tsar's court. And she had this rule that whoever could outwit her should marry her. And she announced to the poor and the rich: "Whoever can outwit me can take me in marriage!"

But whoever went into her room found that it was heated so hot that they couldn't talk there, they could just say, "Greetings, why is it so hot in here?"

"My father has been roasting cocks."

There lived three brothers, two of them clever and the third Ivan the Fool. And these brothers intended to go to the princess. "Brothers, take me with you," said the Fool.

"Get on with you!"

So he readied a goat and climbed up on its back. He rode along and he found a worn-out shoe. He stuck it in his belt. He set off further and he found a dead crow lying there. Again he put it in his belt. He rode along on his goat and there was some frozen mud. He stuck it in his pocket. He rode up and went straight in to her, into her home.

"Greetings, my beauty," he said. "It's me! What is that devilish heat?"

She replied, "My father has been roasting some cocks."

"Could you not roast one for me too?"

"I could roast one but there's no frying pan!"

He pulled the worn-out boot out from his belt.

"Here's a frying pan for you."

"Great, but I've got no cock!"

He pulled the crow out from behind his belt. "Here's a cock for you."

"That would be fine but there's no sauce."

He pulled the mud out from behind his belt. "Here's some sauce."

Now then, they were married, and they loved each other. I was there, I drank mead, it flowed over my lips but none got into my mouth.

61. The Philosopher and the Cripple

This, too, is rarely found among the East Slavs. Afanas'ev collected one that was included in his papers. It was first published in 1940 and in the 1986 edition it may be found among the "Dopolneniia," no. 30. The plot likely originated in India but it is known throughout Europe. Onchukov recorded the tale from Grigorii Petrovich Kashin, a twenty-six-year-old from Nionoksa. He had visited Arkhangelsk and served as a seaman since the age of ten. He was widely traveled throughout the north and had even visited Norway. He was apparently a careful teller of tales, although Onchukov notes that he was not always certain that what he told was "true." SUS 854.

There lived and dwelt this poor peasant, who collapsed from exhaustion in the evenings, took his supper, but there was nothing to eat. He would get up but his family was hungry. So this once he tumbled off to sleep and in the night he had this dream. In his dream he saw someone say to him: "You have this treasure, but you don't know where to find it. Call the philosopher and he will figure it out for you."

The peasant got up in the morning, happy, and set off after the philosopher. So he arrived at the philosopher's. "Come, let's figure out this dream." The philosopher agreed and they rode off. They came to a village and caught up with an old man and an old woman. They had a twelve-year-old son. He was a cripple and couldn't speak, nor could he walk, and he couldn't do anything with his hands. The old man and the old woman came out of their hut.

The cripple said, "Philosopher, I know where you are going but you won't figure out the dream until I say so."

The philosopher asked, "Where is it? Tell me."

"Search in the peasant's backyard, at the fifteenth charred log, and there you'll find the treasure." (Formerly the peasant had had a large house, but it burned down, and charred logs don't rot in the ground.) They rode to the poor peasant's and began digging. They dug until they dug up the fifteenth charred log. They raised it and money poured out.

The peasant gave the philosopher as much as was proper and he himself began living well and even as a rich man. The philosopher, riding back home, stopped in the same village and in the same hut. He started drinking tea and the cripple said to him, "Well, philosopher, did you figure out the dream?"

"I figured it out."

"Buy me from my father and my mother and in time I will be of use to you. They will part with me for very little." So then the old man and the old woman came and the philosopher said, "This lad lives with you and you just beat him. Sell him to me."

"What do you need him for?"

"I'll keep him instead of a museum."

They settled on a hundred fifty thousand rubles and then the philosopher got ready to depart. The cripple jumped up and bowed deeply to his mother and father and then he said, "Thank you for feeding me these twelve years and giving me something to drink when I was thirsty. But now I am not your servant."

The father and the mother howled and begged for their son back, but the philosopher wouldn't return him.

They went to the philosopher's house and he lived with the philosopher for a while. Then the tsar had a dream. He summoned the philosopher and said, "I've dreamed this dream; now interpret it."

The philosopher tried and tried, but there was no way he could figure it out. He turned to the tsar and said, "I have this servant and he will certainly be able to interpret it." The tsar ordered him to summon the servant.

The servant came and said, "The philosopher is a literate man and I was a cripple until I was twelve years old, and I am illiterate, so how can I figure out the dream?"

The philosopher came home and fell to thinking. His wife was a proud woman and sly, and she said, "Well, what have you thought up? Take that servant and murder him. Take out his heart, eat it, and you will be just like him: you'll know everything." The philosopher ordered his servants to kill the servant.

His servants led him away and were about to kill him when he said to them: "It's no use your killing me; let me go free and murder a dog. Take out the dog's heart and take it on a plate to the philosopher. The servant who carries it should stumble on the threshold and fall, and the heart will fall on the floor. Two dogs will come running up and eat that heart, but the philosopher won't curse, he'll just say 'A dog's death for a dog.'"

So that's what the servants did. The philosopher was given three full days to guess the meaning of the dream. He thought and thought but he couldn't figure out the dream and on the third day he went out onto the porch to cool off and weep, and the servants said, "If you had been a faithful servant, you'd have guessed it."

And he replied, "No, there was no way to solve it."

Suddenly out of nowhere that servant came out and said, "Well, philosopher, let me guess it for you." They went in to the tsar and he said, "I won't be able to figure out your dream until you chop off the philosopher's head."

The tsar ordered the philosopher's head chopped off and then the servant said, "Now, tsar, whatever I say, good or bad, release me for as long as I ask you." The tsar gave his word. When they had eaten their fill, the servant said, "Well, your royal highness, you dreamed this dream that in three years I will fuck your daughter." The tsar wanted to arrest the servant, but the people wouldn't permit it.

"Take courage before you give your word and afterward keep your word."

The tsar gave the servant a passport for three years and he went abroad for three years. There he learned to play every sort of musical instrument and he made for himself a silver lion. He put together a boat in order to go back to that tsardom. When he began to approach it, he ordered the captain and all the deck hands: "When the tsar comes, you will have this lion to sell, but don't sell it to him. Loan him the one from that jacket for three thousand rubles a day, and if the lion breaks, thirty thousand to repair it, but take the lion back."

So they began heading for the country and he himself went into the silver lion, sat down, and began to play on every sort of musical instrument. The tsar heard it, came up to it, and began asking them to sell the lion. They wouldn't sell it to him and the tsar agreed to pay for all their transport. They took the lion away and placed it in the tsar's daughter's dining room. The tsar began to prepare a feast.

Everyone lay down to sleep. "What is that noise you're making?"

"In my dreams I dreamt that a man had come and was intending to rape me."

"Oh you nasty thing. You listen to every sort of conversation. In your dreams you wander about, disturbing your parents."

The tsar raised his saber higher than his daughter's head and said, "If you shout again, I'll come and chop off your head: don't disturb me." Her father went away and once more the servant came out.

She was still awake and would have been frightened but he said, "If you shout, it will be death for you in any case." Then he went back into the silver lion and fell fast asleep from all the unpleasantness.

In the morning the tsar woke up. The lion didn't play; it was broken. So they tried to fix it but there was no way to fix it. They sent the lion away on a boat and the servant came out of it. The time came for him. They searched for him everywhere. At the very last moment the servant appeared at the palace himself. His majesty asked him, "Well, will you go quickly to your execution?"

"We'll see whether I go or not."

"And what are you going to do with my daughter?"

"I'll have to do what I promised to do."

The tsar went to his daughter and she said, "Yes, in fact that's what happened." The servant told them how it had all been. And the tsar said: "Well, alright, if you could do that so cleverly, you can take my daughter." So he gave away his daughter and half the tsardom as well. (Heard at sea from a Pomor of Mud'iuga.)

62. The Soldier Erema the Crafty

A very popular tale among the Russians, but little known among the other East Slavs. This version, published as recently as 1983, is from the Trans-Baikal region. Azadovskii collected it on the Upper Lena (*Verkhnelenskie skazki*, 27), also in eastern Siberia. Aarne–Thompson lists only one related version, that from India. SUS 855*.

This happened long ago, in the reign of Peter the Great. He was a good tsar, a man of great soul. He loved people who were a little more daring.

There was this soldier who served in the tsar's guards, and on account of his agility they called him Erema the Crafty. In those days soldiers served twenty-five years. And most of the officers were Germans. This Erema somehow got acquainted with the son of an officer and started learning German from him. And after two or three years he spoke German tolerably well.

A soldier's duty was difficult—they were beaten and insulted. In short, the soldiers were badly maintained and poorly fed. At first Erema tolerated everything, but then he decided to get back at some officers and the brigadier. He waited for the right opportunity and then such an opportunity arose.

Once Erema the Crafty had finished his tasks and was returning to his unit. He was walking through a field. He saw two officers—Germans. Erema thought, "Now I'll spoil their disposition." He quickly thrust his rifle and bayonet into the ground in front of him and sat down straight up, right behind the bayonet.

The officers were talking among themselves and the junior one said, "Speaking of our brigadier's daughter—what a daughter! I'd give ten thousand for her!"

"And where would you get it, that much money?"

"I'd stand guard over the unit's money coffers and I'd steal from it. There'd be no great loss to the tsar." Erema sat there, stroking his moustache.

The second officer said, "I wouldn't get involved in such petty thievery. I'd simply sell half the country for her."

And then they glimpsed the soldier sitting there, "hidden" behind his bayonet. "What are you doing here, you son-of-a-bitch? Would you drag yourself off into some hole?"

"What kind of wide-eyed lads are you, officers and gentlemen? You'll even be after fool's gold."

Well, they called him over, as you can imagine. They slapped him on the cheeks and led him off to court. "Let's go to the tsar, our little father!" They'd do whatever it takes to make a Russian soldier out as a fool. But Peter the Great had himself created the court and the judgment. They brought Erema to the tsar.

"It was like this, your majesty. He didn't greet us gentlemen officers and besides he was in a place he wasn't supposed to be. He must be sent to prison."

"We'll just see who ought to be sent up. It's you who should be sent to prison," said Erema.

The tsar said: "How's that? Why do you say that?"

"This is why, Little Father Tsar. We serve twenty-five years, protecting the state, and for some flit of a girl they're pleased to sell half of Russia or rob it blind. What measures up to that?"

The tsar immediately put it to them, of course. They started fumbling for excuses but confessed. The matter was as stated. The tsar ordered the officers sent to prison. They were led away and he said to Erema: "I see you're a very capable soldier. What's your name?"

"Erema the Crafty, your highness."

"Tell me, what would you give for this beautiful maiden?"

"I would marry her for three rubles, only I don't have three rubles."

"Go get them, if you're so clever."

"But Little Father Tsar, I'm in the army. Give me leave for a week or two and I'll earn the money and then I'll marry this girl, the brigadier's daughter."

So Peter the Great said to him, "Here are three rubles. I'll give you no more. You'll have to get hold of the others, but I'll tell you how to do it. Spare the royal treasury and I'll spare it too." That's what the tsar said to the soldier. "I have this merchant millionaire. He's a tightwad and a thief. I'll arrest him and put him in jail with you. And I'll set you this condition: whoever answers my three riddles, I'll let out. You figure out what to do and how."

Then they imprisoned the soldier in a cell and then they brought in the millionaire merchant. He cried as if he didn't understand why he was being imprisoned. A little later the tsar came and said to the millionaire: "You know your sins very well. Now listen to my conditions: I'm giving you three riddles. If you guess them, I'll let you out tomorrow; if you don't, you'll stay here."

The tsar went away, but first he set the merchant the three riddles. The merchant thought and thought, but he couldn't solve them. In the morning he asked them to call the tsar to him.

The tsar came. "Well?"

"Oh Little Father Tsar! Let me visit my servants. Perhaps I'll be able to collect my wits. The surroundings here aren't so very conducive."

"Go then."

But the merchant was really relying on his wife. She was a fine woman and he thought she could solve the riddles. He came home very unhappy.

His wife asked him, "What's the matter?"

"Here's what's the matter! I've been put in jail and given three riddles to guess. 'Guess them,' said the tsar, 'and I'll let you out of jail. If you don't guess them, you will sit here until you do.'"

"What are they?"

They lay down to sleep and he started telling her the riddles. "The first riddle," he said, "was this: 'What is dearest on earth?'"

"What? Who couldn't guess that one? Who is dearest of all? Am I not dear to you?"

"Why, that's true! You are dearest of all!"

"Now then, give me the second riddle."

"What is fastest of all on earth?"

"Fastest of all? You soaring high. . . . Do you remember when we went to liturgy? Our old bay Pegashka pulled us such that the wheels flew off our cart. That's who's fastest."

"Right. Now the last: What is richest of all on earth?"

"Oh lad, just look! Our boar can't walk any longer; he's gotten so fat. He's richest of all." The merchant rejoiced and he slept the night through with his old woman.

In the morning they led him back to jail. When they had led him in, the tsar came. "Well, have you guessed them?"

"I've guessed them, Father Tsar."

"Then tell me who is dearest on earth."

"Little Father Tsar, for me my wife is dearest of all on earth."

"You lie, you villain! And what is fastest?"

"Our Pegashka. He pulled us so fast that the wheels flew off our cart."

"You fool! And now what is richest, fattest?"

"Oh, Little Father Tsar! We have this boar that's so overfed that he can't walk on his own feet!"

"Fool! Just keep sitting here."

So then the merchant was in deep sorrow. He thought, "Since I didn't guess these riddles and my wife didn't guess them, that's it. All my life I'm going to suffer in prison."

But the soldier heard all this so he went to the merchant and started up a conversation. "Why are you sitting here in jail? Why are you so sorrowful?"

In his grief the merchant told him, "It was like this, you see. I was supposed to guess these three riddles and until I guess them, I won't be let out of jail."

"Perhaps I can help you in your distress. Of course, if you will help me!"

"What kind of help do you need?"

"I need to get home. I've neither money nor clothing."

"Oh, I've got plenty of all that."

"And I've one more request to make of you if I guess your riddles: to get me somewhere the uniform of a German, of a German prince."

"But I've got ten shops in all the cities. It's nothing to find such a German uniform. We'll find it! Only guess these riddles."

So the soldier said, "When the little father tsar comes tomorrow, he'll ask 'What is dearest on earth?' and you say 'The sun.' And what is fastest? 'A thought.' And what is richest? 'That's our Mother Earth.'" So the merchant remembered all this. They slept until morning.

In the morning the tsar came. "Have you guessed the riddles?"

"I've guessed them, Little Father Tsar."

"Tell me, what is dearest on earth?"

"The sun."

"And what is fastest?"

"A thought."

"And what is fattest and richest?"

"Our Mother Earth."

"Correct. You may go."

The door was opened and they released the merchant. Then he ordered the soldier released. The soldier waited, looking around. The merchant caught sight of him. "Oh, my savior! Come in, come!" And so Erema went in. "Whatever you need, soldier, just ask." He explained to his wife. "He's the one who rescued me."

Now what's a thousand or two to a millionaire? It's no problem, is it? So he gave him ten thousand, brought him a hat with a plume in it from his shop, and the uniform of a German duke. The next morning Erema appeared before the tsar, who didn't recognize him. He chuckled, "Truly, Erema the Crafty, you are clever, very clever. I love the crafty and the clever. Ask for whatever you need."

"Whatever, Little Father? We had an agreement for me to marry the general's daughter. And I've been toting around these three rubles all the time."

"You didn't drink them up?"

"Not at all. Should I drink the tsar's gift? I use it as is proper."

"Go, take two weeks' leave. If you get married, I'll let you out of the army altogether."

So the soldier put on the uniform of the German prince (sic!) and set off. And that brigadier who was persecuting him lived in a village. He was the son of a landowner. The landowner had died and he was his heir. He had a fine estate and in general he lived well. He was a widower. He had just the one daughter and she was a beauty. So the soldier arrived and asked where so-and-so lived. They showed him. He went there and asked to be admitted. They let him in, but not into the main room, not into the hall—into an anteroom. "You may spend the night here."

So he went in there and the daughter had a secret meeting arranged with this other prince, concealed from her father. So then the soldier got wind of this matter and hid behind the draperies. At about seven or eight in the evening this other prince came. They sat, engaged in a little tittle-tattle. She said, "Today I'm going to sleep on the second floor. I'll let down a rope ladder. At the same time I'll be testing your courage to see whether you're afraid to climb up here on that rope ladder. I'll open the window and you come, pull on the ladder, and I'll know you're there. I'll already have opened the window. Crawl in and spend the night with me."

The soldier heard all this—what the appointed hour was and everything. The prince went away. About fifteen minutes before the agreed hour, the soldier came to the rope ladder and pulled on it. She said, "What's this? It's clear he's in a hurry!" She meant that he loved her a lot if he had come running. She quickly opened the door and he climbed up the rope ladder. He spoke German with her; he greeted her in German.

"Don't light the lamp. That would arouse suspicion. Your papa might come." Of course she didn't light it. So then they played games, embracing and kissing, and maybe something else as well. Oho! In general, she found him very pleasing! But then it was nine o'clock. And there was a pulling at that ladder. She went over. And Erema knew who was pulling on that ladder—it was her fiancé.

He crawled up the ladder. Erema opened the window and let him have it, that prince, her fiancé. He worked him over, but the prince cursed her out roundly: "You whore and prostitute! You decided to disgrace yourself." And he ran away and shot himself.

In the morning her father found out. Can you imagine the fuss there was? The prince shot himself! For what reason? Why? Her father organized the funeral. They buried him over two days but then Erema started drinking and lay with a hangover for a couple of days more. But the soldier was enjoying himself with her. It turned out that he was more pleasing to her than the other. She mulled it over: "It's good that he shot himself. Now I'll tell father that I want to marry this one. There'll be nothing standing in the way."

Finally her father had finished all the funeral services. He came and she fell at his feet. "Father, I've fallen in love with this German prince. Whatever you say, I'm going to marry him." And she was the heiress to all his capital. There were no other children. Out of decorum he pretended to be all broken up over it, but then he granted her permission. So then they got married and the soldier got some evidence of his marriage. He had to give the evidence to the tsar. He was married! He was alive!

Then the general set off on an inspection tour, maybe just visiting. This general had a working uniform and a dress uniform. He went away in his work uniform and he left his parade uniform behind. So then the soldier thought that he needed to go to his regiment and teach the officers a lesson for all the beatings and everything. He put on the dress uniform, told his wife he'd be gone for a week, and then he rode off. "Why in papa's uniform?"

"What do you mean why? It's more proper. It'll give me more prestige." She was satisfied. "But papa has a gemstone on his finger. You should wear one if you're going to pretend." She took an emerald ring out of a little casket, put it on him, and he rode off. Just then they were selecting the most handsome soldiers among the guards and in general those most full of life—it was the tsar's guard. And then suddenly here was

---

this general who was a splendid sight. His wife almost cried as she accompanied him, even when they parted. They kissed so loudly you could hear it!

So he rode to St. Petersburg, to his unit, to the regiment of the guards. He went to the garrison where he had formerly lived, back to his friends. At first they were all at ease, then they came to attention: a general had entered the garrison. He said, "At last!"

"It's true, it's Eremka! What are you doing here?"

"It's all right. Sit down. Quiet. Let's talk. I'm a general now."

"What will we talk about?"

"This is what. I served with you, I know all the procedures, how they beat us, how badly they fed us, and how poorly they clothed us. How are things now?"

"How are things now? Even worse. They feed us any old way, our boots are all worn out, and the soles have gone right through."

"Alright, tomorrow all will be put right. I'll gather you for a parade and don't you be bashful. Alesha, I'll ask you first 'How do they feed you?' Don't be bashful. Tell the whole truth. Really pour it on. You there, Vasia, talk about the boots. And you, Petia, go on about your winter greatcoats, alright?"

He did all this and lay down; he slept with the soldiers. In the morning he gathered the regiment for parade on the square, probably on the Senate Square.* "Brother soldiers, I wish you good health!" And they said, "Good health, Sir General."

"Well, how are you serving?"

"Alright, we're serving somehow."

"Tell me the whole truth. I'm now on inspection. How is it with your food?" And the first one whom he had coached stepped up. "With food it's worse than before. The rations are less and less. They never give us any butter. They used to give us a hundred grams of vodka, but now it's only fifty."

"You, Vasia, don't be bashful. Speak!"

"Our boots, as you can see, are full of holes. The time for changing them is long past, but these bastards, they sell them and drink and we are almost barefoot."

The third added, "Our coats are worn out."

"Who's in charge of the food?"

An officer flew up. "I am."

And he slapped him twice on the cheeks. "Put him in the hole for three days, hungry, because he's starving the soldiers." They put him in handcuffs and marched him off to the hole. Then they called the second officer. "How are your boots? Take them off. You, Vasia, take off your worn-out ones and put on these. To the hole for ten days." The third one got fifteen days for the overcoats. "Let all the soldiers in the Russian army be outfitted like this! How will they fight for the motherland?"

So he dealt with the officers. The soldiers were satisfied. He increased their vodka ration to two hundred grams and gave them three days' leave. And so after a week, what the hell! The tsar himself summoned the general. They had never

---

*The main square in St. Petersburg.

thought, the high command, that it was Erema the Crafty. They thought it was a real general.

Peter the Great said to him, "You German mug! Decided to ignore the tsar's orders, to introduce your own procedures? You've got away with the whole treasury. You've emptied all our stores. You've distributed all our boots! And who ordered you to increase the rations? If you fed the whole army that way, we wouldn't have enough of anything. To prison with him!"

So they imprisoned the general and when he arrived, Erema the Crafty hung up his uniform as if nothing was amiss. Then he said to her, "I have to go out for a minute. The tsar is summoning me." He came and appeared before Peter the Great. They let him in.

The tsar said, "What's going on, Erema the Crafty?"

"It's like this, Peter Alekseevich." (He spoke in the familiar Thou to the tsar.) "I got married, acquired a little capital, and here are your three rubles. I didn't even spend the three. Take them."

"Can it be that you are married? Perhaps you're deceiving me."

"Here's my marriage certificate."

"That's great. Did you marry that girl, the brigadier's daughter?"

"I did; it's a done deed."

"Good lad, Eremka. Now I'm pleased to release you from the army. Is there someone at home?"

"Of course. My mother, brothers, and sisters."

"Go home. Whatever you need let it be known now. You can take it from the royal treasury. I love resourceful people."

"I don't need anything very much, Father Tsar. I have everything."

"Wait a minute. Where is your father-in-law?"

"I really don't know. He rode off a month and a half ago and is gone."

"If you don't know, I'll tell you where he is. I've locked him up in jail, the son-of-a-bitch! I'll shoot him today so he won't alter the tsar's procedures. When you get there, to your wife's, take all his estate and everything else for yourself."

"She will probably give it to me."

"Whatever. If she won't, there'll be a royal decree in this matter."

So he came home and became master of the whole estate. I used to drop in to see him. They don't live badly; everything is neat and tidy. As for the mistress, it's true: there's nothing more to say. She's a woman like any other.

63. The Peasant and the Devil

Recorded in 1897 by Kosogorov in the village of Kaluzhkino. There were, in theory at least, four mealtimes in peasant Russia: two breakfasts, a substantial lunch or dinner, and supper. SUS 859F.

There lived this woman and her husband. The woman was evil but the husband was kind. The woman tormented and scolded her husband. The husband rode to work, he plowed, and he said, "Wife, bring me my breakfast."

And his wife said, "No, I won't bring it, you useless trash."

So the husband worked until lunch without eating. He came home and the woman cursed him once more. So her husband thought and thought and it finally occurred to him: "Now then, wife, don't bring me any breakfast."

"Oh, I'll bring it to you, you useless trash."

"And don't butcher that red rooster!"

"No, I'll butcher it, you useless trash."

"And don't bake any *bliny*."

"No, you useless trash; I'll bake some."

"And don't bring any breakfast."

"You're lying, you trash. I'll bring some."

As soon as the peasant had harnessed the horse, his wife had already caught the rooster. The husband thought, "Now I'll have some breakfast today." The moment the peasant rode away to plow, his wife began preparing breakfast. The peasant hadn't managed to complete the rounds of his field when he saw his woman carrying out the breakfast. "Now," thought the peasant, "I've found out how to deceive my wife, I'll have to try to deceive her again."

Not far away was a bottomless ravine. He took a very thin log and put it over the ravine. When he had had breakfast, he thanked his wife, and said, "Now, wife, don't go over that log and don't shake. There's a ravine there and the log is thin."

"No, you trash, I'll shake." And so she set off over the ravine on the log and when she got to the middle, she shook and flew into the ravine.

When the peasant came home, his wife was not there. He thought, "No matter what kind of wife she was, now my children are shouting, the cattle haven't been driven in, and the house isn't tidy." He had to put things in order, clean, and he still had nothing to eat. He spent the night and thought, "Regardless of what kind of woman she was, even if I didn't eat, everything was tidy. I'll go and try. Maybe I can get her." He took and tied two ropes together and went off. He went up to the ravine and dropped the rope into it. A devil grabbed hold of the rope but the peasant pulled back. He pulled him up to the edge and saw that it wasn't his woman but a devil with horns. The peasant got frightened and began shaking the rope, hoping to shake the devil off the rope and back into the ravine.

The devil started shouting, "Peasant, be so kind! Pull me out of here and I will give you great riches—money, goods, all that you could want. But some woman came tumbling down with a stick and beat me, and she broke all my ribs, and she bit, and she was about to bite off my ears." The peasant agreed to put the devil out of the ravine. He thought, "If I pull out my wife, it will be too bad for me. She tried to bite off the devil's ears and she beat him up. I won't even live if she beats me. She'll be even more evil and that will be bad indeed."

So the peasant pulled the devil out of the ravine and then the devil said, "Well, peasant, this is for you. Shake this purse and you'll have money for every need, and I'll help you in all your affairs and in your misfortune."

So the peasant took the devil's purse and set off home. When he got home, he saw that the children were sad and longing for their mother. The peasant said, "Well, children, don't long for her." He shook the purse, and he hit it against the bench. "Money! We need some money, children!" the father said to the children. But the children longed for their mother because their father's appearance had somehow changed and was like their mother's. And they were in torn clothing and dirty, and they were unwashed and filthy.

For a time the children lived without their mother but after a time they died. The peasant buried the children without their mother and was left alone. He was bored and sad, and from his boredom he began drinking vodka and going from tavern to tavern. Day or night he staggered along—either in the mud or in the dust—but no one would take him in.

Once late in the evening he was going home drunk from a tavern and the devil came to meet him and asked him, "Who is that coming here?" And the peasant answered, "A drunkard, and who are you?"

"I am the devil."

The peasant said, "And are you the very same one I pulled out of the ravine?"

The devil said, "I'm the same."

"Well, devil, you promised to help me in my misfortune," said the peasant.

"And what sort of misfortune do you have, peasant?"

"What sort of misfortune? I don't have a wife and because of you my children died."

"Don't grieve, peasant, we'll find you a wife."

"But how will you find her? Who would marry me? I don't have a hut and who would marry a drunkard?"

"Well, peasant," said the devil, "sign up for just three years not to drink vodka, not to smoke a pipe, not to cut your hair, not to bathe, and go around in nothing but your shirt (not changing your underclothing), in old bast shoes, in a poor, home-made coat, and in a big, torn hat, and not changing any of this for three years and not going outside for three years, then I'll give you a home and a young wife." The peasant agreed to fulfill all this.

In a certain place there lived a rich merchant and he had a fine house. The peasant liked it and said to the devil: "If only you could build a house like that for me."

The devil said, "We can buy this house. When he sells it, don't yawn, buy it quickly, there'll be money." So then the devil went to drive out the merchant. He made his way into the house and began playing tricks. He would make a racket in one corner and howl in another, then the table would dance and the chairs would hop about. All this gave no peace to the merchant, neither in the day nor at night. The merchant went out among the old women and sorcerers, he engaged in sorcery himself, and he tried divination. He brought the old women and the sorcerers, and he whispered and attempted fortune telling, and then he drove them all out and asked, but no one could do anything and there was no way he could live there. He was advised to sell the house and buy himself another. So the merchant began to try to sell the house. He tried to get merchants and gentlemen to buy it, but no one wanted to. So the peasant heard about this and started to buy the house. The merchant said, "How can you buy it, you don't have any money?"

The peasant pulled out his purse: "Here's my money!"

The merchant sold the peasant the house and saw that there wasn't much money in the purse. But the peasant began pulling out of the purse first some gold and then some silver until he had pulled out about twice as much as the merchant had asked for the house. The merchant stared and thought, "That purse, even though it's quite small—so small you can't see it—still has much money jingling in it." The peasant counted it out, as he should have done, and then he put the remainder back into the purse. The merchant took his money and said to the peasant, "Well, you won't live in this house; something has taken over in it. It whistles and makes a noise all the time, and gives you no rest, neither in the daytime nor at night."

Then the peasant said, "We'll find out how to chase it out, we'll chase it out and it won't play jokes on me."

So the peasant moved into that house and began living there. So then the joker (devil) said to the peasant, "Now then, peasant, you will tell fortunes and I will give you hints about them." The peasant became well known as a fortune teller. Peasants came to him, as did merchants, and gentlemen came to have their fortunes read. Whenever someone had some misfortune, he would soon find it out and if someone came with a misfortune, he would tell him everything and then the peasant would go into the other room and talk with the joker. The joker would tell him everything and then the peasant would tell it to the one who came with it. If something disappeared or was stolen, he would find it out, and then they would pay him a lot of money. He became very rich and began loaning money out at high rates of interest.

In this town there lived this gentleman and he had many children. Three girls were already of marriageable age. The gentleman had to feed them, supply them with drink, clothe and shoe them, and buy fine costumes. He was fast becoming poor. He heard that this peasant had a lot of money and that he loaned out money at a percentage. So the gentleman rode over to the peasant's house. When he got there, he went into the house and saw that the peasant was sitting there, counting his money. He was fierce looking, disheveled, dirty, unwashed, with some teeth missing. The house was filled with smoke. The gentleman went up to him and greeted him. The peasant said, "Why have you come to us, master?" The gentleman said, "I heard that you will loan money at a percentage."

"Yes, I do that," said the peasant, "only you would need to sign something."

"And what would I have to sign?" said the gentleman. "I've nothing at all to sign for."

"If that's the case, then I won't give you any money. But let me go and think about it."

So he went to consult with the devil and the joker said, "Well, peasant, the gentleman has three daughters. He'll sign if you don't give him any money. Let him give you one of his daughters in marriage." So the peasant went back to the gentleman and said, "Here's what I've thought up. You have three unmarried daughters and if you sign, then you can give me one, any one, to marry and I'll give you as much money as you want."

The gentleman agreed to give any one of his daughters to him in marriage and he signed. The peasant gave him the money and the gentleman took the money and went home, happy to have become rich. "But the girls won't marry him," thought the gentleman.

So the time passed for which the gentleman had taken the money, but he didn't return it because he had nowhere to get it from. The peasant waited and waited for the gentleman and the money. He said, "Now it's time to go courting the maiden," and he set off to the gentleman's. When he was riding up to the gentleman's house, the gentleman looked out the window from the second story and said, "Well, daughters, that groom is riding for you. I took some money from him for your outfits and signed an agreement to give it back by now. If I don't return it, then I'm to give any one of you daughters to him in marriage. But I've nowhere to get the money so obviously you're going to have to rescue me." The oldest daughter looked and took fright. She went up into the loft and strangled herself.

The gentleman met the peasant and the peasant said, "Well, fulfill your agreement. You didn't bring the money as agreed."

The gentleman said, "There is no money."

"Alright. Then I'll take a bride. Where are they?"

The gentleman went to look for the girls. He found the two younger ones but not the oldest. He looked and looked but she had disappeared. The peasant didn't want to take either of the younger ones. "Give me the oldest one; nothing else will do."

So the gentleman climbed up into the loft but she was already dead. He jumped down from the loft and said, "A misfortune has taken place with us!"

The peasant said, "What sort of bad luck?"

"My oldest daughter has hanged herself. Choose one of these two."

The peasant said, "I'll take the middle one."

But the middle one said, "No, I won't marry him, papa."

"Well, youngest daughter, save me—marry him!" The peasant took the youngest daughter and went off to get married, and they buried the oldest one.

So the peasant came to his house. The joker ordered him to cut his hair, shave his beard, throw off his ripped coat and worn-out bast shoes, go to the bathhouse, wash, and put on some scent. The peasant did all this. He cut his hair, shaved his beard, threw off his ripped coat and shirt, and his worn-out bast shoes, steamed in the bathhouse, washed, dressed as a merchant, put on some scent, and went off to be married. He was married and went to his father-in-law's with his young bride. They were riding up to the house and from the second story her parents and sister looked at them. "Who is that coming up here?" said the middle sister. The gentleman said, "That's my son-in-law and my daughter!" The middle daughter looked again and said, "Oh, how handsome he is! Why didn't I marry him?" She was frowning.

The parents met their son-in-law and daughter and invited them into the house with joy. They invited other guests and they had a great feast. The middle daughter climbed up into the loft from shame and there she stabbed herself because her youngest sister had married such a handsome man and she was left an unmarried maid.

The gentleman was grieving but he forgot about it in his happiness that his favorite daughter had married such a handsome, rich man. He looked about for his middle daughter but she wasn't at the feast and she wasn't walking about with the other young ladies. He looked in another room but the daughter wasn't there either. He dashed into the loft and there she lay, stabbed to death. Out of fright he jumped down from the loft to his guests and said, "Well, dear guests, I am now without any daughters at all. The eldest hanged herself, the middle one stabbed herself, and I have married the youngest one off." And so the ball ended.

They buried the other one and the son-in-law and his wife went home. When they were approaching their home, the joker popped out to greet them, laughing, but the peasant said, "Why are you laughing?"

"Why should I not laugh? You took one for yourself but I got two!"

And thus the hapless wedding came to an end. They buried two in their misfortune but the other got married and the two began living while the joker went away. He took himself far away from them.

64. The White-Bearded Old Man

Primarily recorded among the Russians. Aarne–Thompson lists only one Russian variant but there are several. Onchukov collected this tale from Grigorii Ivanovich Chuprov, who was also a *bylina* singer, although not among the best known. Onchukov considered him one of the most outstanding narrators he encountered. He lived on the River Pechora in the Far North. His tales are characterized by their good-natured humor. SUS 860B*.

There were these two merchants, two brothers, and then one merchant died, and he left a young son. The merchant began trading beyond the seas, trading by ship, but his nephew started begging his mother, "Let me go trading with my uncle." His mother let him go and she gave him a hundred rubles in cash.

They set off. They sailed over the seas; they arrived, and docked at the wharf.

Then they went to announce themselves to the foreign tsar and register their papers. They appeared and the foreign tsar said, "Lads, go ahead and trade, only in our town there's this white-bearded old man. He will out-trade you, he will rob you, and there's nothing that can be done."

The uncle was silent, but his nephew spoke: "But if anyone out-trades him and robs him, will he be taken to court?"

"No, he will not be tried."

The nephew said, "May we not, your royal highness, ask for a letter with your seal?" The tsar ordered the letter written, signed it in his own hand, and gave them the letter with his seal. And he and his uncle set off.

The nephew walked by the shop where the white-bearded old man was trading. "So, young man, where are you going? You don't even take a look at our goods, or would you like to play cards?"

"Your goods aren't worth looking at."

"But I have something at home, to tickle the imagination, and for a look it's just a hundred rubles."

They went into his house. He led him into his rooms, and then the old man ordered his woman to undress completely, and he led her through the rooms naked. "Now give me the hundred rubles."

The lad gave him the hundred rubles. The next morning the uncle loaded his ship but his nephew had nothing to load. They set off back to their own place.

They came sailing in and docked at the wharf. The next day the uncle began unloading his ship and the lad's mother asked him, "Well, didn't you do anything at all?"

"I bought up plenty of goods, mama, but I didn't have enough cash and so they wouldn't hand them over to me."

"Oh, you foolish son! Your father used to trade such that he would buy up as many goods as he had cash."

Whether for a long time or a short time after this, the uncle again got ready to go abroad to trade. The nephew once more asked his mother, "Let me go with uncle." His mother let him, and she gave him a hundred rubles in cash.*

They set off. They sailed over the seas; they arrived, and docked at the wharf. Then they went to announce themselves to the foreign tsar and register their papers. They appeared and the foreign tsar said, "Lads, go ahead and trade, only in our town there's this white-bearded old man. He will out-trade you, he will rob you, and there's nothing that can be done."

The uncle was silent, but his nephew spoke: "But if anyone out-trades him and robs him, will he be taken to court?"

"No, he will not be tried."

The nephew said, "May we not, your royal highness, ask for a letter with your

---

*The preceding passage is repeated three times word for word in the original story.

seal?" The tsar ordered the letter written, signed it in his own hand, and gave them the letter with his seal. And he and his uncle set off.

The nephew walked by the shop where the white-bearded old man was trading. "So, young man, where are you going? You don't even take a look at our goods, or would you like to play cards?"

"Your goods aren't worth looking at."

"But I have something at home, to tickle the imagination, and for a look it's just a hundred rubles."

They went into his house. He led him into his rooms, and then the old man ordered his woman to undress completely, and he led her through the rooms naked. "Now give me the hundred rubles."

The lad gave him the hundred rubles. The next morning the uncle loaded his ship but his nephew had nothing to load. Then he caught on. But his uncle's sails were already raised. The boy began walking about the town with nothing to do and he caught sight of the wife of the white-bearded old man. "Hello, dear! I've already given you a couple of hundred rubles and still haven't been with you. You should agree to go with me just once."

So then the woman agreed and she invited him to her house, and she kept him in her house secretly, in some special rooms. And the woman said, "If you come, will you play cards with the old man?"

"That's possible."

"Only take his cap, put it on and play, and the old man will look at the hat, but don't you yawn."

So the lad went by the shop and the old man shouted, "You don't even take a look at our goods, or would you like to play cards?"

"I'd like to play cards."

"Come on then, and we'll play cards."

The boy went and they began playing. He put the hat nearby. The first time they played the old man lost a hundred rubles Then they played a second time and the old man lost a hundred rubles, They played a third time and the old man lost another hundred rubles. The old man decided to end the game and go home. The boy took the hat, said "farewell," and went away.

He went to their home, hung up the hat where it had always hung, and stealthily went into the other room. The old man came home and asked his wife about the hat, "Oh, you bitch, you so-and-so, where's my hat?"

"What are you on about, old man? Are you stupid, or clever? Your hat is where it always was."

"Well, some peasant or other came to play cards with me, and I kept looking at my hat, and I lost three hundred rubles."

The old man's woman began scolding him. "You old fool! You've lost three hundred rubles for no reason. Isn't your hat where it always was? And your boots where your boots were, and a man is just what he always was too, so why not a hat?"

So they went on living, for a long time or a short time, and after that the woman once more said to the boy: "Hey, wouldn't you like to go play cards with the old man again?"

"That's possible."

"Put on his boots and go play."

And three times he won nine hundred rubles from the old man. They went on living for a long time or a short time and then the woman said to the boy: "Why do we live like thieves? We should live openly."

"What do you mean, 'live openly'?"

"You dress in poor clothing, and come and hire on as a worker. We need a worker."

So the boy put on poor clothing and came at the right time when the old man was dining. He hired on to the old man as a worker, not asking for much pay, and the old man was glad to have him on the cheap. Soon, in two or three words, he and the old man had come to an agreement.

He lived for a long time or a short time as a worker in the old man's house. Then the wife said to the old man, "You've hired that worker for yourself, and I have no one to help me. Either hire a girl to help out or marry off the worker." So they asked the worker, "Would you like to get married?"

And he said, "I would."

So the white-bearded old man asked, "Where should we find a bride?"

And his wife answered, "Our neighbor has a girl, we could take her."

And the old man said, "I've never seen this girl."

"You maybe haven't seen her, but when it gets light, she comes out onto the porch to sweep and then you'll see her."

It got light and the old man dressed and went out to look. The woman changed clothes, went out through the back door, and went out onto the neighbor's porch. The old man came up, took a look, and went back. The woman ran back through the rear door, met the old man, and asked, "Well, what's she like? Did she please you?"

"She's alright. A bold girl. In a word, she's not so small, and she quite resembles you. You look like her! How shall we recognize her?"

"Oh, you old fool of an old man! You don't recognize someone by her face but by her clothes. A mistress is in a fine dress but a hired girl is in a poor one."

"That's probably so."

And so with a feast and a banquet they got ready to be married, and the neighbor began the courting and giving away money for wine. And they started drinking for a wedding festival, and they feasted for three days. The old man got totally drunk and even fell down. But he raised his head and said, "Let's drink to the wedding, to the wedding!"

So he drank and fell asleep. And at that time the songs and music played, the drums beat, and the old man raised his head, and they repeated it all to him.

So then the men and women loaded up the ship with goods from the storehouse, and they took everything from the shop, and they loaded it all on the ship. When the old man woke up he started walking through the rooms and the first room was empty and there was nothing in the second, and his wife was gone; nor could he find the worker and his young wife. He looked at all his stores, barns, shops, but everywhere there was nothing. Cleaned out. He called the police. "They've robbed me, they've stolen everything."

They started searching, they found the lad with the old man's wife at the wharf. They took the boy, led him to the tsar, and the tsar questioned him.

"Why did you rob the old man?"

So then the lad said to him, "Forgive me, your royal highness. In a certain year a document was issued, in a certain other year another one, and then this is the third. He drew out the three documents and put them on the table. The tsar looked at them. "There is nothing to be done. The tsar's word cannot be retracted."

He said to the white-bearded old man: "Formerly you out-traded everybody, you robbed them all, and were you taken to court? Of course you were not."

So then the tsar let the boy go and the boy went onto the ship, raised sail, and set off for home with the old man's wife. They sailed for a long time or a short time over the seas, and then they sailed into his town. He came to his mother, explained about his marriage, and brought in a whole ship full of goods.

65. The Tsar and the Two Craftsmen

Several versions of the type are known among the Russians, but none among the Ukrainians or Belarusians. This one is from Saratov on the lower Volga. Told by Savikhin, a horse herder, who was born in 1900. This tale was recorded in 1936. SUS 575 + 873.

In two towns there lived two craftsmen. One was a joiner, and the other a metal worker. So then the metal worker decided to move to the other town. And the joiner moved from his town to the other. And they set off. Along the way they met and talked. One asked the other, "Are you going far?"

"Oh, just to such and such a town."

"Why?"

"To take up work there."

"It's useless. I'm from there. You won't find work there, I'm leaving there."

"And why is that?"

"I'm also going to look for work. Things are bad there. There's no place to take work."

What should they do? Together they thought about it and then they came up with this: "Let's go to the capital city of Moscow. I've heard that there our tsar takes all craftsmen into his employ. Only there's this one thing: he takes from each master an example of his craft."

"Well, let's go then."

And they set off and then they arrived. They reported to the tsar and the tsar said to them, "In this little amount of time make me an example of your craft and bring it to me. Here is a pass."

So they went and thought, "What should we do?" And they decided to help each other. "Let's not either of us abandon the other." And then they went to their quarters. And one said, "I will make this sort of thing, and you make the motor for me."

And quickly, easily, they finished. They had made a model airplane. They took their sample and brought it in. And there were a lot of entrepreneurs sitting with him and he asked them, "Well, what have you made?"

And the joiner said, "My skill was to put together and construct and thus to make this airplane."

And the other said, "And my skill was to add the motor to this airplane."

So next what? Well, they attached the motor to the airplane and sent it flying about the hall. Everyone was frightened and said, "We don't need such people. Let's send them abroad."

And so they were exiled. And they took along their airplane and put it in a storeroom for the storage of all sorts of crafts [a museum].

The tsar's son was growing up. He was getting tall. He began going about and once he wandered into this museum. He looked over a great many objects there but most of all he liked the airplane. And through all these years he kept it in mind. When he got to be eighteen years of age, the tsarevich became interested in seeing his entire country and other lands as well. But how could he do it? That was the question. So then he thought again about the airplane. And so he entrusted his fate to the airplane, to make a journey on it. And he asked his father, "Papa, permit me to travel about my country, give me some money. I feel like seeing where all our riches are."

His father didn't hold him back; he released him. "Go, my son, and have a look at where our riches are." And he gave him quite a lot of money.

He set off. And he took that airplane, went out of the city, and flew away. But their tsardom wasn't so very large. He quickly became acquainted with it and it seemed awfully small to him. He wrote a letter to his father, "Papa, I have been over all our country but I don't have enough money. I ask you to send me more with your best courier. I am in such and such a place." And he waited. When the tsar received his letter, he counted out the money and sent his runner with it and the runner brought it to him.

So now that the tsarevich had received the money, he went farther into other lands. But his father knew nothing about this. He came to another country; he saw a town. He hadn't flown to this town yet when he stopped in a little village. Suddenly everybody was frightened. What was this? It had flown in the air, like a bird. . . . And then out of this bird stepped a man. That was frightening. And nobody would go up close.

He went up to this one hut where there lived a man and his wife, but they had no children. The wife, who was rather sharp, asked him, "Where are you from, good man?"

"I am from a far-off land. I've flown here to visit your territory. Perhaps you will tell me what sort of town that is up ahead."

"That is our capital city. The tsar of our country lives there."

"And what is that turret standing in your town?"

"This is what sort it is. A daughter was born to our tsar," the mistress began telling him, "and the tsar keeps on having this dream that his daughter is going to give birth to a child while still a maiden. And that's why he built this turret and put her there, so that she should never see any men."

He thought about it. "But why is it obligatory that she not see men? Couldn't she see her father?"

"No, she can't even see her father. No one but her nanny and her mother."

It seemed to him extraordinary that she couldn't see any men. "And then if she gives birth as a maiden, such commotion will take place, but what is to become of her?"

His hostess said, "Our ruler says that if this takes place, his daughter will be publicly executed."

He asked the maiden's age and then in the evening he readied the airplane. He wrote a note and quietly threw it onto the balcony. He wrote, "Listen, princess, your life is interesting to me since you have been put in the turret; you don't know even half of the world . . . ," and he finished. Then he went back to his host and hostess.

In the morning the maiden went out onto the balcony and saw the paper, which she took and read. What was this all about? She was astonished: "Who can write like that? Only I can." And she fell to thinking about it and then at that very minute she wrote a note: "It would be interesting to know a person who is of my learning. But we can only converse in writing." And then she put it on the balcony.

So then he quietly got into his airplane, landed on the balcony, took and read the note, and wrote that "you can see such a person only if no one notices us." Again she read his note, rejoiced, and gave her consent to meet with him.

When the hour came, he got into his airplane and flew up to her. And then they met. At first she was terrified. But at the same time she liked him. And they were for a while in a secret place and then they were secretly married, but no one knew anything about it. But they started noticing her in that secret place. All her nannies and her mother were just sick at heart about her because they knew the orders of the tsar. And they thought that he would never permit her to have a child and that he would execute her for it. But anyway, in a short or long time, they had to tell the tsar.

Angrily, furiously, he ordered them to build a platform in the central part of the city. And on that platform he ordered the executioners to appear in front of an enormous crowd and said he was going to execute his daughter. He set the day for the execution and announced it to all his people who had come from all over for the day. And she explained to her husband that he must watch her execution.

When the people were all assembled, they led her out onto that platform. She stood there in heavy chains—pale, ever so pale, and she saw an enormous number of people all about her. She forgot about her execution. She was just interested to know what was going on in the real world. She asked her father to let her offer some final words. "Papa, in my final hour and minute let me say a word to these people whom I've never seen in my whole life."

He granted her permission. She began speaking and the executioners stood there, waiting for the end of her speech. They greedily wanted to make use of her head! But when she had said several words and was about to say "Farewell, all you people, I am about to depart," suddenly her husband descended in his airplane, put her in it, and carried her off.

All were terrified and in fright from this. They couldn't understand her disappearance. Even the tsar himself said, "I've probably buried her!" So they landed in that village where his rooms were and began living and dwelling there until their son was born. They called him Ivan the Fortunate and gave him to their hostess to be brought up while they themselves disappeared. But they left an uncountable financial capital with him and said, "Raise him up, teach him what he is capable of learning. And if you don't have enough, then we'll get more for you."

They flew home. His father had been waiting for the hour and the minute. And when he saw them, he died from fear. He was left with his mother, who inherited the tsardom. When the hostess had raised that infant, he stopped going to school and the hostess sent him into the city. When he had finished his middle schooling, he was interested in becoming a soldier and so he went to officer training school. He studied well. He had a gold *grivna* with the royal insignia hung round his neck for recognition. He stayed there in his rooms but he would often run back to the hostess. But he found it very strange that they lived in a village. He wanted to take them away to the city. But the old folks had no desire to go there. Still, they fulfilled his wish. Moreover, the old woman persuaded the old man, "We'll live somehow. I'll take in laundry and you'll cut wood. And so we'll live." She hoped, she said, that they would live out their days in the city. But she had an uncountable amount of money that the tsarevich had left for the child. So they rented rooms and started living there. But his fellow officers, who studied with him in the same school, lived in luxury. He came and said, "Granny, we live very poorly. Look at my comrades, what fine suits they have and what quarters. They live splendidly and their relatives always appear intelligent. They invited me to visit them and I've been there. But I've nothing to greet them with here." She answered, "Don't worry about it. Go to a good shop. Get us a cab and we'll go."

This seemed very strange to him. "Where will she get the money from? It will be embarrassing to leave the shop with nothing." So she said, "Let's go." And they set off. They came to the very best shop. And they went in. She said to him, "Listen, Vania, look for a suit of clothes for yourself, the very best and most costly, according to your wishes." Vania requested such a suit, but he had no hope of buying it. When he put it on, she asked, "Do you like it? Take it."

"Yes, it's fine, granny." So she paid for it and asked him, "Now, what else do you need?"

And so they bought him an entire outfit. Then he said, "This is still too little, granny. In such an outfit I can go about, but no one will believe me. Let's buy you such an outfit too." They pacified Ivan the Fortunate. Then he invited all his comrades to his rooms, entertained them just as they had entertained him. And then they had to write their exams, and all the students who had studied with Ivan the Fortunate passed them, as did he.

But then after some time he was dissatisfied and he thought about opening a shop. He asked his granny's permission and she granted it, and he began to trade. And Ivan the Fortunate traded completely openly. Sometimes he would take money for his goods and sometimes not. But the amount of his goods kept growing and growing. And so it was that he was called Ivan the Fortunate. Then all the other traders became angry with him because he had taken all the profits from them. He was forced to leave. And he moved to another city. There he didn't open a shop, but just apprenticed himself to a stallholder. He said, "Listen, mister, take me on to trade with you."

And the man answered, "What do you have to trade? I've nothing even by myself."

"Never mind. We'll expand the trade, only take me on."

So he took him on. Ivan the Fortunate, whatever he received, he gave away, and still his goods kept accumulating. After a little while he had not just a little stall but a huge, well-known shop. But then trading became boring to him. He asked his comrade, "Listen, release me from our agreement."

The shopkeeper was sad. "Why should I let him go when things are going so well with him?" But they had to part. He took more money from him. And he left all the goods for the use of his comrade.

Ivan the Fortunate got on the train. He rode to a city that bordered on his father's tsardom. And his palace was there. And all this family. And his father had three daughters.

So Ivan the Fortunate stayed in this town and opened a little shop. And he invited his comrade and they began to trade. It went as before. Whatever he received, he would give away and he would always have better and better goods from the whole town. He put all the other traders out of business. His goods were foreign, the very best silks and even clothes. Then even the tsar's daughters selected their materials from his store.

Ivan the Fortunate was a very handsome young man and the tsar's daughters loved him and sent him all sorts of little notes. Then because they were young, they concocted a plot; they took some cunning steps and let no one know they were to meet each other at a given time. But their plot was soon discovered and even the tsar found out about it. And he began to investigate them and he decided to execute Ivan the Fortunate.

When the day came for the execution of Ivan the Fortunate, he asked that he be executed publicly and in front of the tsar himself. The hour came to call him forth for the execution. He came out and said, "Well, put me where you want me."

So they took off his underclothing, as they wanted to cut off his head. But suddenly the tsar took him by the hand and led him off by himself. The people asked, "How can this be explained that the execution has been postponed?" Later this turned out to be the tsar's heir. The tsar took off the *grivna* and gave it to his mother and said, "This is your son who was given away when he was born."

So then there was a feast and not just for the tsardom but for the whole world. And how cheerful it was! And I was there, and I drank mead and wine and it flowed over my moustache, but none got into my mouth.

66. The Wise Seven-Year-Old Girl

One of the most popular tales among the East Slavs. It is also widely known throughout Europe and has been recorded in India, China, and Indonesia, as well as in Africa and in the Americas. Mitropol'skaia recorded this tale in 1969 from E.F. Vasiliev, who was eighty-three years old. SUS 875.

The wife of a poor peasant died. He was left with a seven-year-old daughter. So he nicknamed her "the seven-year-old." She grew up and was no longer a little girl but he still called her "Seven-Year-Old." Once he and a rich merchant were quarreling about something. At that time military governors called *voevodas* governed the world. They set off for the *voevoda* so that he might judge their affairs. They came to the *voevoda* and told him their case. The *voevoda* heard them out and said, "Go home and come tomorrow and tell me who is kindest of all to man."

So the father went home and his daughter asked, "Well, how did your case go, father?"

"Badly, daughter. The *voevoda* ordered us to come tomorrow and tell him what on earth is kindest of all to man."

The daughter said, "Don't be sad, father. Have your supper and go to bed. Morning is wiser than evening." In the morning he got up and his daughter said, "Go to the *voevoda* and tell him that dreams are kinder than anything else to man, for in a dream all woes are forgotten."

So they went again to the *voevoda,* who asked them, "Now tell me, what is kinder than anything else on earth to man?" The rich man got up and said, "A wife is kindest of all." The *voevoda* laughed. "And what do you say?" He turned to the poor man. "A dream is kindest to man for in a dream all woes are forgotten."

"Who taught you that?" asked the *voevoda*.

"My daughter, Seven-Year-Old," answered the peasant.

"Well, alright," said the *voevoda,* "Go home and come tomorrow and tell me what the richest thing in the whole world is."

The father went home and his daughter asked him what had happened. Her father said, "Things are bad, daughter, tomorrow the *voevoda* has ordered us to come and tell him what in the world is the richest of all."

The daughter said, "Do not grieve, Father. Eat your supper and go to sleep. Morning is wiser than evening."

In the morning the father arose and his daughter said, "Go to the *voevoda* and tell him that the earth is richest of all, for she produces every sort of fruit."

They went and the *voevoda* asked, "Well, what is richest of all on earth?"

The rich man jumped up and said, "I have a boar, so rich in fat that richer than he there is nothing on earth."

The *voevoda* laughed. "And what do you say?" he said to the poor man.

"The earth is richest of all because it produces fruits of every sort," said the poor man.

"Who taught you that?" asked the *voevoda*.

"My daughter, Seven-Year-Old," the peasant answered.

"Well, go home now and come tomorrow and tell me what is fastest of all on earth."

So the father came home and again he was miserable. His daughter asked, "What happened?"

He said, "Things are bad. Tomorrow the *voevoda* has ordered us to come and tell him what is fastest of all on earth."

"Don't be sad. Eat your supper and go to bed. Morning is wiser than evening." The next morning the daughter said, "Tell the *voevoda* that human thought is quickest of all."

They went to the *voevoda* and he asked them, "What is fastest of all on earth?"

The rich man jumped up and said, "I have a horse so fast that there is none faster on earth."

"And what do you say, poor man?" And he turned to the poor man.

"A man's thought is fastest of all," the old man answered.

"Who taught you that?" asked the *voevoda*.

"My daughter, Seven-Year-Old," the old man replied.

"Go home and let her come to me tomorrow not naked, not clad, and let her bring neither a gift nor no gift."

Again the father grieved. "The *voevoda* has ordered you to go tomorrow neither naked nor clad and to bring neither a gift nor no gift."

"Don't fret about it," the daughter replied. "Eat your supper and go to bed. Morning is wiser than evening."

In the morning Seven-Year-Old got up, sewed herself a dress of muslin net, caught a dove, and went to the *voevoda*. She gave the *voevoda* the dove, it struggled and flew away. Seven-Year-Old had outwitted the *voevoda,* so he fell in love with her and married her.

67. Tsar Peter and the Clever Woman

This is apparently a northern tale, known only from the Novgorod and Pustozersk regions. The narrator here is Aleksei Ivanovich Ditiatev, who was seventy-one. Although he was blind, he worked as a woodcutter and even went hunting at sea. SUS 875*.

There lived and dwelt this tsar, Peter the First. He was clever, wise. He collected his boyars for a council. "What do you think, my wise boyars? I want to harvest an unsown field. Can you guess this riddle?"

"We do not know, your royal highness."

"If you can't guess it, then your heads from your shoulders. I will give you three full days to answer it."

So they went through the streets pondering it. They went through all the cross-roads, returned, and went along all the long streets. They saw an old house. It was broad, big, but the doors were poor and falling apart and not hung properly. They went into this old house and in it a maid was washing the floors. At first she hid behind the stove, then she put on her blouse, came out, and said, "Oh Lord, let there not be a dull eye nor an earless window." She finished washing the floors, carried the dirty water outside, washed her hands, and sat down on the bench. "Where are you headed, my lord ministers?"

"The tsar has assigned us the task of answering the riddle, but we can't guess it. He wants to harvest an unsown field."

"Don't you know the answer to that? Go and tell the tsar: 'You begin and we will help you.'"

"But, mother, we want to eat something."

"And what do you want, some spat out or some licked and then spat?"*

She placed some clean crockery out on the table for them and some white fish. They sat down and ate. Then they went out and prayed to God. "What is this 'spat out' and some 'licked and then spat'?"

"Surely you know that!"

---

*Two ways of sowing small amounts of seeds.

"We don't know it, mother."

"You are eating the tsar's bread in vain. You ought to have asked me for some of the spat-out and I would have given you a bowl of stickleback fish. You would have eaten it and spat it out [because of the bones]. Then you would have asked for the licked and I would have given you some clear *ukha** and you would have eaten the fish and licked the bowl clean.

The ministers left her. They came to the tsar and said, "Your royal highness, you begin and we'll help you."

"Who told you that?"

"A lovely maiden on the street."

"Take this maid this length of silk; let her weave a towel** for me."

So they took it to the maid and handed it over to her. "The tsar orders you to weave him a towel." The maiden gave them some mahogany with a sewing needle. "Let the tsar make for me a shuttle and loom out of this and I'll weave it for him."

So the ministers went to the tsar and handed the wood and sewing needle over to him. "She orders you to make a shuttle and loom for her out of this."

The tsar took it and shook his head. "Well, ministers, court this maiden for me."

So the ministers went and bowed to her. "Will you marry the tsar?"

"My lord ministers! I am not responsible to the tsar."

The ministers scurried back to the tsar neither to brew beer nor to age wine*** but to prepare a happy feast and quick wedding. The tsar came for the maiden in his carriage. He took her and they went off to God's holy church to be married.

The tsar lived with his young wife and whatever he thought in his mind to do, his wife supported him. Once more the tsar summoned his councilors. "What do you think, my councilors and advisors? My wife wishes to be slyer than I am. How shall I live with her? I want to execute her for this. I am going to take myself off to foreign lands and take an ambler stallion with me and the tsaritsa will be left at home with her mare. Perhaps this mare can give birth to a colt. So now she will not be pregnant from me. How can she give birth to a child without me, the tsar? I will leave her a separate suitcase with twelve locks and I will take the key with me. Can she pack some gold and silver and not damage a single lock?"

He outfitted a ship and went away to a foreign land. A little while later the tsaritsa outfitted a ship just like his and she took the empty suitcase, put the gold and silver in bags, took her mare with her, and set off for a different land. She found out where the tsar was and docked in the same town. She asked, "Where is the tsar quartered?"

---

*A popular fish soup.

**Making a special towel is one of the bride's task before the wedding.

***Brewing beer (*kanun*) on the eve of celebrations and distilling vodka, frequently called wine to give it "status," feature in many festivities. See also Glossary, "wine/vodka."

"Just opposite the prince's palace."

She asked the prince for quarters. She led her mare into the white stone stables, cut her hair in men's fashion, called herself a prince, and observed the movements of the tsar. The tsar went to a tavern and some inns and he saw some good card games. "These cards, I'd like to play."

The prince protested. "Why should you play those cards for no purpose? Let's make a wager. We'll play and put down a wager and if I lose, then a hundred rubles from me as the fool, but if you lose, I'll keep your twelve keys for the night."

So they went to where they were to play and the tsar lost and he handed over his twelve keys to the prince for the night. The tsaritsa brought the twelve keys and opened the suitcase. "I'll fill it with gold and silver." In the morning she put the keys back and once more watched where the tsar was going and then she (as the prince) went after him. The tsar went into taverns and inns and saw some good card games. "I'd like to play some cards."

The prince spoke out: "Why waste your time with those cards? If I lose, then you take twelve rubles from me for being the fool. But if you lose, then your ambler stallion is mine to keep for the night." The tsar lost his ambler stallion to the prince for the night and they left their game and went home. They led away the ambler stallion and let him loose in the white stone stables. They tied him to a pillar but the mare was walking about freely. The stallion longed for her and he tore loose from his pillar. He mounted the mare and the mare got pregnant. In the morning the stallion was already at home.

Again the prince watched the tsar. The tsar went to the taverns and the inns with the prince after him. Again the tsar saw some good cards and said, "I'd like to play some cards."

Again the prince said, "Why waste your time with those cards? Let's make a bet. If you lose, it's three hundred rubles for being the fool and if I lose it's my ass for you for the night." They started playing and the prince lost. The prince said, "Come to me at two in the night."

Then the tsaritsa took off her man's clothing and put on her woman's. She braided her hair and went about setting the tables with various foods. The tsar came running at two at night and ran up to the doors. She heard him, went out, and let him in. The tsar sat down at the table and she treated him to some vodka from a shot glass. Then she offered him something to eat but he was in a hurry to tumble onto the bed. She said, "Be silent. There's still a lot of time in the night."

Finally, they went off to bed and slept. In the morning they got up, said farewell, and the tsaritsa readied her ship and set off for her own land.

Three years passed. The tsar readied his ship and set off home. He got home and the senators welcomed him at the ship docks. The tsar came out on the deck; his wife came, carrying a son. They greeted each other and he entered his house. He grabbed the suitcase, broke open the seal, and it was filled with gold and silver. He looked at the green gardens and said, "The mare's in the garden and there's a yearling with her: a colt just like my stallion." He summoned his ministers and questioned them: "How had she managed to do this?" He took his son into his arms and went to the mirror. "He's just like me." The tsar said, "I'm going to execute her for this. What do you think?"

The ministers said, "You cannot execute a person who is not guilty."

His wife said, "Your royal highness! In that foreign land did you not frequent taverns and inns?"

"I did."

"Did you not play cards with a prince? Did you lose your stallion for a night?"

"I lost him for a night."

"You lost him to me and I led him to my mare and let her be with him, and then did you not lose your keys for a night?"

"I lost them."

"You lost them to me. And then did you play for a third time?"

"I did."

"Did you win the prince's ass for a night?"

"I won it."

"So you beat me and spent the night playing in bed with me. Here's your son!"

68. The Clever Daughter (or the Dispute over a Colt)

Represented in all three branches of the East Slavic tradition, this tale is also known in India, but not, apparently, in Europe. SUS 875E*.

There lived and dwelt two brothers, one rich and the other poor. The rich one's barns were bursting with prosperity, but besides a fertile mare the poor brother had nothing. Spring came, time to plow the earth. The poor brother set off to the rich one to ask for a plow and a cart. He said, "Brother, give me a cart with harness and a plow. I'll sow the grain and in autumn I'll pay you back."

The rich brother gave him an old cart and a plow. The poor man went into the field. He plowed until dusk and when it was dark, he unhitched his mare, lay down in the cart, and went to sleep. In the morning he woke up and saw a colt lying under the cart. "Oh, my mare has foaled," he said. And then for his sins the rich brother came riding up. He saw the colt beneath the cart and rejoiced: "My cart has foaled!"

They began quarrelling, but how could it be proved to the rich man? They went to a judge. They came to the judge and told him what the case was about. The judge thought and thought, and then said, "Whichever of you can answer three riddles will receive the colt. The first riddle is 'What is richest on earth?' The second is 'What is fastest on earth?' and the third, 'What is the very softest?'"

The rich man and the poor man went to their homes to think about it. The judge ordered them to come in the morning with the answers. The rich man told his wife everything and she said, "Those are easy riddles. Count on it: the colt is already ours. We've fed the sow and she's eaten everything. There's nothing fatter, richer. The fastest is our horse, and the softest is my pillow."

The poor man came home and his daughter met him. She asked him why he was so unhappy. Her father told her everything and the daughter said, "Lie down, papa, and sleep. Morning is wiser than evening. All will be well. I'll teach you."

Morning came. Again the poor man and the rich man went before the judge. The rich man spoke first. "I've guessed all the riddles. There's nothing richer than our sow, nothing faster than our horse, and softest of all is my wife's pillow."

Then the poor man answered, "The richest is our Mother Moist Earth, the fastest is our thought, the softest is my hand. No matter what you sleep on, you can put your hand under your head."

The judge heard them out and asked the rich man, "Who taught you that?"
"My wife."
"And you?"
"My daughter."
"Hear this then. Let your daughter guess three more riddles. If she does, it's your colt. If she doesn't, it isn't. Let her bring me a gift that is no gift, come in a dress that is no dress, and neither on foot nor not on foot."

The poor man was very upset. He came home and told his daughter everything. She again put him to bed. Morning came and she put two doves in a sieve, tied it up with a kerchief, and on top of her dress she threw a cape over her shoulders, mounted a goat with her feet just touching the ground, and set off for the judge. She arrived on the goat, threw off the cape, and was now in her dress. She gave the judge the sieve and he untied the kerchief. The doves flew away. The judge praised the girl and ordered her father to take the colt. And he himself sent the matchmakers to the poor man and married his son to the girl.

69. How I Became Head of the Division

From Tiumen region of the Urals. The tale was told in 1926 by Ivan Elizarovich Bogdanov, when he was thirty-three years old. This version differs considerably from the usual Ural type, (see Zelenin: Perm 66). The differences are not significant except that in the Onchukov version some episodes are omitted. Aarne–Thompson does not list any examples of the type other than the Russian, although it is known among the Ukrainians as well. SUS 880*.

They inducted me into the army. I studied a while, learned how to handle a rifle, and then I thought, "Why should I bang my head on this?" I pretended that I didn't understand anything. They beat me and beat me, but to no purpose, so they sent me to the kitchen to scrub potatoes. I was glad: it was warm and the work was easy, and I could eat all I wanted. One holiday I put on my greatcoat, set off for the town, went into a tavern, and ordered a bottle of beer. I sat there, sipping the beer. Suddenly a general came in, the head of our division. He sat down at a table and also ordered a beer. I thought, "Oh, you son-of-a-bitch!" There was nowhere to hide so I just sat there.

The general recognized me and waved me over with his finger. I went up to him. "Soldier, wouldn't you like to play cards with me?"

"With pleasure, your excellency, but I have no money."

"Sit down, brother. I'll loan you three rubles." He took out his wallet and gave me three rubles.

There was nothing else to do; I took them. We began playing cards and I kept winning and the general kept losing. I won ten rubles and gave the general back his three. "Take your money, your excellency." We played on and I kept winning while the general kept losing. The general lost a hundred rubles.

"That's enough, brother," he said. "I've lost all my money. But wait! My frock coat for the kitty." But then he lost his frock coat, and he lost his boots; he was left in just his underwear. He had nothing more to lose. I took the money and things, left the tavern, took the very best room in the hotel, and spent the night there. In the morning I got dressed in the general's uniform and went about the town and the soldiers and officers saluted me. In the evening I went for a walk in the garden. There were also some officers there and the head of the division, a general with his daughter. The daughter said, "Papa, he's so young and already a full general." Her father answered, "Well, once you have such an educated man, it can happen."

"Could you not introduce me to him, papa?"

"Of course I can." So the general came up to me. "My daughter wishes to become acquainted with you. Permit me to invite you to visit."

I didn't refuse and went to visit the general. For about a week I visited them every day and the general's daughter fell in love with me. "I'll marry the general's daughter," I thought. So I married her and we lived together for about a week. But then my leave ended and I was supposed to return to the kitchen in the barracks. I told my wife that I would be going on duty for the whole day and I took off the general's clothing in the barracks and put on my soldier's. I spent the entire day on duty in the kitchen, longing for my wife. "Well," I thought, "How can I get away to my wife?" I asked to see the duty officer. "You see, mister duty officer, my parents have come here from the village. Couldn't I visit them for just one evening? Maybe you'll do a favor and come; we'll have some drinks."

"I agree. What's your address?"

"Such and such a street and such and such a number."

"Alright, I'll come."

So I changed into the general's uniform and went to my wife. We sat and drank with my father-in-law. The duty officer came to the house.

"Why are you here?" asked the sentry.

"I need to see a friend of mine."

"Alright, go in."

The duty officer came flying into the general's apartment, opened the door, and saw two generals sitting there, drinking. He was taken aback. He saw that he had come to the wrong place. "I'm sorry," he said, "I got the wrong address." I jumped up to him and was about to punch him in the nose, remembering how he beat us in the ranks.

"Leave him," said my father-in-law. "Don't get so upset. There are lots of such peasants and you can't beat them all!"

I led him out and in the morning appeared in the barracks again. The duty officer looked at me with hatred but he didn't say a word. The day passed and once more I was longing for my wife. I didn't dare go to the duty officer so I went to a section commander. "So you see, my parents have come from the village. . . ." (The section commander let me go and came visiting where he received one in the teeth. The third day the same story was repeated with the sergeant major.)

His majesty the emperor came to the town and made an inspection of the troops. My wife said, "I'd be interested in seeing this inspection; I'll come to it."

I said, "Please don't come!"

"No, don't say that. I'll certainly come. I want to see how you prance around on a horse before the emperor." His majesty conducted the inspection but my wife didn't see me at the inspection. She went up to the tsar and said, "Your imperial majesty, I've lost my husband. He left the house for the inspection but he isn't here." His majesty ordered them to bring out for inspection all those who were not in regular ranks. There was nothing else to do. I had to go out with all the other cook's assistants. My wife went around all the regiments with his majesty, but she couldn't find her husband. She went to the last regiment and saw me, and she said to his majesty, "There he is, there's my husband." His majesty called me over and ordered me to tell him everything without hiding a thing. I told him everything conscientiously. Then his majesty called up the old general, the head of the division, and ordered him to take his rifle and march forth. The tsar ordered me, despite my youth, to take command. Then his majesty the emperor sent the head of the division into retirement and appointed me in his place.

70. The Merchant's Daughter

Very common in the Russian tradition and throughout Europe. Balashov recorded this tale in Varzuga in 1957 from Evdokiia Dmitrievna Koneva, born in 1898. SUS 883A.

There lived a merchant with his wife and they had two children, a son and a daughter. The wife died and so this husband was left with two children. Then the children grew up. He had to travel with his goods—he was after all a merchant—so he locked up his daughter. Because she was grown, he was afraid to let her out. And so he got ready to go traveling with his son. But nannies would come and go and could let her out. So he thought: "I'll carry her off to her uncle in the monastery."

Well, the uncle said, "Fine, fine, leave us; she'll live with me a while." (But why shouldn't he have taken her on board his ship?) Well, anyway, the ship left, and this uncle (and he was a blood relative!) began to importune her. . . .

Well, she said, "Get yourself some street clothes and then it will be fine."

So he set off to get some street clothes. And he himself closed everything up—the doors and the windows and their shutters. She didn't know what to do and thought. She pulled herself up through the chimney and went away beyond the monastery. The uncle returned and she was gone! So she cut off her hair and dressed in men's clothing (perhaps the father worried about his daughter, but the daughter had much the better mind!). And so she set off wherever her eyes would take her. She walked and walked and came to a city. She hired herself to one merchant as an order clerk. And so she lived among the other order clerks and worked well for her master, and he could not praise her enough.

Now her father had bought up trading goods there and he turned back to where the uncle was. And the uncle said (well, he wouldn't say how it really was!), "Well, I was absent for a short while, and she went away," he said.

The father was so furious with his daughter that he couldn't put words together. So he sent off his son: "Go, look for your sister." He sharpened his knife, cooked up some provisions for the road, and baked them. "Well," he said, "Wherever you catch sight of your sister, stab her." So that brother went to search. Well, so he went to more than one city, but he couldn't see her (or in the villages) and so he came to this city. He came and started going around the shops. And then something notable struck him—as if that voice was indicating something. Well, that man looked like any other man, but the voice was his sister's. And she immediately recognized that he was her brother. And he said to her, "Let's go, sister, we'll walk about the city; I have some business with you."

(He'd guessed it was his sister.) Well, she agreed, seeing that it was her brother. So they set off. And he said, "Father gave me this knife and ordered me, when I saw you, to kill you, but I can't bear to kill you, so here's what I'll do: I'll put you in a barrel and put you out to sea."

Well, she agreed. So he put her in a barrel, called some drunks, and they rolled the barrel into the sea. So the barrel was carried and carried away and thrown up on a shore and it was lashed by waves against the beach and the barrel fell apart and she stepped out. She stepped out, and right into a city. In this city there lived a tsar. So she became one of the tsar's servants, one of the cooks. This tsar had a son and so she cooked away there and he found her pleasing and then he began to court her. She agreed and married him. She told him her whole life story, how it had all been, how they had taken her to her uncle, and everything.

So they lived and got on, and they had the thought of her going to visit her father, and then later, after a month, he, the tsarevich, would come. So the tsar fitted out a ship and sent sailors, boatmen, and machinists, and they set off. They sailed and sailed, and she sat in a cabin and suddenly one sailor came up and asked her the same thing her uncle had asked. She poured him a glass of wine. "Drink it, it will be easier for you!" she said. And he fell asleep, so she went down and said to turn up the heat, and then they really started flying.

They covered about fifty kilometers and he again woke up and began begging her. "Otherwise I'll throw you into the sea!"

So she gave him another glass of wine. "Drink it, and maybe then," she said. So he drank it and again fell asleep. So she went down again and ordered them to add still more heat. They had just managed to arrive where her father lived, in that very city, when he woke up. So she got dressed, only she put on a poorer dress and started applying for a cook's position with her father. Well, her father thought she was dead and her brother didn't think of her at all. She wasn't dressed right. "We already have two cooks," they said, "we don't need any more."

"Take me on to deal with the cows then!" Well, they took her on to deal with the cows. So they are dealing with the cows, these cooks, and she said, "One day soon the tsar will come in ships and he'll come here seeking quarters." They laughed. They said, "And he'll tumble into bed with you!" Soon nearly a month had passed. And she said, "Soon the tsar will come on ships and will come here seeking quarters." Again they laughed. "To tumble into bed with you, with such a perfect beauty!"

So she was silent. And time passed and the ships were under way. "Well, the tsar is coming," she said, and later: "They're coming here for quarters."

And again they laughed: "And he'll tumble off to sleep with you, with such a perfect beauty."

"Well, the tsar is coming," she said, and later, "They're coming here for quarters."

And again they laughed: "And he'll tumble off to sleep with you, with such a beauty." She already went around like that, dirty.

A ship docked in the harbor and the tsar came off it. He had already been told what the house was like and everything so he went directly to it. "It's true," they said, "the tsar's coming!"

Well, the merchant took fright. He led the tsar up to the upper chambers, up to the upper rooms. They began to treat him to drinks. And that monk, the uncle, was there too. And the sailors had all come with him. "Well," said the tsar, "I love listening to tales; isn't there someone who can tell a tale?" Then the father said, "We don't know any tales to tell; we're not accustomed to that."

"Well," he said, "you have cooks, maybe they know." So they called out one; she came and bowed. "No, I don't know any tales," she said. They called another and she also said, "I don't know any tales."

"You have one more cook."

"What?" they said, "She's such shit, a slobbering, sniveling girl, all covered in chicken shit." The tsar said, "Oh, that's nothing once she's in that kind of work, bring her here!"

So she came. She said, "Good health to you." And the tsar said, "Good health to you, miss. I love tales, especially when I drink. Songs, I don't much like songs, but tales I love."

"Well, I can tell you a tale," she said.

"Now then, sit down and tell it!" The order was given that whoever interrupted would go to the noose. They'd already pounded in some nails on the gallows there. And so she began to tell it.

"A merchant was living with his wife and they had two children, a son and a daughter. He put her in his rooms and would not let her out. And then he had to go buy up goods and they didn't know where to put his daughter, and thought, 'Let's take her to her uncle.'

"As soon as the ship had gone, the monk, her uncle, started pleading with her, and she answered, 'If you put on street clothing, then alright!' So he went away. And this maid pulled herself up the chimney and went away beyond the monastery, cut off her hair, dressed in men's clothing, and then she went to the city."

As she was telling this, her uncle said, "Your highness, it's rather inappropriate to speak of such trivialities."

"And why?" He said, "You can't toss a single word from a tale."

"And so now take him to the noose." And he went to the noose.

The girl continued: "and so the girl hired herself out to a merchant as an order clerk. It went well, the merchant could not praise her enough. Well, then her father came back and turned to her uncle.

"And he said, 'I was absent for a little while and she went away.'

"The father was so furious that had she been there, he would have stomped on her. He said to his son, 'Go and wherever you catch sight of your sister, stab her immediately.'

"So the brother set off. And he came to that city and went into the shop and it all became clear to him. He came in once, he came in twice, and the third time said, 'Let's go for a walk, a stroll about the city; I have some business with you.' So they set off. And he said, 'Father gave me this knife and ordered me to kill you but I'm sorry for you, sister, so let's cooper you into a barrel and let you go in the sea.'

"Well, his sister didn't refuse. So he put her in a barrel, called up some drunks, and they rolled the barrel into the sea. The barrel was carried and carried along and finally brought to the shore. And it was lashed about and then it fell apart and the sister came out of it. There was a city there and in this city there lived a tsar. She was taken on as a servant girl. Now this tsar had a son and he courted her. She married him. And so they lived together a while and then they thought she should go to visit her father and her husband would come on in a month. So the tsar equipped a ship and sent it off, and at that time, while they were traveling, one sailor started coming to her cabin and he pleaded with her: 'Otherwise, I'll throw you in the sea,' he threatened her.

"She gave him a glass of wine. 'Drink it, you'll feel better.' He drank it and fell asleep.

"After some time had passed, he again woke up and again threatened her: 'Otherwise, I'll throw you into the sea.'"

Then the sailor said, "Your highness, she is talking absolute nonsense."

But the tsar said, "You can't toss a single word from a tale. Drag him off to the noose." And so they dragged him away.

She continued: "So they docked the ship and she jumped out of her cabin and presented herself to her father as a servant girl. They took her on to mind the cows. So she lived and thrived there and once she said that the tsar would soon come in ships and the cooks laughed at her: 'He'll come and tumble off into bed with you!'

"She once more fell silent. And then a second time she said, 'Soon the tsar will come here in ships and he'll come here looking for quarters.'

"Again the kitchen maids laughed at her: 'The tsar'll come and tumble off to bed with you,' and so then she went silent again. (Her brother had already guessed, but her father hadn't). And so the month passed and the ships arrived. And they said, 'The tsar, the tsar is coming.' And so the ships docked, and the tsar came to her father's looking for quarters. And they led him up to the loft and the tsar asked that someone tell some tales. And the cooks refused: 'We don't know a single tale,' they said. And then they called me. So," she said, "Papa, I am your daughter."

Her father fainted away and then started apologizing. "Never mind, never mind. All is forgiven." She threw off her dress and dressed herself like a tsaritsa and they took her brother and went to live in their city.

71. A Hunter Rescues a Maiden

Tumilevich recorded another version of this tale in 1958. His two texts are the only ones recorded for the East Slavic tradition. Tumilevich collected his tales from among the Cossacks who lived on the lower Don. There are strong elements of satire against the clergy in the tale. SUS 883A*.

An old man lived with his old woman. They found themselves a son and later on a daughter. They called the son Vania and the daughter Masha. They lived and lived on, and then the old man and the old woman died. The brother and sister were left orphans. So the brother and sister lived there a year, then a second and a third. Vania grew and Masha turned fourteen. It came time for the brother to go into the service. He thought, "Who shall I entrust my sister to? She has no family. Entrust her to strangers and they would make fun of her." He thought and thought and then he concluded, "I'll entrust my sister to the priest. The priest is a kind man, devout; he will take care of her."

So Vania handed his sister over to the priest and set off for the service. For a year Masha lived well at the priest's. And Vania wrote to his sister, "I am living well, too." Masha lived a second year at the priest's and she also wrote her brother that she was living well. And her brother answered her that he was living well. The third year came. Masha came of age—she turned seventeen. The priest looked at her and was amazed.

"What a beauty! You'd never find another like her in the whole world!"

He looked at her for a day, then a second and a third, and he then took up having conversations with her. Either he would ask her a question or he would ask something of her, or he'd send her to the shop for something, or to acquaintances. The priest ogled and ogled Masha and started thinking about turning his evil thoughts into evil deeds.

Somehow one evening the priest began proposing an evil deed to Masha. She broke out crying. "How can you, Father? I'm an orphan. You should pity me. That's such a sin and you might drown in your sweat!"

"Never mind, my child. God is gracious. He will forgive me. I will pray for your sins and mine, and people won't know."

So then the priest invited Masha into the bathhouse. They went in and the priest, that pagan-Muslim soul, he laughed at her. How can the earth put up with such an anti-Christ! The maiden didn't remember how she got home. But the next day she got up and thought, "My brother will come and find out and then he'll shoot me." She thought and thought and decided to go away wherever her eyes should take her. She quit the house of the priest, the anti-Christ, and ran into the woods. "Let the wolves tear me apart in the woods," she thought. She wandered about like that in the woods. She wandered to the point where her clothes were all tattered. Then she climbed into a high, high tree and sat there naked. She was sitting up there in the top when she heard three hunters coming. And these hunters had a dog.

The hunters came up to the tree and stopped. Their dog rushed up to the tree and began barking. It barked and barked at the tree. The hunters looked all around, but saw nothing. Right next to the tree there flowed a little stream. One of the hunters bent over the stream to drink some water and in the water there was a human reflection. He looked up into the tree and saw the girl. So he said, "Girl, climb down!"

Then the second hunter said, "Let's throw her some clothing and go on."

But the first hunter had an evil mind. He answered, "No let's kill her, all of us. Maybe she's a savage."

Then the third hunter, the youngest, who was called Ivanushka, said, "Brothers, I have two shirts and two pairs of trousers. I'll take them off and give them to her. Let her get dressed."

Ivanushka threw off his shirt and trousers and threw them to Masha in the tree and then he walked away. He ordered the other hunters to walk away too. Masha put on the shirt and trousers, climbed down from the tree, went over to the stream, and washed. She tidied her hair and stood up. The hunters came up and looked at her and she was a beauty such as you couldn't find anywhere else on earth.

Then two of the hunters started quarrelling. One shouted, "I'll take her!"

The second shouted, "No, I'll take her." They argued and argued but they couldn't resolve it. They kept on quarreling and the one who shouted and quarreled the most was the hunter who had wanted to shoot Masha.

Then the third hunter, the very kindest one called Ivanushka, spoke up: "What are you doing? Neither of you would give her a shirt and now all of a sudden you need her! Let's ask her. Let her go home with whichever one she wants to."

Well, the hunters agreed. So Ivanushka asked her, "With whom will you go?"

Masha answered him, "I'll go with the one who didn't abandon me in my misfortune, who gave me clothes, who didn't want to deprive me of life."

So Ivanushka the little hunter took her and led her home. He led her in and said, "Mama and papa, I was in the woods and found this girl. She agreed to come home with me. She has no family; she was living in the woods. Will you let her stay?"

Ivanushka's mother and father answered, "My son, you must always take in an orphan. Let her live with us as our own daughter." Ivanushka's mother asked Masha, "What is your name, my child?"

"Masha."

"Consider us your parents, Masha, and you may stay." Masha gave her consent.

So Masha began living at Ivanushka's house. She lived there a year and she fell in love with Ivanushka, and he loved her too. Well, they decided to get married. So Ivanushka asked his father and mother, "Father and mother!"

"Yes, son, what is it?"

"Do you like Masha?" They answered that they did. "Give us your blessing!" The parents gave their consent. They blessed their son and adopted daughter. They gathered all their relatives and they all liked Masha. Only the oldest daughter-in-law didn't like her. The father and mother began the wedding rites. Ivanushka was so happy at his wedding but the oldest daughter-in-law took some poison and put it in the wine she gave Masha to drink. But Ivanushka saw the whole evil business of the daughter-in-law, poured out the poison, and he gave the daughter-in-law a good beating!

The wedding came to an end and Ivanushka and Masha separated from the parents. They lived alone and then later on the parents came to live with them. And they heard about the priest. Once the priest had gone out to cut rushes. He had just gone up through the garden when a wild boar ran out of the rushes, attacked the priest, and tore him open with his fangs. Well, that was his path. You can't get away from fate! Neither the horseman nor the foot soldier can pass fate by. But Masha and Ivanushka lived happily, loving each other. I was their guest. I drank vodka and sweet liqueurs. The young woman treated me with pies. How beautiful and kind Masha is! You'll not find such a wife on earth. Even now she and Ivanushka are living well. And I still intend to go on visiting them!

72. The Woman from the Grave

"The Seemingly Dead." Found only among the Russians in the East Slavic territories, although it has been recorded elsewhere in the Baltic region. SUS 885A.

Up until then this boy and girl had played around with each other, for about three years, but then they married the girl to another boy; they married her off to another village and didn't marry her to him. She lived with her husband for three years. Then she became ill and her throat started hurting. Then she died and they buried her. She lived in the ground for six weeks but then in the ground she recovered and in the night came out of the ground and went to her husband. Her husband wouldn't let her in. So she went to her father and her mother but her parents wouldn't let her into their hut during the night. So she went to her godmother but her godmother wouldn't let her in.

Then she thought of something: "I'll go to my old lover to see whether he'll let me in!" She went opposite his window. He was sitting by the window, writing. He could see her well from his window. He woke up a broad-shouldered worker who went after her but the worker came back home when he saw her: he was afraid that she'd eat him, but she said to her former lover: "Take me, my dearest friend. I won't touch you!" He came to her, embraced her, and she said: "Don't hold me too tightly, my bones are brittle." He took her into his room, locked her in the pantry and kept her there for eight weeks, showing her to no one. But he dressed her and fed her.

Then he and she went to church. They entered the church and everyone looked at her—her father and mother, her husband, and her godmother. Her mother said, "That looks like our daughter standing there." They all chattered about it and she heard them and then they left the church and went out into the anteroom, where she spoke to her mother: "I am yours, mother. Don't you remember how I came to you one night but you wouldn't let me in? Then I went to my old lover and he took me in and fed me, and nourished me for eight weeks, and he gave me these clothes."

And then they took her to court. They didn't return her to her old husband. They married her to her old lover who had taken her in during the night. That's my tale, that's my story. Give me a crust to eat. I was in that town and I drank some mead, but my mouth is crooked and the cup had a hole in it so it didn't get into my mouth.

73. About Savvushka

Known in Russian as the "Faithful Shepherd," the role of shepherd can be taken by any menial. The tale involves testing the loyalty of a servant in a contest usually between neighbors. SUS 889.

In this one village there lived and dwelt a husband and his wife. And they had this one son, Savvushka. One time his mother baked some *bliny* and sent Savvushka to his father with them. "And when you have given him the *bliny*, pick some berries for our tea." His father was plowing some new land in a clearing. It was a beautiful day, hot. A host of horseflies and gnats attacked the horse but Savvushka's father didn't wrap him in his horse blanket. The poor horse couldn't stand the biting and tumbled onto the ground, breaking both cart shafts. A piece of them flew off and struck Savvushka's father. Savvushka's father got really angry at the horse and beat it without mercy.

At that very moment Savvushka came up with the hot *bliny* and said to his father: "Father, how ashamed you must be to beat that animal for no reason. How sorry I am for it."

Then his enraged father said threateningly to Savvushka, "How dare you try to teach your father!" He stepped back from the horse and threw himself on Savvushka and he struck Savva with some birch branches and Savva got up from the ground with difficulty. So he left the *bliny* on a plate next to his father and went off in tears to tell his mother about his father. He wasn't up to picking berries just then.

And his mother knew that her husband was plowing just then, and thought Savvushka was picking berries so she set off and invited her favorite neighbor over, for whom she had made the *bliny*. When Savva came home, he called out for his mother, but there was no response. He thought, "Probably after making the *bliny* she's resting in the loft." When he looked in the loft, his mother was in fact lying there and next to her was the neighbor.

He said, "Can it be that the neighbor has no place to rest at home and so he's come to our house?"

Then his mother and the neighbor climbed down from the loft and they both attacked Savvushka and they began to whip and beat him and then they kicked him out on the street. Since Savvushka had no other relatives, he didn't know who to complain to. His father had wrongly beaten him and so had his mother and the neighbor, so he decided to go personally to the tsar and complain about his parents, since the capital city was not far away.

He walked along the road thinking, "I've heard that you don't approach the tsar with empty hands, everybody takes some kind of present. But I don't have any gift at all." So then he came into a clearing in the forest and he saw a little rabbit. He crept up and caught the rabbit. "Now I won't arrive with empty hands."

When he approached the tsar's palace, the tsar's guard wouldn't let him in because he had no pass. So Savvushka went away and began looking over the sentries at all the tsar's gates. And then he saw one sentry standing there and dreaming. Savvushka leapt around him and right into the tsar's court. But again other sentries wouldn't let him into the palace, so he went off a little way and found an open window not too far from the ground. He decided to crawl through that window. "And then I'll find the tsar." But it was unfortunate that he only had one arm free as the other was clutching the little rabbit. He decided to let the little rabbit through the window first and then he leapt up and grabbed hold of the window with both arms and crawled in. But since all of this took place near evening, it was very dark in the room and so Savvushka couldn't find the little rabbit. He began feeling for the door, opened it, but the second room was darker than the first. Then he found a door, opened it, and found himself in a third room and it was really bright in this room and it was decorated with many colors; Savvushka had never seen such beauty in his life. A table stood there and on the table stood various drinks and really tasty little morsels, and there was a beautiful bed with down comforters and pillows and the bed curtain went right down to the floor.

Since Savvushka was very tired and hungry, he wanted to eat but he was afraid, not having permission to do that. So he decided to lie down on the bed and rest. "But they may scold me!"

So then he crawled under the bed but just as soon as he had done so, a beautiful maiden entered. And then a little time later a handsome cavalier entered. He took a drink and a bite to eat and then he said, "My dear, what a beauty you are! A light shines from your face lighting up the whole earth and I see everything that's on it."

So then Savvushka said, "If you, good man, see everything on earth, tell me, please, which corner my little rabbit is hiding in."

The cavalier grabbed Savvushka by the hair and began pulling him and he pushed him out into the passageway, but Savvushka began crying loudly in great pain.

A royal servant grabbed Savvushka and said, "Why have you come here to steal in the tsar's chambers?"

He shouted at them through his tears, "I didn't come here to steal, I came to the tsar with a complaint."

As this racket was going on, the tsar was passing through to his study and he heard Savvushka's voice and he said, "Let him go, let him come in here to me." When Savvushka had entered, the tsar asked him, "What is the complaint you are bringing to me?"

Savvushka explained to him how his mother and the neighbor had beaten him for no good reason and "then they didn't want me to come to you and so I stole away and in my hands I had a fine little present, a little rabbit. First I let it into the room and then I climbed in after it. Then I went into a second room, which was dark just like the first. When I went into a third room, it was very light and various drinks were on the table as well as nice little bites to eat. And there was a very fine bed there with a down comforter and down pillows. Since I was tired, I wanted to lie down on the bed, but I was afraid that someone would curse me, so I crawled under the bed and saw a very beautiful maiden enter and soon after her there came a very handsome cavalier and she began treating him to drinks and bites to eat. When he had eaten and had his drink, he said to her, 'My dear, what a beauty you are! The light from your face brightens all the earth and I see everything on it.' So then I stuck my head out from under the bed and said, 'Tell me, please, my good man, if you can see everything on earth, tell me which corner my little rabbit is sitting in.' So then they grabbed me by the hair, pulled me out, and tossed me here. And then the guard cursed me and beat me and said, 'Why have you come here to steal in the tsar's chambers?'"

When the tsar heard these just words of Savvushka, he said to him, "I shall write a paper to your mother and father that they are not to harm you again for any reason. But if you wish, you may remain with me and I will make you a helper to the groom in the stables." Savvushka loved and took pity on horses and so he was happy to remain. Then they started teaching Savvushka to read and write and he fulfilled all his tasks honorably and conscientiously. The senior groom often praised Savvushka.

And then one beautiful day the senior groom got sick and died. And Savvushka, who had already reached adulthood, was made senior and no one could admire Savvushka's honesty on the job enough. And at that very time there was a war going on and the tsar had frequently said to his ministers and generals: "If you had fulfilled your duties as honorably as Savvushka, we would have conquered the whole world, but you are always acting like traitors for gold. They buy you off for gold."

The commanding general of the forces took offense at these words and said, "Do you want me to show that I can buy even your Savvushka for money?"

But the tsar said, "No."

"Do you want me to purchase your favorite horse?"

Then they made a bet. If the general could buy the horse from Savvushka, the tsar would give him a promotion in rank and half the tsardom. If he didn't succeed in buying it, then off with his head. He was given two months and a special secret guard was posted so that the tsar couldn't warn Savvushka.

So they drew up a document, which all the ministers signed, and after that the general came to Savvushka who was working in the stables and began to make his acquaintance and he said, "Sell me the tsar's favorite horse."

But Savvushka replied, "How could I sell it? The horse isn't mine; it's the tsar's. Go to the tsar. If he'll sell it, I'll hand it over." No matter how much the general implored him, Savvushka wouldn't agree. And the length of the agreement was coming to an end.

Then the general said to his oldest daughter, "Go and try your luck, my daughter, and maybe Savvushka will sell you the tsar's favorite horse. If we don't buy the horse, they'll take off my head and deprive you of the title of general's daughter and you'll be unhappy all your days. So therefore I'm asking you to go to him and promise to give him whatever he wants if only he'll sell us the horse."

So the general's daughter came to Savvushka and said, "Sell me the tsar's horse."

But Savvushka answered, "How could I sell it? The horse isn't mine; it's the tsar's. Go to the tsar. If he'll sell it, then I'll hand over the horse to you." And no matter what she promised, Savvushka wouldn't agree. So then she started to flatter Savvushka, and she moved closer and closer to him and she sat down next to him. Savvushka said to her, "Alright. I'll give you the horse. First you kiss me and then under the condition that if you can lead the horse home, it will be yours, but if the horse tears out of your hands, the horse will be mine."

So the general's daughter kissed Savvushka and Savvushka put a bridle on the horse, led it out of its stall, and handed it over to the general's daughter. She led it off but the horse started being capricious, leapt, started bucking and reared and tore out of the hands of the general's daughter. She took fright and let the horse go. Savvushka caught the horse and led it back to its stall.

Then the general sent his second daughter. No matter what she gave or promised Savvushka, he refused point-blank: "How could I sell it? The horse isn't mine—it's the tsar's and I can't sell it." She begged Savvushka with caresses and flirted with him, and Savvushka said, "Kiss me and I'll give you the horse. If you can lead the horse home, it will be yours under the condition that you lead it home, but if it tears out of your hands, the horse will be mine." And so he handed the horse over to her. It started to play up and jump and then gallop and it tore out of the hands of the general's daughter.

Then the general sent his favorite youngest daughter, saying to her: "You, my dearest, are the most intelligent, most beautiful, and most clever. Go and buy that horse from Savvushka. And give him whatever he wants, for tomorrow is the last day and if we don't buy it, then it's off with my head and they'll deprive you of the rank of general's daughter and you'll be unfortunate forever."

So the youngest daughter set out. She came up to Savvushka and started bartering for the horse. But no matter what she promised, even gold and precious jewels, in a word all that Savvushka could desire, he would not agree to it. Then she started caressing him and his young blood once more began to boil in Savvushka. He said to her, "I will give you the horse if you kiss me just once. But only on the condition that if you lead the horse to your house, the horse will be yours, but if it rears up and tears out of your hands, the horse will be mine." And so he gave her the horse. No matter how much the horse leapt, no matter how much it bucked, she hung on to the reins below the lip. And she led it home.

When the general and his servants saw her, they ran out to meet her and took the tsar's horse. In the morning the general reported to the tsar. He said, "You really trusted Savvushka but I bought your favorite horse from him." And all the ministers and generals were present. And the tsar said, "So there is no justice anywhere. I never thought that Savvushka would betray me. Now he must come to me with a report and we'll see what he says."

All this time Savvushka was pacing the room, thinking, "How can I appear with a report to the tsar?" He took off his field cap and put it on a table. He imagined the field cap was the tsar. "I have the honor to appear, your royal highness."

"Greetings, Savvushka!"

"I wish you good health, your royal highness."

"Is everything in the stables going well?"

"Your favorite horse has been stolen."

"No, that's not the truth."

So he took his field cap and threw it on the floor and then he put it on and took courage. "I'll tell them."

So this time he went to the tsar who was waiting for him with the whole court. "Your favorite horse was kissed by the general's three daughters."

"Good lad, Savvushka."

"I'm pleased to be of service." Then the tsar said to his ministers and generals: "Now you see, he did not sell the horse, he didn't take a single kopeck for it. In addition we had this condition, but why did the general send his daughters? Savvushka didn't sell it—he kissed it."

So they cut off the general's head and they dressed Savvushka in the uniform of a general and said, "Which one of the general's daughters do you want?" Savvushka said he wanted the youngest one. She was happy to marry Savvushka because he was very handsome and besides that he held a high rank. So Savvushka got married and gave a feast for the whole world. And I was at that feast, drank wine and beer, it flowed over my moustaches, but none got into my mouth.

74. The Son-in-Law Teaches His Wife and Mother-in-Law

There are fourteen Russian variants, including some with very strong regional tendencies. This Viatka tale is unusual in that the hero "tames" not only his wife but also his mother-in-law. He teaches his wife to work and punishes his mother-in-law for her bad advice. The appearance of St. Nicholas the Wonderworker is treated in an ironical manner, which is also unusual. The tale was told by G.A. Verkhrubov of Kotel'nicheskii district. SUS 901B*.

There lived this old man and old woman. And the old man and old woman had three daughters. The two older ones were married, but the youngest was still just a girl. The older ones paid no heed to their father, and neither did the youngest one. Once the old man started a conversation with his neighbors: "To anyone who teaches my daughter to be obedient in all things, I will give a samovar and a cart with iron axles as her dowry."

Not far away was this village, about a verst away. And in this village a lad lived with his father who was a peasant. The peasant decided to marry him off and asked him, "Vasia, where could we find a bride that would please you? I'll go make the match."

"Well, father, in the next village this old man has a very fine daughter."

So his father rode over as matchmaker and arranged the marriage for his son. And when the time of the wedding arrived, the old man said to his young son-in-law, "Now son-in-law, if you can teach my daughter to be obedient, I'll give you a samovar and a cart with iron axles as her dowry." The son-in-law bowed to his father-in-law to be. After the wedding and all the feasting they [were led] to the wedding chamber. [And the groom had got a young lad to climb out onto the loft, taking with him a whip made of straps, an axe, and an aspen block. This had all been done.] When the guests had left the wedding chamber, and the doors were locked, the husband said to his wife, "Wife, bow down to my feet!"

"But you still haven't bowed down to me!"

Then he said, "Nicholas, Helper of God, throw down that strap of whips from heaven." Suddenly the whip fell onto the floor. He took the whip and began teaching his wife a lesson. He taught her, oh he taught her! And he said, "Wife, bow down to my feet!"

"You have beaten me and I'm to bow down to you! That's something new! You bow down to me!"

Then he said, "Nicholas, Helper of God, throw me that axe from heaven and the aspen block. I'll cut off my wife's head!" Suddenly the axe and aspen block fell onto the floor. "Now, wife, lie down on that block and I'll cut off your head."

Then his wife started crying and fell at his feet. "Kind husband, have mercy on me. I'll obey you in everything, only don't kill me!"

The husband forgave his wife.

They began living and prospering and so they lived until carnival. And the father-in-law came to invite his son-in-law to eat *bliny*. But the son-in-law treated him and said, "Eat, father, I'll be back by evening." When the father-in-law had left, it began to get dark, and the son-in-law hitched up his horse, put his wife on the sleigh, and set off visiting. They were approaching the village when he stopped, unhitched the horse, hitched his wife to the sleigh tongue, and set off with his wife pulling the sleigh. His father-in-law was looking out the window and laughing. How his son-in-law had taught his daughter! There was nothing more to say about it.

The son-in-law left his wife in the yard and went into the hut and he ordered her to stay there for a while. When he had entered the hut, his mother-in-law said, "What? Didn't our daughter come in with you?"

"Yes, I came on her and she really got up a sweat so she's standing there by that post, resting." Her mother leapt out to the yard and let out a howl. But her daughter said, "Mama, don't howl or else my husband will hear. And then he'll chop off your head. That's just his sort of behavior."

On the husband's orders the mother-in-law and her daughters came into the hut. When they had eaten supper, the father-in-law took an interest in his sons-in-law and said to his oldest son-in-law, "Order your wife to give us each a tankard of beer."

"What sort of host do you think you are? If you want some, get it yourself," said the wife of the oldest son-in-law.

Then he repeated the same thing to the middle daughter.

Then the father-in-law asked the youngest son-in-law, "Son-in-law, order your wife to give us each a tankard of beer!"

The son-in-law said, "Wife!"

"What do you wish?"

"Give us each a tankard of beer." His wife jumped up and started handing round the beer, to her husband, her father, and all the guests. She handed round the beer, sang songs, and even danced.

The next day the father-in-law was saying farewell to his son-in-law and he said, "Go into the stables and take any gelding you want; take the samovar, and the iron cart, and all this because you taught my daughter so well."

So they lived on until summer. And the old woman was still sorry for her daughters. So she set off to find out how they were getting along. How was her youngest daughter getting along? The mother-in-law went through the field and just then her son-in-law was plowing near the road. The old woman turned away from him and passed by, she said nothing. The son-in-law saw that his mother-in-law had gone visiting, so he hitched up his horse and rode home. When he got home, he came up to the porch doors and heard what his mother-in-law was saying to her daughter. She asked her daughter, "How do you get along with your husband?"

And the daughter answered, "Oh mama, I obey him so much that I never eat anything; I take it all to him!"

"You fool! And how does he treat you? You ought to cook for yourself and he could chew on dry bread."

The son-in-law heard these words, got angry with his mother-in-law, put a bridle on her, hitched her to a plow, and started plowing the garden with his mother-in-law. He plowed the entire garden. He got his mother-in-law into such a sweat that it poured from her. Then he brought her over to the fence and tied her to a post and said, "You can stand here for a while and rest. It's not good to give water to someone in such a sweat." Then he went into the hut.

So the mother said to her daughter, "Untie me and I'll go running home!"

Her daughter began trying to persuade her mother. "But mother, because of you my husband will cut off my head. That's the kind of man he is! If he doesn't like something, then off with the head."

But the old woman still got untied and ran home.

Her husband met her on the porch. The old man asked, "Well, my old woman! And how did your son-in-law receive you?"

"Get out of my way, you old goat! He also asked you to go and visit," the old woman said with a sneer. So the old man got ready and set off to visit his son-in-law. The son-in-law was plowing. And he was far from the road. The father-in-law went up to the strip he was plowing and stopped. The son-in-law came up to him by the road. "God help you, son-in-law!"

"You are most welcome!"

"I've come visiting you, to see how you're getting on with your work and to talk about this and that."

So the son-in-law unhitched his horse, put the old man on the horse, and he walked along while his father-in-law rode on the horse's back. When they got home, the son-in-law ran over to the inn and brought back a quart of vodka and he started treating his father-in-law. And he gave him so much to drink that in the evening when the father-in-law set off home, he stood up and fell down. He couldn't walk at all.

His son-in-law harnessed two manure carts, one behind the other, put his father-in-law in them, and set off to take him home (he needed two because his father-in-law was so tall and he couldn't fit him in just one cart.) He brought him to the village, unloaded him from the cart, and went back home so that his mother-in-law wouldn't see him.

The old man could hardly crawl up to the fence on his hands and knees, staggering. The old woman jumped out of the hut and said, "Oh, you old son-of-a bitch! He used me to plow his garden and obviously used you to do the whole field. I could at least walk on my legs, but you're crawling on all fours!"

75. How Peter and a Hunter Went Hunting

This is an interesting tale in that Peter the Great features as the tsar. Versions of the tale were current in the eighteenth century. It was recorded in 1947 from V.S. Isaev, born in 1879, in Kolomna region. Negomozh is a village near Moscow. SUS 921A.

Once Peter I was out with his hunters in the forest and in that forest he got separated from his retinue. The hunters made their way out of the forest and went into a village, perhaps Negomozh, but the tsar went on riding about the forest. And then along a road he happened upon this peasant and the peasant was chopping wood. He was chopping wood and bringing down the limbs from a tree. He wasn't chopping the tree, just bringing down the limbs, and then he climbed up into the tree and climbed back down. Then the tsar went up to that very tree where the peasant was bringing down the branches.

"Greetings, peasant." He didn't know he was the tsar.

"Greetings," he said.

"How might I make my way to Negomozh?" asked the tsar.

"Well, straight ahead, to the left, and to the right." And he said, "I don't know how to read or write, but if you want, I'll take you there, but it will cost a pretty penny."

"Whatever it costs, I'll pay."

He didn't know that it was the tsar he was conversing with, as he was just a simple peasant. "Let me just finish tidying up this tree."

So he finishing tidying up the tree, then he sat down in a double-axled cart, and hitched up his horse.

And then the tsar spoke, "Tell me, peasant, you work here, but then where do you put the money you earn?"

"Where do I put my money? I pay off a debt, I make loans, and I throw some out the window."

The tsar said, "I don't understand your riddle. You will have to explain what you mean."

And the peasant began to explain it. "I pay a debt: I pay my father and mother; I make loans means I take care of my sons, and I throw some out the window means I marry off my daughters. Is that clear? Is that not proper?"

It was time then for them to go out of the woods and go to Negomozh, where the tsar's hunters were resting. And he said, "Well, little peasant, did you ever see the tsar face to face?"

"No, I never saw him."

"And would you desire to look at him?"

"I'd agree to die first in order to see the tsar."

"So ride into Negomozh and you will see that in the village there is a huge crowd of soldiers."

"And will I recognize him among them?"

"You will recognize that none of them will wear a cap. Only he will be in a cap."

So they came into Negomozh and he was staring but he didn't see the tsar. He looked but he didn't see him anywhere.

"No, none of them has a cap."

"Then perhaps one of us?"

Then the peasant said, "Your imperial highness! I apologize for having had such a brazen conversation with you."

"Never mind, never mind. Now those white geese are flying toward you. You should pluck them but don't tell them that riddle you gave me."

So the tsar set off home and with him were the generals and officers. And he said, "I met this peasant and I gave him this question, 'Where do you work, where do you put your money?' And he said, 'Where do I put my money? I pay off a debt, I make loans, and I throw some out the window.' Now be so kind as to explain what this means. This is to be solved by all of you by tomorrow morning."

They thought and they thought but no one could solve the problem. So they turned to that peasant who had brought the tsar out of the forest. They turned to him and he told all of them what he had told the tsar. And then each of them threw half a hundred or a full hundred to him and they made him a rich man. They all went in the morning with the same story and the tsar understood that the peasant had told them the story.

"Call that peasant to meet me. Why did he tell them?" He came and he brought all the money he had got from them.

"Peasant, why did you tell them that story without my permission?"

"I would never tell them without your permission." He showed the tsar the money and there was the tsar featured on every coin.

"Clever lad, peasant."

"I'm happy to help, your highness." And so he was rewarded. He became a big shot.

76. Peter the Great Ate the *Murzovka*

This tale about Peter I's eating a soup called *murzovka* is recorded in the Potiavin version only. *Murzovka* is a soupy mixture of bread, milk, and sour milk or *kvass*. SUS 921H*.

The ruler Peter the Great made an inspection of all Russia at one time in his best. He rode along the road with his coachman and they wanted to eat. The ruler ordered the coachman to drive into a village, to the first house they should encounter. They took care of their horses, tied them up, and went into an inn, which was really just a hovel. They exchanged greetings with the mistress of the house and asked her for something to eat. The mistress answered, "There's nothing to eat, there's nothing to feed you. Perhaps there's a crust of bread and a little *kvass* and a spoonful of butter. And if you wish, I can make you a *murzovka*." She didn't know that this was Peter the Great.

So they agreed. When she had made the *murzovka*, she gave it to them to eat. They really liked this *murzovka*. They ate it and wanted to pay her, but she wouldn't take any money. They thanked the mistress and with this they rode on.

They rode into the courtyard. Peter the Great sent for his valet and ordered the valet to go and fetch the cook. When the cook appeared face to face with the tsar, the ruler said to the cook, "I would like for you to give me some *murzovka* to eat."

"What is this *murzovka*?" thought the cook. He went into the kitchen and decided to go straight to the tsar. He appeared before his majesty and told him that this *murzovka* was in no book of his.

His majesty sent the cook to the stables and ordered him to tell him to harness up a pair of dappled gray horses and ride to that village where he and the coachman had stopped and search the house where they had eaten. There they would find out what this *murzovka* was. So the cook prepared it, although it didn't have the same taste it had had in the village: it was better. And the ruler liked the *murzovka*.

77. The Carefree Monastery

The type is well known in the Russian tradition. Gurevich's version, from Siberia, is particularly well developed. It is related to the tales about the king or kaiser and the abbot known throughout Europe since the Middle Ages. SUS 922.

In a large tract of land there stood a monastery. Many peasants came there to pray. Once as he was driving by, a certain peasant also took it into his head to pray and he knocked at the monastery gates. But no was there. The gates were firmly locked. He listened at the gates and he could hear something—perhaps verses, perhaps even songs. He thought to himself: This must be a carefree monastery. He took out his notebook, tore a page from it, and in large print he wrote: "CAREFREE MONASTERY." He stuck it to the wall.

Soon the tsar came. He also decided to pray here and he saw on the wall the note "CAREFREE MONASTERY." He was greatly astonished. He entered the monastery. The Father Hegumen came to meet him with the cross. He made the sign of the cross over him. The tsar kissed the cross and then asked the Father Hegumen: "It turns out you have a carefree monastery."

The Father Hegumen turned a little bashful and asked the tsar where he learned that this was a carefree monastery.

The tsar led him out onto the street and showed him the note. The Hegumen began begging his forgiveness. Then the tsar said, "I can forgive you only if I set you three riddles. If you can figure them out, then I'll forgive you. Otherwise, I'll execute you all." He got in his carriage and rode away.

The Father Hegumen went away and explained to the monks and brother novices: "When his majesty came here, he put a great sadness on us. Now it is going to be necessary for all of us to labor and endure sadness." They started asking him what sort of sadness it was to be. He explained to them that the tsar had ordered them to find out how many stars there are in the sky. Then the second riddle: is the other world further away or are the heavens higher? Then the third, he ordered them to evaluate him, to see what he is worth. "So brothers, try to solve these riddles; otherwise his majesty will execute us."

So one monk thought. "In any case, I haven't long to live. I'd better go off and take a walk." He came to a tavern and ordered a large measure of vodka.

The tavern keeper was astonished: "Why should a monk need such a large measure of vodka?" he asked him.

The monk told him that his majesty had put a great sadness on them. At that moment a drunkard came up. "What sort of sadness could the tsar place on you?"

The monk told him, "Once you and I had occasion to chat a while."

The other responded, "Perhaps I can help you."

The monk thought and started telling him about it.

Then the drunkard said, "That's easy. I can guess the answers."

So the monk led him to the Father Hegumen and told him that here was a man who could answer the riddles.

The Father Hegumen led him into a room and began asking him: "If only you can, we will reward you with everything you need."

And he replied: "I don't need any reward from you. Only let us exchange clothing. I'll put on your hegumen's clothing, and you put on mine."

No sooner said than done. The drunkard put on the hegumen's clothing and the hegumen put on the drunkard's rags. So now the pretend hegumen asked for several quires of paper. "What for?" asked the Father Hegumen.

"I have to count the number of stars in the sky." A novice quickly brought him the paper and he locked himself in a room and he began writing numbers: twenty here or thirty there, then a thousand, or two or three. And soon he had used up all the paper.

All the monks asked the pretend hegumen how he would deal with the other tasks. He said, "That's not your affair."

On a designated day the tsar came, and Father Hegumen met him with the cross. The tsar kissed the cross and asked, "Well, Father Hegumen, have you figured out my tasks?"

"Of course, your imperial highness, judge for yourself."

He brought him the papers. "You can see that the stars are counted. Only no totals have been entered."

The tsar looked and recounted. He looked again but there were just numbers and numbers. Nothing more. "What is this, Father Hegumen? You've lied to me."

"How so, your imperial highness? If I lied, then count for yourself how many stars are in the sky."

The tsar considered this foolish. He asked about the second riddle. "Well, did you find out? Is that other world further or are the heavens higher?"

"I found that out, too. It must be that that light is further. Since my father went off to the other world, twenty-five years have passed and he still hasn't come back, but in heaven I can hear them chattering and gossiping. So heaven must be closer."

The tsar laughed at this answer. He began asking about the third question. "Did you evaluate me?"

"Yes, I did. You're worth twenty-nine rubles."

This made the tsar furious. "How can that be? A simple day laborer gets thirty rubles a month and you evaluate me at twenty-nine."

"It's very simple," the hegumen said, "because we have this heavenly tsar who was sold for thirty pieces of silver, you ought to be worth at least one ruble less than He."

The tsar was astonished at his wise answer and said, "Can you guess what I am thinking?"

"You are thinking, your imperial highness, that the hegumen of the monastery is quite a lad."

"That is exactly what I am thinking," said the tsar.

"But you are mistaken."

"How so?"

"This fine lad is not the hegumen of the monastery. I'm just a drunkard from the tavern and inn."

"How's that possible?"

They went back and forth with their questions and answers. The hegumen indeed turned out to be a drunkard and the real hegumen was in the drunkard's clothing. The tsar appointed the drunkard as hegumen and forced the former hegumen to leave.

78. Why There Is Treason in Rus

Recounts the ill-fated attempts of Ivan IV to trick a peasant building a church. Rybnikov heard the tale from a Mr. Prozorovskii. SUS 922*.

Tsar Ioann Vasilevich was a stern and powerful tsar, and a fearsome conqueror of other lands, which is why he was called "the Terrible." Once it occurred to him to send his envoys to other lands and demand from their kings and princes the annual tribute due Russia. The envoys reported the tsar's orders to all the foreign kings and princes to whom they had been sent. The kings and princes all gathered in one place and began to hold a council. Should they pay the tribute to the Russian tsar or not? Finally they decided to give the Russian tsar three riddles and if he should solve them, then the kings and princes would immediately give him twelve barrels of gold and pay the annual tribute as well, but if he could not solve them, then not only would they not pay him the tribute, but he would have to quit the tsar's throne. All the kings and princes agreed to this and they sent their envoys with a letter to Tsar Ioann Vasilevich in which they wrote:

> Your royal highness! We are agreed to pay our tribute to Russia according to your demand, and moreover to give you twelve barrels of gold with the condition that you solve our three riddles, which are: What is most daring on earth; what is dearest on earth; and what is sweetest on earth? If you can't solve these riddles, then you will not only receive no tribute from us but you must quit the tsardom. To give your solutions you must come yourself to the East, to the white stone, at such and such a time, where all the kings and princes will gather.

When Tsar Ioann Vasilevich received this letter from the kings and princes and read it, he fell to thinking, and then he gathered all his boyars and princes and clever folk, and presented them with the letter from those foreign kings and princes, and he took counsel with them about how to answer the letter and how to solve the riddles. Some spoke of this or that, but it was not much to the tsar's liking. Finally as a general council they thought of a course of action for the tsar: there is nothing more daring than the wind, and since the tsar had recently become the father of a son they said that there was nothing dearer than he. The tsar agreed with both of these. Then they said that there could be nothing sweeter than honey.

The appointed time came and the tsar prepared to ride to the East to the white stone with all his royal retinue for the solving of the riddles and to receive the annual tribute. Whether he rode far or near, or for a short or long time, the tsar saw in a deserted place a little peasant who was building a church. Most of the church had already been built. He just had to shingle the cupola—in past times they covered cupolas of churches and chapels with shingles—and for every shingle and nail the peasant climbed down from the very top to the ground and then went back up with a single shingle and nail. The tsar rode up to the structure and said to the master: "God help you, old man!"

"Greetings to you, my good man," answered the old man.

"So what are you doing, building a church, old man?"

"That's correct, your grace."

He didn't call him tsar as if he didn't know who it was.

"Why is it, old man, that you go down for a single shingle and nail and then go back up with it? You could take up to ten shingles and nails and carry them up at once. That would be easier for you, wouldn't it?"

"To each his own trade," answered the old man. "And I am asking you, Russian Tsar Ivan Vasilevich the Terrible: where are you going and why? You are going to the East to the white stone to solve the riddles they gave you, aren't you? The foreign kings and princes are already waiting for you there but if you don't resolve those riddles then you will be deprived of your tsardom."

Tsar Ivan Vasilevich thought hard about it and asked the old man, "How can it be that you know all this and could you not help me?"

The old man answered, "Permit me to help you, Tsar Ivan Vasilevich, but only with one condition. You are promised twelve barrels of gold and the annual tribute for solving the riddles. You will get the gold and the tribute but only if you agree to give me one of the barrels. If you agree to this, then I will give you the answers to the riddles and you will go on reigning. If not, your tsardom will end."

The tsar replied, "Take any one of the twelve barrels—just tell me the answers."

So then the old man began. "First they asked you what is most daring on earth, isn't that so?" he asked the tsar.

"That's correct."

"You tell them that that there is nothing more daring than their own eyes. Wherever they look, they see everything in an instant. The second riddle was what is dearest on earth. What could be dearer for us on earth than the bright sun? It warms us and every living thing rejoices. The third was what is sweetest of all. There is nothing sweeter than water on earth. Without it no one and nothing can live. Now go and tell them this and you will have everything."

Tsar Ioann Vasilevich thanked the old man and set off for the East, to the white stone. He arrived at the indicated place where all the foreign kings and princes were already waiting for him. They greeted the tsar appropriately and then began asking him to interpret the riddles they had set him.

The tsar began like this: "Your first riddle was 'what is most daring on earth?'

and I answer that there is nothing more daring than your own eyes. Wherever you look you see everything."

"That is the absolute truth!" said the kings and princes.

"The second: what is dearest of all on earth? Can there be anything dearer on earth than the bright sun? It warms us and every living thing rejoices."

"This is true," answered the kings and princes.

"The third was what is sweetest of all on earth. Can there be anything sweeter than water? Take yourselves for example. If any of us has a great desire to drink and you were told that there is no water and then later you found out that someone else had a supply of water and you still passionately wanted to drink, then you would give God knows what for a spoonful if only you could take a drink. And you would drink hungrily and with such pleasure."

"This is true, absolutely true," shouted the kings and princes, and then they handed over the twelve barrels of gold and promised to pay the annual tribute that was demanded of them.

So Ivan Vasilevich the Terrible took his leave of the foreign kings and princes and set off back to his own tsardom. He approached the place where the old man was building the church. The tsar said to his retinue: "Now, my lords, what do you think: don't you think that giving the old man a barrel of gold is rather too much? We have this army and other forces that need to be maintained and what does the old man have, where would he put the gold? Let's do this instead. Let's take two-thirds of the gold out of one of the barrels and fill up the barrel with sand so that it won't be noticeable and then we'll hand it over to him." They all agreed to this.

No sooner said than done. That's what they did. They took out the gold and filled the barrel two-thirds full with sand and then they put one-third of the gold on top; then they rode up to him. They came to the place where the old man was building the church and the tsar rode up to the old man.

"The Lord help you, old man," he said. "I most humbly thank you for your instruction; I received everything as you promised. So now, old man, you shall receive the barrel of gold that was promised."

The old man said, "Well, Russian Tsar Ivan Vasilevich the Terrible, you yourself will have brought treachery and treason to Orthodox Rus and you will never root it out from this time hence. And the sole reason for this evil is you yourself, Tsar. Why did you try to deceive me? I saved you and your life and you promised me a barrel of gold, but you are paying me with sand and not with gold."

The tsar saw that this was no simple man and he tearfully asked the old man to take any barrel he wished, but the old man replied, "I have no need of your gold and I shall live without your gold. I have no need of your gold plating—I need only the truth. You are a traitor to all this and this treason, I repeat, shall live in Rus for ages and ages and neither you nor anyone else will be able to uproot it. All the cause of all this evil is the Terrible Tsar Ivan Vasilevich. Farewell, tsar," said the old man. "Go forward and rule!"

And in an instant both the church and the old man vanished. All was gone and not a trace remained. Ivan Vasilevich the Terrible concluded that this had been God Himself. He bowed to the earth at this place and set off to rule.

79. Eaten by a Wolf

From the collection of V.I. Dal'. One recalls that St. George (Georgii, Iurii, Egorii) is regarded as the patron saint of wolves by the Russian peasants. SUS 934B*.

Two shepherds were herding a flock of sheep and one of them wanted a drink so he set off through the forest to this well. He walked and he walked and he caught sight of a huge, leafy oak. Beneath it the grass was trampled and dug up. "Let me look and see what's going on here," the shepherd said, and he climbed up to the very top of the tree. He looked down and there came Saint Georgii and right behind him a whole pack of wolves. So Georgii stopped next to the oak and started dispersing the wolves in all directions and he told each one where he should go and what he should eat. He got rid of all of them and then he got ready to ride on.

But then this crippled old wolf dragged himself out and asked him, "So what's to become of me?" Egorii said, "You go wait beneath that oak."

The wolf waited a day and then he waited another for the shepherd to come down from the tree. He went off a little way and hid himself behind this bush. The shepherd looked around, came down, and started to run. But the wolf leapt out from behind the bush, grabbed him, and ate him right there and then.

80. How a Lad Bought Wisdom

The only East Slavic version of this tale type. It tells the story of a prodigal son who solves a murder involving a priest and his lover and is richly rewarded for his efforts. SUS 939A.

A lad got his discharge and went off and he saw this signboard. It said that wisdom could be bought there. He was interested and went into the shop. He came in and said, "Greetings, master!"

"Greetings, young man!"

"What do you sell here?"

"Wisdom."

"And what is wisdom?"

The shopkeeper answered him, "Pay a hundred rubles and then we'll tell you what wisdom is."

So he took out the money and paid the hundred rubles. The shopkeeper tossed the money into a cash box and said to him, "Now, young man, you are thinking of going home. Go as far as a place were there is a road three versts long and another road ten versts long. They will come together, these roads will. You will go along the ten-verst road just as quickly as the three-verst road."

And he asked, "And then what?"

"That's all."

So he thought, "What have I given my hundred rubles for? Well, I've given them away and I won't ever get them back." He went and changed into some other clothes and then set off back along the same road to that shop. When he got there, he said, "Greetings!"

And the man said, "Greetings!"

"What do you sell here?"

"Wisdom."

"And what is wisdom?"

"Pay a hundred rubles and we'll tell you."

So he took out a hundred rubles and gave it to him. The other one threw the money in a cash box and said, "As you're walking home, don't stop in anywhere to spend the night if the master is old and the mistress is young."

"And what else?"

"Nothing else."

He thought, "What a fool I am! I've wasted all my money and now I'll have to go home on foot. And it's a long way."

Nonetheless, he set off home. He walked a whole day.

The next day twelve carts and three peasants caught up to him. They asked him, "Where are you going, young man?"

"I'm going from Petrograd to Petrozavodsk."

"That's where we're going too."

The peasants were all brothers, although with different parents. The two youngest had three horses each and the oldest one had six horses. The one who had the six horses invited him, "Get on a cart. You can help us drive the horses."

They rode along. They came up to this place where this road was and there was a sign there: "This is the three-verst road. The other is the ten-verst road, the post road. But they will join together."

The ones who had the three horses said, "Let's take this road, the one that is three versts long. Why should we ride an extra seven versts?"

Then the young man said, "Well, Uncle, let's take this road. The other could be muddy and the horses will get stuck. You're getting a little old and I'm no specialist in this business."

The older man thought. "Alright, let's go."

Then they said to each other: "Whoever gets there first should wait there at the place where the two roads meet."

And so they rode off. Some took the three-verst road and the others took the ten-verst road. The ones who took the ten-verst road got there first and started waiting for the others. They arrived toward evening and said, "Well, brother, tell that young man 'thank you' since you didn't have to suffer. No matter how much we suffered—we broke the cart tongue. Then we broke a wheel and had to go buy another in the village. We were worn out and wore out the horses."

The young man thought: "My hundred rubles haven't been wasted. He told the truth. Now I'll ride and take a look around."

So they came to the village. Evening was just beginning. They all set off to ask for a place to spend the night. Someone let them in for the night. The young man saw that the wife was young and the man was old. He said to the older brother, "Uncle, this place is a little small. It's not a good place to put up twelve horses. Let's go on out of the village. We still have to feed the horses. We'll start a little fire and have some supper. You'll sleep a little and I'll sit here and then you'll get up and I'll rest. Then the others will arrive and we'll ride off all together."

The older man listened to the young man. "Let's do that!"

The brothers said to him, "Don't you ride too far. Tomorrow we'll ride up to you and then we'll ride together."

So that's what they did. They rode out of town. It was a deserted place. They brought their horses to a halt. They unhitched the horses and tied them up. They fed them. They took something to eat themselves. It soon got pretty dark. The young man said, "Uncle!"

"What?"

"Give me your little hatchet."

"What do you need it for?"

"Well, here, I know, in this forest are a lot of lime trees. I'll cut them and take the bark off them. I'm a master at weaving lime bark for *lapti*. Before we get to Petrozavodsk, I'll have woven lots of bast shoes and there I'll sell them. I'll appear in the village with at least a little money on me."

The older man said, "Well, take my hatchet and go. There are lots of lime trees in that wood and I don't care about them but it will be no small task. The horses will cart them in."

So he took the hatchet and ran off into the village. He came running and jumped under a window. There was a fire burning and the window was curtained. He looked through the transom and there was a priest rolling about with the young mistress. They were discussing something.

"The old man's asleep now. Let's kill him and hand him over to the peasants in a cart. The peasants will set off and you can shout 'you've killed my old man. You put him in a cart and are intending to throw him off somewhere along the road.' And everyone will believe that."

Well, when they had killed the old man, they handed him over to the peasants in the cart but those peasants didn't know that there was this dead body in the cart. Then they all went into the hut and started eating and drinking.

The priest said, "Now, my dearest, we can carouse quite freely."

So the young man went and knocked at the door and then he ran to the window, where he was met by a frightening scene.

"Somebody's trying to get into the hut." She opened the window and said, "Father, jump through that window and run home."

The priest laid his hand on the window and the lad struck him with the hatchet. He chopped two fingers off the priest's hand.

The priest ran off without his fingers.

The young man picked up the fingers, put them in his pocket, and set off to the older brother. He wasn't asleep. 'Uncle, where is your lime tree?"

"Well, it's midnight and I can't see very well. I can't chew with my teeth an alder or a willow and I've never tried chewing on a lime."

The young man threw down the hatchet and came up to him. He placed the hatchet in its place where it had been. "Alright, grandfather, you go on and rest. I'll sit here a while, or else I'll rest and you sit here a while."

So the young man lay down and slept soundly. And then near morning the older man woke him: "Get up and sit awhile and I'll rest for an hour or so."

"Alright, Uncle. You rest."

So the older man lay down to rest and the young man sat around for a while. It became dawn. He woke up the old man: "Grandfather, get up and let's have a little breakfast or else your brothers will soon come and we'll have to go." They got up and ate a bite but the brothers still didn't appear. So he said, "Old man, you go after them."

So he came back to the village and the brothers' hands were all tied behind their backs. They were sitting there, arrested. Just then a constable appeared, the one from the settlement. And this policeman said, "Do you see, travelers, it's clear that they've been doing this crap for some time and they are without faith."

The brothers said to each other, "Tell that young man that he's not to be with us anymore."

So the older brother set off crying to the young man.

He arrived and told him everything: "Thank you for getting me out of there, otherwise you and I would have been bound, too."

And he said, "Uncle."

"What?"

"What if I rescued them?"

"If you rescue them, take any one of those six horses—and anything on that cart—it's all yours. And they'll give you something for each horse, they won't stint, but you must rescue them first."

"I'll do it, grandfather! I'll do it!" he said. "Give me your little hatchet!" He took the hatchet (and it was still covered in blood) and put it under his coat and set off into the village. He arrived; a crowd had already arrived and the corpse was lying there. He went up to the constable and asked, "Is it possible, your honor, that travelers passing by killed this man?"

"Maybe they didn't kill him and he just fell off the cart? The old man perhaps approached that cart for some reason to look at something on it and they suddenly decided that he had come to rob them and so they struck him. Then they saw that he had tumbled off and so they tied him and oiled him and put him on the cart. They rode on and would have thrown him off if the woman hadn't seen it. So, they have no faith, any of them."

He said, "Is it Sunday today?"

"Yes, it's Sunday."

"Isn't it time to go to church to pray to God?"

"What business do you have with prayers?" asked the constable.

"I've no business, only I want to find out why the priest isn't going to church."

"What business do we have with the priest?"

"Your honor, if the priest comes here, perhaps he'll tell us that they didn't kill anybody."

"We've little to do with the priest," the constable said.

"No, your honor, we still need to summon that priest."

So the constable ordered the village elder to go fetch the priest. The night watchman set off. He came to the priest and said, "Father, you are required to go there and sort out some business. Some passersby killed a peasant."

The priest replied, "I'm sick, I can't come. Tell them that the priest said that they certainly did kill him."

So the elder came back to the constable and told him, "Well, the priest is sick and said they were really in the cart and had committed the sin."

So the constable said, "Well, we'll really have to sort it out with these lads!"

And the young man insisted, "Well, your honor, we need to find out what's the matter with that priest. Perhaps you can demand that he come here, and if he doesn't, then we'll bring him here at the point of a bayonet."

Once more the constable spoke: "What business do we have with the priest?"

"You'll see what business we have with the priest! If you are the constable, then you need to work with your head. What people say you should also hear, and bring that priest here."

So the constable saw that the young man had something in mind. He sent two men and a third worker. "Go and fetch that priest here!"

They led up the priest. His right hand was bound. The young man asked him, "Well, Father, is your hand hurting?"

"Yes, it's hurting."

"And why is your hand hurting?"

"I was chopping wood and injured it. I chopped off two fingers."

"And where are those two fingers?"

"What business is it of yours? Why do you ask?"

"You should unbind your hand and show everyone how you can chop off the fingers of your right hand with your left one. Or are you left-handed?"

The constable said, "Alright, father, untie your hand and show us."

The priest untied the bandage. He was missing two fingers.

"And where are those fingers?" the young man asked.

"Once they were cut off, I threw them away. Probably a cat or dog ate them."

The young man took the fingers out of his pocket. "Let's measure them. Won't these fingers fit your hand?" And they fit exactly! "And wasn't this the hatchet I cut them off with?" He went to the window and measured the hatchet. And the fit was exact. "And so you did this and blamed it on the travelers. You and your mistress killed him. I stood here under the window and you killed him and then you carried him to the cart to hide him. Then you discussed what to do and I heard it all. I knocked on the door. You were frightened and she opened the door and you started crawling out. That's when I cut off your fingers."

When they had untied the travelers, they arrested the priest. And the young man set off to his master's. They arrived at his place and he said, "Take a pair of horses and their treasure."

The oldest brother said, "I'll give a horse for having rescued us."

So he rode into the town and he sold one of the horses and he sold some of the goods too. And then on another pair he went home. When he got there, he had brought a lot of money and the pair of horses. And he started living there happily with his mother.

81. Why They Stopped Banishing Old Men

Recorded in 1970 in eastern Lithuania from P.O. Vanagen. In this subtype the robber comes to the aid of the tsar. The tale has been recorded in Russia since the eighteenth century. SUS 951B.

Once a long time ago there was this tsar. He was so greedy that he issued a command: "Anyone who cannot work, or has grown old, must be banished from here."

Now a certain man had an old father. The time came for him to be taken away. What was to be done? The son took him away on a sleigh into the forest during a severe cold spell. When they set off, he took his son to help. When they had brought the old man there, they placed him under a pine. And then the old man's son said to his son, "Let grandfather sit on the sleigh. We don't need to bring it back home."

But the boy said, "How could we leave the sleigh? I'm going to need it when I have to cart you off." This saddened the father and he decided not to abandon the old man in the forest alone. He brought him back home and hid him in a drying shed. There he kept him all winter, spring, and summer.

Autumn began and the harvest failed in that region. Everything that had been planted in the spring had still not come up. Nothing had grown for this man either. He went to the old man and told him everything. So then the old man said, "Take the straw from the threshing floor and plant it." So that's what the old man's son did.

The next morning the old man sent his son, saying, "Go into the fields and see what's to be seen there." So the son went into the field and saw that nothing had grown there.

On the next day the old man again sent off his son: "Go into the fields, put your ear to the ground, and hear what's to be heard."

The son went into the fields, put his ear to the ground, and suddenly he heard some voices: "Where are you going?"

"Where are you?"

"I'm here." He came home and told the old man what he had heard.

The next morning the old man sent his son to the fields once more to hear what could be heard. This time the son heard, "Further, push on further, I haven't got room." He came home and told this to his father. The old man said to him, "Probably the wheat will show through tomorrow."

The next day the son went out and saw that a fine crop of wheat had grown up. But the others in the village had practically none. People began to complain of this to the tsar. The tsar went to see for himself whether what people were saying was true. He rode on his horse and saw that nothing had appeared anywhere except in the field of this one peasant. The tsar went in to the man and asked him why he was the only one who had a crop of wheat. So he was forced to tell the whole story to the tsar. The tsar asked him to show the old man to him. The man begged the tsar not to do anything to the old man and the tsar promised.

The old man came out and the tsar asked him, "If you are so wise, tell me, will I die soon?" The old man said that he would have to think about that. In a day the tsar appeared again and the old man told him that he would soon die. The tsar took fright and said, "Now tell me right away how to save myself from death!" The old man again said that he would have to think about it. In a day the tsar appeared again and the old man said that the tsar wouldn't die if on the very night he was to die he would go out thieving, and that that night was to be the very next one. The tsar was greatly upset but what could he do?

So the tsar waited for the night, dressed in thief's clothing, and left his bedroom, not knowing where to go or what to steal. He walked along and he saw a real thief. He went up to him and said, "Let's steal together!"

The thief agreed and said, "Let's steal something from the royal palace." The tsar agreed. So then the thief dragged out a rope and threw it in one window of the palace. He secured it and started climbing up the wall. And the tsar waited for him below.

Suddenly he saw the thief lowering himself back down and his hands were empty. The tsar asked him why he hadn't stolen anything and the thief said, "There's a council taking place in the palace. They're going to kill the tsar tonight."

So the tsar understood it all. He rewarded the thief with money and let him go. He summoned his guard and executed the plotters. The next day the tsar brought rich presents to the old man and his wife and abolished the law. And from that time they haven't banished old folks.

82. How the Bear Killed the Robbers

Known throughout the Baltic region. This Russian version follows the international type closely. SUS 957.

There was this postal station not far from the town, about fifteen versts from the village. Some robbers heard that the innkeeper had some money. But every evening about fifty men stayed and spent the night there. The robbers said, "Don't keep those people here. It's time to clean up the quarters; the tsar's inspector has announced that he's coming." But they kept on asking to stop over there, even though the innkeeper sent them away. But then here's the upshot: these murderers came in the middle of the night.

But just before they came, there was this bear tamer with his bear. He said, "Let me in to spend the night."

"How can I let you in?"

He said, "You've got to let me in with my bear to spend the night!"

The innkeeper thought and thought and then he said, "You can sleep in the bathhouse." But then, you see, at midnight ten pairs of horses and *tarantases* came up, each pair with two men. They drove up and sat down at the table.

"Give us your money!" He ran about and gathered and gathered it until he had a good stack of money.

"Don't you have some in another place?"

Then he remembered the bear and he went into the bathhouse and said to the bear-tamer, "What should I do? The cutthroats have come."

"Do you have an old axle?"

"Yes, but it's broken."

He brought the axle and a bottle of vodka. The bear drank the vodka and then he put the axle in his paws. The bear went onto the threshold of the hut. He roared as he grabbed the axle, and then he struck out on one side and knocked down six men. He started running and there were another six down. He left them cut down like hay in a pile behind the table.

Then the bear-tamer said, "Mishka, stack them up in the *tarantases*." Mishka put two of them in each *tarantas*, tied them, hitched up the horses and led them out of the yard. The horses went up to the hut with the corpses. And the innkeeper and bear-tamer divided the money between them. It was enough for the innkeeper not to let them in and that's what he did.

83. The Soldier and Death

From the White Sea. Told by an illiterate peasant woman, Tat'iana Ivanovna Chupakova, seventy years old, in 1938. She was related to many of the best narrators of the Far North, including M.D. Krivopolenova. She said she had learned most of her tales from women. A *papirosa* is a hand-rolled cigarette, usually made with cheap tobacco. The aspen is the tree of death in Russian folklore as it is associated with the tree on which Judas hanged himself. SUS 980A*.

There was this soldier returning from service, carrying some bread with him. It was just enough to eat—really only a little. He walked and he walked and he saw this peasant coming. He was healthy and handsome. He came up closer and begged some alms of him. He had only a crust cut in three chunks but he gave the outer one to him. Then the soldier went on and saw a poor cripple coming toward him. So then the cripple said to him, "Soldier, alms for the cripple for the sake of Christ!"

The soldier thought, "What is this? I just gave some to that healthy and vigorous man and now a cripple is asking and I'll have to give him something." So he took the middle chunk and gave it to him.

The cripple said to him, "What can I give you for your aid?"

What did the soldier need? "Do you have any playing cards?" He asked for the cards and he gave him the cards. He gave him the cards and gave him an expanding bag.

He said, "If you are going along and you see something you need, just open the bag and say 'into the bag!' and it will go into the bag!"

They said goodbye. One went one way and the other went the other. The soldier set off. He walked and walked and there was a lake and some wild geese were swimming on the lake. He spread open the bag and said, "Geese, go into the bag!" And then the geese went into the bag, one after the other—three in all. "Alright. That's enough for me." Then he set off further.

He walked and walked and there stood a tavern. "I could use a glass of vodka." The tavern keeper gave him a glass of vodka and he gave him a goose. For one goose he got a glass, for a second he got good service, and for the third: "Prepare something for me to eat with the vodka!"

He got it all from the tavern keeper in an instant. The goose was all prepared in a jiffy. The soldier sat down and drank and looked out the window. There was an empty royal house. "Is that little house empty?"

The mistress said: "You can't sleep in that house. Whoever goes in it, there are no gates and it stands empty."

"How is it that you can't sleep there? I'll go and sleep the night through."

"Oh, soldier, I pity you! I feel sorry for you!"

So he set off to spend the night in the little house. He hung his backpack on a peg, put his bag on the floor, walked about and smoked a *papirosa*. Then he smoked another and thus he walked through half the night.

Suddenly at midnight one of the floorboards opened and a little devil crawled out, and then there were a lot of them. "What are you doing here, soldier?"

"I'm just here, that's all."

"So then. We'll devour you!"

"How can you? I don't sink when I walk on water and I don't burn when I walk on fire. How can you eat me? Nibble! But you can't eat me! Let's play cards instead."

"Yes, let's. Let's play cards."

So they sat down to play cards and the soldier won everything from them, all their money. The oldest devil crawled away and the youngest said, "Run, lads!" to all the other little devils. "He wants to play for a quarter of silver." They wanted to bet everything on the silver, hoping to win back all they'd lost. The youngest devil brought it. But they couldn't beat him.

"Run and bring a quarter of all our gold." But the soldier won all the gold too. So then they had lost everything. "Now we'll just have to eat you."

"No way can you eat me! Why should you? Let's try this." He opened his bag and said, "All you devils, into the bag!" One after the other, all the devils crowded into the bag and the soldier hung the bag on a peg and started pacing about the floor. He had done his work, so why not have a smoke!

In the morning the tsar's servants came and knocked on the doors. "Well now, soldier, are you alive or dead?"

"I'm alive; I'm alive. Go and bring me a large sledgehammer and an anvil!" All the servants came running with them. He said, "Take that bag and put it on the anvil and start pounding."

So they all started pounding the bag on the anvil. "What's that? It's like a barrel full of devils!"

"That's what we are!"

The soldier said to them, "Are you ever going to come here again?"

"No, we'll never come back. We won't. We won't come within forty versts of here."

So he ordered the servants to let them go free. The little devils ran away, but the oldest one crawled out backward and the soldier caught him by a leg. "So, old devil! Cut off one of your legs and write that you won't ever come around here again in your own blood."

The devil cut off his leg and wrote it in his own blood. Then he said, "Soldier, when you're in need of something, remember that I can help you—and that time will come!" and then the devil went away.

So the soldier went to the tsar. "Well, I've cleaned up that little house; you can live in it!"

The tsar thanked him for it and gave him half the tsardom. He said, "What should I do with that? I don't need it. I'll just go home."

He came home, got married, and had a baby. When the baby was already big, in its third year, it was sick all the time. "That old devil wanted to help me. Maybe he could help me now."

And the devil was there. "What do you need, soldier?"

"My little one is sick. We can't do anything to help him. Can you help us out?"

"I can," he said. "Place him on the table, put a glass of water by his head, and then look in the glass. Where do you see death? At his feet or at his head?"

He looked and death was at the head. "If it had been at his feet, I still couldn't have cured him, but since it's at his head this is what you do: wash him with water and then he'll be cured." The soldier did just that and the child was cured.

They then began dragging that soldier everywhere. Whenever someone got sick, they sent for the soldier, and he cured them—he cured them all. Suddenly the tsar fell ill, the one whose little house he had rid of the devils. They sent for the soldier. He looked to see whether death was at the tsar's head or at his feet. He saw that death was at his feet and he said, "I cannot cure you."

But the tsar didn't want to die. "Servants, cut off his head!"

The soldier said, "Why do that? Give me at least three days to go home and say farewell to my wife and child." The tsar let him go.

So he came home, lay down on the bed and lay there smoking, one after the other.

Then the day came and death came and said, "Soldier, have you said farewell to your wife?" He kept on lying there, silently. He smoked another *papirosa*. But death came up to him again the next day.

"Soldier, have you said farewell to your wife and child?" But he kept silent, smoking a *papirosa*. On the third day death came: "Have you said farewell to your wife and child? You only have three more hours to live. Say farewell, soldier." Then he said, "Two more hours to live, soldier."

But the soldier was silent. The bag was at the head of the bed and he opened it and said, "Go into the bag, death!" Death jumped into the bag and he tied her in tightly. Then he ran forty versts into the forest and tied the bag to an aspen.

Old women could not die and old men could not die—there was no death. They asked the soldier, "We need to die now; but there is no more death. Soldier, please let death out of the bag."

So he ran off and brought death in from the aspen, and he said, "Will you come to me?"

"No," death said, "but I'll circle round you." And then the old folks began dying and the children began dying—they all began dying. The soldier aged, too, and he climbed into a cellar for some beer. He fell and lost his grip. He lost consciousness and was hurt—and he started asking for death.

"Come here, and don't just circle round me."

So death came. She wasn't angry; she just came and took him. He died and that's all the tale.

84. The Golden Pitcher

Another story admonishing the fortunate to look after the aged. The narrator, Korol'kova, often told tales with an overt class bias. Her tales were recorded after World War II. SUS 981.

In a certain tsardom, in a certain country, there lived and dwelt a rich, extremely rich, landlord. But he was also ever so stingy. He had three estates. He gobbled up the estates of the old folks and he had begun the third. One of the old men had a favorite son who pitied his father. He dug a shelter for him in the forest, carried wheat for him there, and settled him down.

So the old man sat there and went on living. And his son would check on him secretly. So then the son came to his father.

"How are things?" the old man asked.

"Oh, father, it's the end. He's taken up going after the young maids. This is what he thought up. People must come to him neither in a cart, nor on horseback, nor sitting, nor riding, nor in a shirt, nor bare-naked"

The old man said, "That's not much of a riddle. So you don't ride on horseback. Run and tell whoever is to answer this. Let them ride on a goat, facing the rear, their back to the front, driving it with its tail, and have him put on a loose net rather than a shirt."

So that's what he did. The landlord came out to greet him and he was riding neither in a cart nor on horseback, nor was he on foot, neither clad nor bare-naked. The landowner turned black with rage. He selected another young man.

"Bring me a gift that is and is not."

They thought and they thought. For three days the whole family thought. And then Fetis once more visited the old man. "Father, what is to be done? Tell us. How many people have already been slaughtered!"

"Well, Fetis, scatter some grain, then stick out a sieve, holding a stick, catch a bird, and carry it to the landlord. As he is taking it, let it go. There is your gift that is no gift."

So this young man caught a bullfinch and carried to the landlord. "Here's a gift for you, landlord." The landlord stretched out his hand and the gift flew away. The landlord was furious.

So as soon as the sun came up, the landlord and his wife rode over to a pond. There was a golden goblet in it but they couldn't get hold of it. The landlord said, "All of you try to raise it!" They dove and they dove, but they couldn't get hold of it. He slaughtered them all.

Finally Fetis's turn came. He went to his father, "Father, what's to be done? Now he has ordered me to get it."

The old man thought and he thought, and then he said, "And where is this pond, my son?"

"It's over at the Lopatinskii's."

"And what is next to it?"

"Why, nothing at all."

"What do you mean, 'nothing'? There's an old willow there. And at what time can the goblet be seen?"

"At midday. Then the goblet can be seen, but if you dive in, it's not there."

"So go look. Is the goblet there?"

"It isn't."

"So here's what to do. The goblet is on the willow. When they tell you to get it, go right to the willow."

So then the landlord came. "Well, Fetiska, go into the pond and get me the goblet."

"I'll get the goblet." So he went straight to the willow and got the golden goblet.

The landlord asked him, "Did you think that up or did someone tell you?"

"My father taught me."

"Go and fetch him here." Then the landlord said, "We also need the old folks. Give him what he needs—bread, salt, and water. Let him live out his lifetime."

And since that time the old folks are held in respect on account of their wisdom.

85. Peter the Great and the Three Soldiers

The basic theme of this tale has been known in Russia since the sixteenth century, as *The Tale of Peter and Fevroniia*. The latter entered the folk tradition. Here Peter the Great is made the hero. Peter's first wife was a Livonian peasant girl named Katerina. SUS 983.

This happened in Petersburg. Once three soldiers were walking on a carriageway in Petersburg. Peter the Great was very fond of walking about in uniform. He walked behind these soldiers, following them. At the time they were quite tipsy. They were engaged in conversation among themselves.

Just then an unfamiliar merchant came by in a carriage. One of the soldiers said, "Oh, what a splendid carriage! I would love to go riding in such a carriage." The second said, "What's so good about that carriage? I'd like to ride in a state carriage—that's what I'd ride in." The third: "That's nothing. I would rather sit with the high counselors in a circle. But that's nothing. I would rather [marry] his Ekaterina."

Now this Peter the Great heard all of this and he went up to them: "Permit me, soldiers, to invite you to a restaurant and treat you. I greatly admire soldiers."

"Of course, as that's the way you understand it. There are some who admire our brothers and others who hold them in contempt. But he insists that he admires soldiers. Let's go to a restaurant." So they agreed and went.

He ordered a jug of beer. They drank it and then another. So fine. They he started asking them. "What unit do you serve in?" He asked the first, who told him. He asked the second and then the third. "Fine," he said, "I'll visit you on holidays, during your slack time, and we'll go together to the barracks buffet: I love soldiers passionately." Then they left the restaurant, having gotten really drunk, had these soldiers. "Driver, take these soldiers to their barracks." He paid the driver and sent them off.

So they arrived at the barracks and boasted, "What a good man we met! He got us drunk in the restaurant! He'll come visit us on our holidays. Did you see how much money he has?" They lay down to sleep.

In the morning an orderly came from his majesty the emperor and brought a message to the duty officer of the day. "Are such and such soldiers of this unit here?"

The duty officer took the note and read it. "These men are here."

"Let them immediately report to his imperial majesty in person." They quickly cleaned their ammunition, got ready, and set off.

When they arrived, he came out. "Greetings, brothers!"

"We wish you good health, your imperial highness!"

"Were you in town last night, or not?"

"We were." Then they thought: "Could it be that we failed to pay him proper respect last night because we were drunk?"

"We are guilty, your imperial highness; we were awfully drunk."

"That's nothing, nothing at all. Only as you were walking along, what were you talking about among yourselves?"

"We can't exactly remember because we were so drunk."

"No, when you were still just in a happy mood, what did you say then? Perhaps you said something about me?"

One of them admitted it. "I'm guilty, your imperial highness. I said that I would like to go riding in your carriage."

"Fine!" He shouted to his servants: "Go and take him for a ride." He got in and they rode along the street. "Well, did you like riding in the carriage?"

"It was really great!"

"Here, take this ruble and go and get drunk."

The second said, "This is what I said: 'I would like to sit in a council of the great men.'" He shouted at the great men: "Sit." He sat down for a while and then got up.

His majesty asked him, "Well, did you enjoy that?"

"I certainly did, your imperial highness."

"Here, take this ruble." Then he turned to the third. He beat around the bush. "Never mind, just tell me."

"This is what I said, your imperial highness. . . ."

His majesty ordered them to pour three glasses of the best vodka—gold, silver, and bronze. He drank them all. "Now then? Is there any difference among those glasses of vodka?"

"They are identical," he said, "all magnificent."

"So," said Peter the Great, "all women are identical—mine and a peasant woman."

86. The Monk and the Abbess

Because of the subject matter this tale was not published in Afanas'ev's lifetime. It is also printed in Afanas'ev, vol. 3, no. 23. The collector offered a variant to the beginning of the tale in a note: "A monk began frequenting a nunnery and he deflowered all the nuns. Then first one and then another got pregnant." The monastery on Nevskii was for monks, while the Smol'nyi was a nunnery. SUS 999*.

In a certain town there were two monasteries just like here in Peter: Nevskii and Smol'nyi. In the one there were monks and in the other nuns. So far, so good. Then one young monk started visiting this nun and so that they wouldn't notice him he always dressed in women's clothing. He didn't have a beard yet, but the hair of priests and monks in any case is supposed to be arranged like women's. They noticed that guests were frequently going to the nun, but then there occurred a great misfortune: she became pregnant. The abbess was informed and she gave this order: "If anyone comes to this nun, report it immediately."

So the next day the monk came to his lover. The nuns living in their cells saw him and ran to their little mother and abbess. "Some woman has come to visit." The abbess ordered the bath heated and ordered all those who had just come into the monastery to go and steam themselves. There was nothing to be done, all the nuns gathered together and they led their guest with them. They came into the bathhouse and began to undress. The monk undressed and quickly got onto the highest bench, where he made his way into a corner and wondered what would happen to him next. Around his neck hung a cross on his sash. He untied it (the cross hung lower than his belt) and he covered "his shame." Then the abbess put on her glasses, took a candle, and began walking about all the nuns, noting who might be among them. She began staring at the monk, went up to him, bent over (and here the sash broke and the cross flew to one side). It hit the abbess squarely in the eye.

"Oh, my lord! The most holy Mother of God is with us," shouted the abbess and she grabbed her left eye. The eye had been knocked completely out. Meanwhile, the monk leapt out of the bathhouse and ran off naked. And the abbess was forever deformed.

The time passed and the nun gave birth. And I was at the christening, but I never figured it out: who did God grant, a boy or a girl?

VI

Tales of Clever Fools

The clever fools of this section are fools in name only for they almost invariably outwit their adversaries, whether the village priest, the devil, a landlord, or perhaps Baba Yaga. There is a strong element of satire in tales involving the priest, who is usually depicted as avaricious and unscrupulous. The devil is not really the Christian devil at all, but rather a figure derived from the various malevolent spirits that inhabited the Russian peasant's universe: the forest spirit (*leshii*), the water spirit (*vodianoi*), and others too numerous to mention. The fool will generally encounter his adversary-devil or imp either in a forest or at a lake. Indeed, the Russians have a popular saying to the effect that "in deep waters devils dwell," suggesting the American "to get into deep water." For more on the tales of clever fools, see Haney, *CRF*, vol. 7.

87. Balda the Laborer

Collected from F. Svin'in. This is the only recorded version of the type. Svin'in had a considerable repertoire of tales, but most remain in archival form. The priest is commonly called "little father," his wife "little mother" in Russian tradition. SUS 1001* + 1006***.

In a certain village there lived a priest and his wife. He was so stingy that he wouldn't even keep a laborer. Then one splendid time the priest said to his old wife: "I'm going to go hire a laborer." He got dressed and went off. He walked.

A peasant came toward him. The priest asked him, "Where are you going, peasant?"

"I'm going to hire on as a laborer, father."

"Will you come work for me? I don't have a laborer at the moment."

"Alright, I'll come," said Balda.

The priest asked him, "How much salary are you asking?"

"Only a little, father, just seven days a week I ask."

The priest's eyes bugged out. He didn't understand Balda. Balda explained it to him: "Feed me every day until I'm full, Father, and I will serve you, and I'll just give you three blows to your forehead."

The priest jumped up out of joy. "You're joking, aren't you?" he asked.

"No, father, I'm not joking."

So they set off for the priest's house. When they got there, he said to his wife, "Feed him the best there is. I've hired a laborer for three blows. Every year he'll give me three blows to the forehead and he'll work for that."

So the priest hired him that morning and then they sat down to breakfast. The little mother loaded down the table—there was enough for all three to eat their fill. But Balda ate it all himself. Then he said: "No, father, that was too little. I'll cut no more than fifty *sazhens*."

The priest ordered his wife to gather more food together since Balda had promised not to be back for a whole week. They put everything before him, a whole basket of food. Balda set off for the woods. When he came to the woods, he chopped down the very thinnest pole, one that stretched to the sky no more than five or maybe six *sazhens*. He cut about ten such poles, put them in a pile, and from these ten poles all of a sudden there were fifty *sazhens*! But in fact it didn't make up half a cartload. He spent a week there and chopped three hundred fifty *sazhens*, stacked them in a pile, and went home.

When he got home, the priest asked him, "Well, laborer, did you chop up the wood?"

"I did, Father. Three hundred fifty *sazhens*."

"So now I'll have enough wood for five years. Tomorrow I'll go over there and you can show me the wood."

The next day they set off for the woods. The priest looked around to see where the wood was. They rode up to the coppice. The priest asked, "Where's the wood?"

"You're standing right next to the pile."

"But I told you to chop not this kind of wood—why, this won't amount to a pile of even two *sazhens*."

"But I'm not guilty, father. You said 'five *sazhens*,' but you didn't say what kind, and besides, I chopped three hundred fifty."

The priest thought, "Here's a misfortune! I've exploded at this laborer; somehow I'll have to smooth it over." He went to his wife and told her everything.

"Don't grieve over it, father, we'll get rid of him somehow. We'll send him to the bathhouse and when he falls asleep, we'll unscrew the cast-iron kettle. It will fall and crush him."

Balda heard all this. When evening came, after supper, the priest's wife said, "Go to the bathhouse to sleep. It's dark there and no one will bother you."

"Alright, mother, I'll go right away."

He put on his felt boots, threw on a fur jacket, and took his pillow and his blanket, and then he set off. He came to the bathhouse, brought in a chopping block, put it up on the shelf and put his pillow down next to the block. On a second, small block he laid his hat. He placed his boots by the block. Then he went and covered it with his blanket and it looked just like a man lying there. So he went into the warm room and lay down to sleep on the shelf. He just let out a light snoring. He blocked up the vent so that no one could peer in.

It got dark that evening and the priest and his wife went to the bathhouse to commit their crime. They came into the anteroom and heard this gentle snoring, which meant that he was asleep. They got up into the loft, unscrewed the kettle, which fell down onto the floor with a bang. They shook all over and then they started running. "Well, now we're rid of that laborer. He's dead."

In the morning the priest and his woman were about to go and get the dead man, but by that time the laborer had left the bathhouse. He gave a whistle to the priest, who was in his house. The father looked out and here came the laborer!

"Here's grief! That laborer's alive. What are we going to do now?"

"Don't grieve, father. We've got this ferocious bull, who's broken all his chains. The door is locked; we'll get him to kill that laborer. The bull will charge him and tear him to pieces."

The laborer came into the hut and the priest said, "How did you sleep in the bathhouse?"

"Just fine, father. I never slept better than last night."

The priest and his wife exchanged glances and the priest said, "Sit down and have breakfast with us and then go kill the bull."

"No, father, I'll kill him before breakfast; then I'll take my breakfast."

The priest showed him where the bull was and wondered what would become of the laborer. The priest opened the doors and the bull leapt out with a roar. He flew right at Balda. Balda dodged him and when the bull got close, he gave him a blow. The bull fell down with his legs in the air. The hair on the priest's head stood on end. He ran off to little mother.

"Oh, little mother, I'm completely undone. He killed the bull with a single blow, and I've got three blows coming. He'll knock my whole brain out."

"Don't grieve so, father. There's this lake three versts away. And in that lake there dwells a devil. He drags both cattle and people in—whoever turns up on the shores. Let's send Balda to that lake to collect the rents for the three years they have to pay. They'll drag him in."

All this time Balda was skinning the bull. He hung it up and hung up the meat. Then he came in, washed, and sat down at the table. The priest and little mother fed Balda until he was full. The priest said, "So now, my little worker, there's this lake about three versts from here and some devils live in it. Go and ask them to pay their rents in gold."

"Very well, father, I'll go right away."

He got up from the table, got dressed, and took his sack. Singing a little tune, he set off through the woods. On the way he caught two little hares. Before he had gone as far as the lake, he saw a bear den. He looked in it and there lay an old bear, turning from side to side. He went away from the den and came up to the lake. Then he began weaving sand in long piles just like a rope. A little devil popped out and asked him, "Balda, what are you doing?"

"I'm weaving this rope out of sand and then I'm going to catch all the devils in the lake. If you don't pay the priest the tribute due him for the last three years in gold, then I'm going to strangle you all."

The little devil returned to the lake and went to his old grandfather devil. He said, "Grandfather, Balda wants to chase us out of the lake if we don't give him the tribute for the three years."

The devil was frightened and said, "Run quickly. If you can outrun him in a race around the lake, we won't hand it over; if he outruns you, we will."

The little devil leapt out of the water and said, "Whoever runs around the lake quicker will get the tribute. If I do, then we won't pay; if you do, then we'll give it to you."

"I agree," said Balda. Just then he pulled a little hare out and said, "I can't run myself, so I'll send my little brother. I'll count to three and then run."

At the count of three the devil and hare started running. The devil ran around the lake but the hare ran into the wood. When the devil ran up to him, Balda held up the other little hare, which he dipped in the water; water ran off in little streams. Balda said, "Oh, poor little brother, you've gotten into a mess, but you still ran here first."

The little devil was so frightened that he dove into the lake and quickly ran up to his grandfather. "Grandfather, no matter how fast I ran, he still outran me."

The devil sent this huge, lame giant. He said, "Go and wrestle Balda; if he wins, we'll give him the tribute."

The giant went out onto the shore and said to Balda, "Let's wrestle. If you can defeat me, you'll get the money, but if I defeat you, you will have to serve with us."

"That's fine," said Balda. "Let's go to my middle brother; I don't even want to get my hands dirty with you." He led him to the den where there was this enormous bear. "Go and get him angry; he's lazy. He'll come out and then we'll start the match."

The devil grabbed the bear by a paw and started dragging him. The bear became furious; he tore his paw away and shook the devil's whole body and then he shook his very soul until his bones rattled. The devil tore out of the bear's embrace and limped off to the lake.

"Grandfather, hand over the rent quickly. His other brother has crushed all my sides and my whole body is ripped."

The devil was terrified. He ordered them to bring out three little barrels of gold and then to leave him in peace. The three little devils carried out three little barrels and said to Balda, "Take them. Just leave us in peace."

Balda put the three little barrels in his sack, slung it over his shoulder, singing and whistling some kind of song. He approached the village and the priest and his wife saw him. The priest shouted, "Now I'm done for. The year will soon be up."

At that moment Balda came in, pulled the three little barrels of gold out of his sack, and said, "Here, father, your tribute has been paid."

But the priest wasn't happy about the gold; he was afraid of death. Just then a crier from the count was walking through the street announcing that the count's daughter was going to set some riddles and whoever could solve them and whoever was sharpest of mind would become her husband, she would select him as her groom.

Balda heard all this. Since he was handsome and well built, he put on a three-piece suit and said, "Let's go, father, perhaps we'll be lucky." The priest didn't dare contradict him.

They hitched up a horse, got in the *tarantas,* and set off. When they arrived there were so many people that there was no room to move; everyone was standing in rows. They left their horse. Balda took the priest by the hand and led him, pushing, as the crowd had come to a standstill. They pushed until they stood close to the front row. There was such squeezing, but it didn't matter to Balda.

Then Balda pushed himself into the first row and stood next to a prince. Once Balda had watched the count's daughter bathing, and he had seen that beneath her right arm she had a black spot about the size of a five-kopeck piece. As Balda was standing next to the prince, the prince looked at him sidewise, noticing that this country peasant was standing next to him. Then the count took his daughter by the hand and they both sat down on their chairs, and all was silent. The count's daughter asked the prince, "Well, your excellency, what marks are on me?"

But the prince didn't know and he said, "Your beauty is so extraordinary that no one in your entire duchy can compare with you, and your marvelous eyes strike all."

But the princess didn't laugh. She said, "What else can you say?"

"I can say, your grace, that this uncouth idiot is in the wrong sleigh—he shouldn't be standing next to me."

The count's daughter said, "No, prince, you are wrong; here we have complete equality. Here nobility counts for nothing. Here one needs intelligence and mental agility and reasoning. These are valued most of all."

She turned to Balda, fixing her gaze on him, and his beauty so captivated her that she began to fall in love. "And what can you say?"

"I am a village peasant, countess. Excuse me that I speak as a peasant. Your highness, beneath your right arm, beneath the armpit, you have a black spot."

The count's daughter's eyes opened wide: how could this simple peasant know! "And what else can you say?"

The count was already curious.

"But your grace, this prince is really stupid, worse than a village peasant," said Balda. The prince turned crimson from anger and pushed Balda in the side. Balda said, "Your grace, should he not have to pay for this brazen act?" And then he gave the prince such a punch that the prince was knocked off his feet.

The prince got back on his feet, looked at Balda, shook his head, and quietly made his way to the inn. The priest shook all over at the punch. The count and his daughter saw that the peasant had reasoned correctly and wisely, and that with one punch he had knocked the prince off his feet. They guessed what his strength was. The count's daughter stood up, went up to Balda, took him by the hand, and led him to her father.

"Papa, I don't want to marry anybody but this peasant. He will be my husband and I will be his wife." The count announced to the whole crowd: "My daughter has found her groom; you may all disperse now."

After the count had spoken, Balda said to the priest, "Father, on the occasion of my triumph I am not going to give you three blows at the conclusion of my year's service. But you will give me these three barrels of gold, and if you won't give them to me, then you'll get the three blows."

The priest said to Balda, "I'll bring you the three barrels immediately." He was so happy that he had been saved from certain death. The count, his daughter, and Balda went into the palace. When he was in the palace, the count announced to his entire duchy that his daughter was getting married to a baron because he had just raised Balda to be a baron. The count asked him, "Well now, lord baron, tell me how you served with that priest and why you received the gold from him."

Balda told the count and the count's daughter everything that had happened before their appearance in the palace, the whole story of his year-long service. The count and his daughter laughed until tears flowed at the happenings—how he had deceived the priest in all his dealings, especially with the devil.

By the time he had finished his story and since the village was not far away, the priest carried in the three barrels of gold. The count's servants led the priest before the count. He came in, bowed, took out the barrels, and said, "Worker, I have fulfilled your demand."

But the count said, "He is no worker; he is a baron."

The priest said, "My lord baron, forgive me that I didn't recognize your entitilation [his new title]. May I now depart?" he asked.

The baron said, "You may. But don't you ever hire helpless workers again. If you do, the others will pay you back without the mercy I've shown you."

After these words the priest ran out of the palace, got on his horse, and rode off home. Then the worker, now baron, said to the count: "Master count and you, my bride, allow me to see what was given me in those little barrels by the devils."

The count said, "Yes, of course. It will be interesting to see whether they stuffed them full of some sort of rubbish."

So then they all left the count's office. The count gave his manager an order to send a cooper to open up the little barrels. When the cooper had come and opened them, the entire interior was covered with a gold crust, and gold in all colors of the rainbow gave off such a light that the count and Balda's bride screwed up their eyes. But Balda stood quietly, just chuckling. When the count regained his senses, he said, "Well, baron, this is an uncountable treasure. I haven't a tenth part of it. At the wedding and before all our friends I will proclaim you the heir of my duchy. I will tell all about your inheritance and your wit. And now, baron, go and coo with your bride while I prepare for the marriage feast so that all will be ready."

The count's daughter and the baron left, both sparkling, as this was the first time the count's daughter had fallen in love. All the family was summoned and they all arrived. The next day they celebrated the nuptials and then the wedding. At the wedding the count said with his first toast, "Dear friends, I name my son-in-law my heir over all the duchy. I will only be an advisor because his capital is more than ten times greater than mine. Second, he is clever and strong, and I am already old."

Everyone approved of the count's speech and congratulated the baron on his new rank. Wine poured forth like a river at the festivities. They all talked of nothing but the event, how fate plays with a human being. From a poor man one could become rich but a rich man could also become poor.

The former Balda, now the count's heir governing the province, ruled wisely, helping all his workers and the poor, who loved their new ruler with all their soul. He lived very peaceably with the count and their opinions and counsels always were in agreement. But the main thing was that he loved his wife, and his wife gave him the purest and most dedicated love. They began awaiting children since they had had none before.

88. The Laborer and the Priest

This tale, from Cheliabinsk district of the Urals, is unique in the East Slavic tradition. SUS 1006**.

There lived and dwelt a priest and his wife. And they had this one child. The priest lived well. One time this priest hired a laborer and he said to him, "I am hiring you for a whole year. I'll give you pay—here's this little box of gold—but on the condition that to live here you'll fulfill everything I order you to do and not get angry or curse, because I'm a spiritual father, and I must not sin. If you work well throughout the year, not getting angry and not cursing, then you'll get the gold, but if you don't fulfill this one condition, you'll get nothing."

The laborer worked for a month, then two, three, and finally the whole year. But soon a tale is told; yet not so soon is the deed done. It wasn't easy for the laborer. The priest made the laborer work hard; he fed him poorly; and he hardly gave him anything to wear at all.

Once the laborer rode out in the wintertime to get some hay. He ran alongside his horse to keep himself warm, and he endured everything. The year was nearly at an end. The priest began to worry about his gold. It was apparent that he would have to hand that gold over to the laborer, and that was a pity. So the priest instructed his child: "As soon as the laborer sits down to eat, you ask to go outside." So the child acted up every mealtime. Either he would ask to go outside or he would ask to go play. While the laborer was busy with the child, the mealtime would pass and the laborer would be left with nothing to eat. They so tortured that laborer that he could hardly drag himself about. The laborer could take it no longer—he beat up the child. The priest sent the laborer away for a year and for a whole year his pay was suspended.

All this insulted the laborer. He asked to be hired for another year and with the same conditions. The priest agreed and hired him for another year. This all took place in the spring. The priest accompanied the laborer to the fields to plow and he gave him this order: "When you get to the field to plow, my dog Zhuchka will be with you. Watch after her. Wherever she goes, you do the same. If Zhuchka goes to the cart, that means you are to unhitch the horses for dinner. If Zhuchka goes to the plow, that means you are to hitch up for plowing. And don't come home until Zhuchka runs home herself."

So the laborer plowed for one day, then a second and a third. The laborer never managed to get a meal. Zhuchka ran to the plow. The laborer could hardly drag himself about. The horses were worn out and there was no more bread, but still Zhuchka didn't run home. There was just one more crust. The laborer used the crust to lure Zhuchka, and then he put her in a sack and let her have it with his knout. He thoroughly whacked her sides and then he shook her out of the sack. Did Zhuchka run home then! The laborer hitched up the horses and rode home after Zhuchka. When he got to the yard, Zhuchka nipped under the gates and the laborer took his axe and started whacking the horses about the head, trying to force them under the gates, too. The priest came out and looked at his horses. He asked the laborer: "Why have you killed my horses?"

"It's like this, Father. You yourself said that your laborer was to do exactly what Zhuchka did. Zhuchka nipped under the gates but the gates weren't open for me. And I couldn't stay outside with the horses. So I killed them and I'm pushing them under the gates and then I'll crawl under the gates myself."

The priest didn't answer since he had ordered the laborer to do just what Zhuchka did. But the priest was annoyed about the horses. The priest decided to take revenge on the laborer for his loss. He hired the deacon to kill the laborer. The deacon turned a sheepskin coat inside out, and then he went to the sheep shed where the priest kept about thirty head. Then the priest sent the laborer to bring him the very largest ram and slaughter it for the holiday.

The laborer took a knife and went off to the sheep shed. He went into the shed and a large ram tried to butt the laborer so he slit its throat with his knife. And thus he killed the deacon. Then he went on to kill all the other sheep. He went and called the priest to the shed. "Let's go take the meat into the cellar, father."

The priest said, "I ordered you to bring a single large ram."

The laborer said, "But why just one ram? We would just have to slaughter another for the next holiday. When winter comes, it will be even worse. It will be too cold to mess around with the meat."

No matter how the priest was sorry about the sheep—he could scarcely contain his anger—nonetheless he kept control of himself. In the night the priest carted the deacon away and buried him in the manure pile.

Then the priest thought, "I've no more horses, no sheep, and I've just got my own brown cow left. The laborer has nothing to do so I'll have to send him off. But if I give him the gold, I'll have to go about the land with cup in hand." About that time the child died. The priest said to his wife, "Alright, Mother, bake some bread, make some hardtack as we're going to have to run away from home."

There was nothing for the laborer to do. He could only watch what the priest was doing. Then the laborer noticed that the master was putting some bread aside and thus he guessed that they were intending to go someplace. The laborer noticed that the bag of hardtack was already full and on top of it was a layer of meat pies.

That evening the priest and his wife went to sleep early. They were intending to run away in the night. The laborer also lay down. When the priest and his wife were asleep, the laborer went, shook the hardtack out of the bag, crawled into it, covered himself over with the hard biscuits, took some wine with him, and placed the pies on his head.

That night the priest and his wife woke up and got ready to run. The wife took the little casket of gold and the priest swung the bag with the laborer and hardtack in it onto his shoulders. They walked quickly so that the laborer couldn't catch up to them.

It was already midday. The priest and his wife stopped next to a spring, had a bite to eat, and then pushed on. But the laborer sat in the sack and nibbled on those sweet little pies, sipped some wine, but then a great misfortune arose: the laborer needed to piss. He held it and held it, but then he could hold out no longer and he was forced to let go his water. Mother was walking behind the priest and she said, "What is it, father? There's a stream running from your sack down your neck and back."

"Oh, I've just got up a sweat, little mother."

So they went on further. In the evening they came to a river. It was a big river, seething, and with steep banks. The priest stopped to spend the night there. When they had sat down to eat, the laborer crawled out of the sack and said, "Greetings, dear masters! Where is it you've carried me to?"

"To the town," said the priest. "We're going visiting and we put you in the sack when you were asleep. We didn't want to wake you up—we love you so dearly."

When the laborer had gone off a little way to look at the river, the priest said to his wife, "You lay out the bed on the banks along the river and we'll put the laborer right on the edge next to the river. When he goes to sleep, we'll push him into it."

That's what they did. They lay down to sleep and they put the laborer next to the river's edge. In the middle lay the priest, and on his other side lay his wife. So the priest lay down with his wife and after such an unusual day of physical torture, they fell asleep immediately. But the laborer lay down in the middle between the priest and his wife. So then the priest's wife woke up and whispered to the laborer, thinking that it was the priest, "Push the laborer in!"

They both pressed against the priest and pushed him into the river. The priest just made a splash. They got out of there quickly!

"Well, thank God we're rid of him," said little mother.

"Yes, thank God," said the laborer.

In the morning they got up and little mother looked around. The priest was nowhere to be seen and the laborer was lying there with her. She wanted to run away from him, but the laborer said, "Wait a moment, little mother, you've no place to hurry off to." Then he took her gold.

So you think the laborer got married to the priest's wife? Nothing of the sort. He spat on that old crow. But they went off together. They came to the town and in the town the laborer bought the finest clothes there were in the town and then he began to court the most beautiful girl. He married this beauty and the priest's wife began living with them as a servant. And that's how that laborer has lived ever since. Why, you wouldn't know him now!

89. Horns

A few other versions of this tale exist, but none in Ukrainian and only one in Belarusian. A tale from Zaonezh'ia, this type is well known throughout Europe. This version was told by Anna Antonovna Slepaia. There are several original features in this rendition, especially the beginning. SUS 1060*.

There lived and dwelt this young blacksmith. He was a healthy lad, but he lived in poverty. Then he heard that a serpent was frequently flying to the Tsarevna Mariia. He would fly in and suck her blood. She had fallen seriously ill and wasted. Then the tsar issued this proclamation: "Whoever can rescue Tsarevna Mariia from this serpent shall be given in marriage to her."

The smith said, "I'm going to die anyway; I might as well kill the serpent." So he forged some iron bullets and iron claws. He skinned an ox hide. Then he climbed into the hide and set off. He sat down in the tsarevna's antechamber. The serpent flew up. The smith just sat there, cracking nuts. The serpent said, "What are you doing?"

"I'm cracking nuts."

"Let me crack some."

The smith gave him the iron bullets. The serpent tried to crack them and broke out all his teeth. "Those are the very devil's nuts!" he said.

"Let's play cards instead. Whoever wins will strike the other in the forehead."

"Alright, let's do that." They played and played and the smith lost. The serpent really let fly at his forehead and the smith lost consciousness. The serpent started sucking Tsarevna Mariia's blood again.

The smith stood up. "Just a moment! Now it's my turn to pay you back." They started playing cards again. This time the smith won. "Give me your forehead!" he said. Then he bashed him with his smith's maul and the serpent crumpled to the ground. He got back up after a short while or after a long while.

"So now let's play 'pay back.' Whoever loses, loses his skin." The smith lost and the serpent got ready to tear off his skin. But he was dressed in the ox skin. The serpent pulled it off and the smith said, "I can pay you back without any skin." So they started playing and this time the serpent lost. The smith put on his iron claws and skinned him. And the serpent died right there.

The tsarevna was overjoyed and she got married to the smith. She got fat and beautiful. But then, you see, she no longer wanted to live with the smith. She was educated and he was just a simple peasant. She didn't like that. She ordered her hunters to take the smith into the forest. "Kill him and bring his heart to me."

They led him away. But they felt sorry for him. "Go wherever you want," they said. "But don't go back to the tsar."

Then they killed a dog and took out the heart. The smith walked about, weeping. He wanted to eat. He wanted to eat, dear, and there was an apple tree growing nearby. And on the apple tree hung various kinds of apples—yellow, white, and red. So he ate a red apple and his head began aching. It hurt too much and he decided to go and wash his head with water. He looked in the well and on his head were huge horns! Really enormous! What could be done? Could he show himself to people like this? He stayed in the woods. And then he wanted to eat again so he took and ate a yellow apple. The horns disappeared immediately, as if they'd never been there. Then he took and ate a white apple and he became so handsome, white-skinned, pink-cheeked, and polite. Like a tsarevich. He collected some of the apples and went into the town. He walked around the palace, shouting, "Apples—white, yellow, red!"

The tsarevna sent out a servant: "Go and get some apples, I would really like some." The smith brought some. He knew they were for the tsarevna so he gave the red apples and then he got out of town. She ate one and her head began to hurt. She looked in the mirror and horns had sprouted on her head. What a disgrace! What was to be done? She wept and her servant wept and even the tsar himself wept, and she got sick. She lay down in bed and arranged the horns at the head of the bed. But she got sicker. They called in all the doctors. They couldn't do anything.

Then the tsar made a proclamation. "Whoever can cure my daughter will have half the tsardom, half the country."

The smith heard this and immediately fitted himself out as a doctor. Then he went to the tsar. "I can cure her."

"If you can, then cure her; but if you don't, then it's your head from your shoulders."

"Very well," he said.

And so he went into her antechamber. "The reason you can't get well, tsarevna, is because you offended someone deeply."

"No!" she said.

"How can I cure you if you do not repent?"

She was frightened. "I offended the smith who saved me from the serpent. I ordered him to be killed."

"So, are you sorry for that?"

"Oh, how I do regret it." So then he gave her a yellow apple and the horns immediately disappeared.

"Your servants took pity on the smith. They killed a dog and sent him off to live in the woods."

"If he returned, I would show him my remorse."

"I am that very one," he said. She was so happy. "But you are so handsome and so educated."

He gave her an apple to eat and she became better than all the rest. They began to live happily and, perhaps, they are living still.

90. How Klimka Stole the Landlord's Wife

This is a uniquely Russian tale about a contest to see who can laugh longest. Klimka easily outwits the devil and the landlord, although the laughing horse head plays only a minor role in the tale. Gerasimov's tales were collected in the foothills of the Altai Mountains of southern Siberia. SUS 1080*.

There lived and dwelt this landlord. The landlord quarreled with Klimka. The landlord said to Klimka, "You are not to steal my wife!"

But Klimka said, "I'll steal her." The landlord stationed some watchmen and stood at the doors of his house, while Klimka went out to a grave, pulled the corpse out, crawled up onto the stable roof with the corpse, and then threw the corpse down on the watchmen. They were so frightened that they ran away from the doors and Klimka went into the room. But he still didn't manage to steal the landlord's wife. She was talking with her servants and Klimka overheard all.

The lady said: "Tomorrow the master and I are going for a walk in the fields." Klimka turned around and went out of the room. Then he went to the place where the landlord and his wife were proposing to go. He took a towel and hung it on a tree trunk.

The landlord and his wife were riding along and the landlord caught sight of Klimka and said to his wife: "Just look! Our Klimka has hanged himself!" They quickly rode away from that place and Klimka climbed down from the tree and ran on ahead and hanged himself from another tree. Again the landlord spied him and said, "Can it be that we've got two Klimkas?" He stopped his horse and said to his wife, "You stay here and I'll go and take a look at that Klimka." The landlord got up and walked away while Klimka got down from the tree, sat next to the landlord's wife, and rode away.

They came to a large lake and he sold the landlord's wife to the devils. Then he rode back to the landlord. The landlord asked Klimka, "Did you steal my wife?"

"Yes, I stole her."

"And where have you put her?"

"I sold her to the devils."

"Go buy her back for me."

"I'll buy her back."

So then he went to the place where he had sold the wife and he started stripping bast. A little devil popped up and asked, "What are you doing there?"

Klimka answered, "I'm stripping bast and putting the strips in a pile. I'm going to pull the lake in and snare all you devils."

The little devil asked, "Why?"

"So that you'll give back my landlord's wife."

The little devil went to the biggest devil and said, "Klimka wants the landlord's wife back."

The old devil replied, "Here's a five-*pood* weight. Go to Klimka and tell him that the one of us who can lift this weight higher can have the landlord's wife."

The little devil raised the weight higher than himself. Klimka took the weight and threw it into the lake and pointed up at a cloud. "Do you see?" he asked, "my father and the blacksmith's wife have taken your weight away."

The little devil then proposed to Klimka that whoever should whistle the loudest would have the landlord's wife. Then the little devil whistled, but Klimka managed to stay on his feet. He said to the little devil, "You whistle very well but I will whistle still better. You had better cover your eyes with this towel or they'll pop out." Then he took a cane.

The little devil tied up his eyes. Klimka struck him on the back of his head and the little devil flew into the water and then he said to the oldest devil, "He whistled so loudly that I flew into the water."

"Go tell Klimka that whoever can outlaugh the other can have the woman."

Klimka said, "I can't laugh with you, but I have this old granny." Klimka led the little devil to his granny. A dead horse lay there with its teeth showing all bare. He said, "Laugh with my granny." The little devil laughed but he couldn't outlaugh granny! Then the little devil proposed to Klimka that they have a footrace. Klimka answered, "I can't myself, but I have this brother, Ivashka, in that whitish shirt." He took the devil through the bushes and a hare popped out. Klimka said to the devil, "That's my brother running there."

The little devil set off running after the hare and shouted as loud as he could: "Ivashka in the Whitish Shirt, wait! Let me catch up!" But he couldn't catch Ivashka in the Whitish Shirt! The devil had to give the landlord's wife back to Klimka. Klimka led her home. The landlord saw her and gave Klimka a hundred rubles for her, so Klimka began to prosper and live well on the money.

91. Shabarsha the Laborer

The tale was recorded by D. Khanykov but it is not known who told the tale. The types are all well known throughout the various European traditions but not in this particular combination. There are hints of literary influence, whether from Afanas'ev's editing or from the source he used. SUS 1082 (1045 + 1071 + 1072 + 1084 + 1063 + 1130).

Shall I amuse you with a little tale? It's a wonderful tale. There are marvelous marvels, wondrous wonders, and the laborer Shabarsha, Shabarsha who is a rogue among rogues: oh, well, in for a penny, in for a pound! So Shabarsha set off to work as a laborer, and times were bad. There was no grain at all, and the vegetables didn't grow. But one owner thought a deep thought. How could he chase away his misery, what could he live on, where could he get some money? "Don't worry about it," said Shabarsha to him. "There'll come a day and there will be both grain and money!" And Shabarsha set off for the millpond. "At any rate I can catch some fish. I'll sell them and I'll have some money. But I've no line and no hook. Wait a minute and I'll make one." He asked the miller for a handful of hemp, sat down on the shore, and started weaving his tackle.

He wove and wove, and then a boy in a black shirt and red hat jumped out of the water. "Grandfather! What are you doing here?" he asked.

"I'm weaving a line."

"Why?"

"I intend to cleanse this pond of all you devils by pulling you out of the water."

"Oh, no! Wait a little. I'll go and tell grandfather." The imp dove deep down and Shabarsha went back to his work.

"Wait a minute," he thought, "I'll play a trick on you, you cursed ones. You'll bring me some gold and silver." And Shabarsha began digging a pit and when he had dug it, he placed his hat with a cutout hole over it.

"Shabarsha, oh Shabarsha! Grandfather says that you and I should trade. What will you take not to drag us out of the water?"

"Fill that hat full of gold and silver."

The imp dove back into the water. He came back and said, "Grandfather says that you and I should first wrestle."

"What do you mean, milksop; why should I wrestle with the likes of you? You couldn't even deal with my middle brother, Misha."

"And where is your Misha?"

"Look over there. He's resting in that ravine under a bush."

"How can I call him out?"

"Go up to him and hit him in the side. Then he'll get up of his own accord." The imp went into the ravine, found the bear, and whacked him in the side with his club. Misha rose up on his hind legs and grabbed the imp so that all his bones cracked.

He forced himself out of the bear's claws and ran to the old man in the water. "Well, grandfather," he said in his fright, "Shabarsha has a younger brother, Misha, and he was about to wrestle with me when he cracked all my bones. What would it have been like if I had started to wrestle Shabarsha?"

"Hmm, go and try to have a foot race with Shabarsha; we'll see who can win that."

So the boy in the red hat once more came up to Shabarsha. He repeated his grandfather's words and Shabarsha replied, "Why should I race with the likes of you? My little brother, Bunny, will leave you far behind."

"And where is your little brother Bunny?"

"He's over there, lying in the grass. He wanted a rest. Go up closer to him and touch him on the ear. Then he'll race with you." The imp ran up to Bunny, touched him on the ear, and the hare jumped up with the imp right behind him. "Wait, wait for me, Bunny. Let me come up even with you. Oh, you've got away!"

"Well, grandfather," he said to the water spirit, "I tore after him running. But how? He wouldn't let me catch up to him and he wasn't even Shabarsha—just his youngest brother."

"Hmm," the old man muttered, screwing up his eyebrows. "Go to Shabarsha and tell him to see who can whistle loudest."

"Shabarsha, Shabarsha! Grandfather orders me to see which of us can whistle loudest."

"You whistle first." The imp whistled so loudly that Shabarsha could hardly stand on his own two feet and the leaves started falling off the trees. "You whistle well," said Shabarsha, "but that's not how I do it. When I whistle, you won't stand on your feet and your ears won't be able to stand it. Lie down on your face and cover your ears with your fingers." The imp lay face down on the ground and stuck his fingers in his ears. Shabarsha took his club and with all his might he whacked him on the neck and whistled. He whistled on and on.

"Oh, grandfather, grandfather! You wouldn't believe how Shabarsha whistles. Sparks fell from my eyes and I could hardly get up from the ground, and all the bones in my neck and spine were broken."

"Oho! You see, you're not so strong, imp. Go and take my iron club that's in the rushes and try this: see who can throw it higher into the air."

The imp took the club, put it on his shoulder, and set off for Shabarsha. "Well, Shabarsha, grandfather has ordered us to try one last time. Who can throw this club higher into the air?"

"You throw it first and I'll watch."

The devil threw the club and it flew higher and higher until it was just a black dot in the sky. They waited impatiently for it to come back to earth. Then Shabarsha took the club—it was heavy! He stood it on the toes of one foot, leaned on it with his palm, and began gazing at the sky. "Why don't you throw it? What are you waiting for?" asked the imp.

"I'm waiting until that little cloud comes up, and then I'll throw this club at it. My brother, the blacksmith, is sitting up there and he can use this iron in his business."

"Oh, no, Shabarsha! Don't throw that club into the cloud or else grandfather will be angry." The devil grabbed the club and dove back to his grandfather.

The grandfather heard from his grandson that Shabarsha had nearly thrown his club out of sight and he got seriously afraid and ordered them to drag the money out of the pool and buy him off. The imp dragged up more and more money; he dragged out a whole lot, but the hat still wasn't full. "Well, grandfather, that hat of Shabarsha is a marvel. I've put all your money in it, but it's still empty. There's only that one chest of yours full of money."

"Carry it off to him quickly. Is he still weaving that line?"

"He is." Then was nothing else to do so the imp started with the secret chest and began filling Shabarsha's hat. He poured and poured it in, until finally he had filled it. And since then, since that time, the laborer has lived in glory. They invited me to come and drink mead and beer with them, but I didn't go. The mead was bitter, some said, and the beer was cloudy. Where did such a tale come from?

92. About a Sly Peasant and a Priest

This tale from Kursk province is not otherwise known among the East Slavs. In it the greedy priest tries to steal the poor peasant's crayfish. Aristova notes only that the tale was recorded in the village of Chepukhin in Valuiskii region. SUS 1120*.

There lived and dwelt a poor peasant. Now this peasant was sly! He sowed his grain and reaped hay. His wife fell ill and said to him, "Go to the lake and catch some crayfish; I really love crayfish."

The peasant really didn't want to go to the lake to fetch crayfish, but he set off nonetheless. He came to the lake and started catching crayfish. He caught them and caught them until his sack was full. Then he slung it over his shoulder and set off home.

He walked along and met a priest. "Peace be unto you, God's worker!"

"Thank you, father," said the peasant and bowed. "I wish you the same."

"What's that you're carrying?" the priest asked.

"Some crayfish," answered the peasant.

"The apostle Peter also loved crayfish so I will forgive you your sins for them," said the priest. And he grabbed the sack with one hand and then with the other he made the sign of the cross. Then he took the sack.

The peasant came home without the crayfish and his wife was about to die. Again she asked for some crayfish. So once more the peasant set off for the lake and once more he caught a lot of crayfish. He was carrying them along when once more that same priest appeared, and he said to the peasant. "Your crayfish were very tasty, worker, but your sins are very heavy." Again he took the crayfish.

"Well," thought the peasant. "Just fine, but I'll fix you." He took two sacks, one a little smaller and the other a little larger, and he set off for the lake. He put some crayfish in the smaller one and filled the larger one with devils. He was walking home when the priest was once more standing on the road and waiting for him. The peasant went up to him and said, "So, father, I caught a lot of crayfish today; take whichever sack you want."

The priest was overjoyed and he grabbed the larger. He took it and said, "Well, all your sins are removed, but bring some more crayfish tomorrow."

"Alright," replied the peasant, and he laughed to himself.

The priest came home, untied the sack, and out jumped the devils, who started screeching: "So you're the one who put us in the sack!" They grabbed that priest by his beard and drowned him in a pond. And ever since the peasant goes after crayfish and recalls that priest.

93. About Egibikha (Baba Yaga)

The popular initial episode involves the worker hiding in the sack as the priest and his wife attempt to flee him. Widely known throughout Asia and Europe is the episode of the boy and the witch, here called Egibikha and Egibaba. The Russian version is scatological. SUS 1132.

There lived an old man and an old woman. They had three sons. One they called Grigorii, the second Mikhail, and the third was Ivan. Grigorii and Mikhail set off to sew boots while the third, Ivan the Fool, wanted to go with them, but they wouldn't take him. They packed their backpacks, put in their things, and their lasts. Ivan rummaged around in the chest, pulled out some lasts, and put his in their sack too, and hid in the sack. In the morning the brothers got up, had breakfast, and then ate their dinner. Then they set off. "Let's go before he catches up to us. . . ."

They got tired and thought of resting. They sat down and Ivan shouted, "Brothers, wait for me!" The two brothers threw their packs on their shoulders and started running. Ivan shouted, "Brothers, wait for me. Open your packs and let me out!" So the brothers let him out.

They walked and walked; it was far away. They came to a hut and went in to spend the night. There was no one in the hut. But in that hut lived Egibaba and her three daughters.

Every morning she rode off beyond the river to take a shit in her mortar and then they washed their clothes. The brothers sat down in the cellar, took a kettle, and started boiling up some kasha. Egibaba, hearing them, came; she flew from beyond the lake. She entered her hut. "Phoo, phoo, phoo! A Russian soul! You can't hear them, you can't see them." Baba Egibikha instructed her daughters, "You, Annushka, get up earlier and heat the stove hotter, then roast that Ivashka [Ivan] the little ram." Then she went off to shit beyond the lake.

Annushka heated up the oven. "Ivashka Little Ram, get up." Ivashka got up, sat on the scuttle, spread his arms and legs, and he wouldn't fit into the opening of the oven. She said, "Narrower, narrower!"

"I don't know how. Show me." She got on the scuttle and tucked in her arms and legs. Ivan grabbed the oven door and opened it with the mitts and closed the latch. Then he roasted her, cut up the meat, and put it on the windowsill. Egibaba came from beyond the lake and cursed her daughter. "Where have you been?"

She ate and threw the bones on the floor and then she said, "I would like to take a drive, to take a ride on Ivashka's bones."

From the cellar Ivan replied, "Go take your drive and your ride on Annushka's bones."

Night passed and in the morning she rode off again. The next day she said to her second daughter, "You are to roast Grishka [Grigorii] today."

In just the same way Motrena heated up the oven and called out: "Get up, Grishka."

Ivan said, "Wait, I'll go." So Ivan got on the coalscuttle, spread his arms and legs, and he wouldn't fit into the oven.

She said, "Narrower, narrower."

"I don't know how; you show me."

She sat on the coalscuttle and tucked in her arms and legs. Ivan got Motrena into the oven and burned her up. Ivanushka prepared the meat and put it on the windowsill. Egibaba came riding back and ate up her daughter.

"Egibaba, Egibaba, we've made some kasha, don't step in it!" But Egibaba stepped in the kasha—she put her foot right in it! She scorched her legs and cursed her daughters.

On the third morning there was nothing else to be done and she heated the oven by herself. No way could she ride off beyond the lake. She heated up the oven and said, "Get up, Mikhailushka [Mikhail], and come out of the cellar."

Ivan stepped back again, spread open his arms and legs, and couldn't crawl into the oven. Egibikha said, "Narrower, narrower!"

"I don't know how."

When she sat down to show him, he grabbed the mitts and put her into the oven. It got too hot for Egibikha in the oven and she twisted and turned and then she backed her ass into the latch and got stuck. Ivan said to his brothers, "Come out from the cellar now; no one will eat you." The brothers climbed out, ate, and they all set off. Ivan of the Oven said, "I'll take the old woman with me."

"What do you need her for?"

"No, I'll take her." And they set off.

They walked and walked and then stopped beneath a fir tree for the night. They crawled under the fir. Ivan tied the old woman up to the fir. Twelve robbers came up to the fir. They came up and lit a fire. Ivan said, "Brothers, they've decided to rob us."

One brother said, "Piss on them."

The robbers put a kettle on to boil beneath the fir. Ivan started to piss right in their kettle. The robbers said, "God's dew is falling."

Then Ivan said, "Oh, brothers, I need to shit."

His brothers said, "Shit in a boot." He started shitting into the kettle.

The robbers said, "The little goddess is dropping crumbs."

Ivan said, "Brothers, I can't hold my old woman any longer."

The brothers said, "Let us hold her."

Ivan let the old woman loose. Egibishna got out of the fir, she started flying, and she fell right into the kettle. The robbers were counting out some money. The old woman fell into the kettle—she closed it with the latch. The robbers got frightened, ran away, and one was left behind. Ivan cut out the robber's tongue. The robber ran to catch up to the others and shouted, "Brothers, give me some water."

The robbers waited for him and asked, "Were there a lot of them?"

The robber said, "Twee, twee, tweetee." They thought he meant thirty. The brothers took the money and flew off home. That's a tale for you and a string of pretzels for me.

94. A Lad Who Watched *Rusalki*

This is the only East Slavic version of this tale of the lad who watched the *rusalki* and their guardian, a one-eyed ogre. The *rusalki* were (are!) maidens inhabiting streams. They entice young men to their deaths, often by seduction. They are thought to derive from the souls of girls who die or drown without confession or the sacrament of chrismation. SUS 1135.

A certain man was a great wizard. He knew everything and could see *rusalki*. A young lad found out about this and thought: "I'll go to him and talk with him. I'll find out about these *rusalki*."

So the lad set off to talk to the wizard and the wizard told him that he could see some *rusalki*. So then the lad asked him: "Teach me to see the *rusalki*."

"I can," answered the wizard, "only you must take three pairs of boot soles, then butcher a piglet, put it on a spit about a *sazhen* in length, go into the steppe, light a fire, and roast the piglet on the fire. When you've lit the fire, it will be visible far into the steppe. When midnight comes, the *rusalki* will come running with shouts, songs, and whistles, like at a wedding, and they'll all be in different clothing. You sit there and don't move from your place. The *rusalki* will run up to the fire but you look and don't blink. If you blink, you won't see the *rusalki*—they will just disappear.

"And when they come, there will be a devil with them. He will stand apart from the *rusalki*. This devil has lost one eye and the other is completely crossed. He will sit down next to you and start questioning you: 'Man, man, what are you roasting?'

"Don't you answer, don't blink, just watch so that he doesn't snitch a bit of the piglet or the *rusalki* will throw themselves at you and tear you to bits. All around you there will be an unbelievable host of *rusalki*, but you just look at them. When you've looked enough, then when the devil asks you, 'Man, man, what are you roasting?' you say 'Frog.'

"'And where do they catch them?' he'll ask.

"'Over there, in the river,' you tell him and point with your hand toward the steppe, toward the woods. But there's no river there. The *rusalki* will hear this and rush off toward the river, searching for the river. The one-eyed devil will stay behind to guard you and again he will question you. Then you ask him why he's one-eyed and if he asks you, 'Can you cure me?' say to him 'I can, but only on one condition. Lie down, screw up your eye, and don't look at what I am doing. If you look, you will lose your last eye.' When he's screwed up his eye, pull out the red-hot spit and poke it in his eye. Then when you've done that, throw everything down and run off with the boot soles in your hands. Along the way as the *rusalki* begin to catch up to you, toss one pair of the soles down and run on. And then a second pair, and finally the third."

The lad listened to all this and then went away. He waited for evening, butchered the piglet, dressed it out, and set off for the steppe. When midnight came, the lad laid and lit the fire and began roasting the piglet.

The fire burned brightly and could be seen far away. The *rusalki* saw it and ran toward it. They ran to the fire, giggling, noisily, with their songs and whistling.

They ran up to the fire and the one-eyed devil was with them. They surrounded the youth, standing there. The lad looked at them and watched everything. The *rusalki* surrounded the lad, questioning him, but especially the one-eyed devil did.

"Man!"

"What?"

"Man, what are you roasting?"

"A frog."

"And where did you catch it?"

"Over there, beyond that hill, there's a little river in the steppe and I caught the frog in it."

The *rusalki* all ran toward the river while the one-eyed devil stayed behind to guard the youth. He sat there and asked, "Man!"

"What?"

"Man, what are you doing?"

"I'm roasting this frog."

"And what will you do with it?"

"When I've roasted it, I'll feed you and there'll be enough for the *rusalki*." And then he asked him, "Why are you one-eyed?"

The devil didn't answer the lad as to why he was one-eyed. He just asked, "Can you cure me?"

"I can."

"Then cure me."

"I could cure you but you devils are a hopeless lot. If I cure you, you'll just make a racket."

"No, I won't make a racket. Cure my eye!" said the devil.

"If you won't make a racket, then I'll cure you," said the lad.

"Only tell me, what is your name?" asked the devil.

"I'm called MeMyself."

"Alright, I'm me myself, too. Cure me."

"I will cure you, but you must squint your eye and not peek. If you peek, then your last eye will disappear. Watch out and don't peek!"

"I won't peek—just cure me, lad."

So the devil closed his eyes, lay down on the ground, and the youth drew the red-hot spit out of the fire and poked it into the devil's crossed eye. The devil roared out with every swear word such that it was terrible to hear him. The hair on the youth's head stood on end.

The *rusalki* heard the shouts of the one-eyed devil and stopped looking for the river. They ran back to the fire where they had left the devil. When they had run up, the devil was still shouting. The *rusalki* asked him, "Why are you shouting?"

"He burned out my eye!"

"Who did it?"

"MeMyself."

"Well, if it was you yourself, then just sit there. There's nothing to shout about. Why bother us? We looked for the river and you just bothered us."

The *rusalki* looked and the lad wasn't there. They ran after the youth. They started to catch up to him. The lad saw they were catching up and he threw down one pair of soles. The *rusalki* grabbed the boot soles and tried them on their feet. One would try them, and then the second would grab them and try them. They tried them until they were worn out.

They started running again. The youth threw another pair of the boot soles down and ran on. The *rusalki* rushed up and grabbed the soles and started trying them on. They kept trying them until they were worn out. Then they threw them down and started running after the youth again.

They started catching up to him so the lad threw the third pair down. The *rusalki* started trying them but then they stopped trying them on and rushed after the lad. By now the youth had run nearly to his home.

They were just about to grab him when the clever youth took his hat and threw it at them. The *rusalki* thought it would be interesting to try on the hat. They tried it on and laughed while the lad went into his own yard. When they had all tried on the hat, they set off running after the youth. They rushed to the gates, but just then the cock crowed. Then the *rusalki* all disappeared right into the earth.

95. The Tsar and the Peasant

There is one other version of this tale in the Russian tradition. From the Pomor'e area of Arkhangelsk province. SUS 1138*.

There lived and dwelt this tsar and his tsaritsa. They had a daughter and there was an old woman who lived with them. A certain peasant decided to fool the tsar. He took a bucket of pitch and walked along shouting: "Are there any skins to gild?" He went to the tsaritsa and said, "May I perhaps gild you?"

She said, "Gild away!"

So he gilded her, took a hundred rubles and said, "Lie down so that the gilt doesn't run off."

He entered the next room. There he found the tsar's daughter. He asked her, "May I gild you?"

She replied, "Gild me!"

He gilded her, took a hundred rubles, and told her the same thing as he had the tsaritsa.

Then he went into the third room. There was the old woman. "Well, may I gild you?"

"Gild me in my old age," she mumbled.

He gilded her, took a hundred rubles, and went away.

The tsar came to see the tsaritsa. The tsaritsa said to him, "Easy, easy, my lord. Don't disturb the gilt. It cost a hundred rubles."

The tsar said to her, "What are you saying? You haven't been gilded—that's pitch." Then the tsar went in to his daughter and to the old woman. It was the same. So the tsar asked, "Who smeared you with that pitch?"

They said, "Some peasant came and gilded us."

The tsar returned, took a horse, and galloped after the peasant. The peasant walked along the road and met an old woman. He said to her, "Old woman, take off your clothes. The tsar is coming and he'll beat you." The old woman took off her clothes and the peasant covered her in moss and then he put on the old woman's clothes.

The tsar rode by. "What are you doing there, granny?"

"I'm mixing sourdough."

"Did you see a traveler, a robber and peasant?"

"Yes, not long ago such a robber passed by."

"Do you think I can catch up with him, granny?"

"Oh, father! You can. Only give me your clothing."

The tsar gave the peasant his clothing. The peasant put it on and he dressed the tsar in the old woman's clothing and said to him, "Hold this sourdough and don't stir it. I'll go catch him."

The peasant rode away. The tsar waited and waited. Then he heard the old woman grumbling beneath the moss. He went and dug away the moss and saw that the old woman was alive. The old woman said to the tsar, "Why of course, father, some robber was here. He took off my clothes and buried me in the moss."

What was the tsar to do? He gave the old woman her clothes, put on the peasant's, which the old woman had, and set off home.

He got home but the soldiers wouldn't let him in. They didn't recognize him. Then he pleaded with the soldiers, "What is this, brothers, I am your tsar!" Then they let him in.

The peasant came home with the money and even now he is alive and prospering. And he laughed at the tsar, at how easy it was to fool him.

96. The Peasant and the Devil

Narrated by Nataliia Mikhailovna Dement'eva, in her mid-thirties. She lived on the shore of Lake Onega. Onchukov claimed she was among the best narrators he encountered in the north. Further, Onchukov noted that several of her tales were "pornographic" and thus unsuitable for printing. No other East Slavic tales belonging to this type are known. SUS 1161A.

Once a peasant was fishing at a lake, but the fish weren't biting, and he thought, "If only the devil would give me some fish!" He thought that and then he set off for home. On the way he met a man who said, "What were you thinking, peasant?"

"I wasn't thinking anything."

"What do you mean, you weren't thinking? Think hard."

"I said, 'If only the devil would give me some fish!'"

"That's right, but what of your goods will you give me?"

"I would be glad to give you something, but I haven't anything. There's just a black bull. I could give you that."

"But you won't deceive me?"

"No, I won't deceive you."

"Alright then, bring your bull tomorrow." The next day in the morning the peasant got up and remembered about yesterday, and he was sorry to part with the bull. He thought, "Maybe I'll be sly. I'll take a rotten old rope and tie it to a sapling." That's what he thought and that's what he did.

He went off to the lake to check his fish traps. There were a whole lot of fish in them. The devil came out of the lake and said, "Here are your fish; now where is your bull?"

"I tied the bull to a sapling." They went over to the tree and there was just the rope tied there. The peasant said, "Oh, brother, the bull has broken loose!"

"Alright, there's nothing to be done; look for him and bring him tomorrow." The peasant was happy and once more tied some rotten rope to a tree and went to check his fish traps. Once more he saw that there were a lot of fish, and he was overjoyed. He was about to go home when the devil came out of the lake again and asked for the bull. The peasant said that the bull had once more broken loose from the tree. Then the devil said to the peasant, "Look here, peasant, don't deceive me. Bring that bull you promised or you're going to suffer from me."

He came the third day and the peasant saw a bear on the other side of the lake. The bear dove into the water and swam and the devil came out of the lake and demanded the bull. The clever peasant answered the devil, "I brought the bull here, but he got loose again. There he is, swimming in the lake. Grab him right now!"

The devil ran up to the shore and grabbed the bear, but he couldn't overcome it. Another devil came out of the lake and the two tried to get control of the bear. Then the first devil went up to the peasant and said, "Well brother, alone I couldn't handle that bull, and if my grandfather hadn't come to help me, he would have gotten away from me. But he clobbered my grandfather with a hoof and nearly knocked an eye out."

97. The Devil Takes the Soldier's Watch

Although this tale may have been derived from the Old Russian story about the journey of Archpriest Ioann to Jerusalem, this version is much different. From the V.I. Dal' collection of folktales. Piter is of course St. Petersburg. Irkutsk is scarcely close to St. Petersburg; it is located in Eastern Siberia near Lake Baikal. SUS 1166*.

In olden times when devils weren't opposed to training to be soldiers, to march and handle a rifle, there lived in Piter this soldier, and how brave and courageous he was!

He served neither to well nor too badly; he never asked to go on duty and he never hesitated to loaf. But once it fell to him to stand watch in the Galley Port and, as it happened, at very midnight. So he went off with God at his side, crossing himself, and took the place of his comrade. He stood there and because he had nothing else to do, he gave a signal with his rifle while on guard. He looked up and saw the Unclean One coming toward him. The soldier wasn't timid, and even if he had been a coward, what was there to do? You can't leap into the water to escape the devil! "Greetings, soldier," the devil said. "I wish you good health. Teach me how to do your watch. I've been studying you for a long time, but I can't grasp it."

"You're some devil!" said the soldier. "And just how are you going to understand? I've been serving for ten years and I have a stripe, but I'm still learning. I've been on night duty more than a thousand times. And you want to learn how by just watching! No, brother, that would be too quick and too cheap."

"Teach me, soldier!"

"Perhaps; only for what I paid for it, I'll sell it to you."

The soldier put the devil in front of him and for a beginning he whistled with all his might right at the crown of his head so that the devil stumbled. "Oh, you really get bent over at the front," said the soldier. And then he let him have it as never before. He struck him about ten times and saw that the devil was hardly standing on his feet and that he had stopped shouting. "Now, come here! That's enough for the first time. Although I'm sorry for you, you can't get along without it. You know yourself that being a soldier is the highest there is, and there's nothing at all like being at the front." The devil thanked him for the training and gave the soldier ten gold rubles before he left. "Oho," thought the soldier, "I'm only sorry that I beat him so little! If I'd given him some more, he'd have given me twenty!"

Exactly a week later the soldier had to go on duty at the same hour and at the same place. He was standing there, holding his rifle in various poses, thinking, "If that devil appears again, I'll make up for lost time." At midnight out of somewhere the Unclean One appeared.

"Greetings, soldier!"

"Greetings, brother. Why have you come?"

"What do you mean? I've come for training."

"So that's it. And you wanted to get it all in one go. No, my little friend, 'Do it quickly, they'll be born blind.' Fall in!" the soldier commanded. "Chest out, belly tucked in, and eyes focused on the commander." He fussed for a long time with the devil, loading him up with a dress outfit with stripes and in this way he taught the Unclean One to handle a rifle on his shoulder, on his foot, and standing guard. "Well," he said, "now you could be foot soldier to Satan and not fall on your face in the mud! Only there's still a small problem. Your tail is too big from the back. Turn around to the left." The Unclean One turned and the soldier pulled a neck cross out of his pocket and quietly pinned it to the devil. The devil jumped and screamed bloody hell! "Why, isn't this part of the inner life of you devils?"

the soldier asked. The devil saw that he was simply lost, so he promised the soldier some silver and gold and every sort of riches. The soldier wasn't against the money but he demanded that the devil deliver neither a little nor a lot but just a whole cartload! In a moment all was ready. The devil had delivered a whole heap of money, which the soldier hid in a ravine and made the sign of the cross over. "So that bastard devil thought he could deceive our Orthodox brother! He gave me charcoal and not gold."

"What's the matter, soldier?" the devil asked. "Let me go now and take off your cross."

"No, brother, wait a little. I want you to do me one more little service. It's been ten years since I was last at home and I left my wife and children there. Before my death I want to visit the land of my birth and see my family. Take me home. It isn't far, my brother, just to Irkutsk gubernia. When you've taken me there, I'll remove the cross." The devil frowned and frowned but then he agreed. The next day the soldier went to headquarters and asked for two days leave to celebrate—there were some holidays at that time—and then he went straight to the Unclean One. He got on his back and held on tightly to his horns. The devil whistled and carried him like lightning. The soldier could only look on as towns and villages flashed by him. "Oh, my fine lad! I love to speed along!" He had hardly had time to say this when they arrived. The soldier got off the devil and said, "Thank you! One good turn deserves another! Go wherever you like now, but come back tomorrow evening and then we'll go back." He visited with his friends and feasted for a whole two days and then toward night he said goodbye to his relatives and returned on the devil to Piter just in time. But oh, how he had tormented that Unclean One! He had nearly broken his horns off. He removed the cross and hadn't even managed to put it in his pocket when the devil had already disappeared! All traces were cold! He picked up the devil's money and lived in clover.

98. Whence Came Baba Yaga

This is an amusing tale that reflects the general attitude toward women among peasant men in the nineteenth century. It is unknown elsewhere among the East Slavs. Serebrennikov's tales were collected in the Kama River area of north-central Perm province before the 1917 revolution. There is no mention of this tale type in the A–T index. SUS 1169*.

A certain devil wanted to make Baba Yaga. He gathered twelve of the very nastiest women and began boiling them in a kettle. He tasted it and then he boiled them for a whole day. He tasted it, sneezed, and the gates opened. Once more he sipped the soup and he spat it out. And then Baba Yaga jumped out of the kettle.

99. The Wizard

Recorded in Tver province. This is the only version of this tale type known among the Russians, but there is a single version recorded from the Ukrainian tradition. Type 1180 has several analogues but there appear to be none to 1199C*. SUS 1180 + 1199C*.

This soldier had taken quarters. He practiced black magic and possessed such books. Once he was not at home and a friend came to visit him. He saw that his countryman wasn't home, but he found his books and started reading them in his boredom. It was nighttime. He was reading with a night-light. Some sorts of names were written down. He read half of them and then looked back: a whole shelf of devils was standing there. The soldier was frightened and he quickly took to reading the book again. He read and read, and then he glanced back and there were still more devils. So he started reading some more and he read to the end. He turned around and there were now so many more devils that only with difficulty could they fit in the soldier's quarters. One devil was sitting on another and they were chasing each other around. The soldier saw that things were bad. He closed the book, frowned, and sat there, waiting for his friend. Meanwhile, the devils came closer and they were pestering him. "Come on, give us some work!"

The soldier thought and thought and said, "Carry all the water from all the barrels and kettles to the town bathhouses in a sieve." The devils ran off but in about two minutes they came running back. "We've carried it all. Give us some new work!"

The soldier gave them an order: "Take the *voevoda*'s house apart brick by brick, but don't touch the people in it, don't bother them, and then put it all back together as it was."

The devils ran off but in about two minutes they were back. "Finished," the said. "Give us some more work!"

The soldier said, "Go make a mountain with some crushed sand in such and such a place."

The devils ran off. In a minute they were back. "Finished," they said. "Give us some more work."

"Count the number of grains of sand lying on the bottom of the Volga from its source to where it enters the sea, the number of drops of water, and the number of fish!" The devils ran off but in a minute they came back and they had fulfilled all his orders.

They didn't give the soldier a chance to think things through very well because they always wanted more work and had always fulfilled the old tasks. The moment the soldier thought of something, the devils started pestering him. They gave him no rest; they even threatened to beat him if he left them for any length of time without a task. The soldier was feeling completely tortured and his friend still wasn't there. What could he do? How could he be rid of the devils? Then he thought: while he had been reading the book, not a single devil approached him. "Let me try reading it again and maybe things will get better."

He started reading the book from the beginning but then he noticed that there were more devils than before—so many that the light from the nightlight hardly came through, such a host of the pagan forces had gathered around him. And every time the soldier stumbled on a word, or cleared his throat, they would immediately press him more than ever. "Give us some more work!"

The soldier broke free from that devilish apparition but he didn't know how to get himself out of his misfortune. Then suddenly it occurred to him: "The devil's children began appearing when I was reading the book from the beginning; let me read it from the end. Maybe they'll all go away."

He immediately opened the book upside down and started reading from the end. He read and read and he noticed that there were fewer and fewer devils. The light from his nightlight got brighter and there was more space in the hut. The soldier was overjoyed and kept on reading. He read and read until he had read it all backward. And thus he was saved from those pagan devils.

Soon his friend came home and he told him what had been going on with him. "Well," said his friend, "You're lucky that you managed to read it all the way through backward; if you had not, then at midnight they would have devoured you!" Since then the soldier has had enough of reading books of sorcery but his friend kept on using them as before.

Anecdotes

Anecdotes make up nearly half of the tales classified in the Russian SUS. Most, but not all, of them consist of a single plot per tale. They are characterized by their strong tendency to humor often bordering on the ridiculous. The Russian versions frequently vary considerably from the international tale type, suggesting that their resemblance to the standard type is coincidental. Jokes and jests, mostly of the two- or three-line variety, have never been catalogued and thus are not included here. These tend to have a short life span, particularly the political jokes and the off-color ones for which the Russians are rightly famous.

100. The Dog Tsuvarnachka

Collected in Tobolsk, western Siberia, by the student Khudiakov. The tale differs from the standard versions of this tale known sporadically throughout Europe where a sickle is thrown into deep water as punishment for a fault. SUS 1202.

There lived an old man with his old woman and they had three sons: Tsupravor, Tsudozor, and Tsuvanko, and they had this little dog Tsuvarnachka. The brothers went into the woods to cut hay and the dog went with them. They mowed and mowed but the little dog Tsuvarnachka got left behind. They looked and looked for her all over the woods, but they didn't find her. They found a great huge cave, a kennel. "Tsupravor," they said, "you go into that cave."

But the very moment he stuck his head in, wolves ate it right up! "What should we do now? Wolves have eaten our brother's head." So they walked and wandered about but they still didn't find their dog Tsuvarnachka. Then they found a big pile of wood, so they lit a fire in the pile of wood. Tsuvarnachka had been hiding in that pile of wood and she got roasted! The brothers found her and said, "Is this our little dog or is this a hare?" They took and ate her, deciding it was a hare. Then they set off for home. When they got home, they told their father and mother that they had lost the dog and that wolves had eaten their brother. Their parents scolded them, but then they just went on living as before.

101. Those Folk from Pskov

Originally collected by P. Sakharov, it is otherwise unknown. Pskov is an important and ancient city on the shores of Lake Peipus. SUS 1250***.

Once it had been wet for a very long time in Pskov; the clouds came round very low, so low that good Orthodox Christians thought that the sky was going to fall onto the very earth. The whole community came together to discuss how to avoid this calamity. The good people of Pskov debated this for three days and then on the fourth they decided on a course of action: they would take apart the town stockade and prop up the sky with the stakes.

They disassembled the stockade and stuck the stakes up at all the corners of the city. Good weather came and the clouds passed by. One councilor went about the city, stroking his beard, and looking at the people. Then he stopped in the middle of the square and said aloud: "Great, isn't it, Orthodox Christians! The calamity has been avoided; now you may all go to your homes."

102. A Tailor or a Crayfish

The Chuvash are a Turkic people inhabiting the central Urals. A Belarusian version of the tale is also known. SUS 1310.

After his regular work was finished, a tailor decided to go on the road. He set off for the land of the Chuvash. He was walking along a river and when he came up to the river, he said, "I'll feel along the banks. Maybe there are some crayfish nests." So he started feeling around. He found a lot of nests but they were all empty. He pulled out just one crayfish from a nest. But what a crawdad it was! As big as a worn-out boot! He stuck the crawdad behind his belt and set off for the Chuvash village. He came into the village and asked at every window beginning at the first yard into the village whether somebody didn't need some sewing done. In one house they told him to come in. He went in and in that hut there was just this one Chuvash woman. Word for word that Chuvash woman said to him, "Now I'm the only one here at home; my husband and I live alone. He's gone off to the woods to get some firewood in for the winter. He's slept out two nights in the woods and he still hasn't come back." She nattered a while with the tailor and then she went off to milk the cows.

It wasn't very late and it was still possible to go asking for work. So the tailor thought, "Maybe I could sew some clothing for this Chuvash woman while her husband isn't here? Maybe I could just earn a little with a good word? She's no doubt the mistress but she doesn't own the house. Would the master cuss her out just for some new clothes? But maybe he wouldn't pay me for my work. . . . He'll say, 'And why did you pay attention to a woman when her master isn't at home? Take the money from her.' But how do you get it from the woman? They tell the truth who say, 'Whoever gets mixed up with a woman is a woman himself.' But wait just a moment; I'm not going to leave just yet. I'll play a little joke on you!"

The tailor looked at all the corners in the hut. Then he saw the stove standing there with the old woman's bread dough rising. He took the crawdad out from his pouch and stuck it into the dough. The Chuvash woman and the milkmaid came into the hut. The tailor said, "What can I sew for you, mother?"

She said, "I'll have a white *kaftan*."

"No, I wouldn't dare sew you a *kaftan* without the master's consent. I'll come back, but for now 'Goodbye.' I need to find some work."

"Goodbye," the Chuvash woman said, "but take heed and come back here day after tomorrow without fail."

The night passed. The next day in the morning the Chuvash woman looked at her bread dough and there was this crawdad struggling to crawl out of it! She had never seen a crayfish before in her whole life and she was frightened. She ran outside and called out for the sentries. All the Chuvashes came running to her yard and said, "What are you yelling about?"

"The devil's in my bread dough." They all tumbled into her hut and the tailor brought up the rear. He went up to the dough and looked. Somebody else took a look but they were all afraid to grab hold of it.

The mayor heard them and came into the Chuvash's hut. "What's going on in here?"

"I don't know. Something's crawled into the woman's bread dough."

"Here, let me take a look." He looked at the dough and said to all the Chuvashes, "What's that in the bread dough?"

One said, "It's the devil!"

Another: "It's the cursed one!"

"No, you're all liars," the mayor said. "That's no devil and it's not the cursed one; it's something else! Maybe it's a tailor. Take a look: he's got scissors in his hands with teeth on their ends."

"Brilliant! You're brilliant, Foma Eremeich!" they all shouted together. "Apparently none of them had guessed it, but you guessed it! That is certainly a tailor. Just look how he wiggles his scissors."

"So now carry him outside and let him go wherever he wants. But wash him off," said the mayor, "as he's really covered in dough."

So the Chuvashes washed the crawdad in a whole bucket of water and the crawdad tore loose and went straight to the bottom of the bucket and started crawling around on the bottom backward. "You guys," said the tailor, "I'm a tailor and I know tailors. They sew clothing for water devils that live in the water. See how he takes to the water! Let's take him over to the water. That woman started hollering because she didn't get her white *kaftan*."

"You are right," said the Chuvashes. Thank you for teaching us that lesson." So they took the crayfish in the bucket and tossed him into the pond: the tailor, the crayfish, and the whole joker's clothing!

103. The Mare's Egg

The tale was told to Zelenin by a twenty-eight-year-old peasant, Gavriil Nikolaevich Opalev, who said he had heard the tale from his father. This is a common story among the East Slavs. It is quite different from West European tales classified under the same rubric. SUS 1319.

A certain priest had a laborer. He would go into the woods to cut firewood. He found a giant puffball, brought it home, and showed it to the priest. The priest asked him, "What's that?"

"That, Father, is a mare's egg."

"And what's a mare's egg?"

"From just such an egg you can hatch out a colt."

"And how do you hatch out a colt?"

"Just like a hen sits on her eggs: you have to sit four weeks on it." And he put the priest on the stove.

The time was up, the four weeks. The laborer kept thinking it over: "What am I to do?" He knew that no colt was going to hatch out of the puffball. He went into the woods and somehow caught a rabbit. He went up to the priest on the stove and said, "Father, turn around! It's about time for that colt to come out!" The priest moved and the puffball burst. At that very moment the laborer let the rabbit loose—the priest didn't see him—and as the door was wide open, the rabbit ran right outside. They both ran after him, trying to catch him. They couldn't though: the rabbit was a rabbit after all.

The priest said, "Oh, laborer! That probably was a very good colt: his hind legs were really long."

"Yes, Father, it was probably a very good one."

104. Kostia

This is a common tale among the East Slavs and it is well known throughout Europe as well. The tale was told to Onchukov by A.I. Ditiatev, an elderly blind man from Pustozersk. As a younger man he spent the summers hunting at sea. In old age he was poor and forced to work as a sawyer. SUS 1380.

There lived and dwelt an old man and an old woman. The old woman had a lover, Kostia, who lived over the river and who had red boots. Kostia would come visiting the old woman and she would pray to God that her old man would go deaf or blind. The old man heard her and said, "Old woman! In the open steppe there's a dry oak and in that oak is St. Nikola of the Hollow. Go and pray, for he is very merciful."

Night passed and in the morning they got up. The old man harnessed his horses and set off for the woods. He hid his little horse, climbed into the hollow oak, and sat down. At home the old woman got her things together and set off for the steppe where the dead oak stood. "Oh Lord," she said, "Blind and deafen the old man!"

From inside the oak the old man responded, "I shall blind him, old woman, and I shall deafen him."

"Glory to Thee, oh Lord." Toward evening the old man came home, shamming blindness and deafness, wandered about the garden, but he still couldn't find the harness yoke; he was lost. The old woman jumped up and shouted at the old man, "Oh, my poor, poor old man! He can't hear a thing! He wanders about, he stumbles, and he can't find anything!" But she was thinking, "Oh Glory to Thee, oh Lord! He is blinded and he is deafened."

The little old man came into the hut and flopped down in the rafters to sleep. Toward morning the old woman got up, heated up the stove, and baked and cooked some *bliny* and potato fritters. Kostia came visiting and the old woman seated him at the head of the table, and then she brought him the food and entertained him. The old man lay up in the rafters and called down: "Oh, my poor old woman! Bring me my bow and arrow!"

She threw them up to him and said, "Here, you blind and deaf old fool!" She went on entertaining Kostia, placed the *bliny* on the table, but she'd forgotten to bring the butter, so she went down into the cellar for it. The old man opened his eyes and shot Kostia right in the chest. He jumped down from the rafters, pulled out the arrow, opened Kostia's mouth, grabbed the potato fritters off the plate, and stuffed them in his mouth, and then rolled him over toward the wall. The old woman came bringing the butter. She thought Kostia had choked. "Oh, this is just horrible!"

The old man heard her: "So, my poor old woman, why are you oohing and aahing?"

"Oh, shut up, you old deaf and blind! You've ruined everything."

Evening came and night was approaching. The old man said, "Where are we going to put Kostia?" He went and dressed him out in fine clothing and then carried him away to a rich peasant's turnip field. The old man stole a turnip and then he took a barrel and placed Kostia next to the barrel. He stuffed the turnip in his mouth and went away.

In the morning the merchant's workers saw Kostia and reported: "Kostia is stealing your turnips!"

"Go and beat that thief Kostia!" The lads ran off and struck Kostia with a post and Kostia fell down, dead.

"Where shall we put Kostia?"

The merchant said, "Drag him off to a garbage pit somewhere." They dragged Kostia off and dumped him in a garbage pit.

The old man was standing watch and in the night he brought Kostia back to the rich merchant's home, laid him out, and then went into the barn. He carried out as much flour as he could and put a sack in Kostia's hands, he put a scoop next to him. In the morning the workers came and saw that the barn was open. They reported it to the merchant: "Kostia is stealing flour!"

The merchant said, "Run, beat him!"

The servants ran and struck him with a post and Kostia fell down dead. "Where should we put him?"

"Drag him out beyond all the houses!"

They dragged him out beyond all the houses but again that night the old man brought him back. He went to the rich merchant's and stole a fine horse; he put the bridle on it and then sat Kostia in the saddle. He put the reins in his hands and the horse ran about the town. In the morning the merchant's workmen saw this and caught the horse. They poked Kostia and Kostia fell down, dead. "Where should we put Kostia?"

"Just drag him off somewhere!"

In the night the old man once more carried off Kostia, placed him in a boat on the river, stuck two oars in his hands, and pushed him off. Kostia sat there, not rowing and not steering, just letting the water carry him along. Some fishermen were catching fish:

"Kostia, come back! You're heading into the nets!" But Kostia didn't turn back and he sailed right into the nets. The peasants shouted, "Go on then, beat Kostia! Why did he go right into the nets?" They all went their separate ways, but some of them poked Kostia in the chest and he fell in and drowned.

So Kostia was carried along by the river and into a mill run and then Kostia got into a fish trap. They came to empty out the trap, pulled Kostia out of it, and threw him in the water.

---

105. The Lord of the Manor

Only one other telling of this type is known to exist among the Russians and there are apparently none among the Ukrainians or Belarusians. The tale is also known among the Finns and Estonians. The attitude of Korol'kova to the lord of the manor is reflected in this and some of her other tales. SUS 1440.

There lived and dwelt this rich lord of a manor. He had had three estates. He had already devoured one estate and he was on the second. Once he went out into a field where his serfs were working and he saw a peasant girl. He found her very attractive. He asked his overseer, "Which girl is that? Who are her mother and father?"

And the overseer replied, "She has no mother and father; she is an orphan. Her grandfather raised her and he is now one hundred twenty. They live together."

The gentleman went up to her and asked her, "What is your name?"

"Katiusha."

"Well, Katiusha, come to me at the summer house this evening when work is finished; I'll be waiting for you. He took her long braid in his hand and tugged on it, flirting a little. "Will you come?"

"Yes, I'll come."

Then he rode off. When the sun had set and work was finished, all the people went home, but she didn't go to him on her way, so the next day the gentleman came again, went up to her, and asked, "Katiusha, why didn't you come?"

"Sir, I was there, I walked about the estate until the cocks crowed. Even the dogs were barking and I was afraid they'd tear me to shreds so I went away."

"Will you come now then?"

"Yes, I'll come, sir."

"I'll be waiting at the gates." And so that night the gentleman waited until the cocks crowed, but she didn't come. He came again and asked her, "Why didn't you come, Katiusha?"

"My grandfather wouldn't let me out: 'Where would the winds be carrying you of a night? Go lie down!' And then he said that he would never let me go out anywhere in the evening."

"Alright," said the gentleman. He went to her grandfather and said, "Why won't you let your granddaughter out? I'll send a servant and if you won't let her out, then it will be to the stables with you and for a whipping!"

"Very well, sir!"

The gentleman went to his estate and said to a servant, "Go to Old Man Fokin. Tell him the lord of the manor has sent you and that he will hand her over and you then bring her here."

Meanwhile, the old man asked his granddaughter, "Why does the gentleman need you?"

"I don't know. He has ordered me to come and spend the night."

"So this is what he's thought up, but we'll shift all the blame for your ruin onto him!"

The old man had a really ramshackle hut—the passages were just wicker. There were only two doors, one onto the street and the other into the backyard. Katiusha was then brushing her hair out, weeping and looking out the window. She saw the servant approaching through the window. She jumped up and ran out into the backyard. Next to the neighbor's drying rack stood an old, old bay mare. It was hardly standing, dozing.

Katiusha hid behind the horse and her grandfather saw that that's where she had disappeared. When the servant came in, she leapt over the fence to the neighbors and hid there.

The servant came in: "Well, grandfather, where is she?"

"She's out there by the drying rack."

The servant went out into the yard. Next to the drying rack stood the bay mare. He thought, "Why would the gentleman need such an old nag?" But he led her off anyway. He brought her into the estate yard, and went into the hallway where the gentleman was entertaining guests.

The gentleman asked, "Did you bring her?"

"I brought her."

"Take her into the bedroom."

Now the gentleman's bedroom was on the second floor. The servant said, "But sir, she'll make an awful racket; she's shod!"

"All these villagers are alike, they're all shod. Take some galoshes; they're lying over there near the guests; then lead her upstairs."

The servant came up to the gentleman and stated: "I've tried to lead her by force, but she won't budge."

"Take a box of gingerbreads and some honey sticks. Offer her some tea and feed her."

The servant took the gingerbreads and honey sticks and tea to her. She ate the gingerbreads and honey sticks out of his hands but she wouldn't touch the tea. "Sir, she ate up the gingerbread and honey sticks, but she wouldn't have the tea; she just snorted."

"Oh, these village ones are all alike. Throw her down on the bed, put out the light, and go yourself. Here's a silver ruble for you!"

The servant ran into the bedroom and thought: "How am I to lay her down?" He placed her alongside the bed. The mare was really old, scarcely standing. He pushed her and she collapsed onto the down comforter. He covered her with a blanket and went off by himself.

The guests started leaving but there were four galoshes missing; the servant had taken them without choosing—just grabbed them up. They looked and looked but they were nowhere to be found. Then they left.

The gentleman quickly went into the bedroom, quickly undressed and made a dash for the bed. He collided with her legs. He wanted to hug her and he pawed her—but she was already dead!

When they had taken the horse away, they tidied up the room, and hauled out a good measure of shit. The gentleman turned purple in his rage and had a stroke. They brought the doctors in but they couldn't cure him. The lord of the manor croaked and life for his serfs got better. Katiusha was especially happy. She would go out to work, she sang, danced, and never covered her face. Now she knew that the gentleman was no more and that no one would take her away in the night.

106. How the Soldier Stole the Speck

No other Russian versions are known, although it is known in Ukrainian and Belarusian. Speck is the fat from the back of a pig, regarded as a delicacy by the Slavic peasantry. SUS 1525M*.

There weren't any cars yet. In those long-ago years they transferred soldiers from here to there and they moved them from town to town on foot. They even transferred them from distant cities. Then they would transfer them into some village and quarter them there. They'd put two or three men in each dwelling. So it happened that this one soldier looked about and saw that this peasant had hung a chunk of speck from the ceiling. He thought to himself: "I wonder how I'd go about pulling that speck down a bit."

He waited for night. The roofs there were all made of thatch. He climbed up on the roof and broke through the roof, through the thatch. The speck was hanging right there and so he cut through the rope that held it. Then it occurred to him: "How can I get it back up here? I won't be able to lift it." He thought, "I'll let myself down into the hallway, then I'll open it up and carry it out."

He started getting down and then he knocked something and it made a noise—a bag of something fell. The owner heard it and thought to himself, "What was that bang?" He opened the door into the hut and there stood the soldier, who said, "Master, will you buy some speck?"

The owner said, "No, I already have enough speck; I don't need any more."

"Well, if you don't need any, then help me get this up onto my shoulder."

The owner took it and gave it to him—he helped him put it on his shoulder. So he set off, the soldier set off with the speck. He walked along and came to a stream. There was a board over the stream, so he crossed over it singing:

> A soldier walked along a plank,
> The soldier wasn't carrying trifles;
> He didn't steal, he didn't thieve,
> The master gave it to him himself,
> And even put it on his shoulders!

107. Unsalted Custard

No other versions known among the East Slavs. Oatmeal custard is simply oat porridge steamed and slightly soured. Collected in Kostroma province. SUS 1687***.

A girl got married and became mistress of her own house. She had to have something to feed her husband, but she didn't know how to cook—she had always watched her mother from a distance. Her husband asked his young wife for some oatmeal custard. But how was she to do it? Was she to salt the custard when she cooked it? But she'd heard all sorts of things: some said salt it, others said it wasn't necessary. Maybe she should ask her neighbor, but that would be embarrassing—they'd laugh at her all over the village.

She went outside and noticed a wool-beater passing by. She started cursing him for this and then for that: "You are just unsalted custard, you old grump!"

"You fool of a woman! Whoever heard of salting custard?"

She was so happy to hear him say it that she didn't even take offense at his calling her "fool"; now she had found out how to make the custard. She cooked the custard and fed her husband.

108. If You Don't Like It, Don't Listen!

Although some of the types represented in this tale are found elsewhere in the East Slavic repertoire, SUS 1960L* (the big clutch of duck eggs) is found only in this one tale. The motif of obtaining fire by story telling is, according to ATU, found only in Russian, Turkish, and Greek but in fact it is common in Ukrainian and Belarusian as well. SUS 1920H + 1960M + 1889P + 1960L* +1886 + 1889K.

In a certain tsardom, in a certain land, there lived and dwelt a peasant and he had three sons: two were clever but the third was a fool. Their father sent them out to plow the land. They plowed and plowed—right up until evening. They had to spend the night in the field; they had to cook their kasha for their supper and there was no one to go after any fire. The oldest brother climbed up in a tree and looked here and there and when he spied off to one side it was as if a fire was burning. He climbed back down and went off to get some fire.

He walked along, just by himself, and then he saw this little hut on cock's legs, on dog's paws, on the path, and in the hut sat a gray little old man. "Greetings, Grandfather!"

"Greetings, neighbor!"

"Give me some fire!"

"Tell me a tale!"

"I don't know how."

"Just tell me the beginning!"

"I can't do that."

"If that's the case, then you'll answer with your back!" He ripped a strip from his back, sprinkled ashes on the spot, and sent him off without any fire.

The lad came back to his brothers and told them that he couldn't find any. "Oh, you goose! I suppose I'll have to go," said the middle brother. He set off but the same thing happened with him. "Alright, fool! Now it's your turn."

The fool set off, stumbling along and he found that little hut on cock's legs, on dog's paws, and in that hut was the gray little old man. "Greetings, Grandfather!"

"Greetings, neighbor!"

"Give me some fire!"

"Tell me a tale!"

"I'll do it, but you mustn't interrupt."

"No, I won't; I love it when someone tells me tales."

"Alright then. We'll have this deal: whoever interrupts the other will have a strip taken out of his back!"

"Agreed!"

And so the fool began: "You see, grandfather, there were the three of us brothers and we set out to mow the grass. We got there but, guess what? There wasn't a single scythe—we'd forgotten them all at home. What were we to do? How were we to mow? But you see, we were pretty inventive, we decided to mow with harness bows. We cut and cut and piled up three stacks. We started getting ready to go back home. We were riding by the wood and we heard this great racket: crash, bang! What could it be? It was a bear fighting with a bumblebee. The bumblebee was shrieking: 'Help me!' and the bear was shrieking: 'Help me!' Now what? Which one should we help? If we helped the bumblebee, it would get away and fly off. We helped the bear; we killed the bumblebee and filled about seven basins of wax and we collected honey to the amount of a whole hay shock. From the wax I sculpted myself a mare and rode about on her for three years. Once I rode out into some meadows for some reason. I was riding along, knowing nothing, and I looked back and half my horse was gone! I was sitting on the front half while the rear half was galloping about the meadow. I chased and chased it, and finally I caught it. I took and sewed the two halves together with some bast and I've been riding it for another three years since then.

"Another time I happened to be riding along a lake and there was a duck weaving her nest on that lake. I immediately cut three saplings: one lime, one stripped lime, and the third the kind they use to strip bast. I threw one but I didn't hit it. I threw the second and overshot it. I threw the third and hit the duck. The duck started flying and I, Grandfather, pulled the nest in and filled half the boat with eggs. You won't eat them all in a whole year!

"I felt like having a drink so I waded into the lake up to my throat, but I didn't have anything to draw the water with, so I took off my skull and used that to drink from. I looked back—my horse had gone far away. I ran after it and forgot my skull. By the time I had caught the horse my skull had floated away. The duck flew back and carried off some eggs in it and then hatched out some babies. I grabbed the whole nest, put my skull back on, roasted the birds, and ate.

"After that I rode through the woods. There was a peasant grinding peas on an oak. A pea rolled off onto the ground and the others sat on the branches. I climbed up to collect the peas, Grandfather, and here I was, sitting in the tree, collecting away, and knowing nothing at all! The oak grew and grew and it grew right up to the heaven. I climbed up into the heaven to have a look around and see what was going on. There was just our priest sitting there with his jealous eyes: he went and cut down that oak and dragged it off to his yard. How's that? Thanks very much—cows are cheap there. A calf costs the same as a fly and they'll give you a gadfly for a bull. So I caught a whole purse full of flies and bought some calves. I started butchering them and skinning them to make straps. I attached the strap to one edge of heaven and started going down. I went down and down and then I saw that I was at the end of the strap but it was still far down to earth. If I were to jump, I'd kill myself! To my good fortune a peasant was hauling in some oats. I grabbed hold of the straw and wove a rope. But the rope broke. I fell and nearly killed myself—I ended up in the otherworld and there I saw all these dead people. My father was there carrying water on your grandfather. . . ."

"What is this, fool? Is this the truth?" the old man broke in.

The fool knocked him over and cut the strip from his back, took the fire, and returned to his brothers: "Here's your fire, now cook the kasha."

109. The Turnip

An original treatment of a common motif. SUS 1960G + 37.

There lived this old man and old woman. They had nothing to eat. So the old man thought something up: "Let's go sow some turnips on the bathhouse!" And so they sowed the turnips.

The turnips grew. Now soon a tale is told; not so soon is the deed done. The old man went for a turnip and they ate that turnip. "Now, old woman, you go; I've already gone there."

But the old woman was poorly—poorly, really sick. "I can't crawl up there, old man!" she said.

"Well, climb into that sack and I'll lift you up." So the old woman got into the sack. The old man lifted her up somehow onto the bathhouse. She cut out a turnip and said, "Now, old man, you need to let me down!"

The old man put her into the sack and began to go down. He was lowering her when he dropped her. He dropped her, went down from the bathhouse, and looked in the sack: the old woman had given up the ghost, she had died in her fall.

The old man began howling. He was so sorry for that old woman. A hare came running up and said, "Why, old man, do you howl so much? Hire me to do your lamenting for you! I'm a master at keening!"

"You're hired, cousin! You're hired, my dear!"

And so she started in. "Alas, alas, alas . . . !" But no matter how she tried, nothing much came of it.

A wolf came running up. "Old man, hire me to howl for you! What will you give me?"

"You're hired, you're hired, wolf! I'll give you a turnip."

So the wolf started in: "Yee—ee-ee!" He howled away. The dogs in the village heard him and started barking. People came running with pitchforks—to kill the wolf.

So the wolf grabbed the old woman and flung her on his back and was off along the road. He dragged her into the woods. And that's how it ended for you; that's how it was all decided.

110. Roundsides

The familiar gingerbread man in its Russian version. A good example of a cumulative tale. SUS 2025.

An old man lived and dwelt with an old woman. The old man said, "Bake a gingerbread, old woman."

And what should I bake it with? There's no flour."

"Oh no! Scrape around that flour bin and then you'll find enough flour."

The old woman took a feather brush and scraped around in the bin, then swept it up and she collected about two handfuls of flour. She let it rise with some sour cream, baked it in butter, and put it on the windowsill to cool.

The gingerbread lay there for a while, then suddenly he started to roll, from the sill to the bench, from the bench onto the floor, from the floor to the door; it leapt over the threshold, into the passageway, from the passageway to the porch, from the porch to the yard, from the yard to the gates, and on and on. The gingerbread rolled along the road and he encountered a hare: "Gingerbread, gingerbread, I'll eat you up!"

"Don't eat me, cross-eyed hare! I'll sing you a song," said little Roundsides, and then he started to sing:

> I've been scraped from the flour bin
> Swept up from the flour bin,
> Mixed with sour cream
> And made into a gingerbread with butter.
> I was cooled on a windowsill,
> I got away from a grandfather,
> I got away from a grandmother,
> And from you, hare, it's not hard to get away!

And then Roundsides rolled himself further: the hare could just look on. The gingerbread rolled on, and it encountered a wolf. "Gingerbread, gingerbread, I'll eat you up!"

"Don't eat me, gray wolf! I'll sing you a song!"

> I've been scraped from the flour bin
> Swept up from the flour bin,
> Mixed with sour cream
> And made into a gingerbread with butter.
> I was cooled on a windowsill,
> I got away from a grandfather,
> I got away from a grandmother,
> I got away from a hare,
> And from you, gray wolf, it's not hard to get away!

And then Roundsides rolled himself further: the wolf could just look on. The gingerbread rolled on, and it encountered a bear. "Gingerbread, gingerbread, I'll eat you up!"

"How are you going to eat me, Pigeon-toes? I'll sing you a song!"

> I've been scraped from the flour bin
> Swept up from the flour bin,
> Mixed with sour cream
> And made into a gingerbread with butter.
> I was cooled on a windowsill,
> I got away from a grandfather,
> I got away from a grandmother,
> I got away from a hare,
> I got away from a gray wolf,
> And from you, Pigeon-toes, it's not hard to get away!

And again he rolled away, and the bear could just look on! Roundsides rolled and rolled and he encountered a fox. "Good health to you, Gingerbread! What a fine gingerbread you are!"

And Roundsides started singing:

> I've been scraped from the flour bin
> Swept up from the flour bin,
> Mixed with sour cream
> And made into a gingerbread with butter.
> I was cooled on a windowsill,
> I got away from a grandfather,
> I got away from a grandmother,
> I got away from a hare,
> I got away from a gray wolf,
> I got away from a bear,
> And from you, fox, I'll get away in a jiffy!

"What a splendid song!" said the fox. "But I've grown old, Gingerbread, and I hear poorly. Sit on my muzzle and sing it again a little louder." Roundsides jumped onto the fox's muzzle and started singing the same song. "Thank you, Gingerbread, that's a splendid song. I'd like to hear it again. Sit on my tongue and sing it through one last time," said the fox, and she stuck out her tongue. Roundsides, the little fool, jumped onto the fox's tongue, and the fox—snap! And she gobbled up the gingerbread.

111. The Sad Story of a Raven

An example of an "endless tale." Russian knows many such tales and there are several recorded in Ukrainian, but few are attested in Belarusian. SUS 2300.

There lived and dwelt a rich peasant and he had an orchard. And in this orchard stood an apple tree, and apples grew on it. A raven had the habit of flying there and knocking apples off. The peasant thought: he made a slash and poured pitch into it. The raven flew up, dropped an apple into the slash, and tried to get it out with its beak, but the beak got stuck in the pitch. It finally got its beak unstuck and then its tail got stuck. It finally got its tail unstuck and then its beak got stuck. It finally got its beak unstuck but then its tail got stuck. It finally got its tail unstuck but then its beak got stuck. . . . The poor raven went on struggling its whole life to its very death.

Serial Tales from the Far North

Several narrators of the very far north of European Russia responded to conditions of their employment by creating long, highly ornamental tales known as *dolgie skazki*. The term is difficult to translate into English. The adjective *dolgii* generally refers to long in time, not distance, and the majority of narrators who created these tales told them serially, over the course of considerable time (several evenings perhaps). Generally, the *skazochniki,* the narrators, combined several tale types into one tale, and because of the manner of narration and their length we have termed them serial tales in this anthology. Most of the tales recorded in the twentieth century show traces of literary influence. Those of M.M. Korguev are certainly no exception.

112. Fear-Bogatyr

Fedor Fedorovich Kabrenov told this tale in 1938 to V. Dmitrichenko. Kabrenov was regarded as one of the best *skazochniki* of Pudozh region. More than fifty of his tales were recorded, none so long and involved as this one, however. He generally preferred wondertales but also told tales of everyday life and some anecdotes. Kabrenov spent his entire life working in the lumberyards of the north and learned his tales from other workers and from passersby. He was literate and loved to read but that fact does not seem to have influenced his repertoire, although traces of his reading are to be seen in his vocabulary. Traditionally, parish priests in the Russian Church were required to be married; if the priest's wife died, he had either to remarry or enter a monastery. The iconostasis is the icon screen that separates the nave from the altar in the Orthodox church. The mythical island of Buian is encountered in the *byliny* as well as in the wondertales. To refer to an elder man as "grandfather" or "uncle" is a sign of respect and does not necessarily infer a blood relationship. Note Kabrenov's predilection for the wondertale in this serial tale. SUS 510B + 315A.

There lived and dwelt this priest. The priest had a daughter, a wife, and a servant. He had lived for a long time and the priest's wife had gotten old. She went to a shop, bought some material for a dress and some new slippers. The priest asked her, "Why, little mother, did you buy all this? You are old: a colorful dress doesn't suit you, and these slippers!"

She answered, "Well, you see, father, I'll soon die and you won't want to live like that; you will get married, so choose a bride such that this dress will fit her bones and the slippers her little feet."

After a short time the priest's wife died. The priest went forth in search of a bride. He took the dress and slippers with him. But though he went round everywhere, the dress didn't fit anybody, nor did the slippers fit any feet. He came home. This took place on a Sunday. He went off to the church. His daughter wanted to pay her respects to her mother. She put on the dress and slippers—and set off for church. But priests' daughters according to custom didn't stand in the back of the church. She made her way forward to the royal gates. The priest was serving the liturgy at the altar at the time; he came out with his censer to cense the iconostasis; he censed the iconostasis; then he turned to the congregation to cense the congregation. He waved the censer once or twice, noted his daughter, and saw the dress. He looked and there were the slippers on her feet. He quit serving the liturgy and ran home. He bought some white flour and whatever else was needed for a wedding. Then he ordered his servant to bake some pies for a wedding and told her to say nothing to anyone as to why. The servant made the pies, while he ran off to summon the guests to the wedding. His daughter questioned the servant at length: "Why are you baking all these pies?"

No way would the servant answer. Then the priest's daughter tricked the servant: she cut a hot pie in half, smelled it, and said to the servant, "Servant, sniff this: is this pie done?"

The servant had a long nose. She bent over to sniff the pie and just then the priest's daughter poked her nose in it. The servant's nose started burning and she asked the priest's daughter to let her nose out of the hot pie. But the priest's daughter said, "I won't let your nose out of the pie until you tell me for whom these pies are being prepared."

There was nothing else for the servant to do. She would have to confess all and tell all as to why the pies were being prepared.

"Father ran off to summon the guests to a wedding. He wants to marry you." (Gads, what a business this is!)

On account of this unpleasantness, and still in the dress and slippers, the priest's daughter ran off into the woods. For a long time she wandered about the forest. The slippers wore out and the dress was ripped to shreds. She was now embarrassed to go about naked so she crept into a hollow tree. Just then the tsar's son was out hunting and his dogs sensed that a person was in the hollow and began to bark. Ivan the tsar's son came up to the hollow and examined it carefully: there was no one there.

He said, "Whoever's in that hollow, come out, or else I'll let fly a tempered arrow and take this oak apart and into tiny pieces."

Then the priest's daughter said, "I would come out to you but I'm ashamed because I'm naked. Take off your overcoat and give it to me: I'll get dressed and come out."

So then Ivan the tsar's son took off his overcoat and threw it into the hollow. The priest's daughter put it on and came out to Tsarevich Ivan. The priest's daughter was beautiful and Ivan immediately fell for her. He questioned her, whose daughter she was and from where she came, and then he led her off to his tsardom or country. The tsar's son got up earlier that morning and went in to his tsar to say good morning and wish him all the best, and then he told him that he had found the priest's daughter and that that is why he had not appeared before his father for three whole days. When on that fourth day he appeared, the tsar began questioning him: "Why haven't you been here for three days, Vania? Probably you've been thinking of getting married."

Ivan Tsarevich had to admit it. Then the tsar said: "Since that's the case, go into my bedroom and there on the wall you'll find a lot of portraits hanging. Whichever one is to your liking will be the one we'll marry you to."

Formerly the tsar had ridden through all the tsardoms and all the countries, taking pictures of the daughters of all the tsars and rulers, but Vania went and looked at all those pictures, came back to his father, and said, "No, papa, I don't like your pictures (or portraits). If you like, I'll show you a living portrait that I have in my bedroom."

During this time, during these three days, Ivan Tsarevich had gone to a shop, bought an engagement dress for the priest's daughter, which was so beautiful that she put it on and she was beautiful but in this dress she was an indescribable beauty. Then the tsar said, "If you have such a portrait, then bring it out and show it to me."

So then Vania led the priest's daughter out to the tsar. The tsar looked at her beauty and from his amazement at her beauty he fell down flat and for three days he was unconscious. When he got up, he began questioning her: "Tell me, from what land, from which horde, are you, and who are your father and mother?"

The priest's daughter told him: "I am from the least family and clan, I am a priest's daughter."

Then the tsar turned to his son and said, "Vania, can it be that a tsar's son could marry a priest's daughter?"

And in answer the son said, "Papa, who is to know that I married a priest's daughter? We will say that she is from a foreign tsar—and no one will know the difference."

Then the tsar gave him permission for Vania to marry the priest's daughter. They had the wedding. After a short time the priest's daughter was pregnant. It came time for her to give birth. Just before giving birth she fainted. They carried her off into a separate bedroom and the tsar was worried that she was unwell so he began searching for doctors.

The priest meanwhile came home and having summoned the guests, he found out that his daughter wasn't at home. He went out of his mind. He said that he was a doctor and went out to cure people. So then he came into that country and recognized the sick tsarevna, and he said to the tsar: "I will cure your daughter-in-law."

So the tsar led the doctor into the room where his daughter-in-law was lying. But she had already given birth. The priest recognized his daughter and took and tore the little boy in half, smeared the mother's lips with blood, then came out to the tsar and said (after having given birth she was still in a faint): "Your royal highness, this is my very villainous daughter. This isn't the first infant she has eaten. Go and see, she has started eating the baby. If you don't send her off somewhere, it will be bad for you."

The tsar took fright and ordered that the bride and her little boy be taken off into a deep forest and left there alone. She lay there for a long time and then she saw the torn-up child, her son. She cried but there was nothing to be done. She lay there for a little longer and then she saw that not far off there was a large pool of water. Out of nowhere, two little ravens came flying up and began pecking each other. One defeated the other and flew off. Then the mother raven flew up, took up the little raven, and bathed it in the pool. The little raven shook himself off and flew away. Then the royal bride took her little boy, brought him over, and wet him in the pool too. The little boy grew back together and started crying. The little boy grew not by the days but by the hours. When he was just seven years old, they set off on a journey. For a long time they walked about the woods, and then they chanced upon a bear. The little boy asked his mother: "Mama, what is that thing coming over here?"

His mother answered, "That, my child, is a bear, a destroyer of peasants. He brings much harm to the people."

Then the little boy asked, "Do people eat them?"

"Yes, they eat them. Even great lords eat them because their meat is very fatty."

The little boy responded, "Mama, I'll kill him."

But his mother said to him, "Well, my son, even hunters, if they shoot him in a soft spot, their bullet will go right through, and the bear will walk away."

But the little boy said anyway, "Mama, I'll kill him." He ripped up a tree and killed the bear. "Mama, now what? Will we eat him?"

His mother said, "We'll have to roast him, we'll have to make a fire."

"And how will we make a fire?"

In olden times there were no matches, they made fire by friction. His mother said, "So, my son, go and rub a twig against another twig, and a fire will start up."

Not thinking about it for even an instant, the son tore up a tree, brought it to earth, and then did the same with a second tree. He bashed one tree against the other, and immediately a fire started up. For a bit he fanned the fire. Then his mother tore off a chunk of meat, about two pounds, which she roasted in the fire while the son ate the rest of the bear—without roasting it at all. Then they set off farther. A little bit further along the way and road they met a deer, but with the deer he didn't ask his mother's permission. He killed the deer and they ate it.

They walked on through the forest for a long time and then they stopped in at a house. It was a large house. They went in, but there was no one at home. So then the mother said to her son: "Go and look in the stove: perhaps there's something in it."

The son opened the stove, looked inside, and saw that there was a meat pie in it. The son had no idea what a meat pie was. He said to his mother: "There's some round thing in there."

Then his mother said to him, "Look on the table: perhaps there's something else there."

So her son turned the table so that its legs were up, pulled out a drawer, and saw that there was something else round.

His mother said, "That's enough, son, put everything back in its place." And she herself got a pot from the stove, pulled out a loaf of bread from the cupboard, and they began eating. They would have eaten everything up with their big appetites as they hadn't seen bread for so long, but his mother said, "Now then, son, obviously someone lives here. Let's leave them something to nibble on."

And so then they hid themselves. Suddenly an old man came into the house. He looked at the table and saw there a crust of bread; he looked in the oven and saw just a little cooked cabbage soup. He got angry but then he thought it over and said, "It's probably someone baptized who ate for himself and left some for me." And he began shouting, "Whoever is in this house come out! I won't do anything to you."

So then the mother and her son came out. The old man asked the woman, "What is your son's name?"

And she answered, "I don't know his name since he still hasn't been baptized."

The old man said, "Then I will baptize him."

He carried a forty-bucket barrel of water over, dipped the son in it, and said, "His name will be 'Fear-Bogatyr' since he has extraordinary strength."

After that the mother and son lived in that house, and the old man went out hunting and brought them food. This is what happened: the old man went away into the woods and didn't return for a long time. They lived there a little, but then there was no more food. So then Fear-Bogatyr set off hunting himself. He began bringing in food and his mother would prepare meals. And they never saw the old man again. They lived there a long time. When Fear-Bogatyr was out hunting, his mother got bored sitting alone at home. She went to the pond: she strolled about the woods. One day she went far away from home; she stopped for a moment and saw a fiery river; and beyond the river stood a cavalier, one whom you couldn't describe in a tale or depict with a pen—he was so handsome.

And he said to this woman: "Bring me across the river: we'll make love and live together as husband and wife."

Then she said to him: "And how am I to get you across? I have neither boat nor steamer."

He responded: "Go and get that tablecloth you have on the table. Bring it here, wave it over the river, and a sturdy bridge will appear. Then I'll come across."

So she ran off, took the tablecloth, and brought him over the river (it's quicker to tell this—I can't describe it all). Now this was the devil himself. He entered the house and said, "Do you live alone?"

She answered, "No, I have a son whose name is Fear-Bogatyr."

"At all costs you must kill off your son, or else I won't be able to live with you."

So Fear-Bogatyr's mother took on the devil's spirit, abandoned all hopes for her son, and said to the devil: "And how am I to kill him?"

The devil responded, "Pretend to be sick and tell your son to go beyond the thrice-nine lands, beyond the thrice-nice seas, to the thrice-nine tsardom, to the thrice-nine land, beyond the seas, to the island of Buian and there kill the sow Ramida, strain her blood, and bring it back to you. Then you'll recover. He loves you and will go then. But whoever has gone there has never come back."

Her son came home from his hunting and the devil hid, not showing himself to Fear-Bogatyr. His mother sighed and said, "Oh, my son, you must go here and then there (just as the devil had taught her).

Now the son loved his mother and he said to her, "Don't despair, mama, I'll go."

In the morning he got up pretty early (let's describe it, shall we!); he washed himself clean, prayed to God, and set out on the path and way. He walked near or far, low or high, for soon a tale is told but the deed is done by good efforts. He found this grandfather in the forest. The grandfather was lying there blind. He went up to him a little closer and said, "Good health to you, Uncle."

At the same time he took a birch branch and handed it to the grandfather. The old man took the branch and the branch turned into ashes. Then the grandfather said, "So, Fear-Bogatyr, you've done well to give me that branch and not your hand; if you'd given me your hand, nothing would have remained of it but ash. Now tell me, Fear-Bogatyr, where are you going?"

Fear-Bogatyr said, "I've set off for the thrice-nine land, for the thrice-nine tsardom, the thrice-ten country beyond the sea, on the island of Buian, to kill the sow Ramida and strain her blood, and then to carry it to my mother and smear it on her—so that my mother will be well."

"You've thought up quite a long journey," the old man said to him. "Whoever has gone there has never come back. But since you've set out on it, you'd best go. Watch out. You'll meet up with a gray wolf and you aim at it. It will plead with you not to kill it. He will do you a favor."

Fear-Bogatyr took his leave of the grandfather and set off again. He had only gone a little way when he met the gray wolf. Fear-Bogatyr took his rifle in his hand, getting ready to shoot it. But the wolf spoke in a human voice: "Don't kill me, Fear-Bogatyr: whatever you need I'll do for you."

Then Fear-Bogatyr told him that he had set off for the thrice-nine land in the thrice-ten tsardom, in the thrice-nine land, beyond the sea, on the island of Buian. (He had to repeat this just the first time to the wolf.) "I must kill the sow Ramida, strain her blood, and take the blood home to cure my mother."

Then the gray wolf said, "Fear-Bogatyr, get on my back and hold on to me. I will take you to the island of Buian."

They crossed the sea and came out on the island of Buian. Then the gray wolf spoke to Fear-Bogatyr: "Get behind that bush. In a moment the sow Ramida and her twelve piglets will come by. Let the first eleven piglets go, but catch the twelfth."

The wolf hardly managed to speak these words—Fear-Bogatyr crept behind a bush and saw the sow Ramida coming: his heart began pounding. Fear-Bogatyr leapt out from behind the bush and started chasing the little pig. The great wolf ran up to him and helped him catch it. Fear-Bogatyr jumped onto the wolf with the piglet and they set off over the sea. When they came out on the shore, the wolf said to Fear-Bogatyr, "Kill me, Fear-Bogatyr, or else I'll devour you."

But Fear-Bogatyr said, "Gray wolf, I don't know how to thank you for your great service."

"No," said the gray wolf, "If you don't kill me, you'll nonetheless not remain alive. When I was swimming across the sea, I strained myself; yet it's all the same: if you don't kill me, then I'll do away with you."

So then Fear-Bogatyr took his rifle in his hands and killed the wolf. He came home and said to his mother, "So I killed the sow Ramida and brought you a whole piglet."

His mother looked at the piglet and said, "Hand it to me."

"You've seen it, mother, you'll be well."

Then he took the piglet and carried it off to the woods, dug out its eyes, and let the blind little piglet go loose; he put the piglet's eyes in a secret pocket. While he was wandering about with the piglet in the woods, the devil once more tried to convince his mother that she must without fail murder her son. She said to the devil, "How shall I do away with him?"

The devil instructed her: "Fall ill and tell your son to go to the thrice-nine land, to the thrice-nine tsardom, to the thrice-nine country. (It wasn't stated to which tsar he was to go.) This tsar has a tree standing in the middle of his garden, and he is to pluck the leaves from this tree and bring them to you—then you will be cured." But this was the tsardom of Koshchei the Deathless, and whoever went there never ever came back because Koshchei the Deathless burns up all within thirty versts.

When Fear-Bogatyr returned from the woods, his mother told him everything. But this time Fear-Bogatyr didn't tell his mother not to feel sorry for herself. Once more he got up early in the morning, washed himself clean, prayed to God and set off down the road. He walked near or far, low or high, for soon a tale may be told but a deed is done by good efforts. And again he came upon the grandfather. Grandfather asked him, "Where are you going, Fear-Bogatyr? Where is your journey taking you?"

Fear-Bogatyr told the grandfather everything, and the grandfather responded: "You have taken up a great deed; I myself went there and now I lie here blind, but if you will submit to me and submit to my years, I will help you."

So then Fear-Bogatyr didn't think about that for very long; he submitted to the grandfather and to his old age. Out of nowhere a coal-black horse appeared: you couldn't describe it in a tale or depict it with a pen. The old man said, "Take the horse, put on my armor, and ride wherever your journey takes you!"

Fear-Bogatyr rode off for a long way and fell to thinking: "What sort of Fear-Bogatyr am I if I submitted to an old man and his old age?" He hadn't finished saying the last word when he turned up at the grandfather's again.

The old man said to him: "So, Fear-Bogatyr, why did you start thinking about me? You will not get away from me until you bow to me and to my old age. But I ask you not to recall me on your journey."

So Fear-Bogatyr bowed to the old man and his old age, mounted his horse, and rode off. And the horse spoke in a human voice: "So then, Fear-Bogatyr, how shall we go: over the earth or shall we go through that standing forest, or shall we rise up higher than the standing forest, yet beneath the wandering clouds?"

Fear-Bogatyr answered, "If we go over the earth, we shall have to ride for many years; if we go through the forest, all my clothing will be ripped off and your sides scratched up; if you can, let us rise up higher than the standing forest, yet beneath the wandering clouds."

So then they got to the thrice-nine land, to the thrice-nine tsardom, to the thrice-ten country, to Koshchei the Deathless, that very night. All were asleep in the tsardom of Koshchei the Deathless; they leapt over the town palisade and he let his horse rest in the orchard, next to that tree from which he was to pluck the leaves. But Fear-Bogatyr started thinking: "Why should I pluck them one at a time?"

He tore out the whole tree, got on his horse, and they started out on their way back. The roots clanged against the strings around the town and the strings began singing, the bells began ringing; Koshchei the Deathless woke up and shouted: "Bring me my seven-legged, seven-winged mare and my fiery shield. I'll go catch that thief. Who would dare to carry off my tree?"

That tree was enchanted. It contained a tsarevna, whom Koshchei had carried away from some tsar. When Koshchei the Deathless was already catching the thief, he saw it and said to himself, "That can't be the one who stole my tree. Bogatyrs don't ride beneath the clouds: they ride over the earth. Some god must have taken a liking to that tree: let him carry it off." So he went back.

Fear-Bogatyr rode for a long time with the tree until he finally decided to feed his horse. He went down onto green pastures, and he himself lay down to rest. The tsarevna in the tree sensed that the tree had stopped and so she went out to see who was carrying her and there she saw a man lying on the ground: he was so handsome that she immediately fell in love with him. She said to him, "Tell me, good man, how did you manage to carry me away from that horrible Koshchei the Deathless?"

And Fear-Bogatyr said to her, "Tell me, miss, whose daughter are you and where are you from? From which tsardom are you and who is your tsar?"

Then she told him that she was the daughter of such and such a tsar. "If you will take me to my father, I will marry you."

So Fear-Bogatyr left the tree in the meadow, he and the tsarevna got on his horse, and they galloped off to her tsardom. All the other bogatyrs had gathered at the tsar's, and they were all of one thought: how should they go to search for the tsarevna? In the middle of the courtyard a pillar had been raised and rings had been attached to the pillar. The bogatyrs came and attached their horses to the pillar according to their own strength: the weaker ones attached theirs to the lower ring, those with more strength attached their higher up. Just one ring—the very top one—remained free. Then he descended from up above into the courtyard, tied his horse to the very highest ring, and went into the royal chambers. His horse snorted and from his snorting all the bogatyrs' horses reared up on their reins. The bogatyrs looked out the windows and saw their horses rearing up. They didn't have time to go looking for the tsar's daughter when Fear-Bogatyr entered and said, "Your royal highness! I have brought your daughter!"

Then all the other bogatyrs saw that things weren't too good, weren't too healthy for them, and they quietly departed so that no one would know. The tsar was overjoyed and wanted to put on the wedding there and now, but Fear-Bogatyr said, "Your royal majesty, I have no family, no kin, except my mother, so I'll go and bring her here for the wedding."

"Why should you go yourself?" said the tsar. "I have horses; we'll send a troika; we'll hitch them to the very best carriage. We'll bring your mother to the wedding without you."

But Fear-Bogatyr didn't agree. "No, I'll go and get her myself."

He took his leave of the tsar and set off for his mother's. He arrived and gave her the leaves, and then he went off into the forest hunting. Once more the devil spoke to his mother: "Whatever happens, you have to kill off Fear-Bogatyr."

But she replied, "And how am I to kill him off?"

The devil instructed her. "Here's how. When Fear-Bogatyr comes back, ask him to play cards. Whoever loses must have his hands tied."

So Fear-Bogatyr came back from his hunting and his mother said to him, "Fear-Bogatyr, let's play cards. Whoever loses must have his hands tied."

They started playing. Fear-Bogatyr beat his mother, and then he tied her hands together with a towel. His mother struggled for a long time, but she couldn't get untied. Fear-Bogatyr took pity on his mother and untied her. Then she said once more: "Let's play cards."

They played for a long time, but the mother beat her son and tied his hands together with a two-inch truss. Fear-Bogatyr struggled, and as they played, the trusses broke. She went down into the cellar where the devil was sitting, and said to him: "I beat my son and tied his hands with trusses, but he strained and the trusses broke."

Then the devil said, "Here, take this strap, and beat your son at cards again; then tie him up with the strap."

Once more his mother came and persuaded her son to play cards. She beat her son and tied his hands with the belt. But Fear-Bogatyr strained, tightening his muscles to the very bone: he still couldn't tear off the strap. Then his mother took a little knife; gouged out Fear-Bogatyr's eyes; and dispatched him to the woods. All alone Fear-Bogatyr shouted for his good horse, got on it, and rode off. The blind man rode for a long time, and then he decided to let his horse feed. He let him loose in a place where not even shoreweed grows (it only grows in sandy places). Then he lay down to rest on his stomach.

His horse thought it over: "I've very likely got a blind master to let me out where there's no grass while he himself goes to sleep on his stomach (bogatyrs only sleep on their elbows). I think I'll give him the slip. If my master isn't blind, he'll find me. If he is blind, he won't." He hid behind a bush. Fear-Bogatyr woke up and began calling his horse. He wandered about but he couldn't find him anywhere. Then his horse called out in a human voice: "We don't serve blind masters. You will not find me until you have some eyes."

So then Fear-Bogatyr remembered that in his secret pocket he had that piglet's eyes; he put them in. He found his horse, got on it, and set off. As he rode along, he could see where all the puddles of water were and the mud holes, and he would stop and turn somersaults in the mud. He rode for a long time before he came to the grandfather. He exchanged greetings with him, and the old man asked him: "Well, how have you been getting along, Fear-Bogatyr?"

"I'm fine, only my mother gouged out my eyes. I put the pig's eyes in, but the sad thing about that is that they see where there's lots of mud and draw me to it, to bathe in it. (Pigs' eyes, so pigs love the mud.)

The old man replied: "Well, you fetched that tree that you went after?"

So Fear-Bogatyr told him everything. Then the grandfather said, "Do you want to be that same Fear-Bogatyr? Here, take my walking stick. Bang with the lower end of it on the ground and you'll become an old man; but if you want to be young, then bang with the top and you'll become the same youth as you were before—Fear-Bogatyr."

He thanked the old man, banged with the top, and became a youth; then he rode off to his tsarevna, to find out whether she had perhaps forgotten him. He was riding through the woods when he heard the sound of axes. He rode up a little closer and saw some carpenters. He got off his horse, banged the bottom of his stick against the ground, and became an old, old man. He went up to the workers and asked them, "What are you building?"

They answered, "In our country the tsar's daughter got lost; some Fear-Bogatyr found her and rode off to get his mother, to bring her to the wedding, but he still hasn't returned. So our tsarevna went to church, ordered a liturgy sung, and now she has decided this: to build a nunnery here and bring some nuns here, and then to become hegumeness, and then pray just for Fear-Bogatyr."

Then Fear-Bogatyr understood that his tsarevna hadn't forgotten him. He said to the workmen: "So then, old men, won't you take me to the tsar and tsarevna so I might beg for alms?"

They answered him, "We'll soon finish off this work and then we'll take you to the tsar."

The workmen finished their work and they led Fear-Bogatyr to the court, where Fear-Bogatyr saw a large crowd of people in the courtyard, begging for alms, which the tsarevna herself was giving out. But Fear-Bogatyr didn't stand in line. He set off to push himself closer to the tsarevna, and whichever beggar he touched with his finger would fall down. He came up to the porch itself. The tsarevna was giving out alms for the repose of Fear-Bogatyr. Then Fear-Bogatyr said to the tsarevna: "Give me some alms for the health of Fear-Bogatyr."

The tsarevna stopped giving out alms and said to the old man: "And so, have you seen Fear-Bogatyr?"

"How could I not have seen him? I parted from him not very long ago."

Then the tsarevna took the old man by the hand and led him to her bedroom so that he might tell her something about Fear-Bogatyr. They entered the bedroom and Fear-Bogatyr asked her, "Do you really pity Fear-Bogatyr so very much? If you do, I'll lead you to him."

The tsarevna agreed. Then Fear-Bogatyr went behind a door, banged with his stick with the top down—and became the handsome Fear-Bogatyr, and then he came out to her in her bedroom. In her joy the tsarevna called her father to her, and the tsar immediately wanted to put on the wedding, but Fear-Bogatyr said, "Your royal highness, I set off to get my mother but I didn't get that far. I'll go again and bring her to the wedding."

For a long time the tsar didn't agree, saying "You'll go away and not come back to us."

But he still couldn't convince Fear-Bogatyr. Fear-Bogatyr set off for his mother. He came to his mother's and said, "Mama, I want to get married. But if I get married, I won't be coming back here to live. We will have to divide up the property. And as we do so, I won't be harming you, mama; you take the upper story where there's a stove and all, and I'll take the lower one."

Then his mother said, "Thank you my son, that you won't be insulting your mother."

"So, mama, I'll deal with my portion as I wish; I don't want to trick you."

She answered, "Do as you know best."

"I'm going to burn my portion up. And you can live with yours, keep it separate."

He poured kerosene and gas all over and lit his floor, and he didn't let his mother out of the house, and she and the devil burned up. And Fear-Bogatyr went back to the tsar, they held the wedding, and now, even nowadays, they are living there. And that's it.

I was at the wedding, drank some beer and wine; it flowed over my moustache, but not a drop got into my mouth.

113. Ondrei the Shooter

Typical of the serial tales, never told better than by Matvei Mikhailovich Korguev, is "Ondrei the Shooter." Korguev, who related more than one hundred twenty different tales to A.N. Nechaev from 1936 to 1938, was born in 1883 in Keret, Karelia. He was frequently hired by ships' captains to sail on their long hunting and fishing expeditions throughout the White Sea. In his own words he would tell a tale "until all fell asleep, then I would be silent and stop narrating. The next day they would ask for more . . ." and thus until he ended one tale or began another (T.I. Sen'kina, *Russkaia skazka Karelii*, Petrozavodsk, 1988, p. 56). Like other serial-tale narrators, Korguev preferred heroes with supernatural strength and he does not usually rely on magic to advance the movement of the tale. His tales are also noted for their adherence to the traditional relating of the tale type. This tale type is very common in Eastern Europe as the Quest for the Unknown. SUS 465A (repeated with variations).

In no certain tsardom, in no certain country, there lived and dwelt a tsar, and he was single. Now then, he kept twelve shooters about him, and one of them was the Shooter Ondrei. This Ondrei could shoot a falcon in flight and thus was considered to be the senior shooter. Yes. And their hunting took place for six days when they worked for the tsar, but the seventh day was just for themselves.

So he spent five years at the tsar's and all at the same work. But it seemed to him that he was not paid well at all. He decided to go elsewhere. Then he thought: "Let me get through this month, I'll go out hunting once more for myself, and then I'll leave."

So. Then this once he went out hunting for himself as it was the seventh day. He went out, of course, and for the whole day he walked about the forest, but he didn't see a living thing. So then he came back near to the city and he saw a falcon on a fox's prey.

"Well, let's go ahead and shoot her." So he shot her and wounded her and she fell. He picked her up and was about to wring her neck when the female falcon spoke up in human voice and said, "Listen to me, Ondrei the Shooter, don't wring my head off. Take me home. When you get home, sit down to drink something and put me on the windowsill. Then throw me out the window and see what happens. If you want, keep it for yourself; if not, give it to other people."

So then when he started to drink tea, he put the falcon on the sill and finally threw it out the window. And there it turned into a beautiful maiden, just like a flower. He looked at her but he couldn't say a word. She asked, "Well, Ondrei the Shooter, will you give me away or keep me for yourself?"

"I'll keep you for myself."

"If for yourself, that's fine, only know how to keep me."

So then she came in and she started living with him. They lived together for a week and then she said, "Ondrei, you obviously live pretty humbly, don't you?"

"As you can see for yourself."

So then she said, "Here's what, Ondrei, do you have an acquaintance who would loan you a hundred rubles? If so, go and ask him. When you get the money, go into the shop and bring me a length of silk and I'll make a carpet from it."

So then Ondrei went straight away to a merchant whom he knew, who was of course also called Ivan. So then he said, "Give me, please, twenty rubles."

"What do you need them for?"

"You know—I have this need."

"What use are twenty? I'll give you forty."

So then he thanked him and went to another merchant he knew. "Well, my friend, give me twenty rubles; I really need them."

"What's this to me, Ondrei? I'll give you forty."

So he took them and thus he had eighty and needed only twenty more. He went away and went straight to a third merchant. "Can you loan me ten rubles, my friend?" That one gave him twenty and he had the full hundred. When he got all the money, he went into the shop, bought the length of silk, and brought it to his wife: "Here you are, Elena the Beautiful, here's the silk; I've brought it."

Then she said to him, "From whom did you take this money, from one merchant or from three, and how much did each of them give you?"

"From the first merchant, Ivan, I asked for twenty and he gave me forty, from the second I asked for twenty and he gave me forty, and from the third I asked for ten and he gave me twenty; so here are the hundred rubles."

"So Ondrei, you have taken this money and will be returning it, give it back double. From the one of whom you asked twenty and he gave you forty, give him back eighty and so on."

So then Ondrei set to work for six days and she set about her work and began weaving the carpet. And when Ondrei had hunted for the six days, he came home of course on Saturday, and on Sunday morning she gave him the carpet and said, "Now, Ondrei, go to the market and sell the carpet—only don't hike up the price; whoever offers you something, take it."

So he took the carpet and was setting off, and she said, "Listen, Ondrei, when you get the money, be sure to pay back double what they gave you."

So yes, Ondrei the Shooter took the carpet and set off for the market. He came to the market, carrying the carpet, spread it out and a crowd gathered about to look at the carpet such that you couldn't pass by. No one offered to buy it: they all just looked. And this carpet was really beautifully designed: on it were a wood, rivers, lakes, a sea, birds, fish—everything on earth. And they all just stood there. Then the tsar's day orderly chanced to ride by. "Well, why have all these people gathered here? Clear the path!"

Of course he forced his way into the crowd and came to look at the carpet. And then this orderly examined the carpet all over, for about three hours, and he really liked it, and he began asking: "Whose carpet is this and how much does it cost?"

Then Ondrei came up to the orderly and said, "This carpet is mine."

"And how much does it cost?"

"I'll take whatever you give me for it."

Then the royal orderly said, "I'll give you thirty thousand for it, Ondrei. Will that be enough?"

"That's enough."

He took the money out of his pocket, gave it to him, and set off. So Ondrei went to the first merchant and gave him eighty; the merchant asked him, "Why eighty, Ondrei? I gave you forty."

"Because I asked for twenty and you gave me double; therefore, I'll pay you back double."

Then he went to the second merchant and then to the third. These merchants thanked Ondrei, and then he brought the rest of the money home to his wife. "Here, Lenochka, I brought you the money."

"And how much did you get?"

"Thirty thousand."

"And did you pay back the money?"

"I did."

"So now do you see my profit, Ondrei?"

"Yes, not bad!"

"Now you can live well."

Then when the royal orderly had put the carpet on the wall, it just happened that the young tsarevich came to see the orderly at that very time and he looked at the carpet. When he had looked it over, he really liked it and started asking, "Where did you get this carpet, orderly? And how much did you pay for it?"

"I bought it at the market and paid thirty thousand for it."

"From whom?"

"From the shooter Ondrei."

"Sell it to me—I'll give you thirty-five."

So then he said, "Please, take it. I'll go around to Ondrei and order a new one."

So he took the money and that evening at about ten o'clock he went to Ondrei to order the carpet. Ondrei had already gone to bed and the doors were barred. He came up and knocked. Ondrei said, "We'll have to open up, Lenochka, there's probably somebody there; I'll go and get dressed, open up, and there'll be someone from the tsar's servants.

She said, "Calm down, you're already undressed; go to sleep, and I'll go and open it myself."

She went to the doors and opened them. When she had opened them, the tsar's orderly looked at her, put one leg over the threshold, but he couldn't bring over the other; he was silent; he couldn't say another word. She began questioning him: "Why have you come here, royal orderly? Do you need Ondrei yourself, or is it for the tsar? You yourself know that he has gone to sleep and that tomorrow morning he has to go to work for the tsar."

But he just remained silent. She waited for his answer for a long time and finally she could wait no longer: she turned him out and closed the door. He just kept silent and set off home. Finally, he had gone about a hundred *sazhens* when he remembered: "I went to order a carpet and forgot—Ondrei's wife is so fine, just like a picture."

When he got home, at that same time the tsarevich came. "Well, did you order the carpet?"

"No, I didn't."

"Why not?"

"I couldn't be bothered with a carpet, Ondrei's wife is so fine, and I just didn't remember. What a beauty she is!"

Then he said to him, "Well, alright, then I myself will go and order the carpet and take a look at this wife of Ondrei."

So the young tsarevich went to Ondrei's about eight o'clock. When he came, Ondrei had already undressed and was ready to go to bed. The doors, of course, were closed. When they knocked, he, that is Ondrei, said, "Elena the Beautiful, I'll have to go; I'll get dressed and go out."

"No, no Ondrei, since you've already undressed, I'll go and open up myself."

When Elena went to the doors, she opened up, and the young tsarevich put his foot across the threshold and then he saw such a picture before him that he just stood there dumbly, shuffling his feet. She looked at him for a long time and then she asked, "Well, young tsarevich, what do you want of Ondrei? Tell me please, I'm waiting. You know very well that Ondrei must rest; he has to go to work in the morning."

But the young tsarevich couldn't say a thing; he just couldn't; he kept looking at her. She turned him out by the shoulders. "Go now, young tsarevich, if you can't say a thing. Ondrei must sleep."

He went out. When he had gone only a little way away, he thought to himself, "Ai, ai, Ondrei's wife is so fine that one way or another I'll have to take her away from him, or maybe he'll somehow give her to me freely."

When he got home, he summoned his boyars and began a conversation with them: "How can I get Ondrei's wife away from him? I can't execute him, nor can I take her away by force; in a word we'll have to think up some sort of task for him."

And all were agreed to give him a task such that he would either repudiate his wife or as a result of the task he would give her up voluntarily. They began pondering it. They thought about it for a long time, but they couldn't think up a thing.

Finally one of the noblemen took it upon himself to think up the task in three days for ten thousand rubles. "You know what? I'll give you the money," and he gave him the order. He took out the money. "If you don't think something up, then in three days it's off with your head!"

And with those words he left the room. That nobleman thought for two whole days but he couldn't think up a thing; he realized he was in danger. On the third day he went into the forest. "Somehow I'll think up something; if not, I'll hang myself. It's all the same: I'm to lose my head!"

He was walking through the forest all sad and unhappy, but he couldn't think of a thing, and toward evening there was no point to his returning back home. Suddenly he met an old woman coming toward him and she said to him, "What are you pondering, little man?"

He answered her coarsely: "What do you want of me?" He passed her by a little way and then he changed his mind, "So probably I should ask the old woman. Maybe she knows something. Excuse me, granny, excuse a brazen word, but maybe you know what I'm thinking about."

Then she said to him, "Now listen to me, my dear, in the future don't avoid your elders. Go and tell the tsar. Let Ondrei go beyond the thrice-nine lands, beyond the thrice-nine mountains, to the thrice-ten tsardom on the island of Buian, and bring back the sheep with the golden head. Give him a sailing ship and a drinking crew and he will go away and never come back. But give him four months, no longer, and he will divorce his wife."

Then that nobleman thanked the granny and said, "Thank you, I'll go right away."

He went to the tsar and said, "Your highness, I have thought of something. Give Ondrei this task: Let Ondrei go beyond the thrice-nine lands, beyond the thrice-nine mountains, to the thrice-ten tsardom on the island of Buian and bring back the sheep with the golden head. Give him a sailing ship and a drinking crew and he will go away and never come back."

So then the tsarevich said to him: "Well, thank you." And he immediately sent a servant for Ondrei. "Summon him; we'll see what he says to me."

So now then. When the servant came, he announced to him that the tsar was summoning him, and Ondrei thought, "Why is the tsar summoning me?" he said to Elena the Beautiful.

"I don't know." Then Elena said, "Listen, Ondrei, go to the tsar; I know they have a task for you. When you come to the tsar, he will say to you 'Here it is, Ondrei, hand over your wife and I won't give you this task or say anything more to you. If you won't hand her over, then there'll be a task for you.' But you say to him, 'Alright, load a ship with wine and bread.' And agree to this with him but don't agree to be gone less than four months."

So now then. Our Ondrei set off to see the tsar. He came before the tsar and they exchanged greetings.

"This is what's been decided, Ondrei. Give me your wife. If you give her to me, I won't set you any tasks; if you won't give her to me, then there will be one."

So then Ondrei answered the tsar like this: "I got married, your majesty, for myself and not for other folk; I don't agree. Load a ship with wine and bread."

Then they agreed on a time limit of four months. "If you don't bring it back by then, then it's your head from your shoulders," the tsar commanded.

And with that he set off home. "Well," he thought, "There's no way I can save my head: I won't manage to get anything in four months." So Ondrei came home and broke out into bitter tears. "So Elenochka, I won't ever see you again."

She replied to him, "Listen, Ondrei, that's no task—it's just a little task—the big task is still ahead. Let's eat and you go to sleep. Morning is wiser than evening."

They ate their supper and lay down to sleep. She slept for a little and rested until midnight; then she got up, took a magic kerchief out of her pocket, and waved it. Yes! Three young lads jumped out: "How can we be of service to you, Elena the Beautiful?"

"Well, lads, this is what we need: run within two hours beyond the thrice-nine seas, beyond the thrice-nine mountains to the thrice-ten tsardom to the island of Buian and bring back from there the little sheep with the golden head."

The lads brought back the little sheep with the golden head in two hours, she took it, and she put it in a trunk; then she put it at the head of her bed and lay down to sleep. They slept until six o'clock. Elena got up first, heated up the samovar, and woke up Ondrei: "Ondrei, get up, you need to drink your tea, eat, and set off."

So yes, when he had drunk his tea and eaten, he got ready to set off along the road and he burst out crying: "Elenochka, farewell, I'll never see you again!"

"Don't cry, Ondrei, you think the tsar will get me? No, he'll no more see me than his own ears." She gave him a little trunk. Ondrei took the little trunk. "When you come onto the ship, two months will pass and there'll be still weather. While the weather is still, get all your crew drunk to the very last one and turn the ship back. When you get back, you'll see that the sheep with the golden head is in this trunk and you can hand it over to the tsar."

As he started to say goodbye, he began crying. She took a kerchief out of her pocket, wiped away his tears, and said, "Well, Ondrei, go. Don't be afraid of anything. I won't go anywhere." And with these words Ondrei set off for the pier.

No sooner had Ondrei left than the tsarevich sent a detachment to Elena the Beautiful. They searched for her for a long time, they turned the house upside down, they lifted up the floorboards, but they couldn't find her and they decided that Ondrei had taken her with him.

So then Ondrei came to the pier and the ship was already completely ready. He got on board and they set out over the sea. He went over the sea for two whole months before the sea was becalmed, and then he said, "Now then, lads, because of the good weather, let's all have a drink together." The drinking got started.

When he had got all of them drunk, it was quiet on the ship, so he went up to the wheel and quietly turned the ship back. There was a breeze and he said, "Well, lads, can any one of you take the wheel?"

"Listen, Ondrei the Shooter! We can get up but our heads ache."

"Then you'll have to take a drink and sober up!"

They drank a little and once more went on and continued their journey. So they sailed along and the weather was fine: there was a good breeze. They sailed and sailed and then suddenly they sailed back to their own country. When they had sailed back home, the crew asked him, "Well, Ondrei the Shooter, where were we? Why did we go? Why did we all get drunk? And why did we come back home? Did we bring back, or rather, did we get what we went for?"

Then he replied to them: "Well, lads, how is it that you don't remember?"

"But how can we remember when we were all drunk?"

"We got what we went for."

"Well, thanks be to God!"

With these words they came off onto the pier and when they were on the pier, they were met by the young tsarevich, his saber in his hand. When Ondrei met the tsarevich, he said, "Well, Ondrei, did you get it?"

"See for yourself."

And he handed him the little trunk. The tsarevich took it and went home and Ondrei also went home. When he was approaching his house, Elena ran out onto the porch, embraced him, and kissed him, and then led him into the room where the samovar was ready. He sat down to drink tea. Elena asked him, "Well, Ondrei, were you successful?"

"It was nothing, it went well."

"You will have to go once more."

And then not two days had passed when the young tsarevich found out that Ondrei's wife was with him. "No matter what happens, I must take his wife away from him."

He summoned the nobleman and told him to think up another task. "Very well, your highness, I'll think up something quickly."

Once more he went to search out the old woman. He went along the forest path. When he caught sight of her, he immediately stepped to one side. "Well, my friend, did Ondrei manage it?"

"Yes, he was successful."

"Well, it's not so hard to deceive Ondrei, but you won't soon deceive his wife."

"So help me think up another task for him, granny."

Granny replied: "Alright, I'll soon think of something. Let Ondrei go once more beyond the thrice-nine lands and the thrice-nine seas to the thrice-ten tsardom on the island of Buian, and have him fetch the pig with the golden bristles. Give him a hard-drinking crew and a good sailing ship. He'll go away but he won't come back."

With these words the nobleman went to the tsarevich. "Well, your highness, again I've thought up something: let Ondrei go to the thrice-nine lands to the thrice-nine mountains to the thrice-ten tsardom on the island of Buian and fetch the pig with the golden bristles. Give him a hard-drinking crew and a good sailing ship. And a time limit of four months, no longer."

So very soon they called Ondrei again to the tsar. He said to his Elena: "Once again something, some sort of misfortune is brewing and again I am summoned to the tsar."

Then she said, "Tell the tsar that they must load a ship with wine and bread. You yourself know that you married me for yourself and not for others. You know how to guard me."

So he left and came there, of course, to the tsar. He came there and he said, "What do you need of me, your highness?"

And the tsar said to him, "Tell me, Ondrei, where do you hide your wife when you go away?"

"She's at home."

"Hand her over to me or else I'll give you another task."

"No," he said, "I won't hand her over. I married her for myself."

So. "If you won't hand her over, then I'll give you a task: to go to the thrice-nine lands to the thrice-nine mountains to the thrice-ten tsardom on the island of Buian and fetch the pig with the golden bristles. We'll give you a time limit of four months. If you don't bring it back, then it's your head from your shoulders!"

And Ondrei replied, "Well, then, your highness, load a ship with wine and bread and I'll be ready!"

With these words Ondrei went away home. When he got back to Elena, she asked him, "Well, Ondrei?"

"Another task, to the same place as before."

"Well, Ondrei, don't be sad: morning is wiser than evening. This is not a real task, Ondrei; there'll be a third task and we shall have to ponder this third task carefully."

Then they had supper and tumbled in to bed. She slept with him until twelve o'clock. At twelve o'clock she got up, pulled out her magic kerchief, waved it, and there appeared three lads who bowed to her. "What do you command us to do, Elena?"

"Now then, lads, within two hours run to the thrice-nine tsardom, to the thrice-ten land on the island of Buian and bring back the pig with the golden bristles."

The lads bowed and ran off. Not two hours had passed when the lads came running back, dragging along the pig. She took the pig, packed it in a trunk, and went back to sleep. She got up at six o'clock, put on the samovar, and woke up Ondrei.

"Get up, Ondrei, you need to take a drink, eat something, and set off along the road."

Ondrei drank his tea, of course, got dressed, and started crying. "Well, Elenochka, probably I won't see you again."

"Don't cry, Ondrei, nothing will happen." When he had dressed, she gave him the trunk. "Here's this little trunk, Ondrei, and the pig with the golden bristles is in it. After two months get your crew drunk, turn the ship back and come back here: you don't have to go anywhere. Everything is in the trunk."

"But won't the tsar find you?"

"No, he won't find me, he'll no more see me than his own ears!"

When Ondrei had gone, the tsarevich went to his house and tore everything apart: he lifted up the floors, took apart the stove, tore up everything on earth, but she wasn't there. "Probably," he thought, "Ondrei took her with him."

And so Ondrei set off for the ship. He got there and went on board the ship, and they set off on their journey. They sailed for two months, until they were becalmed, that is, the weather was tranquil. Now then. When the weather had quieted down, he got his whole crew drunk and when it was already quiet on the ship, he went up to the wheel and turned the wheel, and then he began awakening his crew from their sleep. "Get up, my friends, will someone take the wheel, if you can?"

They answered, "It's fine to steer the ship, but the head hurts!"

"Well, then, you'll have to take a drink and sober up!"

Soon they began to approach their own country. Here it was, their own country, and they began asking again, "Ondrei the Shooter, did we get what we went for?"

"We got it."

"Alright then, that's fine."

"So can't you remember then?"

"How can we remember when we were dead drunk?"

"Well, you got it."

So then when they had sailed in, they went out onto the pier, and the young tsarevich with his sword came over and asked, "Well, Ondrei, did you manage to acquire it?"

"I got it. You can have it, your highness, the task is completed." And then he went home.

He was just coming up to the house, when Elena leapt out onto the porch, kissed him, and led him into the room. The samovar was already hot and they sat down at the table. They drank their tea and she asked him, "Well, Ondrei, how was your trip?"

"It was fine, really alright."

"Good, and it will be fine next time."

Not two days had passed before the tsarevich found out that Ondrei's wife was there. He sought out that noble man to think up a third task so that no matter what else, he could take away Ondrei's wife. So they found Ondrei's wife and the tsarevich said to him, "Now, my friend, go and think up some third task for Ondrei."

He answered, "Good. It won't take long to think something up."

He was relying on the old woman. Then the noble set off along the forest path. He had walked a long time when he met the old woman. "Greetings, granny!"

"Greetings, my son."

She asked him, "Well, did Ondrei manage it?"

"He managed it."

"Hmm. It isn't so hard to deceive Ondrei but you can't deceive his wife. Never mind, I'll think of something: I'll separate him from his wife for seven years."

Then she said to him, "Go around to the tsar and tell him this: 'Let Ondrei go he doesn't know where and fetch he doesn't know what. And give him a set time, not less than seven years. Maybe he won't undertake it. But during this time the tsar can marry Elena the Beautiful."

You see she didn't know that Elena could disappear. That nobleman immediately went to the tsar and reported: "So, your highness, let Ondrei go he doesn't know where and fetch he doesn't know what. And give him a set time, not less than seven years. During that time you can get hold of his wife." (Did this really happen?)

When the tsar heard these words from the noble, he impatiently sent for Ondrei. When the messenger came, he ordered Ondrei to come to the tsar; he summoned him immediately. Ondrei answered, "Alright." Then he said once more to his Elena the Beautiful: "Elena, the tsar has probably thought up something bad again."

"Yes, there's to be another task. But don't refuse the task; take it on; all will be clear."

Now then. So Ondrei went to the tsar and the tsar led him into a separate room and began treating him. He was thinking of getting him drunk so that Ondrei would more readily agree. But his wife had warned him: "Look out, Ondrei, and don't drink any vodka."

So then Ondrei, of course, didn't refuse and went with him to the table, sat down, and drank just one small flagon, and the tsar started speaking to him. Now then. "So, Ondrei, you hand over your wife and I'll marry you to a fine daughter of a general, and you'll live happily, with no particular worries; otherwise, I'll assign you a really big task."

But Ondrei wouldn't agree for anything, no matter what the conditions, and he said, "I'd rather go than give up my wife."

And he refused the vodka absolutely.

"Then do you know what, Ondrei, I'll give you a task: to go where—you don't know where—and bring back—you don't know what. I am giving you an unlimited length of time. If you can't bring it back and you return, then it's your head from your shoulders."

And so with those words Ondrei went out and came home to Elena the Beautiful. He came in gloomy and sad with tears in his eyes. Elena asked Ondrei, "Why are you crying?"

"How should I not cry, Elena? He's given me this task: to go you know not where and bring back you know not what."

She answered him, "Listen, Ondrei, don't be sad, drink something and eat, go to sleep—the morning is wiser than the evening, and by morning all will be clear."

They had supper and went off to bed. She slept for a little, got up, took down her magic book and began looking for something: "go you don't know where. . . ." She looked for a long time, but of course she couldn't find it, so she threw down the magic book, took out her magic kerchief, shook it, and out leapt the three lads.

"What do you order us to do, Elena the Beautiful?"

"So now then, lads, you don't know where 'you don't know where' is, do you?"

One said, "I don't know." The second said, "I don't know." They all said the same thing. She hid the kerchief back in her pocket, took a big hank of yarn, and began to make it into a ball. When she had twisted it into a large ball, such that she could scarcely carry it, she took it outside and put it on the porch. This took her until about six o'clock in the morning. She put on the samovar and woke up Ondrei.

"Get up, Ondreiushko, my dear friend, you have work to do and a long journey to go on."

So they sat down, drank their tea, and she said, "Now then, Ondrei, there's a ball on the porch. This ball will roll along the road, and you go after it. As long as this ball goes along the road, you go after it and keep on going until the ball stops. The thread will stretch out along the road and you'll see a palace. Enter the palace: you'll be met there."

So Ondrei got ready to go. She got a sack ready for him, a knapsack, and he started crying: "Well, Elenochka, I won't ever see you again; you don't know where I am going!"

"Don't even think about that, Ondrei; the tsar won't take me and I'll wait for you; of course we won't see each other for a long time." And then she added, "Here's a little bag for you. When you come to the palace, you will be met and fed, and given something to drink, and then they will give you a bed. When you get up in the morning, you will wash and they will bring you a towel. Don't dry yourself with their towel—take the one out of this little bag and dry yourself with it."

So then he wandered around a little and he felt very sorry for her and he cried. She comforted him. She wiped his face with a cloth and together they went outside onto the porch. He set off down the road and the ball rolled along in front of him. And so Ondrei departed on his journey.

When the tsar found out that Ondrei had gone away, he immediately put guards around her house and began a search of the entire home. But he couldn't find her and finally he got angry and burned down the whole house.

Ondrei continued his journey farther, and the ball rolled on, getting smaller and smaller. Ondrei was bored walking along—he just kept thinking about Elena the Beautiful. So he walked and walked, continuing on his way, and the ball got to be really small—about the size of a chicken's head. Ondrei was really bored; there wasn't a single dwelling around and the smaller the ball of yarn got, the more Ondrei was in despair. Finally the ball got so small that you couldn't even see it on the road: the thread was stretched out all along the road. Ondrei lifted up his eyes and looked: there stood the palace. He went up to the porch, the main porch. As he was approaching the porch, two girls came down a ladder and ran toward him. One of them was just like his Elenochka, but he didn't dare say so. They took him by the hand and led him up to the second floor. When they had led him in, they quickly set the table with cloths, and there were drinks of all sorts—foreign wines, too—and they gave him some drinks and fed him, and then let him go to sleep with a down comforter. And then they went away. So he slept through the night. In the morning they came running in at eight o'clock to wake him from his sleep. When he got up, they brought him some water to wash with and they brought him a towel. Ondrei washed, of course. And they gave him their towel.

"No, girls, I have my own towel that I brought with me."

He took the towel out of his knapsack; he had only just managed to put the towel on his face when one of the girls grabbed it and ran away. And the other went after her. Ondrei remained standing in deep sorrow, and he thought, "What will happen to me now since she ordered me to wipe myself with that towel?"

So then those girls took the towel to their mother and said, "Do you know what, Mama; our Ondrei has come!"

"Yes, yes! I know why he has come!"

And there was his towel. On account of it she had ordered him to dry himself with that towel so that they would know who he was and why he had come there, that was why she had ordered him to dry himself. So then the old woman jumped up from her chair and with her daughters she went out to him: "Greetings, son-in-law!"

"Greetings, mama!"

"I know why you've come. The tsar wants to take my Elena. But ha, ha! He won't manage that! I'll help you, which is why you came here. You'll stay here with me for a few days. You see, he thought it up, that young tsarevich, to seize my Elena, but let him just try, let him try for even a hundred years—he still won't find her."

Then Ondrei sat down at the table and began eating; he calmed down. A little later this is what she said, "Alright then, son-in-law, you'll stay here for three days, and I'll go have a look."

She went away and when she came back, she took her magic book down and began looking for the words "that which you don't know." She looked for a long time, threw down the book, and yanked at her hair, but she couldn't find it. She thought and she thought, and then she said, "Finally I've thought of it."

She took two brooms and flew off through the air. She flew for a whole day and then she flew back, but she couldn't find it. She took up the book of magic and again began searching. She looked and looked but she couldn't find it so she threw down the book and started thinking. She thought for about eight hours and then she said, "Now I've thought it through and found out where it is. Skokushka-babushka has been living in the swamp for three hundred years and she likely knows; I'll fly over to her."

She took her two brooms and flew off. When she had arrived at Skokushka-babushka's and the swamp, she asked, "Skokushka-babushka, do you know where 'that which you don't know' is?"

"I know," she said.

"Then tell me."

"No, I won't tell you. I'll tell you when you carry me to the fiery river of steaming milk. Then I'll tell you but before that I won't tell you."

She took Skokushka on her back and carried her there. She took a jug of milk and started steaming her. When she had bathed, she took Granny Skokushka (she was a frog), and brought her to her son-in-law.

"Well, son-in-law, get dressed and go: I'll give you my horse."

So our Ondrei the Shooter got dressed and she led out her horse. Then the granny said to him, "Now you fly to the fiery river, and next to the fiery river the horse will disappear; ask the old woman there how to go on farther."

So he went to the fiery river and the horse disappeared. There remained just the jug and he began pulling the frog out by a string. When he had pulled out Skokushka, she said to him: "Get on me, Ondrei, before it's too late."

And he said to her, "But granny, you are so small; I'll crush you."

"Get on!"

He hesitated for a time and didn't mount her, but finally he said, "Well, I'll get on."

He got on and that frog began rising upward and upward, and she was higher than the woods, and she kept on swallowing him up until only his head was visible. Then she spoke: "Now hold on tighter."

Then the frog leapt and she jumped across the fiery river. She let him out. He questioned her. "Tell me, granny, where is 'that which I don't know'?"

"Now then, if you hadn't asked me, you wouldn't have found out. But now I'll tell you."

And so granny began: "Here's where 'that which you don't know' lives. Go along this path, and it will be a long way, of course, and where it looks like you have to go, just go! You'll see a house, well not a house but a barn; not a barn but an estate, and yet no estate. Enter it. The building will be completely empty and falling down. There'll be just a stove. So you enter this building and get on the stove. Two lads will come out and say, 'Svat-Naum, drink and eat!' Then some sort of music will start playing, ironed tablecloths will appear, drinks, liquors, and foreign wines. You just wait until they go away and the room will be completely empty. Then you go and say 'Svat-Naum, drink and eat!' And you do the same. When you drink and eat, treat Svat-Naum to a shot. Then he won't leave you. And that will be 'that which you don't know.'"

So then Granny Skokushka finished all that. He thanked her and set off down the road. He walked for a long time and finally he saw it: a house that was no house, a barn that was no barn. He went in and it was completely empty and falling down—there was just a stove. Yes, and then suddenly out came two young men and they said, "Svat-Naum, eat and drink!"

Then out of nowhere, there appeared ironed tablecloths, drinks, liquors, various foreign wines, and the room was transformed—it was completely different. And when they had eaten, they left, and once more the room was empty. Then Ondrei came out from behind the stove. When he came out from behind the stove, he started speaking: "Svat-Naum, drink and eat."

And the same thing happened. There appeared ironed tablecloths, drinks, liquors, various foreign wines, and also vodka and a shot glass, and everything on earth. So he sat down at the table and started eating and he said, "Svat-Naum, might I have a second shot?" And Svat-Naum poured him a second shot.

"Svat-Naum, treat yourself to a second glass, from me, a traveling man."

So then Svat-Naum drank a second shot and started talking: "Well, Ondrei the Shooter, you've given me a shot and now I'll not leave you. I've been feeding two fools for thirty years and I haven't seen hide nor hair of them!"

"Svat-Naum, show yourself!"

"No," he said, "I am the spirit that no one can see. I am 'that which you can't know.'"

So Ondrei drank, ate, and began to gather his things. "Well, Svat-Naum, will you come with me?"

"Of course, I am always behind you."

"Where?"

"Well, let's go!"

So Ondrei was walking along the road and he kept on asking, "Svat-Naum, are you there?"

"I'm here; I'll never leave you."

Finally Ondrei came to the sea. When he got to the sea, he said, "Svat-Naum, and where will we go now?"

"Wait a little, Ondrei; soon a ship will come sailing by and we'll sail off on it."

Suddenly out of nowhere the ship! A little sloop came over to them and carried them to the ship, and he asked, "Svat-Naum, are you there?"

"I am, I am. I'll never leave you."

Well, on that ship there wasn't a single person, no people at all. "How can this be, Svat-Naum? We have no people who can sail the ship—no navigators and no sailors."

Then Svat-Naum said, "Go to sleep; I'll manage it by myself."

So Ondrei went to bed, slept, and then got up. Then Svat-Naum said to him, "Well, Ondrei, we'll sail to this one island, and we'll go off the ship and settle there, that is."

So they sailed up to this island, and then let a boat down from the ship that carried them to the island, and then the ship disappeared. So they went out onto the island. The island was standing in the sea. Svat-Naum said, "Here's what, Ondrei, on this island we'll build a palace and surround it with orchards. Then three ships will sail by this island and they'll come to visit us."

So Svat-Naum immediately built the palace and surrounded it with orchards, and they started living there; they lived on and on. And then Svat-Naum said to him, "In three days the three ships will come sailing up, and they never will have seen such a marvel: they've been sailing by this place for thirty years and have never seen anyone living here. So they'll drop anchor and come to us. The captains of these three ships have three wondrous things that we need to take in exchange for me. They will agree, but I'll never leave you. When we've given them plenty to drink and to eat, we'll get them drunk, and they'll boast about these wondrous things and ask you, 'What will you take for Svat-Naum?'"

So then a little time passed and the three ships came sailing up. They met up and started discussing this astonishing thing. "What is this? For thirty years we've been sailing here, but we've never seen such an amazing thing: someone has come here and built a palace; we'll have to take a look!"

So all together they stopped their three ships. All the captains, the sailors, and the navigators lowered boats and set off for the hill. When they had come to the hill and entered the palace, Ondrei the Shooter met them and said, "Svat-Naum! Offer drink and food to treat these sailors!"

And ironed tablecloths appeared, and drinks, and liquors, and various foreign wines. And all this was done. The guests all sat down at the table. When they began drinking the vodka, they soon got quite tipsy. They began asking him, "What is this Svat-Naum that you have, Ondrei the Shooter. What sort of person, and have you been living on this island for a long time?"

Then he said to them, "This Svat-Naum is my friend; he fulfills all my desires, and wherever I wish to reside, I could go with him and live there."

"And what sort of person is he? How can we take a look at him?"

"I don't know. I've never seen him myself. He's a spirit of a sort that no one can see."

When these guests were all quite drunk, they began boasting. And one captain said, "Well, Ondrei, I also have an amazing thing: when I wish it, I have this axe and I say to a tree, 'Axe, whack, whack, and make me a ship,' and it's ready in a minute."

Then the second captain spoke up: "What you have is nothing! I have this saber. If I walk along a shore and hit next to the water with it, it will make a crystal bridge. But if I strike across the water, nothing will happen. And if I decide to make a palace, I go out onto a fine square and walk three times around my saber and make such a palace as I'll show you."

Then the third captain said to the second one: "I have a very fine thing indeed. I've got this little trumpet and I can go into the steppe, blow it, and an army will appear as big as I command, and they'll do what I ask."

So then when all the captains had told their stories, Svat-Naum said to Ondrei, he whispered in his ear, "Listen, Ondrei the Shooter, let's exchange for me. We need all these things, but I'll never leave you; they'll agree."

So after all this Ondrei the Shooter said to the captains, "Now then, comrade captains, let's exchange. I'll hand over Svat-Naum and you'll give me all these things."

The captains thought about it and talked among themselves, and finally they said, "Alright." And then they decided: "Comrades, let's do this: let's go home and bring our wives here and we'll live on this island, and Svat-Naum will feed us and we won't have to work anymore."

They immediately went onto their ships for their things. When they got to their ships, they took their things and came back onto the mountain. And just then Svat-Naum spoke to Ondrei: "When they've come back here, get them all drunk, collect their things, and go to the end of the island."

So when they came back, these captains, they sat down at the table and had a great drinking bout. Yes. These captains handed over the things to him and he said to Svat-Naum, "Well, Svat-Naum, you stay here with these captains and serve them as you have served me, and I'll go away."

They said goodbye; he took their things, and set off. He went off a little way and thought: "Svat-Naum, are you here?"

"I'm always with you. Wait a little and they'll drink a little more before they fall asleep. They'll wake up on bare rocks: there'll be nothing more around them."

Meanwhile, those captains drank so much that they fell asleep. They woke up, jumped up, but they were left on the bare rocks. There was nothing else, no palace, no gardens. Ondrei's traces were long gone cold.

Then Ondrei came to the end of the island and asked Svat-Naum: "Well, Svat-Naum, what are we going to do?"

"It would seem that you yourself already know; don't you have an axe?"

"I have."

"Well, build a ship!"

Ondrei quickly located a tree and struck it with his axe. "Whack, whack! Make a ship!" At that very moment the ship was ready and waiting in the water. Then he said, "And now, Svat-Naum, how are we to get onto the ship?"

"Don't you have that thing?"

He took his saber, struck the water with it, and a little bridge appeared. They crossed it onto the ship. He struck it crisscross, took the bridge away, and they sailed off on the ship.

And so they sailed for a long time or a short time, low or high, near or far—they just kept on sailing. Ondrei sailed up to the country where he had started out from and saw that all was just the same. When they came sailing in on course, Ondrei took his saber, struck the water with it, and there appeared a little bridge. They got up onto it and went over onto the mountain. When they had come out onto the shore, they walked through the town. Ondrei walked among the same dwellings where his hut had been. When he recognized the spot, he looked carefully at it and saw that the place had been entirely burned down and grass was growing all over the spot. He looked at it and said, "Obviously, my Elena has perished; the idiot has burned everything up."

Then there was nothing left for Ondrei to do. He asked Svat-Naum, "What are we going to do now, Svat-Naum?"

Svat-Naum replied to him, "Build a house and your Elena will be found."

So Ondrei the Shooter took his saber and twirled it round and then he said, "Build me a palace three times better than the tsar's."

Immediately the palace was built with a silver nameplate on it: "Ondrei the Shooter." When he saw that such a splendid palace had been built, he joyfully went up to the second story and began walking through the rooms. Finally, he entered the bedroom. When he had entered the bedroom, he pulled the curtain aside and saw that Elena was sleeping on the bed. He woke her. She opened her eyes, rushed to him, and began kissing him. She said, "Is it you I see, my dear shooter Ondrei?"

"It's me!" he said. "Let's go to the hall now and put on a splendid feast, and I'll tell you about my whole journey!"

When they had entered the hall, they sat down at the table, and she asked, "Well, did you get 'that which you can't know'?"

He said, "I got it."

Then Ondrei spoke: "Now then, Svat-Naum, let's live and eat, be happy, feed yourself, me, and my wife."

Then she began asking him, "Svat-Naum, who are you? Show yourself to me!"

"No, Elena the Beautiful, since my birth I've never shown myself to anybody. I am such a spirit that no one can see me: I am 'that which you can't know.'"

She didn't ask him anything further. Now Ondrei questioned him: "Now then, Svat-Naum, what are we going to do now? Will you go to the tsar or will you live with me?"

Svat-Naum replied: "No, Ondrei, I will not go to the tsar; the tsar didn't get me: you did, Ondrei the Shooter, and I will serve you. We shall deal with the tsar in another way."

And then Svat-Naum said to him: "Take a horn, like a bugle, Ondrei, and let's go into the steppe. When we've got to the open steppe, blow it just once."

So Ondrei took his horn and went into the open steppe. When he had come to the steppe, he immediately blew the horn. And there poured out of it so many soldiers that he didn't know what to make of it: they just kept on coming. Their main atamans galloped up to him and bowed to the waist. "What do you need, Ondrei the Shooter?"

He didn't know what to say to them. Then Svat-Naum said to Ondrei, "Order them to shell the city with blank shells and order them to call out the tsar himself, or let him send an army."

So yes. When the tsar heard of this dangerous situation, he was beside himself and didn't know what to do. He sent twenty-five soldiers to reconnoiter, to find out what they needed and what army had come. When the soldiers came, Ondrei asked, "Svat-Naum, what shall we do with these soldiers?"

"Here's what: tie twenty of them to the grass by the hair and send the other five back, saying not to send so many to us—either send your army or come yourself."

That's what they did. They tied up the twenty and sent the others back with the answer. When the soldiers had returned to the tsar and reported the situation, the tsar fell into deep thought: what was he to do? Finally he decided to go himself. When the tsar came to the steppe, Ondrei the Shooter saw him and said to Svat-Naum: "Svat-Naum, how are we to receive the tsar now?"

Svat-Naum answered, "In my opinion, we should deal with him very simply: execute him and you should mount the throne."

Ondrei replied, "No, Svat-Naum, I've no intention of executing him, let him live with that evil; it would be better to do something else with him and find out what he will say."

When the tsar came up to Ondrei the Shooter, he was very frightened and began begging for forgiveness. "Ondrei the Shooter, do what you want with me, only don't take off my head."

And then he saw the enormous army.

"I don't need anything from you—whatever you've brought or haven't brought—I don't need anything. Only don't execute me."

"Well, alright."

"I'll hand over my throne: mount my throne, and I'll abandon it."

And then Ondrei said to the tsar: "Alright, I'll leave you your life, but you will spend forty years as a shepherd."

So then he blew twice on his horn and his army completely disappeared.

They entered the royal rooms. The tsar quietly handed everything over to him and he left to become a shepherd. Then Ondrei the Shooter mounted the throne and began the wedding. When the wedding was over, of course he began ruling the tsardom until deep old age.

114. Ivan Medvedevich the Bear's Son

This is a little tale of murders—patricide, infanticide, and matricide among the several. Korguev frequently employed supernatural births as a motif. Most commonly a bear, for millennia a much-tabooed ancestor of East Slavs, plays the role of parent, as in this tale, but the bull, horse, and cow may figure in other tales. The water tsar or water spirit was believed to inhabit various bodies of water and was a particular threat to the young heroes. In more recent tales his role is often fulfilled by a devil and his brood. The priest (and the tsar) was called "Batiushka" or little father, the priest's wife "Matushka." As is often the case, vodka is referred to as "wine," to give it more status. SUS 650A + 315A + 300A + 301A + 302.

Now then in no certain tsardom, in no certain country there lived and dwelt a priest with his wife (there are few unmarried priests: only when the wife dies, that's when). He had a vegetable garden that wasn't particularly close to his house. There he grew potatoes and other vegetables.

So then Matushka set off one fine day to collect some vegetables. It was an autumn evening, and Batiushka somehow wasn't free. Suddenly a bear came running by and grabbed this priest's wife and dragged her off to his little house, you know, the place where he lived—in a cave. So he kept her there: he wouldn't let her out. He kept her in place of his wife; he fed her and gave her whatever she wanted, she was never in need. So then, you see, he kept her for two years and she got pregnant by him.

The priest had come home late. He looked and looked for her, but when he couldn't find her, he went back and that was that.

So then, you see, the priest's wife, she had a son. They gave him the name Ivan Medvedevich, the Bear's Son, because his father was a bear! So! And this little boy in three years grew up to be big and he became very strong. But his mother didn't know this, that he was so strong. Once he asked his mother, "Mama, why do we live in the ground and don't see any people when there are people not far away?"

He could hear dogs barking and sometimes people talking. At the time the bear wasn't at home.

"Oh, my child, I've been living here for five years since he dragged me in here, you were born here, and since then three years have passed. I used to be a priest's wife."

"So, mama, let's leave here and live somewhere else. There are people there, and it would be more fun to live with people."

"No, my child, I don't dare go; why if he met us, he would devour us; you couldn't deal with him—you're still too young."

But even if he was young, he was of a very substantial size! "Let's go, mama, I'm not afraid of him."

They had just gone out when the bear flew at them. He came running up and said, "I've told you, both of you. . . . How dare you leave the house?"

He drew even with them and was ready to throw himself on them when the son took him by his hind legs and struck him against a fallen log such that all his flesh flew off and only his skin remained in the boy's hands. With that the bear perished.

"Now where, mama? I think we should go into the city; in any case there's no point in our going back to our village."

So they set off for the city. And he grabbed the bearskin and took it with him. "We'll sell it at our first chance."

So they went along. They were coming into the city and they stopped at the edge of it at a certain little widow's. She let them in to stay. The next day he said to his mother, "Well, mama, I'll go and sell this skin; maybe someone will give me something for it."

He came into the city and went to the bazaar. "Where do they sell skins?"

Someone pointed it out to him. He stood in line, as you're supposed to, and when it was his turn, he started trading with the merchants. They asked him, "Well, lad, are you wanting to sell this skin?"

"I am."

"But why is this skin whole and not taken off as you're supposed to?"

He said, "I didn't have a knife or an axe, and I had no time to skin it properly. My mother and I had just left home when the bear attacked us. He was about to devour us, so I grabbed him by the legs and hit him against a log, and all his flesh fell off. If you like, take it for whatever price you want."

One of the merchants said to him, "How much do you want for this skin?"

"Whatever you'll give me will be just fine."

"Well, I'll give you a hundred rubles—will that be enough?"

"Alright, that will be enough," he said.

So then the merchant handed over the money and said, "Well, you're a fit lad if you killed a bear with your hands; you could earn good money from the tsar. The tsar needs such people."

He took the money and went home to his mother. He gave his mother the money and said, "Go buy something to eat and I'll go into the city and look around."

So he took a few rubles for himself and set off. His mother went and of course bought everything that they needed. And he went and bought nothing because, it must be said, he didn't have much money. He came home, but then after that a great rumor spread throughout the city. This merchant had told how the youth had killed a bear without any knife or axe. And the news got to the tsar. The tsar gave an order: "Seek out this young man and ask him whether he doesn't wish to come to me so that I may find out who he is." So they began searching throughout the city: the royal servants ran here and there, searching for that youth. They went about all the houses, and finally came to that very last house that stood on the edge of the city. And when they went into that last house, they saw the old woman and the woman and the youth.

"Tell us, how much strength do you have and what is your name?"

"What is my name? It's a simple name: Ivan Medvedevich."

"And tell us how much strength you have."

"I don't know how much strength I have. It's just that once my mother and I were going from our home to the city and we met up with a bear and I took him by his hind legs and struck him against a log and all his flesh came out of his skin and then I sold his skin at the bazaar for a hundred rubles."

Then the servants said to him: "Now then, Ivan Medvedevich, the tsar has asked that you come to visit him; he wishes to see you. And we've been going everywhere, looking for you."

"Alright, go. And I'll come: once he's asked, I'll have to come and visit him."

So the servants went away and he remained at home with his mother and with the old granny. When they had left, his mother said to him: "My son, you killed the bear, so you've done these things and the tsar will arrest you if you go to him."

And he replied: "Oh, stop it, mother, there's nothing to worry about. Why would he arrest me? I killed the bear to protect myself and you; I had to." And with these words he set off to see the tsar.

Now of course when he came to the tsar's palace, the servants met him. "Tell us, young man, who are you?"

"I am Ivan Medvedevich, and since the tsar ordered me to come, here I am."

They took him by the hand and presented him to the tsar. When he came before the tsar, he said to him: "Greetings, your majesty!"

"Greetings, Ivan Medvedevich. Sit down here with me." He sat him down at the table, brought a little vodka and something to eat, and he began entertaining him. When he had entertained him, of course he began questioning him: "So tell me, Ivan Medvedevich, how much strength do you have? I've heard that you have a lot of strength in you and perhaps you wouldn't mind being in the bodyguard of our tsardom: we have no one."

He said, "Your highness, I don't know what strength I have because I've never had occasion to use it—only that instance when I met the bear, and I killed it and I sold its skin at the bazaar: maybe you heard about that occasion."

"Listen, Ivan Medvedevich, you have great strength since you killed the bear: you struck him against the log and the flesh flew off. And so I would ask you to remain in our tsardom. I shall set you a great task."

"Very well, your majesty, I wish to remain here but the fact of the matter is that I am illiterate; I grew up in the woods; I can serve, however."

"Don't worry about that, Ivan Medvedevich; we can introduce you to reading, and writing too, only indicate your desire to be here."

"Well, as I said I'll be here, I will be."

They immediately started teaching him reading and writing and within a month he had figured out how to write and to read. Then the tsar asked, "What relatives do you have with you now?"

"I have only my mother."

While he had been studying, his mother hadn't been there, but when he finished with his learning, the tsar had asked that. "So bring your mother here and I will give you a separate room in which you can live."

So then he went to his mother, of course, and told her how he had been with the tsar and how he had studied, and he said, "Let's go, mama, to the tsar; that's where we are going to live."

He thanked that old granny, gave her some money, and they left. Of course, then they came to the tsar, where they were given a room all ready for them. And they began living there and he went on with his studies. Of course, we aren't going to talk about their food—it was all prepared.

Then the tsar summoned him once more: "Now then, Ivan Medvedevich, we have this big problem, you know. Eleven bogatyrs are going to attack me and I must repulse them at any cost. There is a high mountain and on this mountain there is a club, and the bogatyrs who get this club will conquer all our tsardom. So you go round to these bogatyrs and hang around there; you are still young and they'll take you for a mere stripling. It would be great if you could get hold of this club and kill all those bogatyrs. I'll make you famous throughout the whole tsardom and you will be my heir. Only I don't have a daughter or else I would marry you to her and you would live here in our tsardom."

He said, "Alright, I'll try; and if I manage it, I'll do your majesty this favor; I'll have a go."

So the next day after that and having said nothing to his mother, he set off. And he came to that mountain, and when he had come to the mountain, he climbed up to the top and looked: eleven bogatyrs were standing there so he went up to them and greeted them.

"Greetings, lads! What are you doing here?" he asked them.

And they answered him, "Hello, young man. You are still young—why have you come here?"

"To find out what you're doing here, and to help you."

"That's good. You are still young; if you found out what we are doing and helped us, that would be good."

"But I don't know what you are attempting—maybe I could help you."

"Now then, where are you from? From which city, and how are we to call you? Will you come with us to conquer this tsardom?" they asked him.

He said, "I came here not long ago so I don't know who rules here and it makes no difference to me and thus I can go with you."

And they said, "Very well, if that's the case, you can join us and we'll show you what to get. And when you get it, you can hand it over to us."

"Alright."

So they took him to the place where the club was fastened and each in turn tried to pull it out, all the bogatyrs. And they all tried, but none of them could. It just shook, but they couldn't lift it out. He said to them: "You are trying one at a time; take about five men and maybe you will be able to pull it out."

They took five men and rocked it, but nonetheless it wouldn't come out, so six of them grabbed hold, but nonetheless it wouldn't come out.

"Well, now you Ivan Medvedevich, you try it, maybe something will come of that."

"Alright, let me have a go."

So he grabbed hold of the club, you see, and once he turned it, it creaked; so he turned it the other way and he pulled it out. They all clapped their hands: "The power will be ours, young man, Ivan Medvedevich!"

Then the oldest of the bogatyrs spoke: "Now then, Ivan Medvedevich, give me the club and we'll go into the city, we'll conquer the city and no one will want to fight with us anymore. And you will be if not the oldest, then a bogatyr alongside me."

Then without saying a word, Ivan Medvedevich swung the club to one side, and that flattened four of them. Then he swung it another time in his great passion, and another four fell; he looked—and there were just two remaining. He laid these two flat but the eleventh bogatyr had disappeared. He hadn't known in his passion that while he was striking them, the senior bogatyr had disappeared. He didn't know where he had gone. So fine. So then he began going down the mountain, to go back to the tsar, and he thought: "Now then I have this club as a fine bodyguard."

It seemed light to him. Then he came, of course, to that tsar: he marched right into his palace and went in to him with the club. In actual fact it wasn't so light, and he wasn't so light, so all the rooms shook. When he came in to the tsar, the tsar was delighted, and he said, "So, your majesty, I've brought this club that you wanted me to bring here and I've destroyed those bogatyrs."

Then he said to him: "Good lad, Ivan Medvedevich! You have done us such a service, for our tsardom, that now we are ruling firmly, and I am proposing to have you be my heir, if that is satisfactory to you, and I will reward you with half the tsardom. You have done a great deed for me, and in a very short time, but you did it very well."

But at that time that bogatyr who had disappeared began courting his mother, and Ivan Medvedevich knew nothing about any of it. He even began living with her. Of course, he used to visit his mother but he didn't suspect anything. The bogatyr advised her: "Listen, pretend to be ill when your son comes and I'll think something up and destroy him, and then your and my affair will prosper. When you are ill, he will come and ask 'What is the matter with you, Mother?' and you say to him 'Well, my son, when I fell ill, I saw in a dream that there was this lake and that if you were to bring some water from this lake and I were to drink some of that water, I would be cured.' Well, from here it isn't near, perhaps about two hundred versts. In this lake there lives the water tsar and from a distance of fifty versts around he drags people into that lake so that no one can cross over his boundaries because he will grab them and drown them. He [your son] will go, he'll serve you."

So now then. Ivan Medvedevich was with the tsar at that time, and he said, "Your majesty, everything would be fine for me to live in your tsardom except there's one thing wrong."

"What is that, Ivan Medvedevich? Tell me and perhaps we can right this one thing. If it's possible tell me; I'll do everything for you."

He replied: "I would like a horse that would be able to carry me, but very likely there isn't such a horse in your tsardom."

"Listen, Ivan Medvedevich, perhaps there is; there are many horses in this tsardom. I'll immediately give an order and you go about the stables: there are many horses there—you can choose one."

So he wrote out an order to the grooms: "Bring out all your horses and show them to Ivan Medvedevich!" So he went to the stables, gave the grooms the order, and they led out a whole yard full of horses.

"So, Ivan Medvedevich, choose any one you like; other than these we've no more in the tsardom."

So Ivan Medvedevich began walking around among them. Whichever one he laid a hand on would go down on its knees. He said, "No, in this tsardom there isn't a horse for me; I'll go search for a horse elsewhere."

So he left the tsardom and set off looking. He walked and walked, he walked along the road, and then he saw a little hut. "I'll stop by this little hut and get some advice from whoever lives here."

Now in this little hut there lived an enchantress. He entered the little hut and saw an old granny sitting there. "Greetings, granny! Maybe you are my auntie as I have no relatives, excepting only my mother."

"Greetings, Ivan Medvedevich! It's a good thing you came here to see me. I've been waiting for you for a long time and I know why you have come." Granny was very pleased by his little speech where he called her "auntie." "Sit down, my son, I'll tell you."

So he sat down at the table, of course, and the little old granny started questioning him and feeding him.

"So you see, granny, this is the matter I've come to you about: give me a hand or help me or tell me what I'm going to ask you."

"Speak, speak, my son, but I know why you've come here."

"I came here, auntie, because I don't have a horse: where can I get one? I have a good enough club, but I didn't get a horse: there's no horse in the tsardom that will do."

"Yes, Ivan Medvedevich, on account of that club you are going to endure a lot of suffering—you won't even be alive. But I will give you a horse. Listen to me and I will tell you everything. You'll soon get a horse. Just go outside and shout: 'Sivko-Burko—Magic Raven Horse, stand before me like a leaf on grass.' He will appear to you, but don't you immediately take him—just when you need him; just call out his name, and he will be there. And then come back to me in this hut."

He went out and shouted: "Sivko-Burko—Magic Raven Horse, appear before me like a leaf on grass." Suddenly the horse came running, smoke pouring from its ears in a pillar, and from its nostrils flames spurted. It ran up, and stood before him as if fixed to the ground.

"So then, Ivan Medvedevich, tell me, what service may I perform for you? I am always ready: just remember me and I will help you in everything. Only don't make any mistakes yourself!"

"Alright. Go, then Burko, you're not needed right now."

And the horse disappeared. He went back into the hut to his auntie. He came in to that auntie in her hut and she said, "Well, did you see the horse?"

"I saw him."

"Now he will serve you in faith and truth. Now sit down and I will tell you how nonetheless you won't be alive. When you got hold of that club and you killed the ten bogatyrs, the eleventh hid and has taken up with your mother, and he's living even now. And that bogatyr thought up a task for you, and now you will go and fulfill it. There is a lake two hundred versts from here and in it there lives the water spirit, and he drags people into the lake regardless of who is riding by—a bogatyr or anybody else. You will go but just do as your horse tells you, fulfill everything even though it will be difficult for you. Only take that club with you. And when you are coming back—it will be a simple matter to take some water—take some water of course, and they will give you some wine to drink. They'll get you pretty much drunk and ask you, 'Tell us, son, where is your soul? We can't kill you if you don't have a soul.' And you reply to her [mother], 'My soul is in a besom.' And then you leave. They will of course burn that besom, but they won't find anything. And I'll tell you where your soul is—only it won't be your soul but your death. And then you'll go on farther for a second time to where there's a three-headed serpent. And in that garden is a hornless devil, and he'll be complaining that he can't stay mounted on a horse. And your horse will tell you what you have to do there and you will have to bring all the youths back to the tsardom. When you have completed this second task, she [your mother] will again give you much wine to drink and ask, 'Tell me, my son, where is your soul?' And you will tell her, 'My soul is in a horse's tail.' He will go and summon your horse, and he will come and get hold of its tail and pull out a hair, burn it, but you will remain alive. And then when you ride off for the third time, you will come upon a little hut where there are three serpents and where a tsar's daughter has been hidden, but she's not from this tsardom. You and she will get acquainted and you will kill that serpent and you will marry her. For the third time she will give you much to drink. They will give you a lot to drink and you will certainly tell her. And this is where your soul is: on your chest there is a button, and your soul is in this button. Remember this, my son, as she will cut off this button and kill you. Remember all of this, my son, you will not be returning here once your horse comes running to you."

And with these words he went to the tsardom, said goodbye to the old granny and thanked her for everything she had told him. And then he went to his mother.

When he had come to his mother, she was lying there ill, and she said to him: "What is it, my son, why haven't you visited me for so long: I'm really very sick."

"What's the matter with you, mama, tell me. There are many doctors: they will come and perhaps help you. I have been so slow because I was out searching for a horse, but I didn't find one."

Then she said, "I have already been treated, my son, doctors have been here, but they can't find the illness. But just today in a dream I saw that there is a lake two hundred versts from here and if you were to bring some water to me from this lake for me to drink and bathe in, I would be cured."

"Alright, mother, if that's it, I'll go after it. Perhaps you will get well."

And so he set off, but he stopped on the way at the tsar's. The tsar received him and asked, "Well, Ivan Medvedevich, did you find yourself a horse in our tsardom?"

"No, your majesty, I didn't find one in your tsardom, but even if not in yours, I found one that can carry me. Then I was gone for a long time; now I'm going out riding on my horse, to get acquainted with this area, and then I'll come back. Now I'll take my club and set off."

"Go then, Ivan Medvedevich, wherever you like, only don't go across the border where there's that lake—so that the water tsar won't drown you, as I've heard he does."

"No, your majesty, I won't go there."

They parted; he took his club, and set out walking out of the city. When he was out of the city, he shouted for his horse. The horse came running: the ground shook, dust came out of its ears in a pillar, and from its nostrils flames spurted. It drew up next to him and stopped, of course. He took his club and put on his bogatyr's armor, got on, and they rode off. Very soon they crossed that border, and that water tsar started pulling them into the lake. Then the horse said to him, "So now then, Ivan Medvedevich, grab hold of that tree trunk. I can't hold on anymore, but you are still young."

So he grabbed the trunk up next to his belly, and pulled it out by its roots. "Grab hold of another."

He grabbed another, but the water spirit kept on pulling. The lake was already close. The horse said to him, "Well, Ivan Medvedevich, if you can hold on to the last oak, the one standing next to the water, we'll be alright: if not, he'll drown us both."

So he rode up to that oak and grabbed hold tightly, and the water spirit couldn't pull him any further and went back into the water. He stood next to the water waiting to see what would happen next. And the water spirit went to his tsardom and said, "Well, son, go and ask who it is that's come here; I pulled him up to the lake and worked up a great sweat, but I couldn't pull him in. Go and ask whoever it is what he needs. I will pay him tribute since he came here. He was so heavy to pull. So take and carry him a bag of gold and maybe he'll go away."

So the son came, carrying a bag of gold. He came and said, "Who are you, young man, and what do you need? My father has sent you this bag of gold: he's so worn out now that he didn't come himself."

And Ivan Medvedevich answered him, "Leave the bag and go and tell your father that if he doesn't come here himself, I'll stir up your entire lake and torment all you devils, and destroy all your tsardom."

The son came and told his father. The father was very frightened. "He was really a heavy weight; this is probably going to turn out bad. I'll go to him."

He took two more bags of gold, thinking to buy himself off. He hadn't yet got there when the horse said ahead of time: "Listen, Ivan Medvedevich, the moment you see him, he'll give you the gold and you say, 'Leave the gold,' then hit him with your club, jump on him, and ride to his tsardom; I'll be right behind you. There we'll fetter him and he'll never get away from us. I'll grab the gold and bring it to you."

Then the water spirit came with the two bags and said, "What do you need, young man? I've brought you some gold; will this be enough? Then go back home."

So then he said to him, "Listen, water tsar, now you must take me to the tsardom and with the gold, and there I'll let you go back. And if you don't do what I've said, then what I said will happen: I'll tear you all up."

Then he said, "Alright, if that's it, then I'll take you."

And he leapt on him and they rode off, while the horse collected the gold and went on behind them. And as he ran through the woods, the whole wood bowed, and he struck him occasionally with his club, but just lightly. When they came running into the tsardom itself, then he struck that water spirit hard with the club so that he fell down; he immediately fettered him in chains and said, "Now listen! If you howl or frighten people, I'll kill you, but for now just stay here as you are."

Then he let his horse go. "So go now, my good little horse, go and roam until I need you again."

He grabbed up the gold and went to the tsar. He brought it to the tsar and said, "So, your majesty, the water spirit gave me three bags of gold for ransom so that I wouldn't kill him."

The tsar was amazed. "Is it possible that you, Ivan Medvedevich, have been at the water tsar's?"

"Well, come on then, I've even brought him here if you don't believe me: I rode here on him. Let's go and I'll show him to you—and there's nothing to be afraid of."

So that tsar, of course, heard him out with astonishment and he summoned all his boyars and they went to look at that place where the water spirit was chained up. When they got there, all the people were afraid and marveled at him. They had never seen such a thing; they had heard how he dragged off people but they had never seen him. And he [Ivan Medvedevich] walked about him, stroked him, and said, "If you bite anyone or shout out, just you remember what you were told!"

Of course, the water spirit said, "No, Ivan Medvedevich, I won't do anything; I'm just hoping for mercy from you."

"Well, you just get through everything and you'll get your mercy."

And all the people came and got interested, looking at him. And that bogatyr found out that he had arrived on the water spirit. So he said to [Ivan Medvedevich's] mother: "Now there's no other way to kill him except that when he brings you the water, you drink it and say 'No, this won't cure me, but now I'm going to treat you to some vodka.' And then when you've given him the vodka, say 'Likely there's no death for you, if the water spirit can't kill you.' He will tell you where his death is hidden."

So then he came up to his mother and brought her the water. "Now, mama, I've fulfilled your request and brought you the water."

She drank it and said, "Now, my son, since you've fulfilled my request, I'll treat you to some vodka." She brought it in whole buckets in order to get him drunk. And she started giving him all this wine [vodka] to drink. He drank and drank but didn't get drunk and he thought, "I'd better pretend that I'm drunk."

Then she said, "Listen, my son, you've driven that water thing here that used to drag people in, so probably you don't have a soul. Tell me where your soul is kept or where your death is!"

"Why, mother, is my death so necessary to you, what's it to you?"

"Why it's nothing, it's just that I just asked: it would be interesting to know."

"If you want to know, see that whisk broom you use to sweep the hut: that's where my death is!"

She was overjoyed. "Alright, my son, it's all the same where it is; you are mortal just the same."

He left. He went away and came to the tsar and spent some time there, while he was free. The bogatyr returned. "Well, did he tell you?"

"He did."

"And was he really drunk?"

"No, he can handle a lot."

"Well, since he's such a bogatyr, you have to give him a lot. So, where is his death? Did he say?"

"Yes, he told me: it's a simple thing. His death is near us—there, just next to the threshold. Go and burn that little broom: he'll die."

So they were overjoyed. They took the whisk broom and threw it into the stove. And then what? They burned up the broom, but he was still alive! They found out that he was alive, walking about; nothing had worked and he had fooled them.

Then they thought up another trick: it was sure not to fail.

"Listen, pretend once more that you're sick; he'll soon come. Far from here, of course, there is a garden, and in this garden are the living and the dead waters. And in this garden there lives a lion-beast next to a hornless devil, and this very hornless devil is chained to a wall and howls such that people fall down from fright. You tell him to bring a plant from there, but the living and dead waters we don't need. And then when he gets there, the lion-beast will of course kill him. So fine. You pretend to be sick and say: 'I need some of this plant from that garden.' And if he gets it, we'll get him drunk again and find out where his death is: otherwise, nothing good will come of it."

So some time passed and again he came to his mother, and his mother was lying there. "What's the matter with you, mother?"

"Oh, my son, my son! I've fallen ill, and no matter how I've tried to get better,

I can't get well. If only you could fulfill my dream! There is a garden, of course not near here, and in this garden are some plants, and if I could eat them, I would get better."

"Alright, mother, I'll do it for you."

And so he left the hut and went to the tsar. "Well, Ivan Medvedevich, what's new with you, why such despair?"

"It's nothing, your majesty, I need to go away and rid myself of this sadness."

"Go then, but don't go away from me altogether. This tsardom will be yours, as I promised."

So then he went out of the city, of course, taking his club, and he shouted: "Sivko-Burko!" The horse came running.

"So now then, Ivan Medvedevich, where are we going?"

"We're going to such and such a place."

"Oh, Ivan Medvedevich, that won't be good for us, but alright. Along the way there'll be a three-headed serpent, and you will easily deal with that, so mount up."

So he got on, of course, and they rode off. They rode and they rode and they rode. They rode until they came up to three roads. And there was written: "You shall not live—no through passage."

"Let's ride that way!"

They rode off. Then from far off they saw a silver house standing there, incredibly beautiful, shining for all the world. Then the horse spoke: "This is where the serpent lives!" He had no sooner said that than the serpent flew out. "Now deal with it!"

He suddenly swung with his club and two heads flew off; he swung a second time and the third flew off. Having killed it off, he entered the little house. There sat some fair maiden, just like a berry she was. She sat there, crying. So when he had entered the little house, he said, "Greetings, beautiful tsarevna! Why are you crying?"

"Why should I not cry; I was kidnapped by this serpent and have been living here for three years. Now I see, bogatyr, that you have killed the serpent; tell me about yourself, who are you?"

"I am called Ivan Medvedevich, but listen a moment: I'll go out to my horse and give him some wheat: then, we'll talk."

The horse said to him, "Listen, Ivan Medvedevich. Don't marry her right away, but leave her here and when the time is right, then you can take her. Let her live here. She has enough of everything she needs. Only don't forget to take some living and dead water, and either leave it with her or give it to me. Now go to her."

He went in to her. During that time she had prepared everything: the table, everything on it, and some vodka. Then she said to him, "Tell me, Ivan Medvedevich, are you going to take me away from here or not?"

He said: "Alright, beautiful tsarevna, I'll marry you and take you away from here, but in fact it won't be right now. Later on either I myself will come for you, or my horse will. Get on it, don't worry about a thing, and you'll be there! In the meanwhile, go on living here; no one will bother you."

Then he spent a full day with her and set off, and she stayed there crying. "Will Ivan Medvedevich come for me, or not?" She was living well there, you see.

But they rode up to that garden. The horse heard this deep shouting from afar and said, "Listen, Ivan Medvedevich, pull a hair out of my tail and tie it around your head; your head won't be able to stand the shouting: then we'll ride into the garden."

He pulled a hair out and tied it around his head, and then they rode up to the garden. But then the lion-beast rushed at him: he hit him with his club—once, twice—and the lion was pacified and said, "Whatever you need, Ivan Medvedevich, take it."

Meanwhile, the lion-beast strained at the chain and roared with all its might. But Ivan Medvedevich, of course, got down from his horse and took the plant and grabbed some of the living and dead water. He stuck it in his pocket and went up to the lion-beast. He quieted down, sat there, and said nothing to it, as if he had gone away. Then he said, "Listen here, Lion-beast, if you don't pull me to my country, I'll kill all of you, and destroy all your livelihood. But if you pull me there, then so be it."

"Alright, I'll pull you there, but then you go away from here."

"Well, I'll go then."

Right away he handed that living and dead water over to his horse, and then he got on. The lion-beast galloped away and just stumps and roots were scattered after him. And the horse handed over the living and dead water to the girl, and came on afterward. And he rode and rode and rode and then he came to the tsardom to that place where the water tsar was. He took up the chains, forged them together, and said, "If you lunge or roar, I'll kill you."

Well, what could they do? There was nothing they could do. They sat there. He let his horse loose and went in to the tsar. When he came before the tsar: "So now then, your majesty, I went to that garden where there was that lion-beast, maybe you've heard of it, and I brought it here: come and take a look. And there's another wonder there; it will have to be brought in too."

The tsar was greatly astonished. He summoned his subjects and went to look. "Well, Ivan Medvedevich, take my tsardom; if you can deal with them, while they would devour us, probably. . . ."

"Don't be afraid, your majesty, they won't touch you."

So everybody went to have a look, they were all interested. After that he said, "I guess I'll go round to my mother and take her the plant; perhaps it will comfort her."

So he came to his mother and gave her the plant. "So now, mother, get well; since you couldn't before, I brought this for you."

And again they thought of giving him wine to drink and asking him how he was to die. So his mother said, "Well, son, since you have performed such a service for me, I shall treat you to nothing less than some vodka."

And they brought him so much wine; they fixed it all so that he would get drunk. So he sat down, didn't refuse them, and started drinking. He drank; he drank that wine until he had drunk about all of it. And although he got tipsy, he wasn't really drunk. And again she started questioning him: "Now, my son, tell me, where is your soul? If no one on earth can kill you, likely you don't even have one."

"Why do you need my soul, mother? Probably you want to kill me, don't you? Have I done anything harmful to you: I have performed all your requests, but probably you want to kill me."

"Of course not, son, why? I'm only asking point blank: what interest would I have in killing you?"

"Then if you have no interest but you just want to find out, my soul is in my horse's tail; I have no soul about me."

"Oh, alright."

He left and that bogatyr came in and she said, "When he was drunk, he said it was in his horse's tail."

"Oh, alright. I know where that horse is: it's with a certain old woman wizard. I'll shout and it will come out."

He took his sword and, you know, he went out of the city and shouted in a seaman's voice. The horse thought it was his master and flew to him. Suddenly he saw that it wasn't his master, so he flicked his tail, and ran back. But he managed to swing his sword and a hair fell out. He was overjoyed, so he took the hair and went off home. He brought it home and threw it into the stove; they burned it up. It burned of course, but he saw that he was walking around alive!

"So now what! He's deceived us again! Alright, we'll have to send him again."

Again she pretended to be ill and she sent him to that garden again, to fetch some berries from the very highest trees, and that devil, when he breaks his chains, will make quick work of him. But then not very long after he again came to his mother, and his mother once more was lying there ill. He asked, "What is this, mama? Are you sick again?"

"Of course I'm sick—I never got well. If you would only go there again and get some berries from high in the tree, I'll eat a few and get well."

"Oh well, what shall I do? I'll go."

And he went to the tsar again. He came to the tsar and the tsar said to him, "So now then, Ivan Medvedevich, you should get married—that wouldn't be bad at all. I am already old and you should take over the throne."

"But how would I go about finding a bride?"

"But you'll have no trouble finding one. Just say in which tsardom you want to look, and there will be a bride for you because your great fame has gone throughout the entire world. They are already coming here to us taking an interest in such a groom."

"But your highness, I am still young; I have time to get married. First I have to go and bring back one more wonder and then I'll get married."

"Oh, Ivan Medvedevich, then go. I won't say anything to you and then afterward you can get married."

So he took his club and went to his horse. When the horse came running up, he got on and they rode off. They came to that beautiful tsarevna. He rode up to the little silver house, went in, and she was very glad; she began entertaining him and said, "Well, Ivan Medvedevich, will you take me now?"

"No, my beautiful, I can't take you right now; I have to go get that hornless devil, and then I'll come for you."

"What do you mean, Ivan Medvedevich? He'll kill you with just a shout and then I'll remain here my whole life without you."

"No, don't be afraid of a thing; just stay here and I'll come right after you."

So they stayed there one whole day and then he rode off to that devil. They rode up to the garden and the horse said, "Pull out one more hair and tie it around your head. We'll ride into the garden and he'll howl at you with all his might until you hit him with your club."

So he tied the hair around his head, they rode up to the garden and that hornless devil howled so loudly, trying to rush at him. He climbed up the tree, picked the berries to comfort his mother, and went up to it. And that devil, lunging and lunging away, broke free and ran at him. He swung his club and hit it once; he hit it a second time and the devil submitted and began pleading with him. "Don't hit me, Ivan Medvedevich, whatever you need—take it; just leave me in peace. Take this garden, and I will protect you any time: just leave me whole!"

Then he said to the devil: "No, I'm not going to leave you here until I teach you, until you take me to my country; there I'll let you all go."

Then he got on him and let him have it with his club. The devil flew as fast as he could with the horse right behind them. So he came to that country and chained him up—the third wonder right there. He let his horse go and came in to the tsar. He came in and he said to the tsar, "If you want to see, your majesty, I've brought you the last wonder; they are all tied up there. If you want, come and see, and then I'll deal with them—I want to see what they'll do next."

"Listen, Ivan Medvedevich, you've brought these three marvels here, but what if they break loose: they'll destroy all our tsardom."

"Don't worry, your majesty, nothing will happen: strike me among the living he shall not!"

So they all went to look and were amazed. And they were all chained to each other, sitting there quietly. The tsar was greatly overjoyed and he went into his palace. The tsar at that time began collecting various princesses and tsarevnas to look at these animals and to let them take a look at Ivan Medvedevich, to see what he was like.

But he went to his mother. He came there, of course, and gave her the berries, which she ate. "Well, thank you, my son, now I'll get well."

Already before that, of course, there was this plot, this agreement, and there's no need to repeat it. Now she said, "Well, my son, I'll treat you some more, and ask, and maybe you'll tell me."

So there was this feasting. And he drank so much that he was completely drunk, and he forgot what the old woman had told him. When he was drunk, his mother came and said, "Tell me the truth, my son, tell me where your soul is hidden; I won't do anything to you. Since you've conquered all those beasts, and brought them and chained them up, it's likely that you don't have a soul."

"You have this desire to kill me, mother," he said.

"Of course not; why would I? I'm just asking."

She poured him out more and more of the wine. "I'll just drink this one glass and then I'll tell you. So, mother, on my chest there's this button, and if you cut off this button, I'll die." And he fell asleep.

Suddenly in came that bogatyr, cut off his button, took him, chopped him into little pieces, and threw him outside. The tsar, of course, knew nothing of this.

Then this horse found out that he was gone, that his master had perished, and he ran to the old woman and neighed so loudly, and stomped the ground with his hooves until the old woman jumped up: this took place at night. She jumped up and ran out onto the porch, and then she asked, "Well, good horse, what has happened to you or has something happened to Ivan Medvedevich?"

"Yes, granny, give me an empty sack and get on."

"Yes," said the old woman, "That's what I told him—to be careful; he probably said something."

Then the old woman quickly got dressed, took an empty sack, got on the horse, and rode off. The horse came to that place where the pieces had been thrown out; crows were already beginning to drag them off. She quick collected all the pieces, put them in the sack, and brought them to her hut. The horse spoke: "Now, granny, you go in and I'll run to the beautiful tsarevna; both the living and the dead water are there."

And the granny sat down and said, "Alright, little horse, you go and if you can, save Ivan Medvedevich."

The horse ran off there. He got there and struck so hard, he neighed and hit the porch with his hoof. The tsarevna ran out onto the porch, frightened. "What is this, what's happened, I've never heard such a racket." And the horse stood there with the bag on his back. She began questioning him: "Why, dear little horse, are you shouting so loudly? I've never heard such shouting from you before: has something happened to Ivan Medvedevich?"

And he said to her: "Don't ask me now; just get dressed and come out; you'll see your Ivan Medvedevich, but now bring some of the living and dead water."

She gasped. She quickly ran off, got dressed, and brought out the two vials that the horse had brought her. And then when she had come out, he said, "Now take down this sack and shake what's in it, and then you'll see what happens. Sprinkle it with the dead water, and then after the dead water sprinkle it with the living."

She immediately took down the sack and began shaking the bits of the dead human body and she asked, "Who is this?"

"When you've sprinkled it, you'll see, but now I won't say: you mustn't know."

So she right away sprinkled it—and the body came together; she sprinkled it with the living water, and out jumped Ivan Medvedevich. "Oh, how long I slept!"

And standing opposite he saw the beautiful tsarevna and his horse. Then the horse spoke up: "Yes, Ivan Medvedevich, if it weren't for me, you wouldn't be alive. Thanks to your mother, you told her, and they killed you, and if it weren't for me, you wouldn't be alive. And she won't find you again, but she'll try some more if you leave her."

Then the tsarevna took him by the hands, led him into the hut, and began treating him as her guest. "Well, Ivan Medvedevich, tell me the truth: will you take me away from here? Will I have to languish here alone for even longer?"

He said, "No, beautiful tsarevna. You won't be parted from me again; you won't remain behind again. Now all has passed me by: they won't catch me again. Get on and we'll be off."

"She said to him: "But, Ivan Medvedevich, what shall we do with this little house? It's silver after all, and in your tsardom there is no such little house."

"I really don't know; our horse can't carry off our house—only you and me—we'll have to leave it here."

"No, Ivan Medvedevich, we won't leave it here, we'll take it with us." She brought an empty egg and said, "Now, Ivan Medvedevich, blow in this egg and see what happens."

So he blew, and the house disappeared. He stuck the egg in his pocket; they got on and rode off. Along the way she said to him, "Listen, Ivan Medvedevich, you really haven't paid much heed in the past, but listen to me this time."

"What is it, tell me, beautiful tsarevna?"

"I haven't seen my father or my mother, do you know for how long? For eight years. I would really like to see my father and mother. It would really be good to drop in on my father and mother, and then go to your tsardom, where you live. I won't say anything that's bad where you live, I've nothing against it, but I would really like to see my family, since I was their only daughter."

So then he said, "Listen, beautiful tsarevna, and I'll tell you something. We won't be going to your tsardom right now. And here's why: if your father and mother come to our tsardom to look at those animals, those beasts I brought there, then we'll see them, and we'll all be joyful together. But now we have to go to our tsardom because the tsar doesn't know about me, where I have been, whether I've been captured—they don't know."

So then they rode into the tsar's courtyard, and she said, "Now take that egg out and break it on that broad square opposite the palace, and you'll see what happens."

So he pulled the egg out of his pocket, broke it on the broad square opposite the royal palace, and the silver palace appeared. And he tied up his horse and went into the palace. The tsar chanced to look out the window: "What's this? Something's changed. There's a silver palace standing such as has never been in our tsardom before."

And he right away set off to look at the palace. He looked, and Ivan Medvedevich and his wife were sitting at the table. He gasped: "Where did you come from, Ivan Medvedevich, with your young bride?"

"Sit down at the table with me and I'll tell you everything." Then he asked him, "Well then, your majesty, have all the guests gathered for the feast?"

"All were just waiting for you, Ivan Medvedevich, the conqueror, but they were afraid to go out and look at the beasts."

"Are they still here?"

"They are still there chained up."

"Then let's go, and I'll tell you where I've been this time and what happened to me."

They had only just gone in to the feast and first of all her mother and father caught sight of them. "Aha! Our daughter's coming with Ivan Medvedevich, who conquered the eleven bogatyrs and saved our daughter."

The tsar went ahead and sat them down at the place of honor. Her father and mother could not remain seated at the table and came running to their daughter. "Greetings, our dear daughter! Where have you been all this time, what sort of kidnapper kidnapped you, and how were you rescued by this Ivan Medvedevich?"

And then he spoke up, did Ivan Medvedevich: "Listen, papa and mama, you sit down and I'll tell you everything, and she'll affirm it. Now we have time for such a joyful celebration."

They sat down and were just happy that she was alive. And then he said: "Listen and I'll tell my wife to tell about the serpent, and then I'll finish telling the rest."

So then she began: "Listen papa and mama; when I went out walking, you, of course, don't know that a serpent dragged me off and kept me for three years. Of course, I lived well, with plenty of everything, and I had this little silver house, which is now here. And I lived there for these three years until Ivan Medvedevich happened to ride up and he killed that serpent. And he kept me those three years while he dealt with his various affairs. And he was in such an unfortunate situation that his horse brought him on his back all chopped up, but all this business was resolved."

Then she fell silent and Ivan Medvedevich began speaking: "You know, your majesty, that I was gone so long, and your guests were kept so long. I was in such an unfortunate situation because my mother killed me; I was dead, and I know who is responsible for my death. My mother actually killed me, but for whose sake she killed me—this I know, too. When I dragged this club down from the mountain, there were only ten bogatyrs as the eleventh had hidden. He got acquainted with my mother, and they had to kill me off. Twice they got me drunk on wine, and then the third time I drank so much that they killed me. But I have this faithful horse and he saved me and we had enough of the living and dead waters. And then fortunately my horse served me again, gathering my body into a bag, together with an old woman who always gave advice, he brought me to this beautiful tsarevna, which she herself can affirm. And now I've just come from there."

The tsar gasped: "Well, Ivan Medvedevich, you have endured so much: take my throne now: I am renouncing it. And do what you will with your mother and that bogatyr—even kill them if you want."

And all the guests looked at Ivan Medvedevich and at his wife and were amazed at his bravery and strength. Then he said, "Alright, let them live; the time will come when I will deal with them."

And their feast continued for six days. Then after the end of the feast he said, "So now then, guests, come and I'll show you the beasts that I collected."

And he ordered the smiths to forge nine iron rods, and it was done. And all the guests set off to look. When they had all arrived, they all stood back. He said, "Don't be afraid of a thing; nothing will happen to you."

He took an iron rod, went up to the water tsar, and began whipping him. The water tsar pleaded, begging, "Do whatever you wish, only don't kill me; strike me and take what you want: if it's gold or anything else, only leave me alive."

And then he broke three rods and set upon the lion-beast. And when he had beaten up the lion, he left him and said, "Now remember, I'll send people to that garden of yours, and we'll see how you treat them."

Then he took after the hornless devil and gave him the same treatment as he had the others. And then he sent them all back to their places. Then all the guests returned back to the feast and began thanking Ivan Medvedevich for his hospitality and then they departed; only her mother and father remained.

After all that he became tsar, and he invited her mother and father to his palace. "Come and eat with me."

He entertained them for three whole days and then he said, "Well, papa and mama, live here if you like; if not, you are free to go."

Of course, they were sorry to leave, and his father-in-law said to him, "Well, son-in-law, now you come visit us."

"Alright, there will be time for that, and then I'll come, but right now I have some business."

Then, of course, he wished them all the best, and he and his wife went off to sleep. He slept through the night and said to his wife, "Now I'll send some soldiers to that lake and that garden and we'll find out how they are treated, and then I'll deal with those other two."

The next day he sent a detachment of soldiers, of course. When they came to the lake, they began bathing, and the water tsar was so frightened that they were going to drown him: he swam far, far away until he reached the other shore. They swam and then set off for the garden. They came to the garden and the lion-beast stood at the gates, bowing. "Please, do come in!"

And that hornless devil stood next to the oak and he didn't say a word to the soldiers. They walked about, they strolled about the garden, filling their pockets with various fruits, and then they went on. They came back to the tsardom and Ivan Medvedevich asked them, "Well, lads, how did the water tsar greet you?"

"Very well. The water tsar was so frightened that he didn't even set foot on the shore."

"And how were the lion-beast and the devil?"

"The devil didn't say anything, and the lion-beast even bowed. He gave us various fruits and we walked about the garden for a long time."

"Well that's good, that's very good."

Then it was evening, it was about ten o'clock in the evening, and he said, "Well, wife, now I'm going to my mother."

"Why? Why, Ivan Medvedevich? They'll get you drunk and kill you."

"No, that won't happen. They can only kill me if they kill my horse and dry his bones for three years, and the horse won't let them kill him. And I'll tell them nothing about it."

He took his club and set out. He came there and they were sitting and eating supper.

"I've come to visit you, I, Ivan Medvedevich. Do as you wish."

His mother immediately swooned, fell on her knees; he took the club and gave it to that bogatyr such that only a wet spot remained.

"Well, mother, I'll give you no mercy." And he killed her. The next day he ordered them to bury her. He came back to his wife and said, "Well, wife, now I've dealt with them both."

After that he began living and dwelling and ruling his country until old age. And with that we'll finish.

Story Credits

For bibliographic information see the corresponding listing in Sources Cited in Russian. The number following each short citation indicates either a tale number or a page number.

I. Animal Tales

1. Sister Fox and the Wolf. *Afanas'ev 1.*
2. The Peasant, the Bear, and the Fox. *Afanas'ev 24.*
3. The Pig Set Off for the Games. *Pomerantseva 17.*
4. The Fox as Keener. *Afanas'ev 21.*
5. The Fox as Confessor. *Afanas'ev 16.*
6. A Wolf—Gray and Daring. *Pomerantseva 3.*
7. The Fox and the Jug. *Kretov 5.*
8. The Bear and the Beam. *Matveeva 37.*
9. The Peasant, the Bear, the Fox, and the Gadfly. *Afanas'ev 48 and Afanas'ev: Geneva 5.*
10. The Case of the Beekeeper and the Bear. *Zhivaia starina 1911, I, pp. 124–26.*
11. The Bear. *Afanas'ev 57.*
12. The Mushrooms. *Afanas'ev 90.*
13. The Sun, the Wind, and the Moon. *Pudozh 5.*

II. Tales of Heroes and Villains

14. Nikita the Tanner. *Otechestvennye zapiski, 1857, CXIII, pp. 427–30.*
15. Ivan the Mare's Son. *Khudiakov 5.*
16. Maria Morevna. *Afanas'ev 159.*
17. The Witch and the Sun's Sister. *Afanas'ev 93.*
18. The Milk of Wild Beasts. *Afanas'ev 202.*
19. Baba Yaga and the Nimble Youth. *Afanas'ev 106.*
20. Ivan Tsarevich and the Gray Wolf. *Gurevich-Eliasov 24.*

21. The Maiden Tsar. *Afanas'ev 232.*
22. Elena the Wise. *Afanas'ev 237.*
23. The Frog Tsarevna. *Afanas'ev 269.*
24. The Petrified Tsarevna. *Balashov 3.*
25. Fenist the Bright Falcon Feather. *Khudiakov 39.*
26. How the Tsar's Daughter Came to Know Need. *Smirnov 179.*
27. Go Where You Know Not Where, Bring Back You Know Not What. *Afanas'ev 214.*
28. The Mare's Head. *Lutovinova 20.*
29. Baba Yaga. *Afanas'ev 103.*
30. The Swan-Geese. *Afanas'ev 113.*
31. Vasilisa the Beautiful. *Smirnov 294.*

III. Tales of Magic

32. A Prince and His "Uncle." *Afanas'ev 123.*
33. The Golden Slipper. *Afanas'ev 292.*
34. Burenushka the Little Red Cow. *Afanas'ev 101.*
35. Sivko-Burko. *Afanas'ev 179.*
36. The Pig with the Golden Bristles. *Afanas'ev 183.*
37. Dirty Face. *Smirnov 214.*
38. Ivan Tsarevich, the Gray Wolf, and Elena the Most Beautiful. *Azadovskii, Verkhnelenskie skazki 13.*
39. The Rejuvenating Apples. *Balashov 27.*
40. The Three Sons-in-Law. *Azadovskii 30.*
41. The Everlasting Piece. *Bardin 208.*
42. Little Boy Green. *Zhivaia starina 1895, pp. 424–26.*
43. The Fiddler in Hell. *Afanas'ev 371.*
44. The Snow Maiden. *Skazki XIX c. 33.*
45. The Armless Maiden. *Afanas'ev 279.*

IV. Legends

46. The Poor Widow. *Afanas'ev Legends 3a.*
47. The Serpent. *Ivanitskii 18.*
48. The Hermit and the Devil. *Afanas'ev 20b.*
49. The Proud Rich Man. *Afanas'ev Legends (24, pp. 134–37).*
50. The Bigamist. *Smirnov 95.*
51. The Old Woman in Church. *Skazki XVIII, c. p., 9.*
52. The Golden Saucer and the Silver Apple. *Mitropol'skaia 65.*
53. Kas'ian and Nikolai. *Afanas'ev Legends 11.*
54. Why Women Lost Their Rights. *Soboleva 36.*

55. A Tale of a Drunkard. *Afanas'ev Legends 22.*
56. Who Brought Vodka to Rus. *Erlenvein 31.*
57. The Forest Spirit. *Rozhdestvenskaia 60.*
58. The Skomorokh Vavilo. *Sadovnikov 98.*

V. Tales of Love and Life

59. The Self-Playing Gusli. *Afanas'ev 238.*
60. About Ivan the Fool. *Kupriiianikha 65.*
61. The Philosopher and the Cripple. *Onchukov 242.*
62. The Soldier Erema the Crafty. *Zinov'ev 82.*
63. The Peasant and the Devil. *Kaluga, pp. 97–101.*
64. The White-Bearded Old Man. *Onchukov 15.*
65. The Tsar and the Two Craftsmen. *Akimova 383.*
66. The Wise Seven-Year-Old Girl. *Mitropol'skaia 39.*
67. Tsar Peter and the Clever Woman. *Onchukov 49.*
68. The Clever Daughter (or the Dispute over a Colt). *Zinov'ev 64.*
69. How I Became Head of the Division. *Onchukov neizd. 55.*
70. The Merchant's Daughter. *Balashov 66.*
71. A Hunter Rescues a Maiden. *Tumilevich 22.*
72. The Woman from the Grave. *Onchukov 120.*
73. About Savvushka. *Kovalev 29.*
74. The Son-in-Law Teaches His Wife and Mother-in-Law. *Zelenin:Viatka 18.*
75. How Peter and a Hunter Went Hunting. *Moskovskie skazki 73.*
76. Peter the Great Ate the *Murzovka. Potiavin. 31.*
77. The Carefree Monastery. *Gurevich 48.*
78. Why There Is Treason in Rus. *Rybnikov II, 219.*
79. Eaten by a Wolf. *Afanas'ev Legends, no. 32, note on pp. 172–73.*
80. How a Lad Bought Wisdom. *Gospodarev 40.*
81. Why They Stopped Banishing Old Men. *Mitropol'skaia 84.*
82. How the Bear Killed the Robbers. *Kupriiianikha 56.*
83. The Soldier and Death. *Rozhdestvenskaia 12.*
84. The Golden Pitcher. *Korol'kova, pp. 288–90.*
85. Peter the Great and the Three Soldiers. *Zelenin: Perm 97D, pp. 350–51.*
86. The Monk and the Abbess. *Afanas'ev rukopisi 91.*

VI. Tales of Clever Fools

87. Balda the Laborer. *Na rubezhe, 1946, no. 4, pp. 62–66.*
88. The Laborer and the Priest. *Blinova 8.*
89. Horns. *Karnaukhova 3.*
90. How Klimka Stole the Landlord's Wife. *Gerasimov 34.*

91. Shabarsha the Laborer. *Afanas'ev 151.*
92. About a Sly Peasant and a Priest. *Aristova, pp. 51–52.*
93. About Egibikha (Baba Yaga). *Onchukov zavet. 15.*
94. A Lad Who Watched *Rusalki. Tumilevich 17.*
95. The Tsar and the Peasant. *Tseitlin 6.*
96. The Peasant and the Devil. *Onchukov 67.*
97. The Devil Takes the Soldier's Watch. *Afanas'ev Legends, pp. 120–23.*
98. Whence Came Baba Yaga. *Serebrennikov 19.*
99. The Wizard. *Chudinskii 26.*

VII. Anecdotes

100. The Dog Tsuvarnachka. *Khudiakov 35.*
101. Those Folk from Pskov. *Skazki XIX V. 118.*
102. A Tailor or a Crayfish. *Afanas'ev Gruzinskii bb, pp. 417–18.*
103. The Mare's Egg. *Zelenin: Viatka 130.*
104. Kostia. *Onchukov 50.*
105. The Lord of the Manor. *Korol'kova, pp. 351–55.*
106. How the Soldier Stole the Speck. *Soboleva 74.*
107. Unsalted Custard. *Andronikov p. 140.*
108. If You Don't Like It, Don't Listen! *Afanas'ev 422.*
109. The Turnip. *Zelenin: Perm 82.*
110. Roundsides. *Afanas'ev 36, Pomerantseva 21.*
111. The Sad Story of a Raven. *Balashov 94.*

VIII. Serial Tales from the Far North

112. Fear-Bogatyr. *Pudozh 26.*
113. Ondrei the Shooter. *Korguev 2.*
114. Ivan Medvedevich the Bear's Son. *Korguev 14.*

Sources Cited in Russian

Short Citation	Source
Afanas'ev	*Narodnye russkie skazki A.N. Afanas'eva v trekh tomakh.* Ed. L.G. Barag and N.V. Novikov. Moscow, 1984.
Afanas'ev: Geneva	Afanas'ev, A.N. *Russkie zavetnye skazki.* Geneva, 1872. Ed. E. Gracheva and T. Mazepova, Moscow, 1992.
Afanas'ev, Gruzinskii	Afanas'ev, A.N. *Narodnye russkie skazki.* 3rd ed. Moscow, 1897.
Afanas'ev Legends	*Narodnye russkie legendy A.N. Afanas'eva.* Ed. V.S. Kuznetsova. Novosibirsk, 1990.
Afanas'ev rukopisi	Afanas'ev, A.N. *Narodnye russkie skazki ne dlia pechati, zavetnye poslovitsy i pogovorki, sobrannye i obrabotannye A.N. Afans'evym 1857–1862.* Ed. O.V. Alekseeva, V.I. Eremina, E.A. Kostiukhin, and L.V. Bessmertnykh. Moscow, 1997.
Akimova	Akimova, T.N., ed. *Fol'klor Saratovskoi oblasti.* Saratov, 1946.
Andronikov	*Narodnye skazki Kostromskoi gubernii, zapisannye v 90-kh godakh XIX st. A. Andronikovym. Trudy Kostrom. Nauch. Obshchestva po izucheniiu mestnogo kraia.* Issue. I. Kostroma, 1914, pp. 127–41.
Aristova	Aristova, A., and M. Pavlova, eds. *Fol'klor. Chastushki, pesni, skazki, zapisannye v Kurskoi oblasti.* Kursk, 1939.
Azadovskii	Azadovskii, M.K. *Verkhnelenskie skazki. Sbornik M.K. Azadovskogo.* Irkutsk, 1938. (*PSRS,* vol. 13.)
Azadovskii Karelia	Azadovskii, M.K., ed. *Russkie skazki v Karelii (starye zapisi).* Petrozavodsk, 1947.
Balashov	Balashov, D.M., ed. *Skazki Terskogo berega Belogo moria.* Leningrad, 1970.
Bardin	Bardin, A.V., ed. *Fol'klor Chkalovskoi oblasti.* Chkalov (Orenburg), 1940.
Blinova	Blinova, E.M., ed. *Skazy, pesni, chastushki.* Cheliabinsk, 1937.
Chudinskii	Chudinskii, E.A., comp. *Russkie narodnye skazki, pribautki, i pobasenki.* Moscow, 1864. (*PSRS,* vol. 11.)
Erlenvein	Erlenvein, A.A., ed. *Narodnye skazki, sobrannye sel'skimi uchiteliami Tul'skoi gubernii.* Moscow, 1863. (*PSRS,* vol. 11.)

Gerasimov	Gerasimov, B. *Skazki, sobrannye v Zapadnykh predgor'iakh Altaia.* Zap. Semipalatinsk. otd. Russ. geograf. obshchestva, 1913. Part 7, pp. 1–87.
Gospodarev	Novikov, N.V., ed. S*kazki Filippa Pavlovicha Gospodareva.* Petrozavodsk, 1941.
Gurevich	*Russkie skazki Vostochnoi Sibiri. Sbornik A. Gurevicha.* Irkutsk, 1939.
Gurevich-Eliasov	Gurevich, A.V., and L.E. Eliasov. *Staryi fol'klor Pribaikal'ia.* Ulan-Ude, 1939.
Ivanitskii	Ivanitskii, N.A., ed. *Materialy po etnografii Vologodskoi gubernii. Sbornik svedenii dlia izucheniia byta krest'ianskogo naseleniia Rossii.* Vol. 2. Moscow, 1890.
Kaluga	Vedernikova, N.M., comp. *Fol'klor Kaluzhskoi gubernii v zapisiakh i publikatsiiakh XIX–nachala XX veka.* Moscow, 1998.
Karnaukhova	Karnaukhova, I.V., comp. *Skazki i predaniia Severnogo kraia.* Leningrad, 1934. (*PSRS,* vol. 12.)
Khudiakov	Khudiakov, I.A., ed. *Velikorusskie skazki v zapisiakh I.A. Khudiakova.* Moscow-Leningrad, 1964. (*PSRS,* vol. 6.)
Korguev	Nechaev, A.N. *Skazki M.M. Korgueva.* Petrozavodsk, 1939.
Korol'kova	Pomerantseva, E.V., ed. *Russkie narodnye skazki A.N. Korol'kovoi.* Moscow, 1969.
Kovalev	Sokolov, Iu. M., ed. *Skazki I.F. Kovaleva.* Moscow, 1941.
Kretov	Kretov, A.I., ed. *Narodnye skazki Voronezhskoi oblasti. Sovremennye zapisi.* Voronezh, 1977.
Kupriianikha	Novikova, A.M., and I.A. Ossovetskii, eds. *Skazki Kupriianikhi (A.K. Baryshnikova).* Voronezh, 1937. (*PSRS,* vol. 14.)
Lutovinova	Lutovinova, E.I., ed. *Russkie narodnye skazki o machekhe i padcheritse.* Novosibirsk, 1993.
Matveeva	Matveeva, R.P. and T.G. Leonova, eds. *Russie skazki Sibiri i dal'nego Vostoka: Volshebnye i o zhivotnykh.* Novosibirsk, 1993.
Mitropol'skaia	Mitropol'skaia, N.K., ed. *Russkii fol'klor v Litve.* Vilnius, 1975.
Moskovskie skazki	Vedernikova, N.M., and E.A. Samodelova, comps. and eds. *Fol'klornye sokrovishcha Moskovskoi zemli. Skazki i neskazochnaia proza.* Moscow, 1998.
Na rubezhe	*Na rubezhe. Ezhemes. Lit.-khud. i obshchestvenno-polit. zhurnal.* Petrozavodsk, 1940–60.
Nikiforov	Nikiforov, A.I. "Pobeditel' zmeia." *Sovetskii fol'klor,* nos. 4–5. Moscow and Leningrad, 1936.
Onchukov	Onchukov, N.E., ed. *Severnye skazki.* St. Petersburg, 1908. (*PSRS,* vol. 1.)
Onchukov neizd.	Zhekulina, V.I., ed. *Neizdannye skazki iz sobraniia N.E. Onchukova. Tavdinskie, Shokshozerskie, Samarskie.* St. Petersburg, 2000.
Onchukov zavet.	Eremina, V.V., and Zhekulina, eds. *Zavetnye skazki iz sobraniia N.E. Onchukova.* Moscow, 1996.

Otechestvennye zapiski   *Otvechestvennye zapiski,* 1857, CXIII, pp. 427–30. St. Petersburg, 1839–1884.

Pomerantseva   Pomerantseva, E.V., ed. *Russkie narodnye skazki.* Moscow, 1957.

Potiavin   Potiavin, V., ed. *Narodnaia poeziia Gor'kovskoi oblasti.* Gorky, 1960.

Pudozh   Razumova, A.P., and T.I. Sen'kina, comps. *Russkie narodnye skazki Pudozhskogo kraia.* Petrozavodsk, 1982.

PSRS   *Polnoe sobranie russkikh skazok.* St. Petersburg, 1998.

Rozhdestvenskaia   Rozhdestvenskaia, N.I. *Skazy i skazki Belomor'ia i Pinezh'ia.* Arkhangelsk, 1941.

Rybnikov II   Gruzinskii, A.E., ed. *Pesni, sobrannye P.N. Rybnikovym.* Vols. 1–3. 2nd ed. Moscow, 1909–10.

Sadovnikov   Sadovnikov, D.N., ed. *Skazki i predaniia Samarskogo kraia.* Zapiski RGO. St. Petersburg, 1884. (*PSRL,* vol. 10.)

Serebrennikov   Vershinin, T.I., and G.I. Bomshtein, eds. V.N. Serebrennikov, *Metkoe slovo. Pesni. Skazki. Dorevoliutsionnyi fol'klor Prikam'ia.* Perm, 1964.

Skazki XIX c.   Novikov, N.V., comp. *Russkie skazki v zapisiakh i publikatsiiakh pervoi poloviny XIX v.* Moscow-Leningrad, 1961.

Skazki XVIII c.   Novikov, N.V., comp., *Russkie skazki v rannikh zapisiakh i publikatsiiakh (XVI–XVIII vv.).* Leningrad, 1971.

Smirnov   Smirnov, A.M. *Sbornik velikorusskikh skazok arkhiva Russkogo geograficheskogo obshchestva.* Petrograd, 1917. (*PSRS,* vol. 9.)

Soboleva   Soboleva, N.V., and Kargapolov, N.A., comps. *Russkie skazki Sibiri i Dal'nego Vostoka.* Novosibirsk, 1992.

SUS   *Sravnitel'nyi ukazatel' siuzhetov. Vostochnoslavianskaia skazka.* Comp. L.G. Barag, I.P. Berezovskii, K.P. Kabashnikov, and N.V. Novikov. Leningrad, 1979.

Tseitlin   Tseitlin, G. *Pomorskie narodnye skazki.* Arkhangelsk, 1911.

Tumilevich   Tumilevich, F.V., ed. *Skazki i predaniia kazakov-nekrasovtsev.* Rostov, 1961.

Zelenin: Perm   Zelenin, D.K. *Velikorusskie skazki Permskoi gubernii.* Moscow, 1991. See also, edition by T.G. Ivanova, St. Petersburg, 1997.

Zelenin: Viatka   Zelenin, D.K. *Velikorusskie skazki Viatskoi gubernii.* Zapiski RGO. Petrograd, 1915. (*PSRS,* vol. 7.)

Zhivaia starina   *Zhivaia starina.* 1890–1916. St. Petersburg.

Zinov'ev   Zinov'ev, V.P. *Russkie skazki Zabaikal'ia.* Irkutsk, 1983.

Selected Bibliography
of Works in English

Aarne, Antti, and Stith Thompson. *The Types of the Folktale. A Classification and Bibliography.* 2nd ed., Helsinki, 1987.

Afanas'ev, Aleksandr. *Russian Fairy Tales.* Trans. Norbert Guterman. New York, 1973.

Afanasiev (Afanasyev), Aleksandr N. *Russian Secret Tales. Bawdy Folktales of Old Russia.* Baltimore, 1998.

A–T: see Aarne and Thompson.

ATU: see Uther.

Azadovskii, Mark. *A Siberian Tale Teller.* Austin, TX, 1974.

Bailey, James, and Tatyana Ivanova. *An Anthology of Russian Folk Epics.* Armonk, NY, 1998.

CRF: see Haney.

Haney, Jack V. *The Complete Russian Folktale.* 7 vols. Armonk, NY, 1999–2006.

———. *An Introduction to the Russian Folktale* (*CRF* Vol. 1), 1999.

———. *Russian Animal Tales* (*CRF* Vol. 2), 2000.

———. *Russian Wondertales I. Tales of Heroes and Villains* (*CRF* Vol. 3), 2001.

———. *Russian Wondertales II. Tales of Magic and the Supernatural* (*CRF* Vol. 4), 2001.

———. *Russian Legends* (*CRF* Vol. 5), 2003.

———. *Russian Tales of Love and Life* (*CRF* Vol. 6), 2006.

———. *Russian Tales of Clever Fools* (*CRF* Vol. 7), 2006.

Ivanits, Linda J. *Russian Folk Belief.* Armonk, NY, 1989.

Johns, Andreas. *Baba Yaga. The Ambiguous Mother and Witch of the Russian Folktale.* Series: International Folkloristics, vol. 3. New York, 2004.

Lüthi, Max. *Once Upon a Time. On the Nature of Fairy Tales.* Bloomington, 1976.

———. *The European Folktale: Form and Nature.* Bloomington, 1982.

———. *The Fairytale as Art Form and Portrait of Man.* Bloomington, 1987.

Propp, Vladimir. *Morphology of the Folktale.* 2nd ed., Austin, TX, 1968.

———. *Theory and History of Folklore.* ed. Anatoly Liberman. Minneapolis, 1984.

Thompson, Stith. *Motif-Index of Folk-Literature.* Bloomington, 1955.

———. *The Folktale.* Berkeley, CA, 1977.

Uther, Hans-Jörg. *The Types of International Folktales: A Classification and Bibliography, Based on the System of Antti Aarne and Stith Thompson.* Helsinki, 2004.

Zipes, Jack. *Fairy Tale as Myth. Myth as Fairy Tale.* Lexington, KY, 1994.

Index of Tale Types and Motifs

Folklorists classify folktales by tale type and further by motif number so that versions of a tale or plot, or character elements of different stories, can be compared, both within a single linguistic tradition and internationally. The indexes employed in this anthology are: Antti Aarne and Stith Thompson, *The Types of the Folktale: A Classification and Bibliography* (Helsinki, 1961; 1987), expanded by Hans-Jörg Uther in *The Types of International Folktales* (Helsinki, 2004); the Russian (East Slavic) index to tale types, L.G. Barag, I.P. Berezovskii, K.P. Kabashnikov, and N.V. Novikov, *Sravnitel'nyi ukazatel' siuzhetov. Vostochnoslavianskaia skazka* (Leningrad: Nauka, 1979); and Stith Thompson, *Motif-Index of Folk Literature,* 6 vols. (Bloomington, 1955).

Aarne-Thompson (A–T) Tale Types

A–T number and title: story number

1, The Theft of Fish: 1
2, The Tail-Fisher: 1
3, Sham Blood and Brains: 1
4, Carrying the Sham-Sick Trickster: 1
9, Unjust Partner: 2
30, The Fox Tricks the Wolf into Falling into a Pit: 1
37, The Fox as Nursemaid for the Bear: 4, 109
43, The Bear Builds a House of Wood; the Fox, of Ice: 1
61A, Fox as Confessor: 1, 5, 6
68B, Fox Drowns in a Pot: 7
88, Bear Climbs a Tree to Get Honey but Fails: 8
152, Man Paints the Bear: 9
154, "Bear-food": 2, 3, 4
154**, Bear at the Bee-hive: 10
161A*, The Bear with the Wooden Leg: 11

170, Fox Eats His Fellow-lodger: 1
218B, Cock and Hen Plant Bean: 4
297B, War of the Mushrooms: 12
299, Old Man and Sun, Moon, and Wind: 13
300_2, The Dragon-Slayer: 14, 16
300A, The Fight on the Bridge: 39, 114
301A, Quest for a Vanished Princess: 15, 114
301B, The Three Underground Tsardoms: 15
302, The Ogre's Heart in an Egg: 16, 40, 114
306, The Danced-Out Shoes: 22
313H, Flight from the Witch: 29
313J*, The Sorceress and the Sunshine Sister: 17
314A*, The Bullock-savior: 18
315, The Faithless Sister: 18
315A, The Cannibal Sister: 112, 114
327C, The Children and the Ogre: 19
328, The Boy Steals the Giant's Treasure: 20

400_1 The Man on a Quest for His Lost Wife: 16
400_2 Maiden-Tsar: 21
401_1, Princess Transformed into an Animal: 22, 23
402, An Animal as Bride: 21, 23
403, The Substitute Bride: 34
405, Jorinda and Joringel: 24
410, Sleeping Beauty: 24
432, The Prince as Bird: 25
437, The Supplanted Bride: 26
465A, The Quest for the Unknown: 27, 113
465C, A Journey to the Other World: 27
480, Stepmother and Stepdaughter: 28
480A*, Three Sisters Set out to Save Their Brother: 29, 30
480B*, Girl Sent to Watch for Fire: 31
502, The Wild Man: 32
510A, Cinderella: 33
510B, The Dress of Gold, Silver, and Stars: 112
511, The Little Red Cow: 34
530, Princess on the Glass Mountain: 35
530A, The Pig with the Golden Bristles: 36
533**, The Tsarevna and Her Servant: 37
550, Search for the Golden Bird: 20, 38
551, The Apples of Youth: 39
552A, Three Animals as Brothers-in-law: 16, 40
554, The Grateful Animals: 16
575, The Prince's Wings: 65
613D*, The Magic Crust: 41
650A, Strong John: 114
650B*, The Search for the Strong Man: 42
677**, The Fiddler in Hell: 43
703*, The Snow Maiden: 44
706, The Maiden Without Hands: 45
750B****, The Marvelous Travelers: 46
751B, The Old Man with the Golden Coals: 47
753*, Jesus Rejuvenates a Smith: 48
757, The Haughty Tsar: 49
761A*, The Rich Man in Hell: 43
767*, Punishment for Bigamy: 50
778A*, The Old Man and St. Nicholas: 51
780, The Singing Bone: 52
790**, Nicholas and Kas'ian: 53
791, The Savior and Peter in Night-Lodgings: 54
800*, The Drunkard in Heaven: 55
810A, The Devil Does Penance: 56
810C*, The Forest Spirit Works for the Peasant: 57

839A*, The Hermit and the Devils: 48
845B*, Vavilo of Moscow: 58
850, The Birthmarks of the Princess: 59
853, The Hero Catches the Princess with her Own Words: 60
854, The Golden Ram: 61
855*, The Soldier and the Tsarevna: 62
859F, An Inventive Lad: 63
860B*, The Stolen Woman: 64
873, The King Discovers His Unknown Son: 65
875, The Clever Peasant Girl: 66
875*, The Wise Woman: 67
875E*, The Dispute over the Colt: 68
880*, The Gambler's Wife: 69
883A, The Innocent Slandered Maiden: 70
883A*, The Priest as Seducer: 71
885A, The Seemingly Dead: 72
889, The Faithful Servant: 73
901B*, Who Works Not Eats Not: 74
921A, The Four Coins: 75
921H*, Peter the Great Tastes the *Murzovka*: 76
922, The King and the Abbot: 77
922*, Kings Propose Riddles to the Tsar: 78
934B*, Destined to be Eaten by a Wolf: 79
939A, Killing the Returned Son: 80
951B, The Bank Robbery: 81
957, The Bear Chases the Robbers: 82
980A*, Death in the Sack: 83
981, Wisdom of Hidden Old Man Saves the Kingdom: 84
983, The Dishes of the Same Flavor: 85
999*, The Monk and the Abbess: 86
1001*, Cut Wood!: 87
1006**, Kill the Largest Sheep!: 88
1006***, Kill the Bull!: 87
1045, Pulling the Lake Together: 87, 91
1060*, Playing Cards for Nuts: 89
1063, Throwing Contest with Club: 91
1071, Wrestling Match: 91
1072, Race with Little Son: 91
1080*, Laughing Contest: 90
1082, Carrying the Horse: 91
1084, Contest in Whistling: 91
1120*, The Peasant and the Greedy Priest: 92
1130, Counting out Pay: 91
1132, Flight of the Ogre with His Goods in the Bag: 93
1135, Eye-Remedy: 94

1138*, Gilding the Gentry: 95

1161A, The Fatted Cow: 96

1166*, The Devil Keeps Guard in Place of the Soldier: 97

1169*, Whence Came Baba Yaga: 98

1180, Catching Water in a Sieve: 99

1199C*, The Sorcerer and the Devil: 99

1202, The Grain Harvesting: 100

1250***, Holding up the Heavens with Stakes: 101

1310, Drowning the Crayfish: 102

1319, Pumpkin Sold as an Ass's Egg: 103

1380, The Faithless Wife: 104

1440, The Tenant Promises his Daughter to his Master: 105

1525M*, The Theft of Speck: 106

1687***, Unsalted Custard: 107

1886, Man Drinks from his Own Skull: 108

1889K, A Cord Made of Chaff: 4, 108

1889P, Horse Repaired: 108

1920H, Buying Fire by Story-Telling: 108

1960G, The Great Tree: 109

1960L*, The Big Clutch of Duck Eggs: 108

1960M, The Great Insect: 108

2025, The Fleeing Pancake: 110

2300, An Endless Tale: 111

Motifs

Motif number and description: story number

A661.0.1.2, St Peter as porter of heaven: 55

A2611, Plants from body of slain person or animal: 52

A2721.2.1.1, Aspen cursed for serving as cross: 48

B11.10, Sacrifice of human being to dragon: 14, 39

B11.11, Fight with dragon: 14, 15, 20, 22, 39

B11.11.1, Dragon fight: Respite granted and dragon returns with strength: 14, 18

B11.6.1.2, Rescue of hero by dragon: 22

B15.1.2.2.2, Three-headed serpent: 15, 22, 114

B16.2.3, Hero overcomes giant lion: 114

B102.1, Golden Bird: 20, 21, 38

B123.1, Frog with magic knowledge: 23, 113

B126.1, Frog with magic knowledge: 23, 113

B184.1.10, Magic horse makes prodigious jump: 112

B195, Magic animal used by hero in contest: 114

B292, Animal as servant to man: 18

B314, Helpful animal brothers-in-law: 16, 40

B322.1, Hero feeds own flesh to helpful animals: 15

B335, Helpful animal killed by hero's enemy: 34

B360, Animals grateful for rescue from peril of death: 16, 18, 23, 38, 40

B40, Helpful horse: 35, 112, 114

B411, Helpful cow: 34

B411.5, Helpful bullock: 18

B421, Helpful dog: 14, 29

B431, Helpful wild beasts: 18, 38, 40

B457.1, Helpful doves: 15

B470, Fish as helper: 33, 40

B493.2, Helpful frog: 23, 113

B505, Magic object received from animal: 34

B515, Resuscitation by animals: 16, 39, 40, 112, 114

B544, Animal rescues captive: 38

B557.15, Wolf carries man: 20, 38

B557.3, Person carried by frog: 113

B591.2.1, Horse kicks "Death" and saves hero: 16

B615.2, Strong man sent to milk lions (wolf, bear): 18

B620.1, Daughter promised to animal suitor: 16, 40

B631, Human offspring from marriage to animal: 15, 22, 114

B873, Giant insects: 108

C11, The old man and death: 58

C13, The offended skull: 28

C25.1, Child threatened with ogre: 31

C546, Tabu: touching: 20, 38

C611, Forbidden chamber: 16, 18, 22, 40

C615.2, Hero not to swim in lake: 114

C757.1, Not to destroy animal skin of enchanted person too soon: 23

C943.2, Weakness from seeing naked woman: 112

D24.1, Transformation: king to menial: 113

D52.2, Transformation to handsome hero: 36

D56, Magic change in person's age: 112

D150, Transformation: man to bird (feather): 25

D161.2, Transformation: man to goose: 34

D352.3, Transformation: falcon to person: 113

D361.1, Swan Maiden: 27

D364, Goose transformed to person: 34

D421.1, Wolf as changling: 20

D454.7.1, Transformation: comb to mountain (forest): 29

D560, Transformation by various means: 28

D590, Wonderful tree whose fruit Two-eyes alone can pluck: 34

D685, Transformation by magic object: 20

D735.1, Disenchantment of animal (by marriage): 23

D765.1.2, Disenchantment by removal of enchanting pin: 21

D793.2, Burning skin disenchants: 34

D801.1, Magic objects possessed by witch, sorcerer or evil dwarf: 29, 59

D805, Magic object only to be used in extreme need: 29, 30

D813.3, Magic object from otherworld: 25

D814, Magic objects received from sun, moon, stars, etc.: 17

D815, Magic object received from relative: 29

D838, Magic object acquired by stealing: 22

D839.1, Attempt to learn about magic object by spying: 34

D861.6, Magic object stolen during card game: 64

D878, Magic object voluntarily restored to giver: 64

D961, Magic garden: 20, 114

D1046, Magic wine: 24

D1070 Magic amulet: 39

D1226.2, Pursuit of magic arrow leads to adventure: 23

D1244, Magic salve: 24

D1266, Magic book: 99

D1330, Magic object works physical change: 48

D1355, Love-producing magic object: 21

D1381.11, Magic circle protects from devil: 57

D1393, Magic object helps fugitive: 30, 32

D1531.6, Witch flies with aid of magic stick: 29

D1610.5, Speaking head: 28

D1712.3, Interpretation of dreams: 61

D1889.1, Rejuvenation by reading in book: 26, 37

D1891, Transformation to old man to escape recognition: 112

D1960.3, Sleeping Beauty: 24

D1961, Sleepless watcher magically put to sleep: 34

D1962.2, Magic sleep by lousing: 18, 24

D1978.4, Hero wakened from magic sleep by wife (lover) who has purchased place in his bed from false bride: 25

D2074.2.4.3, Helper summoned by calling his name: 113, 114

E80.3, Resuscitation by water: 15, 16, 18, 20, 22, 38, 40, 52, 114

E261.2.1, Coffin bursts, dead arises: 37

E422.1.11.5.1, Ineradicable bloodstain after bloody tragedy: 25

E632, Reincarnation as musical instrument: 52

E711.1, Soul in egg: 40

E752.2, Soul carried off by devil: 63

E761.4.5, Life token: silver object turns dark: 16, 40

E782.1, Hands restored: 45

E782.4.1, Substituted leg: 11

F17, Visit to the land of the sun: 17

F51.1.4, Chaff sky-rope: 108

F142, River of fire as barrier to otherworld: 113

F176., Hero fights ogre in otherworld: 16, 20, 32, 40, 114

F243.4, Food undiminished when eaten: 41

F512.1, Person with one eye: 34

F512.2.1.1, Three-eyed person: 34

F531.6.8.3.1, Giants fight about treasures: 20

F567, Wild man lives alone in forest: 32

F601, Extraordinary companions: 15

F601.3, Extraordinary companions betray hero: 15

F603.1, Princess abducted by ogre: 15, 20, 40, 112

F610, Remarkably strong man: 15, 114

F611.1.1, Strong man son of bear who has stolen his mother: 114

F611.3.2, Hero's precocious strength: 14, 114

F614.10, Strong man fights whole army alone: 42, 114

F615.2, Strong man sent for wild animals: 18

F628.0.1, Strong man as mighty slayer: 14, 114

F628.1.3, Strong man kills serpent: 14, 16, 114

F707, Magic kingdom: 21

F771, Extraordinary castle (house, palace): 26, 114

F783, Extraordinary (flying) carpet: 22, 113

F791.1, Sky lowers on people: 101

F813.1.1, Theft of golden apples: 20, 38

F822, Extraordinary handkerchief: 16, 40, 112

F833, Extraordinary sword: 24

F835, Extraordinary club: 114

F883.1, Extraordinary book: 99

F911.3.1, Thumbling swallowed by animals: 18

F1021, Extraordinary flights through air: 17

F1021.1, Flight on artificial wings: 65

F1041.1.9, Death from jealousy: 45

F1045, Night spent in a tree: 41

F1071, Prodigious jump: 35

F1088, Extraordinary escapes: 18

F147.3, Witch's house at border of otherworld: 16, 21, 23, 25, 39, 114

F451.5.1, Helpful dwarfs: 18

G11.2, Cannibal giant: 31

G33, Child born as cannibal: 17

G83.1, Ogress whets teeth to kill captive: 17, 21, 23

G84, Fee-fie-foe-fum!: 20, 21, 25, 39, 40

G205, Witch as stepmother: 34

G263, Witch injures, enchants, or transforms: 28

G303.10.7, Devil gives luck with fishing or hunting: 96

G303.16.19.17.1, Devil frightened by a woman: 63

G303.16.3.2, Devil cannot endure cross made by straps of knapsack: 97

G303.9.3.1, Devil hires out to a farmer: 56

G401.1, Ogre kills brothers, seizes princess: 20

G442.1, Child-stealing bear: 18

G475.2, Ogre attacks intruders on bridge: 39, 114

G510, Ogre killed, maimed, or captured: 16, 20, 40, 114

G512.3.2, Ogre burned in his own oven: 19

G512.3.2.1, Ogre's daughters burned in his own oven: 19

G512.9.3, Ogress torn to pieces: 18

G526, Ogre deceived by feigned ignorance of hero: 19

G552, Rescue from ogre by helpful animals: 16, 18, 19, 40, 112, 114

G610, Hero steals treasure: 20

G610, Theft from ogre: 114

G671, Wild man released from captivity aids hero: 32

H13.2.7, Recognition by overheard conversation: 37

H31.7.2, Only one man is able to read magic book: 26

H36.1, Slipper test: 33

H38.2.3, Recognition of maidservant substitute bride by her conversation: 26

H51.1, Recognition by birthmark: 59

H94, Identification by ring: 15

H151.6, Heroine in menial disguise: 33

H252.0.1, True stories as test: 70

H311, Inspection test for suitors: 35, 36

H331, Task: to win princess: 36, 112

H331.1, Suitor contests: difficult riding: 35

H363.1, Bride test: wearing deceased wife's clothes: 112

H386, Bride test: obedience: 74

H421, Tests for true lover: 25

H507.1, Princess offered to man who can defeat her in repartee: 60

H507.1.0.1, Princess defeated in repartee by means of objects picked up: 60

H508, Test: finding answer to certain question: 62

H524.1, What am I thinking?: 77

H525, Test: guessing princess's birthmark: 59

H540, Propounding of riddles: 77, 78

H541.1, Riddle pronounced on pain of death: 67, 77

H548, Riddle contests: 66, 67

H561.1, Clever peasant girl asked riddles by king: 66, 68

H561.1.0.1, Clever peasant wife asks king riddles: 67

H561.2, King and abbot: 77

H561.6.1, King and peasant: the plucked fowl: 75

H583, Clever youth: answers king's inquiry in riddles: 62, 75

H585.1, The four coins: 75

H631.3, What is strongest? : 66

H632, What is swiftest: 66, 68

H633, What is sweetest: 66, 78

H636.1, What is richest?: 68

H652.1, What is softest?: 68

H682, Riddles of heavenly distance: 77

H702, How many stars are in the heaven?: 77

H711.1, How much is the king worth?: 77

H901, Tasks imposed on pain of death: 113

H911, Tasks assigned at suggestion of jealous rivals: 113

H915.1, Task assigned because of a hero's boast: 42

H931.1, Prince envious of hero's wife assigns hero tasks: 27

H932, Tasks assigned to devil (ogre): 99

H935, Witch assigns tasks: 29

H971.2, Task performed with help of old person: 113, 114

H974, Task performed with help of supernatural wife: 113

H982, Animals help man perform task: 16, 36, 40, 114

H1010, Impossible tasks: 99

H1023.2, Task: carrying water in sieve: 99

H1053.2, Task: coming neither on horse nor on foot: 68

H1054, Task: coming neither naked nor clad: 66, 68

H1056, Task: coming neither with nor without a present: 66, 68

H1118, Counting grains of sand, drops of water, etc.: 9l

H1118, Task: counting hairs in pig's back, etc.: 108

H1133, Task: building a castle: 99

H1135, Task: annihilating (overcoming) army single-handed: 42

H1144, Task: measuring the ocean: 99

H1150, Tasks: stealing, capturing, or slaying: 113, 114

H1210.1, Quest assigned by father: 20, 23, 38

H1210.2, Quest assigned by king: 27, 36, 38, 42, 113, 114

H1211, Quests assigned in order to get rid of the hero: 27, 113

H1212, Quest assigned because of feigned illness: 112, 114

H1213, Quest for remarkable bird caused by sight of its feathers: 38

H1215, Quest assigned because of a hero's boast: 42

H1217, Quest assigned because of dreams: 61

H1220, Quest voluntarily undertaken: 16, 24, 25, 37, 40, 114

H1226.4, Pursuit of rolling ball: 23, 24, 27, 39, 113

H1229, Quest voluntarily undertaken: 16, 24, 25, 37, 40, 114

H1232.1, Directions on quest given by herdsmen (witch): 25, 114

H1233. 1.2, Old man helps on a quest: 27, 41, 113

H1233.2.1, Quest accomplished with aid of wife: 27, 113

H1233.6, Animals help hero on quest: 20, 36, 38, 114

H1233.6.1, Magic horse: (20), 35, 36, 40, 113, 114

H1241, Series of quests: 20, 38, 113, 114

H1242, Youngest brother alone succeeds on quest: 23

H1250, Quest to the other world: 27, 113, 114

H1254, Journey to other world for magic objects: 16, 27

H1264, Quest for fire: 31, 108

H1319, Quests for the unique—miscellaneous: 113, 114

H1319.3, Quest for the most beautiful rug: 27

H1331.1, Quest for marvelous bird: 20

H1331.4, Quest for marvelous horse: 16, 36, 40, 114

H1378, Paradoxical quest: 37

H1381, Quest for unknown person: 113

H1382, Quest for unknown object or place: 26, 112

H1385.1, Abduction of princess: 14, 15, 40, 114

H1385.5, Quest for vanished lover: 25

H1385.8, Quest for lost brother: 30

H1462, Watch at the grave: 35

H1471, Watch for devastating monster: 20

H1471.1, Watch for thieves in the king's garden: 38

H1510, Attempts at killing hero fail: 14, 16, 114

H1540, Contests in endurance: 20

H1556, Tests of fidelity: 73

H1561.9, Prince chooses more dangerous road: 20, 37, 38

H3815.3, Quest for vanished princess: 16, 21, 22, 24, 40, 112

J152, Wisdom (knowledge) from sage: 79

J163, Wisdom purchased: 79

J246.1, Devil says that his deeds are strong even if not fair: 63

J652.3, Priest seduces man's wife: 78

J675.1, Hero slays father in self-defense: 114

J741.1, The bear builds house of wood; the fox, of ice: 1

J870, Consolation by pretending one does not want the thing one cannot have: 24

J1050, Attention to warnings: 16

J1111.4, Clever peasant daughter: 66

J1112, Clever wife: 67

J1113, Clever youth: 62

J1115.1, Clever gambler: 69

J1146.1, Detection by pitch trap: 33

J1191.1, Reductio ad absurdum: the dispute over the colt: 68

J1264, Multiplying his talents: impregnates nuns: 86

J1615, That which was promised him: 105

J1736.1, Fools ignorant as to what crayfish is: 102

J1772.1, Pumpkin (puffball) thought to be an ass's egg: 103

J1902, Absurd ignorance concerning the hatching of eggs: 103

J2131.5.7, The fox drowns the pot: 7

J2133.5.1, Wife carried up tree in bag in husband's teeth: 109

J2273, Absurd theories concerning the sky: 101

J2351.1, Fox holds conversation with his members, is caught: 2, 3, 4

J2411.3, Unsuccessful imitation of magic production of food: 13

K11.6, Race won by deception: rabbit as "little son" substitute: 90, 91

K12.2, Wrestling match won by deception: bear as "grandfather": 91

K84.1, Contest in shrieking or whistling: 90, 91

K87, Deceptive laughing contest: 90

K218, Devil cheated by religious or magic means: 57, 99

K235, Man goes for geese but brings back dogs in a bag: 2, 3, 4

K264, Deceptive wager: 69

K335.1.6.3, Man Punishes bear for smashing apiary: 10

K341.2, Thief shams death and steals: 1

K371.1, Trickster throws fish off the wagon: 1

K406.4, Object stolen with connivance of owner: 106

K443.7, Fox eats his fellow-lodger: 1

K472, The bear works: the idle peasant cheats the bear: 9

K473, Sham blood and brains: 3

K521.4, Clothes changed so as to escape: 95

K522.0.1, Death feigned to escape unwelcome marriage: 72

K526, Devil captures youth to cook him: 19

K606.1.3, Musician in hell playing for the devils, purposely breaks fiddle strings: 43

K611.4, Man deceives, escapes devil: 43

K649.10, Prisoner escapes by using wolf: 38

K677, Hero tests rope on which he is to be pulled to upper world: 15

K815.1, The fox persuades the cock to come down and talk: 1, 5, 6

K931, Search for mourning woman: 4, 109

K975.2, Secret of external soul learned by deception: 40, 114

K1011, Eye-remedy: 94

K1013, The man paints the bear: 9

K1021, Tail-fisher: 2

K1026, Dupe imitates trickster's theft and is caught: 1

K1034, Climbing bean, man drops wife and kills her: 4

K1058.2, Bear seeking honey bangs head with beam: 8

K1132, Peter receives the blows twice: 54

K1171, The Fox tricks the wolf into falling into a pit: 1

K1241, Trickster rides dupe horseback: 4

K1243, Priest trapped in window and humiliated: 79

K1317.9, Man intercepts love letter and takes lover's place in elopement: 62

K1335, Seduction by stealing clothes of bathing maiden: 27

K1339.3, Sham illness to learn secret: 114

K1341, Entrance to woman's room in hollow animal: 61

K1346, Hero flies to maiden's room: 65

K1358, Girl shows herself naked in return for dancing pig: 59

K1553, Husband feigns blindness and avenges himself on his wife and her paramour: 104

K1613, Poisoner poisoned with his own poison: 50

K1744, Hero threatens to pull lake together with rope: 90, 91, 112

K1810, Deception by disguise: 67, 95

K1811, Gods (saints) in disguise visit mortals: 46

K1812, King in disguise: 65

K1816.03.1, Hero in disguise at heroine's wedding: 15

K1824, Disguise as layman: 112

K1831, Service under a false name: 32

K1837, Disguise of woman in man's clothes: 70

K1875, Escape by sham blood or brains: 3

K1911, The false bride (substitute bride): 34, 37

K1911.1.4, False bride finishes true bride's task and supplants her: 26, 37

K1931.1, Imposters throw hero overboard into the sea: 32

K1931.2, Imposters abandon hero in lower world: 15

K1934, Imposter forces hero to change places with him: 32

K1935, Imposters steal rescued princess: 15

K1945.1.1, Mother-in-law humiliated as cure for wife's malady: 74

K1955, Sham doctor: 112

K1964, Sham churchman: 77

K1971, Man behind tree speaks and pretends to be god (husband): 104

K1971.1, Husband answers behind statue when wife wants to know how to fool him: 104

K2110.1, Calumniated wife: 45

K2114, Man falsely accused of infidelity: 79

K2116.1.1, Innocent woman accused of killing her newborn children: 112

K2117, Calumniated wife: substituted letter (falsified message): 45

K2211, Treacherous brothers kill prince: 20, 38

K2212, Treacherous sister: 25, 52

K2212.0.1, Treacherous sister attempts to kill brother: 17, 18

K2213, Treacherous wife: 64

K2217, Treacherous uncle: 32

K2254, Treacherous cook: 32

K2287, Treacherous maidservant: 37

K2323, War between the mushrooms: 12

L10, Victorious youngest son: 38

L52, Abused youngest daughter: 33

L55, Stepdaughter as heroine: 34

L55, Stepdaughter heroine: 28, 29

L100, Unpromising hero: 14, 15, 27, 35, 36, 38, 42, 61, 62, 64, 95, 114

L102, Unpromising heroine: 33, 112

L111.1, Exile returns and succeeds: 65

L161, Lowly hero marries princess: 15, 20, 27, 32, 35, 61, 62, 114

L162, Lowly heroine marries king (prince): 34, 45, 66, 70

L177, Despised boy wins gambling game: 69

L221, Modest request: present from the journey: 25

L412, Rich man made poor to punish his pride: 49

M101, Punishment for broken oaths: 78

M210, Bargain with the devil: 63

M211, Man sells his soul to the devil: 63

M372, Confinement in tower to avoid fulfillment of prophecy: 18

N0, Wagers and gambling: 69, 73, 112

N25, Wager on truthfulness of servant: 73

N471, Foolish attempt of second man to overhear secrets: 41

N476.3, Secret of vulnerability disclosed: 20, 114

N711.1, King (prince) finds maiden in woods and marries her: 45

N711.4, Prince sees maiden at church and is enamored: 33

N741.4, Husband and wife reunited after long separation and tedious quest: 113

N771, Prince lost on hunt (quest) has adventures: 16

N774.3, Adventures from pursing animals: 25

N819.3.1, Helpful speaking skull: 28

N825, Old person as helper: 113, 114

P231, Mother and son: 114

P233.2, Hero rebuked by his father: 32

P242, Children punished for father's sins: 78

P253, Sister and brother: 30

P294, Aunt: 29

P361, Faithful servant: 73

P426.2, Hermit:48

Q1.1, Gods (saints) in disguise reward hospitality and punish inhospitality: 46

Q2, Kind and unkind: 31

Q68.1, Truth-speaking rewarded: 45

Q111.6, Treasure as reward:61

Q112, Half of kingdom as reward: 32, 36, 39, 60, 61, 65, 73, 83, 89, 114

Q112.0.1, Kingdom as reward: 38, 39, 42

Q113.0.1, High honors as reward: 79

Q113.4, Appointment to priesthood as reward: 77

Q174, Reward: release from hell: 43

Q200, Deeds punished: 25, 114

Q261, Treachery punished: 34, 114

Q262, Imposter punished: 15, 36, 37

Q276, Stinginess punished: 43

Q451.8, Punishment: thong of leather cut from back: 108

Q452, Serpent sucking woman's breast: 47

Q557, Miraculous punishment through animals: 18

Q582.8, Person drinks poison he prepared for another: 50

R11.1, Quest for vanished princess: 16, 20, 23, 40

R41.2, Captivity in tower: 18

R111.1, Rescue of princess: 16, 20, 24, 40, 114

R111.3.1, Girl rescued by traveling through air: 65

R21, Escape from the grave: 50

R215, Escape from execution: 65

R222, Unknown knight: 35, 42

S12, Cruel mother: 114

S12.1.1, Mother and paramour plot son's death: 112, 114

S12.4, Cruel mother blinds son: 112

S31, Cruel stepmother: 28, 29, 34

S42, Cruel grandfather:112

S55, Cruel sister-in-law: 45

S71, Cruel uncle: 21, 32

S123, Burial alive: 50

S181, Wounding by trapping with sharp knives: 25

S221.1, Poor father gives daughters in marriage to Sun, Moon, Wind: 13

S322.1.3, Father condemns daughter to death because he believes her unchaste: 70

S322.4.2, Evil stepmother orders stepdaughter to be killed: 29

S338, Father abandons daughter in forest and leaves axes tied so that they move in wind: 28

S410, Persecuted wife: 45

S451, Outcast wife at last united with husband and children: 45

T16, Man falls in love with woman he sees bathing: 22

T62, Princess to marry first man who asks for her: 40

T68.1, Princess offered as prize to rescuer: 14

T89.1, Woman falls in love with dying warrior: 18

T135.8, Weddings as end of tale: 24, 26,70, 73, 112, 113, 114

T251.2, Taming of the shrew: 74

T311.1, Flight of maiden to escape marriage: 112

T320, Escape from undesired lover: 70, 71, 72

T320.1, Oft-proved fidelity: 70

T381.1.1, Hero sees guarded maiden in other world: 22

T411.1, Lecherous father: 112

T418, Lustful stepmother: 21

T615, Supernatural growth: 15, 112, 114

T617.2, Hero learns name at first adventure: 112

T645, Paramour leaves token with girl to give their son: 65

T1241.1, Hero returning from quest sent upon another: 114

W151, Greed: 87

X1241, Lies about horses: 108

X1280.2, Lies about ferocious insects: 108

X1739.2, Lie: man makes drinking water from own skull: 108

X1813.1, Lie: the great clutch of duck's eggs: 108

Z11, Endless tales: 111

Z33.1, The fleeing pancake: 110

About the Editor

Jack V. Haney received bachelor's degrees in Russian language and literature from the University of Washington (1962) and Oxford University (1964), where he was a Rhodes Scholar. In 1970 he completed a D. Phil. in medieval Russian literature at Oxford with a dissertation on Maxim the Greek. Until his retirement he was professor of Slavic Languages and Literatures at the University of Washington, Seattle, where he taught medieval Russian literature, Russian folklore, and the Russian language. He has also taught at Northwestern and Oxford universities and has lectured at universities in the United States, England, and Russia. He is the author, editor, and translator of *The Complete Russian Folktale*.